# HOW TO START A BUSINESS IN PENNSYLVANIA

*with forms*

## Second Edition

Desiree A. Petrus
Mark Warda
Attorneys at Law

SPHINX® PUBLISHING
AN IMPRINT OF SOURCEBOOKS, INC.®
NAPERVILLE, ILLINOIS

Second Edition, 1999
Information Updated, 4/2001

Published by: **Sphinx® Publishing, An Imprint of Sourcebooks, Inc.**™

Naperville Office
P.O. Box 4410
Naperville, Illinois  60567-4410
630-961-3900
Fax: 630-961-2168
http://www.sourcebooks.com

This publication is designed to provide accurate and authoritative information in regard to the subject matter covered. It is sold with the understanding that the publisher is not engaged in rendering legal, accounting, or other professional service. If legal advice or other expert assistance is required, the services of a competent professional person should be sought.
*From a Declaration of Principles Jointly Adopted by a Committee of the American Bar Association and a Committee of Publishers and Associations*

**This product is not a substitute for legal advice.**

*Disclaimer required by Texas statutes.*

**Library of Congress Cataloging-in-Publication Data**
Petrus, Desiree A.
    How to start a business in Pennsylvania : with forms / Desiree A.
Petrus, Mark Warda. -- 2nd ed.
        p.        cm.
    Includes bibliographical reference and index.
    ISBN 1-57248-112-9 (pbk.)
    1. Business enterprises--Law and legislation--Pennsylvania Popular
works. 2. Business law--Pennsylvania.  I. Warda, Mark.  II. Title.
KFP205.Z9P48        1999
346.748'065--dc21                                    99-32840
                                                     CIP

Printed and bound in the United States of America.
VHG Paperback — 10  9  8  7  6  5  4  3  2

# CONTENTS

# Using Self-Help Law Books

Whenever you shop for a product or service, you are faced with various levels of quality and price. In deciding what product or service to buy, you make a cost/value analysis on the basis of your willingness to pay and the quality you desire.

When buying a car, you decide whether you want transportation, comfort, status, or sex appeal. Accordingly, you decide among such choices as a Neon, a Lincoln, a Rolls Royce, or a Porsche. Before making a decision, you usually weigh the merits of each option against the cost.

When you get a headache, you can take a pain reliever (such as aspirin) or visit a medical specialist for a neurological examination. Given this choice, most people, of course, take a pain reliever, since it costs only pennies; whereas a medical examination costs hundreds of dollars and takes a lot of time. This is often the most logical choice: it's rare to need anything more than a pain reliever for a headache. But in some cases, a headache may indicate a brain tumor, and failing to see a specialist right away can result in complications. Should everyone with a headache go to a specialist? Of course not, but people treating their own illnesses must realize that they are betting on the basis of their cost/value analysis of the situation; they are taking the most logical option.

The same cost/value analysis must be made in deciding to do one's own legal work. Many legal situations are very straight forward, requiring a simple form and no complicated analysis. Anyone with a little intelligence and a book of instructions can handle the matter without outside help.

But there is always the chance that complications are involved that only an attorney would notice. To simplify the law into a book like this, several legal cases often must be condensed into a single sentence or paragraph. Otherwise, the book would be several hundred pages long and too complicated for most people. However, this simplification necessarily leaves out many details and nuances that would apply to special or unusual situations. Also, there are many ways to interpret most legal questions. Your case may come before a judge who disagrees with the analysis of our authors.

Therefore, in deciding to use a self-help law book and to do your own legal work, you must realize that you are making a cost/value analysis. You have decided that the money you will save in doing it yourself outweighs the chance your case will not turn out to your satisfaction. Most people handling their own simple legal matters never have a problem, but occasionally people find that it ended up costing them more to have an attorney straighten out the situation than it would have if they had hired an attorney in the beginning. Also, you may not be able to undo some mistakes. Keep this in mind while handling your case, and be sure to consult an attorney if you feel you might need further guidance.

# INTRODUCTION

With an increasing population, a low cost of living, and a cleaner environment, Pennsylvania is booming. Pennsylvania is the fifth most populous state and is in the top ten states with the most business firms owned by women. Pennsylvania is also in the top fifteen states with businesses owned by African Americans and in the top ten among states with businesses owned by Hispanics.

The best way to take part in this booming and rich atmosphere is to run your own business. Be your own boss and be as successful as you dare to be.

But if you don't follow the laws of the state, your progress can be slowed or stopped by government fines, civil judgments, or even criminal penalties.

This book is intended to give you the framework for legally opening a business in Pennsylvania. It also includes information on where to find special rules for each type of business. If you have problems that are not covered by this book, you should seek an attorney who can be available for your ongoing needs.

In order to cover all of the aspects of any business you are thinking of starting, you should read through this entire book, rather than skipping to the parts that look most important. There are many laws that may not sound as if they apply to you, however, they do have provisions that will affect your business.

In recent years, the government bureaucracies have been amending and lengthening their forms regularly. The forms included in this book were the most recent available at the time of publication. It is possible that some may be revised by the time you read this book, but in most cases they will be similar and require the same information.

# Deciding to Start a Business

# 1

If you are reading this book, you have probably made a serious decision to take the plunge and start your own business. Hundreds of thousands of people make the same decision each year and many of them become very successful. Some merely eke out a living, others become billionaires, but a lot of them also fail. Knowledge can only help your chances of success. You need to know why some succeed while others fail. Some of what follows may seem obvious, but to someone wrapped up in a new business idea, some of this information is occasionally overlooked.

## Know Your Strengths

The last thing a budding entrepreneur wants to hear is that he is not cut out for running his own business. Those "do you have what it takes" quizzes are ignored with the fear that the answer might be one the entrepreneur doesn't want to hear. But even if you lack some skills you can be successful if you know where to get them.

You should consider all of the skills and knowledge that running a successful business means and decide whether you have what it takes. If you don't, it doesn't necessarily mean you are doomed to be an employee all your life. Perhaps you just need a partner who has the skills you lack, or perhaps you can hire the skills you need, or can structure your business to avoid areas where you are weak. If those don't work, maybe you can learn the skills.

For example, if you are not good at dealing with employees (either you are too passive and get taken advantage of or too tough and scare them off), you can:

- ☛ handle product development yourself and have a partner or manager deal with employees;
- ☛ take seminars in employee management; or
- ☛ structure your business so that you don't need employees. Either use independent contractors or set yourself up as an independent contractor.

Here are some of the factors to consider when planning your business:

- ☛ If it takes months or years before your business turns a profit do you have the resources to hold out? Businesses have gone under or were sold just before they were about to take off. Staying power is an important ingredient to success.

- ☛ Are you willing to put in a lot of overtime to make your business a success? Owners of businesses do not set their own hours, the business sets them for the owner. Many business owners work long hours seven days a week, but they enjoy running their business more than family picnics or fishing.

- ☛ Are you willing to do the dirtiest or most unpleasant work of the business? Emergencies come up and employees are not always dependable. You might need to mop up a flooded room, spend a weekend stuffing 10,000 envelopes, or work Christmas if someone calls in sick.

- ☛ Do you know enough about the product or service? Are you aware of the trends in the industry and what changes new technology might bring? Think of the people who started typesetting or printing businesses just before type was replaced by laser printers.

☛ Do you know enough about accounting and inventory to manage the business? Do you have a good "head for business?" Some people naturally know how to save money and do things profitably. Others are in the habit of buying the best and the most expensive of everything. The latter can be fatal to a struggling new business.

☛ Are you good at managing employees?

☛ Do you know how to sell your product or service? You can have the best product on the market but people don't beat a path to your door. If you are a wholesaler, shelf space in major stores is hard to get, especially for a new company without a record, a large line of products, or a large advertising budget.

☛ Do you know enough about getting publicity? The media receive thousands of press releases and announcements each day and most are thrown away. Don't count on free publicity to put your name in front of the public.

# KNOW YOUR BUSINESS

You don't only need to know the concept of a business, you need the experience of working in a business. Maybe you always dreamed of running a bed and breakfast or having your own pizza place and now that you are laid off you think it's time to use your savings to fulfill your dream. Have you ever worked in such a business? If not, you may have no idea of the day-to-day headaches and problems of the business. For example, do you really know how much to allow for theft, spoilage, and unhappy customers.

You might feel silly taking an entry level job at a pizza place when you'd rather start your own, but it might be the most valuable preparation you could have. A few weeks of seeing how a business operates could mean the difference between success and failure.

Working in a business as an employee is one of the best ways to be a success at running such a business. New people with new ideas who work in old stodgy industries have been known to revolutionize them with obvious improvements that no one before dared to try.

# DO THE MATH

Conventional wisdom says you need a business plan before committing yourself to a new venture, but lots of businesses are started successfully without the owner even knowing what a business plan is. They have a great concept, put it on the market, and it takes off. But you at least need to do some basic calculations to see if the business can make a profit. Here are some examples:

☛ If you want to start a retail shop, figure out how many people are close enough to become customers, and how many other stores will be competing for those customers. Visit some of those other shops and see how busy they are. Without giving away your plans to compete, ask some general questions like "how's business?" and maybe they'll share their frustrations or successes.

☛ Whether you sell a good or a service, do the math to find out how much profit is in it. For example: if you plan to start a house painting company, find out what you will have to pay to hire painters; what it will cost you for all of the insurance; bonding and licensing you will need; and what the advertising will cost you. Figure out how many jobs you can do per month and what other painters are charging. In some industries in different areas of the country there may be a large margin of profit or there may be almost no profit.

☛ Find out if there is a demand for your product or service. Suppose you have designed a beautiful new kind of candle and your friends all say you should open a shop because "everyone will want them." Before making a hundred of them and renting a store, bring a few to craft shows or flea markets and see what happens.

☛ Figure out what the income and expenses would be for a typical month of your new business. List monthly expenses such as rent, salaries, utilities, insurance, taxes, supplies, advertising, services, and other overhead. Then figure out how much profit you will average from each sale. Next, figure out how many sales you will need to cover your overhead and divide by the number of business days in the month. Can you reasonably expect that many sales? How will you get those sales?

Most types of businesses have trade associations, which often have figures on how profitable its members are. Some even have start-up kits for people wanting to start businesses. One good source of information on such organizations is the *Encyclopedia of Associations* published by Gale Research Inc. and available in many library reference sections. Producers of products to the trade often give assistance to small companies getting started to win their loyalty. Contact the largest suppliers of the products your business will be using and see if they can be of help.

## SOURCES OF FURTHER GUIDANCE

The following offices offer free or low cost guidance for new businesses:

SCORE     ***Service Corps of Retired Executives.*** this is a group of retired former workers who will give advice to new businesses at no charge.

| | | |
|---|---|---|
| Altoona | 1212 12th Avenue, Altoona, PA 16601 | 814-942-9054 |
| Camp Hill | 4211 Trindle Road, Camp Hill, PA 17011 | 717-761-4304 |
| Carlisle | 212 North Hanover Street, Carlisle, PA 17013 | 717-234-4515 |
| Chambersburg | 75 South 2nd Street, Chambersburg, PA 17201 | 717-264-7101 |
| Eddystone | 2100 Industrial Highway, Eddystone, PA 19022 | 610-447-1300 |
| Erie | 120 West Ninth Street, Erie, PA 16501 | 814-871-5650 |
| Fairless Hills | 409 Hood Boulevard, Fairless Hills, PA 19030 | 215-943-8850 |
| Hanover | 146 Carlisle Street, Hanover, PA 17331 | 717-637-6130 |
| Jenkintown | 1653 The Fairway #204, Jenkintown, PA 19046 | 215-885-3027 |
| Lancaster | 118 West Chesnut Street, Lancaster, PA 17603 | 717-397-3092 |

| Latrobe | 300 Fraser Purchase Rd. 4th Fl., Latrobe, PA 15650 | 724-539-7505 |
| Lebanon | 252 North 8th Street, Lebanon, PA 17042 | 717-273-3727 |
| Lockhaven | 138 E. Walter Street, Lockhaven, PA 17745 | 570-748-5872 |
| Mansfield | RD #1 - Box 513, Mansfield, PA 16933 | 570-724-7977 |
| Meadville | 628 Arch Street, Box A201, Meadville, PA 16335 | 814-337-5194 |
| Media | 602 East Baltimore, Pike, Media, PA 19063 | 610-565-3677 |
| Monessen | 435 Donner Avenue, Monessen, PA 15062 | 724-684-4277 |
| Philadelphia | 1315 Walnut Street #114, Philadelphia, PA 19107 | 215-790-5050 |
| Pittsburgh | 1000 Liberty Avenue #1314, Pittsburgh, PA 15222 | 412-395-6560 |
| Pottstown | 135 High Street, Pottstown, PA 19464 | 610-327-2673 |
| Reading | 645 Penn Street, Reading, PA 19603 | 610-376-6766 |
| Scranton | 235 Washington Ave #104, Scranton, PA 18503 | 570-347-4611 |
| Shamokin | PO Box 10, Shamokin, PA 17876 | 570-743-1221 |
| State College | 200 Innovation Blvd.#242B, St. College, PA 16803 | 814-234-9415 |
| Stroudsburg | 566 Main Street, Stroudsburg, PA 18360 | 570-421-4433 |
| Uniontown | 140 North Beeson Avenue, Uniontown, PA 15401 | 724-437-4222 |
| Warren | 315 Second Avenue - 4th Flr., Warren, PA 16365 | 814-723-9017 |
| West Chester | 601 Westtown Rd., #281, West Chester, PA 19380 | 610-344-6910 |
| Wilkes-Barre | 7 N. Wilkes-Barre Blvd #407, Wilkes-B., PA 18702 | 570-826-6502 |

SMALL BUSINESS DEVELOPMENT CENTERS

Educational programs for small businesses are offered through the Small Business Development Centers at many Pennsylvania colleges and universities. You should see if they have any which could help you in any areas in which you are weak.

Bucknell University
126 Dana Eng. Bldg.,
Lewisburg, PA 17837
717-524-1249

Clarion University
102 Dana Still Building,
Clarion, PA 16214
814-226-2060

Duquesne University
600 Forbes Avenue,
Pittsburgh, PA 15282
412-396-6233

Gannon University
University Square,
Erie, PA 16541
814-871-7714

Indiana University of Pennsylvania
208 Eberly College of Business,
Indiana, PA 15705
724-357-7915

Kutztown University
2986 North 2nd Street,
Harrisburg, PA 17110
717-720-4230

Lehigh University
Rauch Business Center #37,
Bethlehem, PA 18015
610-758-5205

Penn State University
117 Technology Center,
University Park, PA 16802
814-863-4293

St. Francis College
Business Resource Center,
Loretto, PA 15940
814-472-3200

St. Vincent College
Alfred Hall - 4th Floor,
Latrobe, PA 15650
724-537-4572

Temple University
1510 Cecil B. Moore Ave.,
Philadelphia, PA 19121
215-204-7282

University of Pennsylvania
3733 Spruce Street,
Philadelphia, PA 19104
215-898-4861

University of Pittsburgh
208 Bellefield Hall,
Pittsburgh, PA 15213
412-648-1544

University of Scranton
St. Thomas Hall, #588,
Scranton, PA 18510
570-941-7588

West Chester University
211 Carter Drive,
West Chester, PA 19383
610-436-2162

Wilkes University
192 S. Franklin St.,
Wilkes-Barre, PA 18766
570-831-4340

California University
Entrepreneurial Assistance Center
Box 62
250 University Ave.
California, PA 15419
724-938-5885

Drexel University
Department of Management
College of Business
Academic Building, Rm. 314
Philadelphia, PA 19104
215-895-2122

Villanova University
Small Business Institute
Management Department
800 Lancaster, PA 19085
610-519-4382

Washington and Jefferson College
Center for Economic Development
Department of Economics and Business
Washington, PA 15301
724-229-5127

# Choosing the Form of Your Business 2

## Basic Forms of Doing Business

The four most popular forms for a business in Pennsylvania are proprietorship, partnership, corporation, and limited partnership. In 1994, a law was passed that allowed creation of a new type of enterprise, a *limited liability company.* The characteristics, advantages and disadvantages of each are as follows:

PROPRIETORSHIP

*Characteristics:* A proprietorship is one person doing business in his or her own name or under a fictitious name.

*Advantages:* A proprietorship is simple to form. There is a low organizational expense because only the licenses and certificates needed to begin operation are required. A proprietorship allows the greatest freedom from regulation of all four business forms, and there are possible tax advantages. The owner is taxed at individual rate and losses may be deducted from individual return. You may begin as a sole proprietorship and later form another business entity such as a partnership or corporation.

*Disadvantages:* The proprietor is personally liable for all debts and obligations. Also, there is no continuation of the business after death. All profits are directly taxable, certainly a disadvantage for the proprietor, and business affairs are easily mixed with personal affairs. A proprietor has a limited ability to raise capital because he or she must use his or her own money or borrow. Also, if a fictitious name is used, it must be registered with the Corporations Bureau (see page 24).

GENERAL
PARTNERSHIP

***Characteristics***: This involves two or more people carrying on a business together sharing the profits and losses. The rights and privileges of the partnership are defined by the partnership agreement and state law so it is important to put the partner's agreement in writing. Laws covering partnerships are found in Title 15 of the Pennsylvania Consolidated Statutes (Pa.C.S.A.) sections 8101 et seq. and 8301 et seq.

***Advantages:*** Due to low organizational costs, partnerships are easily created. Partners can combine expertise and assets. A general partnership allows liability to be spread among more persons while keeping the same tax advantages as a sole partnership.

***Disadvantages:*** There is unlimited liability for the acts of the other partners. Also, a general partnership has the same problems raising capital as a sole proprietorship. Each partner holds personal liability for partnership debts. In a general partnership, the business is shared; and it is often hard to get rid of a bad partner. Moreover, one partner can commit the firm to any obligation.

CORPORATION

***Characteristics:*** A corporation is an artificial person which carries on a business through its officers for its shareholders. (In Pennsylvania, one person may form a corporation and be the sole shareholder and officer.) Laws covering corporations are contained in Title 15 § 1101 through § 1110, § 1301 through § 1311, and § 1501 through § 1511.

An *S corporation*, formerly known as a *Subchapter S corporation*, is a corporation which has filed IRS Form 2553 choosing to have all profits taxed to the shareholders, rather than to the corporation. An S corporation files a tax return but pays no federal or state tax. The profit shown on the S corporation tax return is reported on the owner's tax returns.

An S corporation has no more than seventy-five shareholders and its income is taxed to the shareholders as if the corporation were a partnership. The shareholders are then able to deduct S corporation losses on their personal income tax returns. Do note that a specific portion of the corporations receipts must come from active business rather than passive investment.

A C *corporation* is a business corporation which has not elected to be taxed as an S corporation. A C corporation pays taxes on its profits. The effect of this is that when the corporation pays dividends to its shareholders there is double taxation, once at the corporate level and again when the shareholders receive them.

A *professional corporation* is a type of corporation where people in regulated professions can practice their professions within a corporate structure. A profession is any kind of personal service that requires a license, admission to practice or other legal authorization. A professional remains personally liable for any wrong-doing in performing personal services.

A *nonprofit corporation* is usually used for such organizations as churches, civic groups, and condominium associations. However, with careful planning, some types of businesses can be set up as nonprofit corporations and save a fortune in taxes. While a nonprofit corporation cannot pay dividends, it can pay its officers and employees fair salaries. Some of the major American nonprofit organizations pay their officers well over $100,000 a year. Pennsylvania's rules for nonprofit corporations are included in 15 Pa.C.S. § 5101 et. seq.

***Advantages:*** The liability of the corporation is limited to amount invested. Shareholders have no liability for corporate debts and lawsuits; and officers usually have no personal liability for their corporate acts. The existence of a corporation may be perpetual. There are possible tax advantages, such as there is a corporate tax rate and the shareholder is taxed only on dividends receive. There is prestige in owning a corporation. Two excellent advantages: capital may be raised by selling shares; and it is easy to transfer ownership at any time, including upon death. A small corporation can be set up as an S corporation to avoid some corporate taxes but still retain corporate advantages. Some types of businesses can be set up as nonprofit corporations which provide significant tax savings.

***Disadvantages:*** A corporation is more difficult to create than a proprietorship or general partnership. There are costs involved for starting up a corporation and for record-keeping; also, corporations are closely regulated because they are governed by state law. Also, separate records must be kept for taxes on dividends to shareholders; and corporations must annually report a capital stock tax, a loans tax, and a corporate net income tax to the department of revenue. A corporation's business activities are restricted to those listed in the corporate charter.

LIMITED
PARTNERSHIP

***Characteristics:*** A limited partnership has characteristics similar to both a corporation and a partnership. There are *general partners* who have the control and liability, and there are *limited partners* who only put up money and whose liability is limited to what they paid for their share of the partnership (like corporate stock). Laws governing limited partnerships are found in title 15 Pa.C.S. sections 8511 et seq.

***Advantages:*** Capital can be contributed by limited partners who have no control of the business or liability for its debts. Limited partners have no liability beyond the amount of money they invested.

***Disadvantages:*** General partners are personally liable for partnership debts and for the acts of each other. There are high start-up costs, and an extensive partnership agreement is required. There is a $200 annual assessment fee payable to the Department of State which will be increased on December 31, 1997 and every third year thereafter (2000, 2003 etc.)

LIMITED
LIABILITY
COMPANY

***Characteristics:*** Pennsylvania adopted the Limited Liability Company Act (106) in 1994. This new invention is like a limited partnership without general partners. It has characteristics of both a corporation and a partnership. None of the partners have liability and all can have some control.

*Advantages:* The limited liability company offers the tax benefits of a partnership with the protection from liability of a corporation. It offers more tax benefits than an S corporation because it may pass through more depreciation and deductions. It may have different classes of ownership and an unlimited number of members.

*Disadvantages:* Besides the start-up costs, limited liability companies must pay Pennsylvania corporate income tax. Because a limited liability company is a new invention, there are not a lot of answers to legal questions which may arise. (However the courts will probably rely on corporation and limited partnership law.) The act makes it clear that a professional will not be relieved of personal liability for malpractice therefore malpractice insurance is a necessity.

LIMITED
LIABILITY
PARTNERSHIP

*Characteristics.* The limited liability partnership is like a general partnership but without personal liability. It was devised to allow partnerships of lawyers and other professionals limit their personal liability without losing their partnership structure. This was important because converting to an LLC could have tax consequences, and some states do not allow professionals to operate as LLCs. Both general and limited partnerships can register as LLPs.

*Advantages.* The limited liability partnership offers the flexibility and tax benefits of a partnership with the protection from liability of a corporation.

*Disadvantages.* Start-up and annual fees are higher for LLPs than for a corporation. Also, the law requires the partnership to maintain certain minimum insurance.

# MAKING YOUR CHOICE

The selection of a form of doing business is best made with the advice of an accountant and an attorney. If you were selling normally harmless objects by mail, a proprietorship would be the easiest way to get started. But if you own a lawn service, it would be important to incorporate to avoid losing your personal assets if one of your drivers were to injure someone in an accident where the damages could exceed your insurance. If you can expect a high cash buildup the first year, a corporation may be the best way to keep taxes low. If you expect the usual start-up losses, a proprietorship, partnership, or S corporation would probably be best.

# START-UP PROCEDURES

PROPRIETORSHIP

All accounts and licenses are registered in the name of the owner. See chapter 3 for using a fictitious name.

PARTNERSHIP

A written agreement should be prepared to spell out rights and obligations of the parties. See chapter 3 for using a fictitious name. Accounts and licenses are usually registered in the names of the partners.

CORPORATION

To form a corporation, articles of Incorporation must be filed with the Secretary of the State in Harrisburg along with $100 in filing fees. An organizational meeting is then held at which officers are elected, stock issued, and other formalities are complied with to avoid the corporate entity being set aside later. Licenses and accounts are titled in the name of the corporation.

LIMITED PARTNERSHIP

A written limited partnership agreement must be drawn up and registered with the Secretary of the State in Harrisburg, and a lengthy disclosure document given to all prospective limited partners. Because of the complexity of securities laws and the criminal penalties for violation, it is advantageous to have an attorney organize a limited partnership.

**LIMITED LIABILITY COMPANY**

Two or more persons may form a limited liability company by filing Articles of Organization with the Secretary of State in Harrisburg. Licenses and accounts are in the name of the company.

**LIMITED LIABILITY PARTNERSHIP**

A limited partnership is a partnership formed by two or more persons having one or more general partners and one or more limited partners. The limited partners have limited exposure to liability and are not involved in the day-to-day operations of the limited partnership. A Pennsylvania limited partnership is formed by filing a Certificate of Limited Partnership on form DSCB: 15-8511 accompanied by a docketing statement in duplicate, form DSCB: 15-134A with the Corporations Bureau, Department of State.

# Business Comparison Chart

| | Sole Proprietorship | General Partnership | Limited Partnership | Limited Liability Co. | Corporation C or S | Nonprofit Corporation |
|---|---|---|---|---|---|---|
| **Liability Protection** | No | No | For limited partners | For all members | For all shareholders | For all members |
| **Taxes** | Pass through | Pass through | Pass through | Pass through | S corps. pass through C corps. pay tax | None on Employees pay on wages |
| **Number of members** | 1 (max.) | 2 or more | 2 or more | 2 or more | 1 | 3 |
| **Start-up fee** | None | None | $100 | $100 | $100 | $100 |
| **Annual fee** | None | None | None | 330 or more | None | None |
| **Diff. classes of ownership** | No | Yes | Yes | Yes | S corps. No C corps. Yes | No ownership Diff. classes of membership |
| **Survives after Death** | No | No | Yes | Yes | Yes | Yes |
| **Best for** | 1 person low-risk business or no assets | low-risk business | low-risk business with silent partners | All types of businesses | All types of businesses | Educational Charitable |

# BUSINESS START-UP CHECKLIST

❑ Make your plan
    ❑ Obtain and read all relevant publications on your type of business
    ❑ Obtain and read all laws and regulations affecting your business
    ❑ Calculate whether your plan will produce a profit
    ❑ Plan your sources of capital
    ❑ Plan your sources of goods or services
    ❑ Plan your marketing efforts
❑ Choose your business name
    ❑ Check other business names and trademarks
    ❑ Register your name, trademark, etc.
❑ Choose the business form
    ❑ Prepare and file organizational papers
    ❑ Prepare and file fictitious name if necessary
❑ Choose the location
    ❑ Check competitors
    ❑ Check zoning
❑ Obtain necessary licenses
    ❑ City?    ❑ State?
    ❑ County?    ❑ Federal?
❑ Choose a bank
    ❑ Checking
    ❑ Credit card processing
    ❑ Loans
❑ Obtain necessary insurance
    ❑ Worker's Comp    ❑ Automobile
    ❑ Liability    ❑ Health
    ❑ Hazard    ❑ Life/disability
❑ File necessary federal tax registrations
❑ File necessary state tax registrations
❑ Set up a bookkeeping system
❑ Plan your hiring
    ❑ Obtain required posters
    ❑ Obtain or prepare employment application
    ❑ Obtain new hire tax forms
    ❑ Prepare employment policies
    ❑ Determine compliance with health and safety laws
❑ Plan your opening
    ❑ Obtain all necessary equipment and supplies
    ❑ Obtain all necessary inventory
    ❑ Do all necessary marketing and publicity
    ❑ Obtain all necessary forms and agreements
    ❑ Prepare your company policies on refunds, exchanges, returns

# Registering the Name of Your Business 3

## Preliminary Considerations

Before deciding upon a name for your business, you should be sure that it is not already being used by someone else. Many business owners have spent thousands of dollars on publicity and printing and then had to throw it all away because another company owned the name. A company that owns a name can take you to court and force you to stop using that name.

If you will be running a small local shop with no plans for expansion you *may* be able to get by with checking only local references, but if you plan to expand or to deal nationally you should do a thorough search of the name you choose. In either case, the potential for being sued is great so it is advisable to check with the Corporation Bureau in Harrisburg to see if another company is using the name you have chosen or something confusingly similar. A preliminary search is free, but a report of the search with the Secretary's seal is $12.

To do a national search, you should check trade directories and phone books of major cities. These can be found at many libraries and are usually reference books which cannot be checked out. The *Trade Names Directory* is a two volume set of names compiled from many sources published by Gale Research Co.

If you have a computer with internet access, you can use it to search all of the yellow page listings in the U.S. at a number of sites at no charge. One website, **http://www.infoseek.com**, offers free searches of yellow pages for all states at once.

To be sure that your use of the name does not violate someone else's trademark rights, you should have a trademark search done of the mark in the United States Patent and Trademark Office. In the past, this required a visit to their offices or the hiring of a search for over a hundred dollars. But in 1999, the USPTO put its trademark records online and you can now search them at: **http://www.uspto.gov/tmdb/index.html**. If you do not have access to the internet, you might be able to do it at a public library or have one of their employees order an online search for you for a small fee. If this is not available to you, you can have the search done through a firm. Once such firm is Government Liaison Services, Inc., P.O. Box 10648, Arlington, VA 22210. Tel. 703-524-8200. They also offer searches of 100 trade directories and 4800 phone books.

The best way to make sure a name you are using is not already owned by someone else is to make one up yourself. Such names as Xerox, Kodak, and Exxon were made up and didn't have any meaning prior to their use by their respective companies. But remember that there are millions of businesses and even something you make up may already be in use. Do a search anyway.

## FICTITIOUS NAMES

In Pennsylvania, as in most states, unless you do business in your own legal name, you must register the name you are using. The name must be registered with the Corporations Bureau in Harrisburg.

Every person who registers a fictitious name must file a report to renew the name in 2000 and every ten years following (54 Pa.C.S. 321).

There is a $500 civil penalty if you fail to register a fictitious name and you may not sue anyone for using your fictitious name unless you are registered. If someone sues you and you are not registered, they may be entitled to attorney's fees and court costs.

If your name is JOHN DOE and you are operating a masonry business, you may operate your business as JOHN DOE, MASON without registering it. Similarly, Doe Masonry, Doe Masonry Company, Doe Company do not need to be registered because the proper last name of the owner is in the name of the business. John's Masonry or any name that does not use the last name of the owner must be registered as a fictitious name.

You cannot use the words, "corporation," "incorporated," "corp.," or "inc." unless you are a corporation. However, corporations do not have to register the name they are using as a fictitious name unless it is different from their registered corporate name (54 P.A.C.S. 301 et. seq.).

Attorneys and professionals licensed by the Bureau of Professional and Occupational Affairs do not have to register the names under which they practice their profession providing that the last name of all the partners are listed.

When you use a fictitious name you are "doing business as" (d/b/a) whatever name you are using. Legally you would use the name "JOHN DOE d/b/a DOE MASONRY."

To register a fictitious name, you must advertise that you have filed or intend to file an application to register a fictitious name in two newspapers. These newspaper ads must appear in a newspaper of general circulation and in a legal newspaper. According to the Fictitious Name Act, the ad must contain the following information: the name of the business; the address of the business's main office; the names and addresses of all parties involved in the registering of the business; and, a statement that you have filed or intend to file an application to register a fictitious name. The ad should usually appear in the classified section of the newspaper and could be worded as follows:

> **FICTITIOUS NAME NOTICE**
>
> Notice is hereby given that an application to register the business name Acme Printing under the Fictitious Name Act has been filed with the Department of State of Pennsylvania. The principal place of business and the main office is located at 456 Main Street, Harrisburg, PA 00000. Jane Doe of 789 Back Street, Harrisburg, PA 00000 is the only individual party to this registration.

Call the classified advertising department of the newspaper and ask for their rates and any other information you may need to know about advertising a fictitious name notice. Don't hesitate to contact more than one paper and shop around for the best rate. Most counties have more than one newspaper of general circulation. Also, most papers have an information sheet they can give you that explains how your ad should be worded and the cost for placing the ad. Some papers will even help you contact a local legal newspaper to place your ad there as well. If the newspaper is unable or unwilling to help you find a legal newspaper, you may find a list of legal newspapers (sometimes called *reporters*) in the appendix that you may contact on your own. The fictitious name notice need only appear once in both papers.

Before or after the ad has appeared, you must file an APPLICATION FOR THE REGISTRATION OF A FICTITIOUS NAME (Form DSCB: 54-311, located on page 161) with the Corporations Bureau. It is important to remember that the fictitious name cannot be the same as or confusingly similar to, the name of any corporation or association authorized to do business in Pennsylvania (partnership, limited partnership, limited liability company) or registered with the Corporations Bureau at 717-787-1057. A written report of a records search can be obtained for $12 (check or money order, the Corporations Bureau will not accept cash for any filing or service) by filing Counter—Corporate Certification and Search Request Form DSCB: PCF3, or by making the request on letterhead stationery. Do not order business stationary, forms, stock certificates, etc. until you have obtained a written report. A phone search is considered a preliminary search and is not a guarantee of the availability of fictitious name.

Some businesses have special requirements for registration of their fictitious names. For example, a fictitious name that implies a business is a bank or trust, an educational institution, or is engaged in engineering, must obtain permission from the Department of Banking, Department of Education or the State Registration Board of Professional Engineers, Land Surveyors and Geologists. Other businesses may have similar requirements. See chapter 6 for a list of state regulated professions with references to the laws which apply to them.

At the end of this chapter are the fictitious name instructions and a sample filled-in form. A blank form is included in the appendix.

# CORPORATE NAMES

A corporation does not have to register a fictitious name because it already has a legal name. The name of a corporation must contain one of the following words:

| | |
|---|---|
| Association | Incorporated |
| Corporation | Inc. |
| Corp. | Limited |
| Company | Ltd. |
| Co. | Syndicate |
| Fund | |

It is not advisable to use only the word "Company" or "Co." because unincorporated businesses also use these words and a person dealing with you might not realize you are incorporated. If this happens you might end up with personal liability for corporate debts. You can use a combination of two of the words, such as ABC Co., Inc.

If the name of the corporation does not contain one of the above words it will be rejected by the Secretary of State. It will also be rejected if the name used by it is already taken or is similar to the name of another corporation, or if it uses a forbidden word such as "bank" or "trust." To check on a name, from 8 A.M. to 5 P.M., you may call the name availability number in Harrisburg: 717-787-1057. Keep trying, they are usually busy.

If a name you pick is taken by another company, you may be able to change it slightly and have it accepted. For example, if there is already a Tri-City, Inc., you may be allowed to use Tri-City Upholstery, Inc. The addition of the locality is not enough to distinguish names but the addition of a description of the business in the names usually is.

Like a fictitious name, don't have anything printed until a written report of a records search and your corporate papers are returned to you. Sometimes a name is approved over the phone and rejected when submitted.

Once you have chosen a corporate name and know it is available, you should immediately register your corporation. A name can be "reserved" for 120 days for $52, by filing form DSCB: PCF3 or placing your request in writing and enclosing a check or money order, but it is easier just to register the corporation than to waste time and money on the name reservation.

If a corporation wants to do business under a name other than its corporate name, it can register a fictitious name such as "Doe Corporation d/b/a Doe Industries." But if the name used leads people to believe that the business is not a corporation, the right to limited liability may be lost. If such a name is used it should always be accompanied by the corporate name.

# PROFESSIONAL CORPORATIONS

Professionals can do business by creating a professional corporation. A profession is defined as any type of personal service that requires a license, admission to practice or some other legal authorization. Under Pennsylvania law, a professional corporation cannot use "Inc.," "Corp.," or "Co." in their name. Instead they must use the words "associates," "and associates" or "professional corporation" or "P.C."

# DOMAIN NAMES

With the internet being so new and changing so rapidly, all of the rules for internet names have not yet been configured. Originally, the first person to reserve a name owned it, and enterprising souls bought up the names of most of the Fortune 500 corporations and held them for ransom. Then a few of the corporations went to court and the rule was developed that if a company had a trademark for a name, that company could stop someone else from using it if the other person didn't have a trademark.

You cannot yet get a trademark merely for using a domain name. Trademarks are granted for the use of a name in commerce. Once you have a valid trademark, you will be safe using it for your domain name.

In the next few years there will probably be several changes to the domain name system to make it more flexible and useful throughout the world. One proposed change is the addition of more generic top level domains (gTLDs) which are the last parts of the names, like *com* and *gov*. Some of the suggested additions are *firm, store, web, arts, rec, nom,* and *info*. This should free up a lot of names since corporations like McDonald's are not in the arts business and would probably not be able to keep the names from legitimate users.

If you wish to protect your domain name, the best thing to do at this point is to get a trademark for it. To do this, you would have to use it on your goods or services. The following section gives some basic information about trademarks. To find out if a domain name is available, go to **http://rs.internic.net**.

# TRADEMARKS

As your business builds goodwill, its name will become more valuable and you will want to protect it from others who may wish to copy it. To protect a name used to describe your goods or services you can register it as a trademark (for goods) or a service mark (for services), with either the Corporations Bureau of the Department of State in Pennsylvania or with the United States Patent and Trademark Office.

You cannot obtain a trademark for only the name of your business, but you can trademark the name you use on your goods and services. In most cases you use your company name on your goods as your trademark, so it, in effect, protects your company name. Another way to protect your company name is to incorporate. A particular corporate name can only be registered by one company in Pennsylvania.

STATE REGISTRATION

State registration would be useful if you only expect to use your trademark within the state of Pennsylvania. Federal registration would protect your mark anywhere in the country. The registration of a mark gives you exclusive use of the mark for the types of goods for which you register it. The only exception is persons who have already been using the mark. You cannot stop people who have been using the mark prior to your registration.

The procedure for state registration is simple and the cost is $52. You should conduct a search for the mark by following the same procedure as you did for a name search. The cost is $12 for a written report and any questions you have about filing an "Application for Registration of Mark" (Form DSCB: 54-1112) can be answered by calling 717-787-1057.

Before a mark can be registered, it must be used in Pennsylvania. For goods this means it must be used on the goods themselves, or on containers, tags, labels or displays of the goods. For services it must be used in the sale or advertising of the services. The use must be in an actual transaction with a customer. Use on a sample mailed to a friend is not acceptable.

The $52 fee will register the mark in only one "class of goods." If the mark is used on more than one class of goods, a separate registration must be filed. The registration is good for ten years. Six months prior to its expiration, it must be renewed. The renewal fee presently is $52 for each class of goods, but could go up in ten years time.

FEDERAL
REGISTRATION

On the following pages are instructions and a sample filled-in form for a Pennsylvania trademark. A blank form is in the appendix of this book.

For federal registration the procedure is a little more complicated. There are two types of applications depending upon whether you have already made use of the mark or whether you merely have an intention to use the mark in the future. For a trademark that has been in use, you must file an application form along with specimens showing actual use and a drawing of the mark which complies with all of the rules of the United States Patent and Trademark Office. For an *intent to use* application you must file two separate forms, one when you make the initial application and the other after you have made actual use of the mark as well as the specimens and drawing. Before a mark can be entitled to federal registration the use of the mark must be in "interstate commerce" or in commerce with another country. The fee for registration is $245, but if you file an intent to use application there is a second fee of $100 for the filing after actual use.

An explanation of the entire trademark registration procedure and the application forms are included in the book *How to Register Your Own Trademark*, published by Sourcebooks, Inc. It is available through most bookstores or directly from the publisher.

DSCB: 54-311 (Rev 90) -3

**Department of State**
**Corporation Bureau**
**P.O. Box 8722**
**Harrisburg, PA 17105-8722**

**Instructions for Completion of Form:**

A. One original of this form is required. The form shall be completed in black or blue-black ink in order to permit reproduction. The filing fee for this form is $52 made payable to the Department of State. PLEASE NOTE: A separate check is required for each form submitted.

B. Under 15 Pa.C.S. § 135(c) (relating to addresses) an actual street or rural route box number must be used as an address, and the Department of State is required to refuse to receive or file any document that sets forth only a post office box address.

C. The following, in addition to the filing fee, shall accompany this form:

    (1) Any necessary copies of form DSCB:17.2 (Consent to Appropriation of Name) or form DSCB:17.3 (Consent to Use of Similar Name).

    (2) An necessary governmental approvals.

D. For general instructions relating to fictitious name registration see 19 Pa. Code Subch. 17C (relating to fictitious names). These instructions relate to such matters as voluntary and mandatory registration, general restrictions on name availability, use of corporate designators, agent for effecting amendments, etc., execution, official advertising when an individual is a party to the registration, and effect of registration and nonregistration.

E. The name of a commercial registered office provider may not be used in Paragraph 3 in lieu of an address.

F. Insert in Paragraph 5 for each entity which is not an individual the following information: (i) the name of the entity and a statement of its form of organization, e.g., corporation, general partnership, limited partnership, business trust, (ii) the name of the jurisdiction under the laws of which it is organized, (iii) the address, including street and number, if any, of its registered office, if any, in this Commonwealth. If any of the entities is an association which has designated the name of a commercial registered office provider in lieu of a registered office address as permitted by 15 Pa. C.S. § 109, the name of the provider and the venue county should be inserted in the last column.

G. Every individual whose name appears in Paragraph 4 of the form must sign the form **exactly** as the name is set forth in Paragraph 4. The name of every other entity listed in Paragraph 5 shall be signed on its behalf by an officer, trustee or other authorized person. See 19 Pa. Code §13.8(b) (relating to execution), which permits execution pursuant to power of attorney. A copy of the underlying power of attorney or other authorization should not be submitted to, and will not be received by or filed in, the Department.

H. If an individual is a party to the registration, the parties are required by 54 Pa. C.S. § 311(g) to advertise their intention to file or the filing of an application for registration of fictitious name. Proofs of publication of such advertising should not be submitted to the Department, and will not be received by or filed in the Department, but should be kept with the permanent records of the business.

I. This form and all accompanying documents shall be mailed to: Department of State, Corporation Bureau, P.O. Box 8722, Harrisburg, PA 17105-8722.

J. To receive confirmation of the file date prior to receiving the microfilmed original, send either a self-addressed, stamped postcard with the filing information noted or a self-addressed, stamped envelope with a copy of the filing document.

Microfilm Number_____

Filed with the Department of State on_____

Entity Number_____

_____
**Secretary of the Commonwealth**

# APPLICATION FOR REGISTRATION OF FICTITIOUS NAME
DCB:54-311 (Rev 90)

In compliance with the requirements of 54 Pa.C.S. §311 (relating to registration), the undersigned entity(ies) desiring to register a fictitious name under 54 Pa.C.S. Ch. 3 (relating to fictitious names), hereby state(s) that:

1. Then fictitious **name** is: _____ Acme Printing _____

2. A brief statement of the character or nature of the business or other activity to be carried on under or through the fictitious name is:

   The printing and reproduction of business and personal documents

3. The **address**, including number and street, if any, of the principal place of business of the business or other activity to be carried on under or through the fictitious name is (P.O. Box alone is **not** acceptable):

   | 456 Main St. | Harrisburg | PA | 00000 | |
   |---|---|---|---|---|
   | Number and Street | City | State | Zip | County |

4. The **name** and **address**, including number and street, if any, of each individual interested in the business is:

   | Name | Number and Street | City | State |
   |---|---|---|---|
   | Jane Roe | 789 Back Street | Harrisburg | PA |

5. Each **entity**, other than an individual, interested in such business is (are):

   | Name | Form of Organization | Organizing Jurisdiction | Principal Office Address | Pa. Registered Office, if any |
   |---|---|---|---|---|
   | None | | | | |

6. The applicant is familiar with the provisions of 54 Pa.C.S. §332 (relating to effect of registration) and understands that filing under the Fictitious Name Act does not create any exclusive or other right in the fictitious name.

7. **(Optional):** The **name(s)** of the agent(s), if any, any one of whom is authorized to execute amendments to, withdrawals from or cancellation of this registration in behalf of all then existing parties to the registration, is (are):

DSCB:54-311 (Rev 90)-2

 

 

IN TESTIMONY WHEREOF, the undersigned have caused this Application for Registration of Fictitious Name to be executed this <u>23rd</u> day of <u>May</u>, 19 <u>98</u> .

 

| | |
|---|---|
| _____ | *Jane Roe* |
| (Individual Signature) | _____ |
| | (Individual Signature) |
| _____ | _____ |
| (Individual Signature) | (Individual Signature) |
| _____ | _____ |
| (Name of Entity) | (Name of Entity) |
| BY: _____ | BY: _____ |
| TITLE: _____ | TITLE: _____ |

DSCB: PCF3
Corporation Bureau
Pennsylvania Dept. of State

## COUNTER - CORPORATE CERTIFICATION & SEARCH REQUEST FORM

ENTITY NAME: Acme Printing _____

_____

_____

_____

_____

DOCUMENT REQUESTED:

_____ Good Standing (Subsistence) Certificate

_____ Certified Copy of Corporate Index

_____ Great Seal Certificate attesting to _____

_____

_____ Certified Copy of _____

_____ Plain Copy of _____

__X___ Corporate Record Search or Plain Copy of Index

_____ Name Reservation

COMMENTS:

REQUESTOR NAME: ___Jane Roe_____

REQUESTOR ADDRESS: _789 Back Street_____

___Harrisburg PA 00000_____

Mail this order when complete. _to above address_

**The undersigned agrees to pay all statutory fees with respect to this request in advance.**

**SIGNATURE OF REQUESTING PARTY:** ___*Jane Roe*_____

__X___ Will pay by check.

_____ Deduct fees from Account# _____.

Total Due: $__12.00_____

DSCB:54-1112 (Rev 90)-2

**Department of State**
**Corporation Bureau**
**P.O. Box 8722**
**Harrisburg, PA 17105-8722**

**Instructions for Completion of Form:**

A. One original of this form is required. The form shall be completed in black or blue-black ink in order to permit reproduction. The filing fee for this form is $52 made payable to the Department of State. PLEASE NOTE: A separate check is required for each form submitted.

B. The name of a commercial registered office provider may not be used in Paragraph 2 in lieu of an address.

C. An application for registration of a mark is limited to a single general class of goods or services, but a mark may be made the subject of multiple registrations in two or more general classes. (See pages 3 and 4 for general classes of goods and services).

D. This registration is effective for a term of ten years from the date of registration. Application to renew for a similar term must be made of form DSCB:54-1114 (Application for Renewal of Registration of Mark) within six months prior to the expiration of such term.

E. This form and all accompanying documents shall be mailed to:

Department of State

Corporation Bureau

P.O. Box 8722

Harrisburg, PA 17105-8722

F. To receive confirmation of the file date prior to receiving the microfilmed original, send either a self-addressed, stamped postcard with the filing information noted or a self-addressed, stamped envelope with a copy of the filing document.

Microfilm Number _____

Entity Number _____

Filed with the Department of State on _____

_____
**Secretary of the Commonwealth**

# APPLICATION FOR REGISTRATION OF MARK
DSCB:54-1112 (REV 90)

In compliance with the requirements of 54 Pa.C.S. § 1112 (relating to application for registration), the undersigned, having adopted and used a trade mark or service mark in this Commonwealth and desiring to register such mark, hereby states that:

1.  The **name** of the applicant is (if a corporation, also give jurisdiction of incorporation): _____

    Acme Lighting Supply, Inc. (a Pennsylvania corporation)

2.  The **residence, location** or **place of business** of the applicant is:

    | 123 Main Street | Harrisburg | PA | 17000 | |
    |---|---|---|---|---|
    | Number and Street | City | State | Zip | County |

3.  The **name and description of the mark** is (A facsimile of the mark to be registered accompanies this application as Exhibit A and is incorporated herein by reference):

    The mark is a blue bulls-eye on a light blue background.

    _____

4.  The general **class** in which such goods or services fall is (use only one of the classifications as set forth in 54 Pa.C.S. § 1103 (relating to classification)): Goods (54 PaCS § 1103(ii))

5.  The **goods and services** in connection with which the mark is used and the mode and manner in which the mark is used in connection with such goods or services are:

    Lighting installations, parts and service

6.  The **date** when the mark was first used anywhere is: 1-1-00

7.  The **date** when the mark was first used in this Commonwealth by the applicant or the predecessor in title of the applicant is: 1-1-00 .

8.  Applicant is the owner of the mark and no other person has the right to use such mark in this Commonwealth, either in the identical form thereof or in any such near resemblance thereto as might be calculated to deceive or to be mistaken therefore.

    IN TESTIMONY WHEREOF, the undersigned person has caused this Application for Registration of Mark to be executed this ____1st____ day of __January__ , 19 _00_ .

    _____John Q. Public_____
    (Name of Applicant)

    BY: _____*John Q. Public*_____
    (Signature)

    TITLE: President and CEO of
    Acme Lighting Supply

DSCB:54-1112 (Rev 90)-3 Classification

The following general classes of goods and services are established for the purpose of administering this chapter. The Department may, by regulation, amend the classification established by this section if such amendment does not limit or extend the rights of any applicant or registrant. An application for registration of a mark shall be limited to a single general class of goods or services. Nothing in this chapter shall be construed as limiting the registration of a mark to one general class. The classes are as follows:

1.  Chemical products used in industry, science, photography, agriculture, horticulture, forestry; artificial and synthetic resins; plastic in the form of powders, liquids or pastes, for industrial use; manures (natural and artificial); fire extinguishing compositions; tempering substances and chemical preparations for soldering; chemical substances for preserving foodstuff; tanning substances; adhesive substances used in industry.

2.  Paints, varnishes, lacquers; preservatives against rust and against deterioration of wood; coloring matters, dyestuffs; mordants; natural resins metals in foil and powder form for painters and decorators.

3.  Bleaching preparations and other substances for laundry use; cleaning, polishing, scouring and abrasive preparations; soaps; perfumery, essential oils, cosmetics, hair lotions; dentifrices.

4.  Industrial oils and greases (other than edible oils and fats and essential oils); lubricants; dust laying and absorbing compositions; fuels (including motor spirit) and illuminants; candles, tapers, night-lights and wicks.

5.  Pharmaceutical, veterinary and sanitary substances; infants' and invalids' foods; plasters, material for bandaging; material for stoping teeth, dental wax; disinfectants; preparations for killing weeds and destroying vermin.

6.  Unwrought and partly wrought common metals and their alloys; anchors, anvils, bells, rolled and cast building materials; rails and other metallic materials for railway tracks; chains (except driving chains for vehicles); cables and wires (non-electric); locksmiths' work; metallic pipes and tubes; safes and cash boxes; steel balls; horseshoes; nails and screws; other goods in nonprecious metal not included in other classes; ores.

7.  Machines and machine tools; motors (except for land vehicles); machine couplings and belting (except for land vehicles); large size agricultural implements; incubators.

8.  Hand tools and instruments; cutlery, forks and spoons; side arms.

9.  Scientific, nautical, surveying and electrical apparatus and instruments (including wireless), photographic, cinematographic, optical, weighing, measuring, signalling, checking (supervision), lifesaving and teaching apparatus and instruments; coin or counter-fed apparatus; talking machines; cash registers; calculating machines; fire extinguishing apparatus.

10.  Surgical, medical, dental and veterinary instruments and apparatus (including artificial limbs, eyes and teeth).

11.  Installations for lighting, heating, steam generating, cooking, refrigerating, drying, ventilating, water supply and sanitary purposes.

12.  Vehicles; apparatus for locomotion by land, air or water.

13.  Firearms; ammunition and projectiles; explosive substances; fireworks.

14.  Precious metals and their alloys and goods in precious metals or coated therewith (except cutlery, forks and spoons); jewelry, precious stones, horological and other chronometric instruments.

15.  Musical instruments (other than talking machines and wireless apparatus).

16.  Paper and paper articles, cardboard and cardboard articles; printed matter, newspapers and periodicals, books; bookbinding material; photographs, stationery, adhesive materials (stationery); artists' materials; paint brushes; typewriters and office requisites (other than furniture); instructional and teaching material (other than apparatus); playing cards; printers' type and cliches (stereotype).

17.  Gutta-percha, India rubber, balata and substitutes, articles made from these substances and not included in other classes; plastics in the form of sheets, blocks and rods, being for use in manufacture; materials for packing, stopping or insulating; asbestos, mica and their products; hose pipes (nonmetallic).

18.  Leather and imitations of leather, and articles made from these materials and not included in other classes; skins, hides; trunks and traveling bags; umbrellas, parasols and walking sticks, whips, harness and saddlery.

19.  Building materials, natural and artificial stone, cement, lime, mortar, plaster and gravel; pipes of earthen ware or cement; road-making materials; asphalt, pitch and bitumen; portable buildings; stone monuments; chimney pots.

20.  Furniture, mirrors, picture frames; articles (not included in other classes) of wood, cork, reeds, cane, wicker, horn, bone, ivory, whalebone, shell, amber, mother-of-pearl, meerschaum, celluloid, substitutes for all these materials, or of plastics.

21.  Small domestic utensils and containers (not of precious metal or coated therewith); combs and sponges; brushes (other than paint brushes); brush-making materials; instruments and material for cleaning purposes; steel wool; glassenware, porcelain and earthenware, not included in other classes.

22. Ropes, string, nets, tents, awnings, tarpaulins, sails, sacks; padding and stuffing materials (hair, capoc, feathers, seaweed, etc.); raw fibrous textile materials.

23. Yarns, threads.

24. Tissues (piece goods); bed and table covers; textile articles not included in other classes.

25. Clothing, including boots, shoes and slippers.

26. Lace and embroidery, ribbons and braid; buttons, press buttons, hooks and eyes, pins and needles; artificial flowers.

27. Carpets, rugs, mats and matting; linoleums and other materials for covering floors; wall hangings (nontextile).

28. Games and playthings; gymnastic and sporting articles (except clothing); ornaments and decorations for Christmas trees.

29. Meat, fish, poultry and game; meat extracts; preserved, dried and cooked fruits and vegetables; jellies, jams; eggs, milk and other dairy products; edible oils and fats; preserves, pickles.

30. Coffee, tea, cocoa, sugar, rice, tapioca, sago, coffee substitutes; flour and preparations made from cereals; bread, biscuits, cakes, pastry and confectionery, ices, honey, treacle; yeast, baking powder; salt, mustard; pepper, vinegar, sauces, spices; ice.

31. Agricultural, horticultural and forestry products and grains not included in other classes; living animals; fresh fruits and vegetables; seeds; live plants and flowers; foodstuff for animals, malt.

32. Beer, ale and porter; mineral and aerated waters and other nonalcoholic drinks; syrups and other preparations for making beverages.

33. Wines, spirits and liqueurs.

34. Tobacco, raw or manufactured; smokers' articles; matches.

## SERVICES

35. Advertising and business.

36. Insurance and financial.

37. Construction and repair.

38. Communication.

39. Transportation and storage.

40. Material treatment.

41. Education and entertainment.

42. Miscellaneous

# FINANCING YOUR BUSINESS 4

The way to finance your business is determined by how fast you want your business to grow and how much risk of failure you are able to handle. Letting the business grow with its own income is the slowest but safest way to grow. Taking out a personal loan against your house to expand quickly is the fastest but riskiest way to grow.

## BOOTSTRAPPING

Many successful businesses have started out with little money and used the profits to grow bigger and bigger. If you have another source of income on which to live (such as a job or a spouse), you can plow all the income of your fledgling business into growth.

Some businesses start as hobbies or part time ventures on the weekend while the entrepreneur holds down a full time job. Many types of goods or service businesses can start this way. Even some multi-million dollar corporations, such as Apple Computer, started out this way.

This allows you to test your idea with little risk. If you find you're not good at running that type of business, or the time or location wasn't right for your idea, all you are out is the time you spent and your start-up capital.

However, a business can only grow so big from its own income. In many cases, as a business grows, it gets to a point where the orders are so big that money must be borrowed to produce the product to fill them. With this kind of order, there is the risk that if the customer can't pay or goes bankrupt, the business will also fail. At such a point, a business owner should investigate the credit worthiness of the customer and weigh the risks. Some businesses have grown rapidly, some have gone under, and others have decided not to take the risk and stayed small. You can worry about that down the road.

# USING YOUR SAVINGS

If you have savings you can tap to get your business started, that is the best source. You won't have to pay high interest rates and you won't have to worry about paying someone back (relatives).

HOME EQUITY

If you have owned your home for several years, it is possible that the equity has grown substantially and you can get a second mortgage to finance your business. If you have been in the home for many years and have a good record of paying your bills, some lenders will make second mortgages that exceed the equity. Just remember, if your business fails, you may lose your house.

RETIREMENT ACCOUNTS

Be careful about borrowing from your retirement savings. There are tax penalties for borrowing from or against certain types of retirement accounts. Also, your future financial security may be lost if your business doesn't succeed.

HAVING TOO MUCH MONEY

It probably doesn't seem possible to have too much money with which to start a business, but many businesses have failed for that reason. With plenty of start-up capital available, a business owner doesn't need to watch expenses and can become wasteful. Employees get used to lavish spending. Once the money runs out and the business must run on its own earnings, it fails.

Starting with the bare minimum forces a business to watch its expenses and be frugal. It necessitates finding the least expensive solutions to problems that crop up and creative ways to be productive.

# BORROWING MONEY

It is extremely tempting to look to others to get the money to start a business. The risk of failure is less worrisome and the pressure is lower, but that is a problem with borrowing. If it is others' money, you don't have quite the same incentive to succeed as if everything you own is on the line.

Actually, you should be even more concerned when using the money of others. Your reputation should be more valuable than the money itself which can always be replaced. Yet that is not always the case. How many people borrow again and again from their parents for failed business ventures?

FAMILY    Depending on how much money your family can spare, it may be the most comfortable or most uncomfortable source of funds for you. If you have been assured a large inheritance and your parents have more funds than they need to live on, you may be able to borrow against your inheritance without worry. It will be your money anyway and you need it much more now than you will ten or twenty or more years from now. If you lose it all, it's your own loss anyway.

However, if you are borrowing your widowed mother's source of income, asking her to cash in a CD she lives on to finance your get-rich-quick scheme, you should have second thoughts about it. Stop and consider all the real reasons your business might not take off and what your mother would do without the income.

FRIENDS    Borrowing from friends is like borrowing from family members. If you know they have the funds available and could survive a loss, you may want to risk it, but if they would be loaning you their only resources, don't chance it.

Financial problems can be the worst thing for a relationship, whether it is a casual friendship or a long term romantic involvement. Before you borrow from a friend, try to imagine what would happen if you couldn't pay it back and how you would feel if it caused the end of your relationship.

The ideal situation is if your friend were a co-venturer in your business and the burden would not be totally on you to see how the funds were spent. Still, realize that such a venture will put extra strain on the relationship.

BANKS      In a way, a bank can be a more comfortable party from which to borrow because you don't have a personal relationship with them as you do with a friend or family member. If you fail, they'll write your loan off rather than disown you. But a bank can also be the least comfortable party to borrow from because they will demand realistic projections and be on top of you to perform. If you don't meet their expectations, they may call your loan just when you need it most.

The best thing about a bank loan is that they will require you to do your homework: you must have plans that make sense to a banker. If they approve your loan, you know that your plans are at least reasonable.

Bank loans aren't cheap or easy. You'll be paying a good interest rate, and you'll have to put up collateral. If your business does not have equipment or receivables, they may require you to put up your house and other personal property to guarantee the loan.

Banks are a little easier to deal with when you get a Small Business Administration (SBA) loan. That is because the SBA guarantees that it will pay the bank if you default on the loan. SBA loans are obtained through local bank branches.

CREDIT CARDS      Borrowing against a credit card is one of the fastest growing ways of financing a business, but it can be one of the most expensive ways. The rates can go higher than twenty percent, but many cards offer lower rates and some people are able to get numerous cards. Some successful businesses have used the partners' credit cards to get off the ground or to weather through a cash crunch, but if the business doesn't begin to generate the cash to make the payments, you could soon end up in bankruptcy. A good strategy is only to use credit cards for a long term asset like a computer or for something that will quickly generate cash, like buying inventory to fill an order. Don't use credit cards to pay expenses that aren't generating revenue.

# A Rich Partner

One of the best business combinations is a young entrepreneur with ideas and ambition and a retired investor with business experience and money. Together they can supply everything the business needs.

How to find such a partner? Be creative. You should have investigated the business you are starting and know others who have been in such businesses. Have any of them had partners retire over the last few years? Are any of them planning to phase out of the business?

# Selling Shares of Your Business

Silent investors are the best source of capital for your business. You retain full control of the business; and if it happens to fail, you have no obligation to them. Unfortunately, few silent investors are interested in a new business. It is only after you have proven your concept to be successful and built up a rather large enterprise, that you will be able to attract such investors.

The most common way to obtain money from investors is to issue stock to them. For this the best type of business entity is the corporation. It gives you almost unlimited flexibility in the number and kinds of shares of stock you can issue.

# SECURITIES LAWS

There is one major problem with selling stock in your business and that is all of the federal and state regulations with which you must comply. Both the state and federal governments have long and complicated laws dealing with the sales of "securities." There are also hundreds of court cases attempting to explain what these laws mean. A thorough explanation of this area of law is obviously beyond the scope of this book.

Basically, securities have been held to exist in any case in which a person provides money to someone with the expectation that he will get a profit through the efforts of that person. This can apply to any situation where someone buys stock in, or makes a loan to your business. What the laws require is disclosure of the risks involved, and in some cases, registration of the securities with the government. There are some exemptions, such as for small amounts of money and for limited numbers of investors.

Penalties for violation of securities laws are severe, including triple damages and prison terms. You should consult a specialist in securities laws before issuing any security. You can often get an introductory consultation at a reasonable rate to learn your options. A limited explanation of the exemptions is contained in the book *How to Form Your Own Corporation*, available from your local bookstore or from Sphinx Publishing by calling 1-800-432-7444.

# USING THE INTERNET TO FIND CAPITAL

In 1995, the owners of Wit Beer made headlines in all the business magazines by successfully raising $1.6 million for their business on the internet. It seemed so easy, every business wanted to try. What wasn't made clear in most of the stories was that the owner was a corporate securities lawyer and that he did all of the necessary legal work to prepare a prospectus and properly register the stock, something which would have cost anyone else over $100,000 in legal fees. Also, most of the interest in the stock came from the articles, not from the internet promotion. Today, a similar effort would probably not be nearly as successful.

Before attempting to market your company's shares on the internet, be sure to get an opinion from a securities lawyer or do some serious research into securities laws. The lawyer who marketed Wit Beer's shares on the internet has started a business to advise others on raising capital. It is Wit Capital located at 826 Broadway, 6th Floor, New York, NY 10003.

The internet does have some sources of capital listed. The following sites may be helpful.

America's Business Funding Directory:
  **http://www.businessfinance.com**
Angel Capital Electronic Network (SBA): **http://www.sba.gov**
FinanceHub: **http://www.financehub.com**
NVST: **http://www.nvst.com**
Private Capital Clearinghouse: **http://www.pricap.com**

# LOCATING YOUR BUSINESS 5

The right location for your business will be determined by what type of business it is, and how fast you expect it to grow. For some types of businesses, the location will not be important to your success or failure, while in others, it will be crucial.

## WORKING OUT OF YOUR HOME

Many small businesses get started out of the home. Chapter 6 discusses the legalities of home businesses. This section discusses the practicalities.

Starting a business out of your home can save you the rent, electricity, insurance, and other costs of setting up at another location. For some people this is ideal, and they can combine their home and work duties easily and efficiently; but for other people it is a disaster. A spouse, children, neighbors, television, and household chores can be so distracting that no other work gets done.

Since residential rates are usually lower than business lines, many people use their residential telephone line to conduct business or add a second residential line. However, if you wish to be listed in the yellow pages, you will need to have a business line in your home. If you are running two or more types of businesses, you can probably add their names as additional listings on the original number and avoid paying for another business line.

You also should consider whether the type of business you are starting is compatible with a home office. For example, if your business mostly consists of making phone calls or calling clients, the home may be an ideal place to run it. If your clients need to visit you or you will need daily pickups and deliveries by truck, the home may not be a good location. This is discussed in more detail in the next chapter.

# CHOOSING A RETAIL SITE

For most types of retail stores the location is of prime importance. Such things to consider are how close it is to your potential customers, how visible it is to the public, and how easily accessible it is to both autos and pedestrians. The attractiveness and safety should also be considered.

Location would be less important for a business which was the only one of its kind in the area. For example, if there was only one moped parts dealer or Armenian restaurant in a metropolitan area, people would have to come to wherever you are if they want your products or services. However, even with such businesses, keep in mind that there is competition. People who want moped parts can order them by mail, and restaurant customers can choose another type of cuisine.

You should look up all the businesses like the one you plan in the phone book and mark them on a map. For some businesses, like a cleaners, you would want to be far from the others. But for other businesses, like antique stores, you would want to be near the others. Since antique stores usually do not carry the same things, they don't compete and people like to go to an "antique district" and visit all the shops.

# Choosing an Office, Manufacturing, or Warehouse Space

If your business will be the type where customers will not come to you, locating it near customers is not as much of a concern and you can probably save money by locating away from the high traffic, central business districts. However, you should consider the convenience for employees and not locate in an area which would be unattractive to them or too far from where they would likely live.

For manufacturing or warehouse operations, you should consider your proximity to a post office, trucking company or rail line. Where several sites are available, you might consider which one has the earliest or most convenient pick-up schedule for the carriers you plan to use.

# Leasing a Site

A lease of space can be one of the biggest expenses of a small business so you should do a lot of homework before signing one. There are a lot of terms in a commercial lease which can make or break your business. These are the most critical:

ZONING         Before signing a lease, you should be sure that everything that your business will need to do is allowed by the zoning of the property.

RESTRICTIONS   In some shopping centers, existing tenants have guarantees that other tenants do not compete with them. For example, if you plan to open a restaurant and bakery you may be forbidden to sell carry out baked goods if the supermarket has a bakery and a noncompete clause.

SIGNS          Business signs are regulated by zoning laws, sign laws, and property restrictions. If you rent a hidden location with no possibility for adequate signage, your business will have a lot smaller chance of success than with a more visible site or much larger sign.

**ADA COMPLIANCE**     The Americans with Disabilities Act requires that reasonable accommodations be made to make businesses accessible to the handicapped. When a business is remodeled, many more changes are required than if no remodeling is done. When renting space you should be sure that it complies with the law, or the landlord will be responsible for compliance, or you are aware of the full costs you will bear.

**EXPANSION**     As your business grows, you may need to expand your space. The time to find out about your options is before you sign the lease. Perhaps you you can take over adjoining units when those leases expire.

**RENEWAL**     Location is a key to success for some businesses. If you spend five years building up a clientele, you don't want someone to take over your locale at the end of your lease. Therefore, you should have a renewal clause on your lease. This usually allows an increase in rent based on inflation.

**GUARANTEE**     Most landlords of commercial space will not rent to a small corporation without a personal guaranty of the lease. This is a very risky thing for a new business owner to do. The lifetime rent on a long term commercial lease can be hundreds of thousands of dollars and if your business fails, the last thing you want to do is be personally responsible for five years of rent.

Where space is scarce or a location is hot, a landlord can get the guarantees he demands and there is nothing you can do about it (except perhaps set up an asset protection plan ahead of time). But where several units are vacant or the commercial rental market is soft, you can often negotiate out of the personal guaranty. If the lease is five years, maybe you can get away with a guaranty of just the first year. Give it a try.

**DUTY TO OPEN**     Some shopping centers have rules requiring all shops to be open certain hours. If you can't afford to staff it the whole time required or if you have religious or other reasons which make this a problem, you should negotiate it out of the lease or find another location.

**SUBLEASE**     At some point you may decide to sell your business, and in many cases the location is the most valuable aspect of it. For this reason you should be sure that you have the right to either assign your lease or to sublease the property. If this is impossible, one way around a prohibition is to incorporate your business before signing the lease and when you sell the business, sell the stock. But some lease clauses prohibit transfer of "any interest" in the business, so read the lease carefully.

For more information about leasing, you should see the book *How to Negotiate Real Estate Leases* by Mark Warda, also published by Sphinx Publishing. It is available at your local bookstore, or by calling the publisher at 1-800-432-7444.

# Buying a Site

If you are experienced with owning rental property, you will probably be more inclined to buy a site for your business. However, you should probably rent and not take on the extra cost and responsibility of property ownership if you have no experience with real estate.

One reason to buy your site is that you can build up equity. You can pay off a mortgage and eventually own the property rather than pay rent to a landlord.

SEPARATING THE OWNERSHIP

One risk in buying a business site is that if the business gets into financial trouble, the creditors may go after the building as well. For this reason, most people who buy a site for their business keep the ownership out of the business. For example, the business will be a corporation and the real estate will be owned personally by the owner or by a trust unrelated to the business.

EXPANSION

Before buying a site, you should consider the growth potential of your business. If it grows quickly, will you be able to expand at that site or will you have to move? Might the property next door be available for sale in the future if you need it? Can you get an option on it?

If the site is a good investment whether or not you have your business, by all means, buy it. But if its main use is for your business, think twice.

ZONING

Some of the concerns when buying a site are the same as when renting. You will want to make sure that the zoning permits the type of business you wish to start, or that you can get a variance without a large expense or delay. Be aware that just because a business is now using the site does not mean that you can expand or remodel the business at that site. Some zoning laws allow businesses to be grandfathered in, but not expanded. Check with the zoning department and find out exactly what is allowed.

SIGNS

Signs are another concern. Some cities have regulated signs and do not allow new ones, or require the new ones to be smaller. Some businesses have used these laws to get publicity. A car dealer who was told to take down a large number of American flags on his lot filed a federal lawsuit and rallied the community behind him. It couldn't have hurt business except for a few over-controlling public officials.

ADA COMPLIANCE

ADA compliance is another concern when buying a commercial building. Find out from the building department if the building is in compliance or what needs to be done to put it in compliance. If you remodel, the requirements may be more strict.

> *Note:* When dealing with public officials always keep in mind they do not always know what the law is, or honestly tell you what it is. They are often overzealous and try to intimidate people into doing things which are not required by law. Read the requirements yourself and question the officials if they seem to be interpreting the requirements wrong. Seek legal advice if they refuse to budge from a clearly erroneous position. But also consider that keeping them happy may be worth the price. If you are already getting away with something they have overlooked, don't make a big deal over a little thing they want changed or they may subject you to a full inspection or audit.

# CHECK GOVERNMENTAL REGULATIONS

When looking for a site for your business, you should investigate the different governmental regulations in your area. For example, a location just outside the city or county limits might have a lower licensing fee, a lower sales tax rate, and less strict sign requirements.

# LICENSING YOUR BUSINESS 6

## OCCUPATIONAL LICENSES AND ZONING

Before opening your business, you are supposed to obtain a county occupational license; and if you will be working within a city, a city occupational license. Businesses which do work in several cities, such as builders, must obtain a license from each city in which they do work. This does not have to be done until you actually begin a job in a particular city.

County occupational licenses can be obtained from the tax collector in the county courthouse. City licenses are usually available at city hall. Be sure to find out if zoning allows your type of business before buying or leasing property because the licensing departments will check the zoning before issuing your license.

If you will be preparing or serving food, you will need to check with the local health department, the Pennsylvania Department of Environment Protection, and in some limited circumstances, the Pennsylvania Department of Agriculture to be sure that the premises complies.

HOME BUSINESS
Problems occasionally arise when persons attempt to start a business in their home. This is often done because small new businesses cannot afford to pay rent for commercial space. However, cities often try to

forbid business in residential areas; and getting a county occupational license or advertising a fictitious name may give notice to the city that a business is being conducted in a residential area.

Some people avoid the problem by starting their businesses without occupational licenses, figuring that the penalties are less expensive than the cost of office space. Others get the county license and ignore the city rules. If a person has commercial trucks and equipment all over his or her property, there will probably be complaints from neighbors and the city will probably take legal action. But if a person's business consists merely of making phone calls out of the home and keeping supplies there, the problem may never arise.

If a problem does appear regarding a home business that does not disturb the neighbors, a good argument can be made that the zoning law that prohibits the business is unconstitutional. When zoning laws were first instituted, they were not meant to stop people from doing things in a residence that had historically been part of the life in a residence. Consider an artist: Should a zoning law prohibit a person from sitting in her home and painting pictures? If the artist sells them for a living is there a difference? Can the government force the artist to rent commercial space just because she decides to sell the paintings that she paints?

Similar arguments can be made for many home businesses. For hundreds of years people performed income-producing activities in their homes. (The authors are waiting for their city fathers to tell them to stop writing books in their home offices.) However, court battles with a city are expensive and probably not worth the effort for a small business. The best course of action is to keep a low profile. Using a post office box is sometimes helpful in diverting attention away from the residence.

# STATE REGULATED PROFESSIONS

Many professionals require special state licenses. You will probably be called upon to produce such a license when applying for an occupational license.

If you are in a regulated profession, you should be aware of the laws which apply to your profession. The following pages contain a list of professions and the Departments or Bureaus covering them. Contact the Department or Bureau directly and ask for an informational packet containing the laws and regulations covering the profession. The information is almost always free, up-to-date, and easier to get than looking for information in the library. If you do not think your profession is regulated, you should read through the list anyway. Some of those included may surprise you.

# THE DEPARTMENT OF STATE, BUREAU OF PROFESSIONAL AND OCCUPATIONAL AFFAIRS

The Department of State has jurisdiction over many professions through its Bureau of Professional and Occupational Affairs. These professions require usually the successful completion of a licensing exam and usually require you to practice your profession in a certain manner (ethically, for example); and if you don't, you may be taken before an administrative law judge and have your license (and livelihood) taken away. There are laws and regulations which govern the practice of these professions. *Laws* are statutes implemented by the legislature and signed into law by the governor. *Regulations* are procedures and requirements contained in the Pennsylvania Code and are created by the body in charge of enforcing the requirements of the law. For example, the law may say that you have to take a test administered by the state to become a chiropractor but the regulations will tell the procedure that you must follow to apply for the test. Of course, you do not need to know the specifics as the application procedure is a fairly standard process; but if you are denied permission to take a test, you know where to go to challenge the decision—knowledge is power!

The following professions are either under the jurisdiction of the Bureau of Professional and Occupational Affairs (BPOA) or some other state department.

Accountants: BPOA—Accountants Board 717-783-1404

Amusement Ride Inspectors: Department of Agriculture 717-787-2291

Anesthetists: BPOA—Cosmetologists and Anesthetists Board 717-783-7130

Approved Food Safety and Laboratory Services Inspectors: Department of Agriculture 717-782-3237

Architects: BPOA—Architect Licensure Board 717-783-3398

Auctioneers: BPOA—Auctioneers Examiners Board 717-783-3397

Auto Appraisers: Department of Insurance 717-783-4312

Bail Bondspersons: Department of Insurance 717-783-4312

Barbers: BPOA—Barber Examiners Board 717-783-3402

Car Dealers: BPOA—Vehicle Board 717-783-1697

Car sales persons: BPOA—Vehicle Board 717-783-1697

Chiropractors: BPOA—Chiropractic Examiners Board 717-783-7156

Cosmetologists: BPOA—Cosmetologists and Anesthetists Board 717-783-7130

Dentists: BPOA—Dentistry Board 717-783-7162

Egg Inspectors: Department of Agriculture 717-787-4211

Emergency Medical Service (EMS) Instructors: Department of Health 717-787-6436

Emergency Medical Technicians (EMT) and Paramedics: Department of Health 717-787-6436

Entertainers: Department of Labor and Industry 717-787-5279

Entertainment Agents: Department of Labor and Industry 717-787-5279

*Exotic Wildlife Dealers: Department of Agriculture 717-783-3181

First Responders: Department of Health 717-787-6436

Funeral Directors: BPOA—Funeral Directors Board 717-783-3397

*Fur Dealers: Department of Agriculture 717-783-3181

Harness Racing Owners and Drivers: Department of Agriculture 717-787-1942

Health Professionals: Department of Health 717-783-1078 and BPOA generally 717-787-1057

Horse Racing Owners and Drivers/Jockeys: Department of Agriculture 717-787-1942

Insurance Adjusters: Department of Insurance 717-787-3840

Insurance Agencies: Department of Insurance 717-783-2142

Insurance Agents: Department of Insurance 717-783-4312

Landscape Architects: BPOA—Landscape Architects Board 717-783-3397

Livestock Brokers: Department of Agriculture 717-787-4737

Livestock Dealers: Department of Agriculture 717-787-4737

Medicine: BPOA—Medicine Board 717-787-2381 or 783-1400

Motion Picture Projectionists: Department of Labor and Industry 717-787-5279

Nursery (plants) Dealers and Agents: Department of Agriculture 717-782-5203

Nurses: BPOA—Nurse Board Division 717-783-7142

Nursing Home Administrators: BPOA—Health Licensing Division 717-783-7155

Occupational Therapists: BPOA—Occupational Therapy Education and Licensure Board 717-783-1389

Optometrists: BPOA—Optometrical Examiners Board 717-783-7134

Osteopathic Doctors: BPOA—Osteopathic Medicine Board 717-783-4858

*Pesticide Dealers: Department of Agriculture 717-787-4737

*Pharmacists: BPOA—Pharmacy Board 717-783-7157

Physical Therapists: BPOA—Physical Therapy Board 717-783-7134

*Pilots: Department of Labor and Industry 717-787-5279

Podiatrists: BPOA—Podiatry Board 717-783-4858

Poultry Technicians: Department of Agriculture 717-783-8555

Professional Engineers: BPOA—Professional Engineers Board 717-783-7049

Psychologists: BPOA—Psychology Board 717-783-7155

Public Weighmasters: Department of Agriculture 717-787-9039

Real Estate Agents: BPOA—Real Estate Commission 717-783-3658

Real Estate Appraisers: BPOA—Certified Real Estate Appraisers Board 717-783-4866

Social Workers: BPOA—Social Work Examiners Board 717-783-1389

Solid Fuel Weighmasters: Department of Agriculture 717-787-9039

Speech-Language and Hearing Therapists: BPOA—Speech-Language and Hearing Examiners Board 717-783-7156

Truck Drivers (Commercial Driver's License—CDL): Department of Transportation 717-787-3130

Vehicle Manufacturers: BPOA—Vehicle Board 717-783-1697

Veterinarians: BPOA—Veterinary Medical Examiners Board 717-783-1389

(Items that have an asterisk (*) by them may have over-lapping federal requirements. Ask when you call the number listed to be sure.)

This list is by no means exhaustive and you are encouraged to contact either your elected state official whose phone number will appear in the government pages of your telephone directory or you may directly contact the department that you think best describes what you plan to do.

ACTIVITIES    In addition to the above required licenses, some *activities* need to be registered, certified, or licensed although the specific individual may not need to be licensed to perform the activity. Again, this list is not at all exhaustive and you are again cautioned to seek help for any questions through your elected official's office or through the appropriate department. Remember, if you don't know—ask! Knowing for sure what you need before you start your business or occupation will save time, money, and heartache later. Besides, your taxes support your elected officials and the departments—so get your money's worth!

If you plan to engage in any of the following activities, you may need to be registered, or to be licensed, or have a permit to do so from the department that follows:

Abortion Clinics: Department of Health (Call your county office.)

Accreditation Medical Command Facilities: Department of Health (Call your county office.)

Accreditation Training Institutes: Department of Health (Call your county office.)

Adoption: Department of Public Welfare 717-772-7015

Adult Day Care Facilities: Department of Public Welfare 717-787-1948

Agricultural Utilization of Sewerage Sludge: Department of Environmental Protection 717-787-7381

Air Quality Plans and Operating: Department of Environmental Protection 717-787-9702

Airport Landing Fields: Department of Transportation 717-783-6677

All Terrain Vehicles: Department of Conservation and Natural Resources 717-783-9227

Ambulance Services: Department of Health (Call your county office.)

Ambulatory Surgery Facilities: Department of Health (Call your county office.)

Animal Feed: Department of Agriculture 717-783-6677

Areas where food is to be prepared for commercial consumption—especially for frozen desserts, non-alcoholic drinks: Department of Agriculture 717-787-4248

Asbestos Removal: Department of Environmental Protection 717-783-2300

Bakeries: Department of Agriculture 717-787-4248

Beneficial Use of Municipal Waste: Department of Environmental Protection 717-783-2300

Beneficial Use of Residual Waste: Department of Environmental Protection 717-787-7381

Birthing Centers: Department of Health (Call your county office.)

Blasting: Department of Environmental Protection 717-787-7846

Boat Launching: Department of Environmental Protection 717-787-2529

Boat Mooring: Department of Environmental Protection 717-787-6826

Boiler Operators: Department of Labor and Industry 717-787-2923

Bottled or Vended Drinking Water: Department of Environmental Protection 717-787-2666

Cattle branding: Department of Agriculture 717-783-6677

Charitable Organizations: Department of State (800)732-0999

Child Day Care: Department of Public Welfare 717-787-8691

Clinical Laboratories: Department of Health (Call your county office.)

Clinical Labs performing: blood alcohol analysis, blood lead analysis, Erythrocyte Protoporphyrin analysis, urine drug tests, and breath alcohol testing devices: Department of Health (Call your county office.)

Coal Mining: Department of Environmental Protection 717-783-8845

Coal Preparation: Department of Environmental Protection 717-783-5338

Coal Refuse Disposal: Department of Environmental Protection 717-783-5338

Coal Surface Mining: Department of Environmental Protection 717-783-8845

Cold Storage Warehouses: Department of Agriculture 717-787-4248

Commercial Fishing: Pennsylvania Fish and Boat Commission 717-657-4528

Commercial Hatchery: Pennsylvania Fish and Boat Commission 814-359-5154

Community Residential Facilities: Department of Public Welfare 717-783-5767

Composting (commercially): Department of Environmental Protection 717-787-5267

Constructing and Demolishing Waste Landfills: Department of Environmental Protection 717-787-6239 or 787-7381

Consumer Discount Companies: Department of Banking 717-783-4721

Corporations: Department of State 717-787-1057

Courier Services: Public Utility Commission 717-783-1740

Dam Safety: Department of Environmental Protection 717-783-1384

Day Treatment Services: Department of Public Welfare 717-787-1948

Deep Mine Blasting and Storage of Explosives: Department of Environmental Protection 717-787-1376

Demonstration of Municipal and Residual Waste Facilities: Department of Environmental Protection 717-787-6239

Drug and Alcohol Facilities: Department of Health (County office)

Drugs, Devices and Cosmetics Sales: Department of Health (County office)

Earth Disturbance: Department of Environmental Protection 717-783-5338

Eating and Drinking Places: Department of Environmental Protection (Call your nearest dept. office from the government pages in your telephone directory.)

Elevator Inspection and Installation: Department of Labor and Industry 717-787-3765

Facility for the Transfer of Municipal and Residual Waste: Department of Environmental Protection 717-787-6239

Fertilizing (commercially): Department of Agriculture 717-772-5203

Fictitious Names: Department of State 717-787-1057

Firewood Gathering from State Forests: Department of Conservation and Natural Resources 717-772-9104

Fishing Agency: Pennsylvania Fish and Boat Commission 717-657-4528

Foster Families: Department of Public Welfare 717-783-7161

"Garbage license" (feeding garbage to pigs): Department of Agriculture 717-783-6677

Gasoline Regulated Distribution: Department of Revenue 717-787-8201

Ginseng Harvesting: Department of Conservation and Natural Resources 717-783-1639

Greenhouses: Department of Agriculture 717-772-5203

Ground Pine Removal: Department of Conservation and Natural Resources 717-787-2703

Health Maintenance Organizations: Department of Insurance 717-783-2107

Home Health Agencies: Department of Health (County office)

Horse Slaughtering: Department of Agriculture 717-772-2852

Hospitals: Department of Health (County office)

Incineration Resource Recovery: Department of Environmental Protection 717-787-9702

Inspection Stations: Department of Transportation 717-787-2795

Intermediate Care Facilities for the Mentally Retarded: Department of Public Welfare 717-787-6443

Intermediate Care Facilities: Department of Public Welfare 717-787-1171

Junkyards: Department of Transportation 717-787-2838

Kennels: Department of Agriculture 717-787-4833

Land Disposal of Sewerage Sludge: Department of Environmental Protection 717-787-7381

Land Reclamation of Sewerage Sludge: Department of Environmental Protection 717-787-7381

Liming (for treating soil): Department of Agriculture 717-772-5203

Limousines: Public Utility Commission 717-783-1740

Live Bait Dealer: Pennsylvania Fish and Boat Commission 717-657-4528

Mammography Screening: Department of Health (County office).

Manufacturing of bedding, upholstery, and stuffed toys: Department of Labor and Industry 717-787-6848

Marina Slips: Department of Environmental Protection 717-787-2529

Meat Packing: Department of Agriculture 814-238-2527

Mineral Prospecting: Department of Environmental Protection 717-783-5338

Mining Authorization Letters: Department of Environmental Protection 717-783-5338

Mining Equipment Approval: Department of Environmental Protection 717-783-5338

Municipal Waste for Landfills: Department of Environmental Protection 717-783-7381

Municipal Waste Processing and Disposal: Department of Environmental Protection 717-783-7381

Non-Coal Surface Mining: Department of Environmental Protection 570-621-3139

Non-community Water Systems: Department of Environmental Protection 717-783-2300

Nurseries (plants): Department of Agriculture 717-772-5203

Nursing Homes: Department of Health (County office).

Occupancy Permits for Health Care Facilities: Department of Health (County office).

Oil and Gas: Department of Environmental Protection 717-772-2199

Out-Of-State Corporation: Department of State 717-787-1057

Passenger Boat Operator's: Pennsylvania Fish and Boat Commission 717-657-4534

Personal Care Homes: Department of Public Welfare 717-783-4505

Portable X-ray Machines: Department of Health (County office).

Poultry Hauling: Department of Agriculture 717-783-8555

Preferred Provider Organizations: Department of Insurance 717-787-2317

Prepaid Capitated Dental Plans: Department of Insurance 717-787-2317

Private Academic Schools: Department of Education 717-783-6788

Private Driver Training Schools: Department of Education 717-783-6788

Private Employment Agencies: Department of Labor and Industry 610-821-6735

Private Licensed Business, Correspondence, and Trade Schools: Department of Education 717-783-6788

Public Water Supply Systems: Department of Environmental Protection 717-787-9037

Radiation-related activities require registration and licensure through the U.S. Nuclear Regulatory Commission as well as licensing and permits through the State, these activities include, but are not limited to: radiation producing machines, radioactive material handling, and storage: Department of Environmental Protection 717-787-2480

Radon Testing and Mitigation: Department of Environmental Protection 1-800-23RADON

Registration of Securities: Pennsylvania Securities Commission 717-787-8061

Regulated Fishing Lake Fishing: Pennsylvania Fish and Boat Commission 717-657-4518

Regulated Hunting Grounds: Pennsylvania Game Commission 717-787-4250

Rendering Plants: Department of Agriculture 717-783-6677

Residential and Maternity Homes: Department of Public Welfare 717-783-4505

Road Use through State Forests: Department of Conservation and Natural Resources 717-787-2703

Sales Finance Companies: Department of Banking 717-787-2665

Sanitation Licenses which include: campgrounds, organized camps, organized camp certificate of registration, private academic school license inspection, seasonal farm camps: Department of Environmental Protection 717-783-2300

Secondary Mortgage Loan Companies: Department of Banking 717-787-2665

Securities Exemption: Pennsylvania Securities Commission 717-787-8061

Seismic Surveying: Department of Environmental Protection 717-783-2300

Selling Milk and Dairy: Department of Agriculture 717-787-4244

Small Games of Chance (you must also get a permit from your county's Office of Treasurer—some counties permit small games of chance and others do not): Department of Revenue 717-787-8201

Snowmobile Registration: Department of Conservation and Natural Resources 717-783-9227

Soil Conditioners and Plant Growth substances: Department of Agriculture 717-787-4737

Stallion-Jack: Department of Agriculture 610-436-3401

State and Local Sales, Use and Occupancy: Department of Revenue 717-783-9227

State Forest Camping: Department of Conservation and Natural Resources 1-800-63PARKS

State Park Camping: Department of Conservation and Natural Resources 1-800-63PARKS

State Park Picnicking: Department of Conservation and Natural Resources 1-800-63PARKS

Storage of Explosives: Department of Environmental Protection 717-783-2300

Submerged Lands Licenses: Department of Environmental Protection 717-783-2300

Taxi Services: Public Utility Commission 717-783-1740

Taxidermy: Pennsylvania Game Commission 717-787-4250

Transportation Companies: Public Utility Commission 717-783-1740

Transporting Chemotherapeutic Waste: Department of Environmental Protection 717-783-2300

Trucking Companies: Public Utility Commission 717-783-1740

Vocational Rehabilitation Facilities: Department of Labor and Industry 717-787-5279

Vulnerable Plant License: Department of Environmental Protection 717-783-2300

Water Obstructions and Encroachment: Department of Environmental Protection 717-783-2300

Wild Plant Management: Department of Conservation and Natural Resources 717-783-1639

Wildlife Menageries: Pennsylvania Game Commission 717-787-4250

Wildlife Pest Control: Pennsylvania Game Commission 717-787-4250

Wildlife Propagation: Pennsylvania Game Commission 717-787-4250

Workmen's Compensation: Department of Labor and Industry 1-800-482-2383

The regional office numbers may be found in the blue pages of your phone book or you may call 1-411 for the general information number for the department and you will be referred to the appropriate person from there.

# FEDERAL LICENSES

So far there are few businesses that require federal registration. If you are in any of the types of businesses listed below, you should check with the federal agency below it.

Radio or television stations or manufacturers of equipment emitting radio waves:

Federal Communications Commission
1919 M Street, NW
Washington, DC 20550

Manufacturers of alcohol, tobacco or fire arms and explosives:

Bureau of Alcohol, Tobacco and Firearms,
Treasury Department
1200 Pennsylvania Ave., NW
Washington, DC 20226

Securities brokers and providers of investment advice:

Securities and Exchange Commission
450 - 5th Street NW
Washington, DC 20549

Manufacturers of drugs and processors of meat:

Food and Drug Administration
5600 Fishers Lane
Rockville, MD 28057

Interstate carriers:

Interstate Commerce Commission
12th St. & Constitution Ave.
Washington, DC 20423

Exporting:

Bureau of Export Administration
Department of Commerce
14th St. & Constitution Ave., NW
Washington, D.C. 20220

# Contract Laws 7

As a business owner, you will need to know the basics of forming a simple contract for your transactions with both customers and vendors. There is a lot of misunderstanding and erroneous information available, and relying on it can cost you money. This chapter will give you a quick overview of the principles that apply to your transactions and pitfalls to avoid. If you face more complicated contract questions, you should consult a law library or an attorney familiar with small business law.

## Traditional Contract Law

One of the first things taught in law school is that a contract is not legal unless three elements are present: offer, acceptance and consideration. The rest of the semester dissects exactly what may be a valid offer, acceptance, and consideration. For your purposes, the important things to remember are:

- ☛ If you make an offer to someone, it may result in a binding contract, even if you change your mind or find out it was a bad deal for you.

- ☛ Unless an offer is accepted and both parties agree to the same contract, there is no contract.

☛ A contract does not always have to be in writing. Some laws require certain contracts to be in writing, but as a general rule an oral contract is legal.

☛ Without consideration (the exchange of something of value or mutual promises), there is not a valid contract.

As mentioned above, an entire semester is spent analyzing each of the three elements of a contract. The most important rules for the business owner are:

☛ An advertisement is not an offer. Suppose you put an ad in the newspaper offering "New IBM computers only $1995!" but there is a typo in the ad and it says $19.95? Can people come in and say "I accept, here's my $19.95" creating a legal contract? Fortunately, no. Courts have ruled that the ad is not an offer that a person can accept. It is an invitation to come in and make offers, that the business can accept or reject.

☛ The same rule applies to the price tag on an item. If someone switches price tags on your merchandise, or if you accidentally put the wrong price on it, you are not required by law to sell it at that price. If you intentionally put the wrong price, you may be liable under the "bait and switch" law. And many merchants honor a mistaken price just because refusing to would constitute bad will and probably lose a customer.

☛ When a person makes an offer, several things may happen. It may be accepted, creating a legal contract. It may be rejected. It may expire before it has been accepted. Or, it may be withdrawn before acceptance. A contract may expire either by a date made in the offer ("This offer remains open until noon on January 29, 1999"), or after a reasonable amount of time. What is reasonable is a legal question that a court must decide. If someone makes you an offer to sell goods, clearly you cannot come back five years later and accept. Can you accept a week later or a month later and create a legal contract? That depends on the type of goods and the circumstances.

☛ A person accepting an offer cannot add any terms to it. If you offer to sell a car for $1,000, and the other party says they accept as long as you put new tires on it, there is not contract. An acceptance with changed terms is considered a rejection and a counteroffer.

☛ When someone rejects your offer and makes a counteroffer, a contract can be created by your acceptance of the counteroffer.

These rules can affect your business on a daily basis. Suppose you offer to sell something to one customer over the phone and five minutes later, another customer walks in and offers you more for it. To protect yourself, you should call the first customer and withdraw your offer before accepting the offer of the second customer. If the first customer accepts before you have withdrawn your offer, you may be sued if you have sold the item to the second customer.

There are a few exceptions to the basic rules of contracts of which you should be aware. These are:

☛ Consent to a contract must be voluntary. If it is made under a threat, the contract is not valid.

☛ Contracts to do illegal acts or acts "against public policy" are not enforceable.

☛ If either party to an offer dies, the offer expires and cannot be accepted by the heirs.

☛ Contracts made under misrepresentation are not enforceable. For example, if someone tells you a car has 35,000 miles on it and you later discover it has 135,000 miles, you may be able to rescind the contract for fraud and misrepresentation.

☛ If there was a mutual mistake, a contract may be rescinded. For example, if both you and the seller thought the car had 35,000 miles on it and both relied on that assumption, the contract could be rescinded. However, if the seller knew the car has 135,000 miles on it, but you assumed it had 35,000 and didn't ask, you probably could not rescind the contract.

# STATUTORY CONTRACT LAW

The previous section discussed the basics of contract law. These are not stated in the statutes, but are the principles decided by judges over the past hundreds of years. But in recent times, the legislature have made numerous exceptions to these principles. In most cases, these laws have been passed when the legislature felt that traditional law was not fair. The important laws that affect contracts are these:

STATUTES OF FRAUD

Statutes of fraud state when a contract must be in writing to be valid. Some people believe a contract isn't valid unless it is in writing, but that is not so. Only those types of contracts mentioned in the statutes of fraud must be in writing. Of course, an oral contract is much harder to prove in court than one that is in writing.

These laws state when a contract must be in writing to be valid. In Pennsylvania some of the contracts that must be in writing are as follows:

- ☞ Sales of any interest in real estate (Act 669 of 1772-SS#1).

- ☞ Leases of real estate over three years (Act 20 of 1951 § 201 and § 202).

- ☞ Guarantees of debts of another person [*Tudor Development Group, Inc v. U.S. Fidelity and Guarantee Co.*, 692 F. Supp. 461 (1988)].

- ☞ Sales of goods of over $500 (13 Pa.C.S. § 2201).

- ☞ Sales of personal property of over $5,000 (13 Pa.C.S. § 1206).

CONSUMER PROTECTION LAWS

Due to the alleged unfair practices by some types of businesses, laws have been passed controlling the types of contracts they may use. Most notable among these are health clubs and door-to-door solicitations. The laws covering these businesses usually give the consumer a certain time to cancel the contract. These laws are described in chapter 11 on advertising and promotion laws.

PLAIN
LANGUAGE
CONSUMER
CONTRACT ACT

The Pennsylvania Plain Language Consumer Contract Act (73 P.S. §§ 2201-2212) requires that consumer contracts be easily readable. Under the regulations (37 Pa. Code §§ 307.1-307.10) both the wording and the look of the contract must be user friendly. For example:

- ☛ words, sentences and paragraphs should be short
- ☛ active verbs should be used
- ☛ double negatives should not be used
- ☛ sentences should have no more than one condition
- ☛ cross references should not be used
- ☛ the ink should contrast with the paper
- ☛ headings should be in bold type

The Office of the Attorney General provides a packet of materials about compliance with the act and will pre-approve contracts submitted to it. For more information, call or write:

Office of Attorney General:
Bureau of Consumer Protection
14th Floor, Strawberry Square, Attn: PLA
Harrisburg, PA 17120
1-717-787-9707 or 1-800-441-2555

# PREPARING YOUR CONTRACTS

Before you open your business, you should obtain or prepare the contracts or policies you will use in your business. In some businesses, such as a restaurant, you will not need much. Perhaps you will want a sign near the entrance stating "shirt and shoes required" or "diners must be seated by 10:30 P.M."

However, if you are a building contractor or a similar business, you will need detailed contracts to use with your customers. If you do not clearly spell out your rights and obligations, you may end up in court and lose thousands of dollars in profits.

Of course, the best way to have an effective contract is to have an attorney, who is experienced in the subject, prepare one to meet the needs of your business. However, since this may be too expensive for your new operation, you may want to go elsewhere. Three sources for the contracts you will need are other business like yours, trade associations, and legal form books. You should obtain as many different contracts as possible, compare them, and decide which terms are most comfortable for you. Also, under certain circumstances, the Pennsylvania Attorney General's office will review a contract which you have drafted and issue a letter stating whether or not such a contract is acceptable. This service is free, but time-consuming. However, if you have a letter of satisfaction from the Attorney General then any questions that may arise from your contract that pertain to its propriety can be answered or defended. Please call 717-787-9707 for information regarding this service.

# INSURANCE 8

There are few laws requiring you to have insurance; but if you do not have insurance, you may face liability which would ruin your business. You should be aware of the types of insurance available and weigh the risks of a loss against the cost of a policy.

Be aware that there can be a wide range of prices and coverage in insurance policies. You should get at least three quotes from different insurance agents and ask each one to explain the benefits of their policy.

## WORKERS' COMPENSATION

If you have *any* full or part-time employees, you are required by law to carry workers' compensation insurance.

This insurance can be obtained from most insurance companies. With such coverage, you are protected against suits by employees or their heirs in case of accident and against potentially ruinous claims.

Failure to provide worker's compensation insurance when required is considered serious. An employer is guilty of a third degree misdemeanor for each failure to provide worker's compensation insurance. If the failure is deemed by the court to be intentional, the employer is guilty of a felony of the third degree for each violation. Each day that there is a failure to carry workers' compensation is considered a separate offense.

There are other requirements of the workers' compensation law, such as reporting any on-the-job deaths of workers within twenty-four hours. Also, it is a misdemeanor to deduct the amount of the premiums from the employee's wages.

Those who are exempt from the law are supposed to file an affidavit each year with the state stating that they are exempt. Also, a notice must be posted in the workplace stating that employees are not entitled to workers' compensation benefits.

This law has been subject to frequent change lately, so you should check with the Bureau of Workers' Compensation for the latest requirements. Ask for the their latest publication. Call 1-800-482-2383 or write:

Bureau of Workers' Compensation
Room 102
1171 S. Cameron St.
Harrisburg, PA 17104-2501

# Liability Insurance

You are not required to carry liability insurance in most cases. A notable exception is physicians. Physicians are required by the state to obtain minimum coverage of $200,000 per incident and $600,000 per year and then pay a surcharge to the Medical Professional Liability Catastrophic Loss Fund (MED-CAT). There is a basic rate surcharge and an emergency surcharge. The basic rate surcharge is based upon the classification of the physician (podiatrist, obstetrician-gynecologist, oncologist, etc.) and the emergency surcharge is a percentage based upon the amount of malpractice claims paid out in the prior year. Information about MED-CAT may be obtained by calling 717-783-3770.

Liability insurance can be divided into two main areas: coverage for injuries on your premises and by your employees, and coverage for injuries caused by your products.

Coverage for the first type of injury is usually very reasonably priced. Injuries in your business or by your employees (such as in an auto accident) are covered by standard premises or auto policies. But coverage for injuries by products may be harder to find and more expensive. In the current liability crisis, juries have awarded ridiculously high judgments for accidents involving products which had little if any impact on the accident. The situation has become so bad that some entire industries have gone out of business or moved overseas.

ASSET
PROTECTION

Hopefully, laws will soon be passed to protect businesses from these unfair awards. For now, if insurance is unavailable or unaffordable, you can go without and use a corporation and other asset protection devices to protect yourself from liability.

UMBRELLA
POLICY

The best way to find out if insurance is available for your type of business is to check with other businesses. If there is a trade group for your industry, their newsletter or magazine may contain ads for insurers.

As a business owner, you will be a more visible target for lawsuits even if there is little merit to them. Lawyers know that a *nuisance suit* is often settled for thousands of dollars. Because of your greater exposure, you should consider getting a personal umbrella policy. This is a policy which covers you for claims of up to a million, or even two or five million dollars and is very reasonably priced.

# HAZARD INSURANCE

One of the worst things that can happen to your business is a fire, flood, or other disaster. With lost customer lists, inventory, and equipment, many businesses have been forced to close after such a disaster.

The premium for such insurance is usually reasonable and could protect you from loss of your business. As an additional protection you should keep backup copies of your important records at your home or another location. Please contact the Pennsylvania Emergency Management Agency at 717-651-2007 or PEMA, Executive Office, PO Box 3221, Harrisburg, PA, 17105-3321 for information on the Federal Flood Insurance Program.

# HOME BUSINESSES

There is a special insurance problem for home businesses. Most homeowner and tenant insurance policies do not cover business activities. In fact, under some policies, you may be denied coverage if you use your home for a business.

If you merely use your home to make business phone calls and send letters, you will probably not have a problem and not need extra coverage. But if you own equipment or have dedicated a portion of your home exclusively to the business, you could have a problem. Check with your insurance agent for the options that are available to you.

If your business is a sole proprietorship, and you have, say, a computer which you use both personally and for your business, it would probably be covered under your homeowners policy. But if you incorporate your business and bought the computer in the name of the corporation, coverage might be denied. If a computer is your main business asset you could get a special insurance policy in the company name covering just the computer. One company which offers such a policy is Safeware at 1-800-723-9273 or 1-800-800-1492.

# Automobile Insurance

If you or any of your employees will be using an automobile for business purposes, be sure that such use is covered. Sometimes a policy may include an exclusion for business use. Check to be sure your liability policy covers you if one of your employees causes an accident while running a business errand.

# Health Insurance

While new businesses can rarely afford health insurance for their employees, the sooner they can obtain it, the better chance they'll have to find and keep good employees. Those starting a business usually need insurance for themselves (unless they have a working spouse who can cover the family), and they can sometimes get a better rate if they get a small business package.

# Employee Theft

If you fear employees may be able to steal from your business, you may want to have them bonded. This can cover all existing and new employees. You may also require a background check of your new employees. Background checks are conducted through the Pennsylvania State Police, and the cost is $10. A check takes about eight weeks. Some employee positions are required by the state to have background check. Most notable are daycare workers and those who come into contact with children, such as coaches and often school personnel.

# HEALTH AND SAFETY LAWS  9

## FEDERAL LAWS

OSHA

The Occupational Safety and Health Administration (OSHA) is a good example of government regulation so severe it strangles businesses out of existence. It is government run amok. Robert D. Moran, a former chairman of the committee that hears appeals from OSHA rulings once said that "there isn't a person on earth who can be certain he is in full compliance with the requirements of this standard at any point in time." The point of the law is to place the duty on the employer to keep the workplace free from recognized hazards that are likely to cause death or serious bodily injury to workers.

For example, OSHA decided analyze repetitive-strain injuries or "RSI," such as carpal tunnel syndrome. The Bureau of Labor Statistics estimated that seven percent of workplace illnesses are RSI and the National Safety Council estimated four percent. OSHA, however, determined that sixty percent is a more accurate figure and came out with a 600 page list of proposed regulations, guidelines, and suggestions. These regulations would have affected over one-half of all businesses in America and cost billions of dollars. Fortunately, these regulations were shot down by Congress in 1995 after an outcry from businesses. Shortly thereafter, OSHA officials ignored Congress' sentiment and promised to launch a new effort.

Fortunately, for small businesses the regulations are not as cumbersome as for larger enterprises. If you have ten or fewer employees or if you are in certain types of businesses, you do not have to keep a record of illnesses, injuries, and exposure to hazardous substances of employees. If you have eleven or more employees, you do have to keep this record, which is called *Log 200*. All employers are required to display a poster that you can get from OSHA.

Within forty-eight hours of an on-the-job death of an employee or injury of five or more employees on the job, the area director of OSHA must be contacted.

For more information, you should write or call an OSHA office:

> U.S. Department of Labor
> 200 Constitution Avenue, NW, Room N-3101
> Washington, DC 20210
> Tel. 202-219-4667

or visit their web site (**http://www.osha-slc.gov**) and obtain copies of their publications, *OSHA Handbook for Small Business* (OSHA 2209), and *OSHA Publications and Audiovisual Programs Catalog* (OSHA 2019). They also have a poster that is required to be posted in the workplace (**http://www.osha-slc.gov/OshDoc/Additional.html**).

The Hazard Communication Standard requires that employees be made aware of the hazards in the workplace (29 CFR 1910.1200). It is especially applicable to those working with chemicals but this can include even offices which use copy machines. Businesses using hazardous chemicals must have a comprehensive program for informing employees of the hazards and for protecting them from contamination.

For more information, you can contact OSHA at the previously-mentioned addresses, phone numbers, or web sites. They can supply a copy of the regulation and a booklet called *OSHA 3084* which explains the law.

EPA    The Worker Protection Standard for Agricultural Pesticides requires safety training, decontamination sites and, of course, posters. The Environmental Protection Agency will provide information on compliance with this law. They can be reached at 1-800-490-9198, or their website at **http://www.epa.gov** or by mail at:

> Environmental Protection Agency
> 401 M St., SW
> Washington, DC 20460

FDA    The Pure Food and Drug Act of 1906 prohibits the misbranding or adulteration of food and drugs. It also created the Food and Drug Administration (FDA) which has promulgated tons of regulations and which must give permission before a new drug can be introduced into the market. If you will be dealing with any food or drugs you should keep abreast of their policies. Their web site is **http://www.fda.gov**, their small business site is **http://www.fda.gov/opacom/morechoices/ smallbusiness/toc.html** and their local small business representative is:

> FDA, Mid-Atlantic Region
> Small Business Representative, Marie T. Falcone
> 900 U.S. Customhouse
> 2nd & Chestnut St.
> Philadelphia, PA 19106
> Phone 215-597-4394 Ext 4003
> Fax 215-597-5798

HAZARDOUS MATERIALS TRANSPORTATION    There are regulations which control the shipping and packing of hazardous materials. For more information contact the Office of Hazardous Materials Transportation at 400 Seventh St., S.W., Washington, DC 20590 or at 202-426-0656.

CPSC   The Consumer Product Safety Commission has a set of rules which cover the safety of products. The commission feels that because its rules cover products, rather than people or companies, they apply to everyone producing such products. However, federal laws do not apply to small businesses which do not affect interstate commerce. Whether a small business would fall under a CPSC rule would depend on the size and nature of your business.

The CPSC rules are contained in Title 16 CFR in the following parts. These can be found at most law libraries, some public libraries, and on the internet at **http://www.access.gpo.gov/nara/cfr/cfr-table-search.html**. The CPSC's site is at: **http://cpsc.gov/index.html**.

| PRODUCT | PART |
| --- | --- |
| Antennas, CB and TV | 1402 |
| Architectural Glazing Material | 1201 |
| Articles Hazardous to Children Under 3 | 1501 |
| Baby Cribs-Full Size | 1508 |
| Baby Cribs-Non-Full Size | 1509 |
| Bicycle Helmets | 1203 |
| Bicycles | 1512 |
| Carpets and Rugs | 1630, 1631 |
| Cellulose Insulation | 1209, 1404 |
| Cigarette Lighters | 1210 |
| Citizens Band Base Station Antennas | 1204 |
| Coal and Wood Burning Appliances | 1406 |
| Consumer Products Containing Chlorofluorocarbons | 1401 |
| Electrically Operated Toys | 1505 |
| Emberizing Materials Containing Asbestos (banned) | 1305 |
| Extremely Flammable Contact Adhesives (banned) | 1302 |
| Fireworks | 1507 |
| Garage Door Openers | 1211 |

| | |
|---|---|
| Hazardous Lawn Darts (banned) | 1306 |
| Hazardous Substances | 1500 |
| Human Subjects | 1028 |
| Lawn Mowers, Walk-Behind | 1205 |
| Lead-Containing Paint (banned) | 1303 |
| Matchbooks | 1202 |
| Mattresses | 1632 |
| Pacifiers | 1511 |
| Patching Compounds Containing Asbestos (banned) | 1304 |
| Poisons | 1700 |
| Rattles | 1510 |
| Self-Pressurized Consumer Products | 1401 |
| Sleepwear-Childrens | 1615, 1616 |
| Swimming Pool Slides | 1207 |
| Toys, Electrical | 1505 |
| Unstable Refuse Bins (banned) | 1301 |

ADDITIONAL REGULATIONS

There are proposals for new laws and regulations every day. It would be impossible to include every conceivable one in this book. To be up to date on the laws that affect your type of business, you should belong to a trade association for your industry and subscribe to newsletters which cover your industry. Attending industry conventions is a good way to learn more and to discover new ways to increase your profits.

# PENNSYLVANIA LAWS

HAZARDOUS OCCUPATIONS

Under Act 177 of 1913, railroading; operating street railways; generating and selling electricity; telegraph and telephone business; express business; blasting and dynamiting; operating automobiles for public use; and boating when the boat is powered by steam, gas or electricity are considered hazardous occupations. The owners of such enterprises are liable for injuries or death of their employees unless they can rebut a presumption against them that they have not used reasonable care. In cases where the employee is at fault, the damages are apportioned. Employers may not contract with employees to avoid the liability of this law.

OCCUPATIONAL
AND INDUSTRIAL
SAFETY

In addition to the Federal Safety requirements under OSHA, Pennsylvania has four specific laws which relate to occupational and industrial safety. These laws are: the Fire and Panic Act which regulate the safety of buildings and assesses fees and penalties for violations thereof; the Required Buildings Be Constructed to Be Usable by the Physically Handicapped Act, which is in addition to the Federal Americans With Disabilities Act; and, the Bedding and Upholstery Act, and Stuffed Toy Manufacturers Act, which regulate safety in the manufacturing of these goods.

The Fire and Panic Act which is embodied in Acts 299 of 1927, 175 of 1990, and 349 of 1992 are very important; very complicated; and compliance can be very costly, especially if you are locating your business in an older building. You are urged to begin the process for submitting your plans for examination and approval as soon as you know where you will be locating your business. You are especially urged to submit your plans for examination as early as possible if you will be leasing or renting property because occupancy will not be permitted until plans are approved. Because the Fire and Panic Act is complicated, rather than break down the Acts here, you are urged to contact the Department of Labor and Industry, Bureau of Occupational and Industrial Safety Building Plans Examination Section in Harrisburg at 717-787-3806. Trained Building Examiners will look at drawings of your building and compare it to the Building Code and will either make notation of areas of noncompliance that must be corrected or approve the drawings. This is not an arbitrary process, it is one of mathematics and measurements. The good news is, your plans will eventually be approved if the required changes are made, the bad news is that the changes may be costly and you have to comply with local ordinance which may (and often does) differ from the State Code. If the local ordinance differs, you may need to seek a variance before the local Zoning Board. Contact the city or municipal government building where you intend to locate your office to determine if there are any local ordinances that may apply.

You know those tags that come on your cushions and furniture that say "do not remove under penalty of law" and you wondered whether the pillow police would come in and inspect your cushions? It is the Bedding and Upholstery Act (Act 249 of 1937) that requires such tags. This Act governs the manufacturing; repairing; renovating; cleansing; sterilizing; and disinfecting of mattresses, pillows, bolsters, feather beds, and other filled bedding, cushions, upholstered furniture, and bulk materials intended for use in such products and for sale or lease. Basically, the Act requires that the above named items be made with new, clean, or disinfected/sterilized materials. Enforcement of this Act lies with the Department of General Services. Their phone number is 717-787-4705.

The Stuffed Toy Manufacturing Act (Act 372 of 1961) regulates the manufacturing of stuffed toys for sale, gift, or use. Manufacturers must pay to register their business with the Department of General Services and obtain a certificate of registration. The Stuffed Toy Act requires that stuffed toys be made with new materials that are free from dangerous or harmful substances and requires a certificate of disinfection of materials of animal origin before their use. Do note, that if you have a business making stuffed toys as a "leisure pursuit" and your gross income from the sale of these toys is less than $1,000 a year, you are exempted from the registration fee, but this does not relieve you of the requirement to comply with the Act's other provisions.

# EMPLOYMENT AND LABOR LAWS 10

## HIRING AND FIRING LAWS

For small businesses, there are not many rules regarding whom you may hire or fire. Fortunately, the ancient law that an employee can be fired at any time (or may quit at any time) still prevails for small businesses. But in certain situations, and as you grow, you will come under a number of laws which affect your hiring and firing practices.

One of the most important things to consider when hiring someone is that if you let them go, they may be entitled to unemployment compensation. If so, your unemployment compensation tax rate will go up and it can cost you a lot of money. Therefore, you should only hire people you are sure you will keep and you should avoid situations where your former employees can make claims against your company.

One way this can be done is by hiring only part time employees. The drawback to this is that you may not be able to attract the best employees. When hiring dishwashers or busboys this may not be an issue, but when hiring someone to develop a software product, you do not want them to leave halfway through the development.

A better solution is to screen applicants to begin with and only hire those whom you feel certain will work out. Of course this is easier said than done. Some people interview well but turn out to be incompetent at the job.

The best record to look for is someone who has stayed at each of their previous jobs for a long time. Next best is someone who has not stayed as long (for good reasons) but has always been employed. The worst type of hire would be someone who has been a job-hopper with no concrete reasons for changing jobs, i.e. "the supervisor didn't like me…" job-loser.

The reason those who have collected compensation are not a good risk is that if they collect in the future, even if it is not your fault, your employment of them could make you chargeable for their claim. For example, you hire someone who has been on unemployment compensation and they work out well for a year, but they quit to take another job and are laid off after a few weeks. In this situation, you would be chargeable for most of their claim because their last five quarters of work are analyzed. Look for a steady job history.

One possible way to avoid an unemployment compensation claim is to only "let go" an employee for "cause." Cause is something the employee did such as not showing up on time day after day or being unable to work a cash register even though they were trained. An employee can collect unemployment compensation if they "lose their job through no fault of their own" such as when a company "downsizes" and lays workers off. But if you let someone go because of tardiness, poor performance, etc., you will probably be able to avoid an unemployment compensation claim. This reason is only probable and not definite because the unemployment compensation offices are traditionally very "pro-employee" and, in most cases, will heavily favor the employee's version of employment termination. You are requested by the office to provide in writing your own version of the termination and you can always appeal and do not necessarily need to engage an attorney to do so.

In the authors' experience, the intelligence of an employee is more important than his or her experience. An employee with years of typing experience may be fast, but unable to figure out how to use your new computer. Whereas an intelligent employee can learn the equipment quickly and eventually gain speed. Of course, common sense is important in all situations.

The bottom line is that you cannot know if an employee will be able to fill your needs from a resume and interview. Once you have found someone whom you think will work out, offer them a job with a ninety day probationary period. If you are not completely satisfied with them after the ninety days, offer to extend the probationary period for ninety additional days rather than end the relationship immediately. Of course, all of this should be in writing.

BACKGROUND CHECKS

Checking references is important, but beware that a former boss may be a good friend, or even a relative. It has always been considered acceptable to exaggerate on resumes, but in recent years, some applicants have been found to be completely fabricating sections of their education and experience.

POLYGRAPH TESTS

Under the federal Employee Polygraph Protection Act you cannot require an employee or prospective employee to take a polygraph test unless you are in the armored car, guard, or pharmaceutical business.

DRUG TESTS

Drug testing in Pennsylvania is discretionary but it must be applied uniformly—in other words, all employees must be required to take a drug test, not just "new hires."

# FIRING

In most cases, unless you have a contract with an employee for a set time period, you can fire him or her at any time. This is only fair since the employee can quit at any time. The exceptions to this are: if you fired someone based on illegal discrimination (see page 99), for filing some sort of health or safety complaint (see page 83), or for refusing your sexual advances (see page 102).

# New Hire Reporting

In order to track down parents who do not pay child support, a federal law was passed in 1996 which requires the reporting of new hires. The Personal Responsibility and Work Opportunity Reconciliation Act of 1996 (PRWORA) provides that such information must be reported by employers to their state government.

Within twenty days of hiring a new employee, an employer must provide the state with information about the employee including the name, social security number, and address. This information can be submitted in several ways including mail, fax, magnetic tape or over the internet. There is a special form which can be used for this reporting; however, an employer can use the W-4 form for this purpose. Since this form must be filled out for all employees anyway, it would be pointless to use a separate form for the new hire reporting. A copy of the W-4 form is included in the appendix and this may be faxed to 1-717-657-4473 or mailed to:

> Pennsylvania New Hire Reporting Program
> P. O. Box 69400
> Harrisburg, PA 17106-9400

For more information about the program you can call them at 1-888-724-9400, visit their web site: **http://www.panewhires.com**, or email them at info@panewhires.com.

# Employment Agreements

To avoid misunderstanding with employees, you should use an employment agreement or an employee handbook. These can spell out in detail the policies of your company and the rights of your employees. They can protect your trade secrets and spell out clearly that employment can be terminated at any time by either party.

While it may be difficult or awkward to ask an existing employee to sign such an agreement, an applicant hoping you will hire them will usually sign whatever is necessary to obtain the job. However, because of the unequal bargaining position, you should not use an agreement which would make you look bad if the matter ever went to court.

If having an employee sign an agreement is awkward, you can usually obtain the same rights by putting the company policies in an employee manual. Each existing and new employee should be given a copy along with a letter stating that the rules apply to all employees and that by accepting or continuing employment at your company, they agree to abide by the rules. Having an employee sign a receipt for the letter and manual is proof that they received it.

One danger of an employment agreement or handbook is that it may be interpreted to create a long term employment contract. To avoid this, be sure that you clearly state in the agreement or handbook that the employment is "at will" and can be terminated at any time by either party.

Some other things to consider in an employment agreement or handbook are:

☞ what the salary and other compensation will be,

☞ what the hours of employment will be,

☞ what the probationary period will be,

☞ that the employee cannot sign any contracts binding the employer, and

☞ that the employee agrees to arbitration rather than filing a lawsuit.

An employment agreement as well as a confidentiality agreement and a non-competition agreement are included in the book *The Most Valuable Business Legal Forms You'll Ever Need* by James C. Ray, published by Sphinx Publishing. It is available at your local bookstore, or by calling the publisher at 1-800-432-7444.

# INDEPENDENT CONTRACTORS

One way to avoid problems with employees and taxes at the same time is to have all of your work done through independent contractors. This can relieve you of most of the burdens of employment laws and the obligation to pay social security and medicare taxes for the workers.

An independent contractor is, in effect, a separate business which you pay to do a job. You pay them just as you pay any company from which you buy products or services. At the end of the year if the amount paid exceeds $600, you will issue a 1099 form instead of a W-2.

This may seem too good to be true; and in some situations, it is. The IRS does not like independent contractor (IC) arrangements because it is too easy for the ICs to cheat on their taxes. To limit the use of ICs, the IRS has strict regulations on who may and may not be classified an independent contractor. Also, companies who do not appear to pay enough in wages for their field of business are audited.

The highest at risk jobs are those which are not traditionally done by independent contractors. For example, you could not get away with hiring a secretary as an independent contractor. One of the most important factors considered in determining if a worker can be an independent contractor is the amount of control the company has over his or her work. If you need someone to paint your building and you agree to pay them a certain price to do it according to their own methods and schedule, you can pay them as an independent contractor. But if you tell them when to work, how to do the job, and provide them with the tools and materials, they will be classified an employee.

If you just need some typing done and you take it to a typing service and pick it up when it is ready, you will be safe in treating them as independent contractors. But, if you need someone to come into your office to type on your machine at your schedule, you will probably be required to treat that person as an employee for tax purposes.

The IRS has a form you can use in determining if a person is an employee or an independent contractor. It is form SS-8 and is included in the appendix of this book.

INDEPENDENT CONTRACTORS V. EMPLOYEES

In deciding whether to make use of independent contractors or employees, you should weigh the following advantages and disadvantages.

*Advantages.*

☛ Lower taxes. You do not have to pay social security, medicare, unemployment, or other employee taxes

☛ Less paperwork. You do not have to handle federal withholding deposits or the monthly employer returns to the state or federal government.

☛ Less insurance. You do not have to pay workers' compensation insurance and since the workers are not your employees you do not have to insure against their possible liabilities.

☛ More flexibility. You can use ICs when you need them and not pay them when business is slow.

*Disadvantages.*

☛ The IRS and state tax offices are strict about when workers may be qualified as ICs. They will audit companies whose use of ICs does not appear to be legitimate.

☛ If your use of ICs is found to be improper, you may have to pay back taxes and penalties and have problems with your pension plan.

☛ While employees usually cannot sue you for their injuries (if you have covered them with workers' compensation), ICs can sue you if their injuries were your fault.

☛ If you are paying someone to produce a creative work (writing, photography, artwork), you receive less rights to the work of an IC. (See *How to Register Your Own Copyright* by Mark Warda, published by Sphinx Publishing, and is available by calling 1-800-432-7444.)

☞ You have less control over the work of an IC and less flexibility in terminating them if you are not satisfied that the job is being done the way you require.

☞ You have less loyalty from an IC who works sporadically for you and possibly others than from your own full time employees.

For some businesses, the advantages outweigh the disadvantages, but for others, they do not. Consider your business plans and the consequences from each type of arrangement. Keep in mind that it will be easier to start with ICs and switch to employees than to hire employees and have to fire them to hire ICs.

# TEMPORARY WORKERS

Another way to avoid the hassles of hiring employees is to get workers from a temporary agency. You may pay a higher amount per hour for the work in this arrangement, but the agency will take care of all of the tax and insurance requirements. Since these requirements can be expensive and time-consuming, the extra cost may be well worth it.

Whether or not temporary workers will work for you depends upon the type of business you are in and tasks you need performed. For such jobs as sales management, you would probably want someone who will stay with you long term and develop relationships with the buyers, but for order fulfillment, temporary workers might work out well.

Another advantage of temporary workers is that you can easily stop using those who do not work out well for you, but if you find one who is ideal, you may be able to hire him or her on a full time basis.

A new wrinkle has developed in the temporary worker area in recent years. Many large companies are beginning to use them because they are so much cheaper than paying the benefits demanded by full time employees. For example, Microsoft Corp. has had as many as 6,000 temporary workers, some of whom have worked for them for years.

Some of the temporary workers recently won a lawsuit declaring that they are really employees and are entitled to the same benefits of other employees (such as pension plans).

The law is not yet settled in this area as to what arrangements will result in a temporary worker being declared an employee. That will take several more court cases, some of which have already been filed. A few things you can do to protect yourself are:

☛ Be sure that any of your benefit plans make it clear that they do not apply to workers obtained through temporary agencies

☛ Do not keep the same temporary workers for longer than a year

☛ Do not list temporary workers in any employee directories or hold them out to the public as your employees

☛ Do not allow them to use your business cards or stationery

# DISCRIMINATION LAWS

FEDERAL LAW    There are numerous federal laws forbidding discrimination based upon race, sex, pregnancy, color, religion, national origin, age, or disability. The laws apply to both hiring and firing and to employment practices such as salaries, promotions, and benefits. Most of these laws only apply to an employer who has fifteen or more employees for twenty weeks of a calendar year or has federal contracts or subcontracts. Therefore, you most likely will not be required to comply with the law immediately upon opening your business. However, there are similar state laws which may apply to your business.

One exception is the Equal Pay Act which applies to employers with two or more employees and requires that women be paid the same as men in the same type of job.

Employers with fifteen or more employees are required to display a poster regarding discrimination. This poster is available from the Equal Employment Opportunity Commission, 2401 E. Street, N.W.,

Washington, DC 20506. Employers with 100 or more employees are required to file an annual report with the EEOC.

When hiring employees, some questions are illegal or inadvisable to ask. The following questions should not be included on your employment application, or in your interviews, unless the information is somehow directly tied to the duties of the job:

☛ Don't ask about an applicant's citizenship or place of birth. But after hiring an employee, you must ask about his or her right to work in this country.

☛ Don't ask a female applicant her maiden name. You can ask if she has been known by any other name in order to do a background check.

☛ Don't ask if applicants have children, plan to have them, or have child care. You can ask if an applicant will be able to work the required hours.

☛ Don't ask if the applicant has religious objections for working Saturday or Sunday. You can mention if the job requires such hours and ask whether the applicant can meet this job requirement.

☛ Don't ask an applicant's age. You can ask if an applicant is eighteen or over, or for a liquor-related job if they are twenty-one or over.

☛ Don't ask an applicant's weight.

☛ Don't ask if an applicant has AIDS or is HIV positive.

☛ Don't ask if the applicant has filed a workers' compensation claim.

☛ Don't ask about the applicant's previous health problems.

☛ Don't ask if the applicant is married or whether their spouse would object to the job, hours, or duties.

☛ Don't ask if the applicant owns a home, furniture, car, as it is considered racially-discriminatory.

☛ Don't ask if the applicant was ever arrested. You can ask if the applicant was ever convicted of a crime.

The most recent discrimination law is the Americans with Disabilities Act of 1990. Under this law, employers who do not make "reasonable accommodations for disabled employees" will face fines of up to $100,000, as well as other civil penalties and civil damage awards.

While the goal of creating more opportunities for people with disabilities is a good one, it is costly to make these accommodations are there are drawbacks. A study released by two MIT economists in late 1998 indicated that since the ADA was passed, employers have hired less rather than more disabled people. It is theorized that this may be due to the expense of the "reasonable accommodations" or the fear of lawsuits by disabled employees.

The ADA currently applies to employers with fifteen or more employees. Employers who need more than fifteen employees might want to consider contracting with independent contractors to avoid problems with this law, particularly if the number of employees is only slightly larger than fifteen.

To find out how this law affects your business, you might want to pay the government $25 for their *ADA Technical Assistance Manual.* You can order it from The Superintendent of Documents, P. O. Box 371954, Pittsburgh, PA 15250-7954, or you can fax your credit card order to 202-512-2233.

***Tax benefits.*** There are three types of tax credits to help small business with the burden of these laws.

☞ Businesses can deduct up to $15,000 a year for making their premises accessible to the disabled and can depreciate the rest (IRC § 190).

☞ Small businesses (under $1,000,000 in revenue and under thirty employees) can get a tax credit each year for fifty percent of the cost of making their premises accessible to the disabled, but this only applies to the amount between $250 and $10,500.

☞ Small businesses can get a credit of up to forty percent of the first $6,000 of wages paid to certain new employees who qualify. See IRS form 8850 and instructions.

***Records.*** To protect against potential claims of discrimination, all employers should keep detailed records showing reasons for hiring or not hiring applicants and for firing employees.

PENNSYLVANIA LAW

Pennsylvania has the Universal Accessibility Act (UAA), Act 235 of 1965 that is applicable in addition to the ADA. Any private building that is used by the public must be accessible by the handicapped pursuant to this Act *if* the building was built or was remodeled after September 1, 1965, the effective date of this Act.

The Pennsylvania Equal Pay Act (Act 694 of 1959) is Pennsylvania's counterpart to the federal law providing for equal pay for the same job to both sexes. This state statute is meant to fill the gap of workers not covered by federal law and, therefore, does not apply to workers who are under the Fair Labor Standards Act, Section 6. The Pennsylvania Equal Pay Act requires employers to post an abstract of Act 694. The abstract is prepared by the Department of Labor and Industry and a copy may be obtained by calling the Bureau of Labor Standards in your region: Altoona, 814-946-7374; Harrisburg, 717-787-4671; Philadelphia, 215-560-1858; Pittsburgh, 412-565-5300; or, Scranton, 570-963-4577.

# SEXUAL HARASSMENT

FEDERAL LAW

What began as protection for employees who were fired or not promoted for failing to succumb to sexual advances of their superiors has been expanded to outlaw nearly any sexual comments or references in the workplace. As an example of how far this has gone, one university was forced to take down a painting by Goya depicting a nude because a teacher felt sexually harassed by its presence!

In the 1980s, the Equal Employment Opportunity Commission interpreted the Title VII of the Civil Rights Act of 1964 to forbid sexual harassment. After that, the courts took over and reviewed all types of conduct in the workplace. The numerous lawsuits that followed began a trend toward expanding the definition of sexual harassment and favoring employees.

Some of the actions which have been considered harassment are:

☞ displaying sexually explicit posters in the workplace;

☞ requiring female employees to wear revealing uniforms;

☞ rating of sexual attractiveness of female employees as they passed male employees' desks

☞ continued sexual jokes and innuendos.

In 1993, the United States Supreme Court ruled that an employee can make a claim for sexual harassment even without proof of a specific injury. However, lower federal courts in more recent cases (such as the Paula Jones case against President Clinton) have dismissed cases where no specific injury was shown (although these cases may be overruled by a higher court). These new cases may indicate that the pendulum has stopped moving toward expanded rights for the employee.

On the other hand, another recent case ruled that an employer can be liable for the harassment of an employee by a supervisor, even if the employer was unaware of the supervisor's conduct, if the employer did not have a system in place to allow complaints against harassment. This area of law is still developing and to avoid a possible lawsuit you should be aware of the things which could potentially cause liability and avoid them.

Some things a business can do to protect against claims of sexual harassment are:

☞ Distribute a written policy against all kinds of sexual harassment to all employees

☛ Encourage employees to report all incidents of sexual harassment

☛ Insure there is no retaliation against those who complain

PENNSYLVANIA LAW

The Pennsylvania Human Relations Act (Act 222 of 1955) prohibits sexual harassment on the job. There are three kinds of sexual harassment as defined in the Act: physical, verbal, and visual. Physical harassment includes touching, fondling, kissing, etc. and can include assault or rape. Verbal harassment includes demands for sexual favors, whistles, jokes of a sexual nature, etc. Visual harassment includes leering, obscene gestures, or crude cartoons, photographs, or posters. Anyone who feels harassment in such a manner and who feels that they must submit or endure this in order to keep their job or get a promotion may file a civil complaint as well as file a complaint before the Pennsylvania Human Relations Commission. In fact, literature published by the Human Relations Commission advises victims to file complaints on several levels: civil court, administrative court (the HRC), their union (if they are unionized employees), and with the police. If you are "the boss" and have not done the harassing, you can and will be sued as well if you know or should have known one of your employees was being victimized and did nothing to stop it. Also, an employee who witnesses the harassment of another can sue the harasser and the boss or supervisor too!

In order to protect yourself, your business, and your employees, you are advised to establish and circulate a policy that explains your position on sexual harassment; defines the behavior that constitutes sexual harassment; and the consequences for violations of the policy. It is advisable to include this sexual harassment policy in the employee handbook that you make each employee sign upon hiring. Also, as an employer, to protect yourself, you should provide a procedure so employees can report incidents, encourage your employees to do so and let them know the incidents will be investigated thoroughly and neutrally and that offenders will be swiftly punished. You should contact the Pennsylvania Human Relations office for assistance in setting up a policy and getting more information about the Human Relations Act.

PA HRC Headquarters
101 S. 2nd St.
Suite 300
Harrisburg, PA 17105-3145
717-787-4410

Harrisburg Regional HRC
Uptown Shopping Plaza
2971-E 7th St.
Harrisburg, PA 17110-2123
717-787-9784

Pittsburgh Regional HRC
11th Floor State Office Building
300 Library Avenue
Pittsburgh, PA 15222-1210
412-565-5395

Philadelphia Regional HRC
711 State Office Building
1400 Spring Garden Street
Philadelphia, PA 19130-4088
215-560-2496

# WAGE AND HOUR LAWS

FEDERAL LAW

***Businesses covered.*** The Fair Labor Standards Act (FLSA) applies to all employers who are engaged in "interstate commerce" or in the production of goods for interstate commerce (anything which will cross the state line) and all employees of hospitals, schools, residential facilities for the disabled or aged, or public agencies. It also applies to all employees of enterprises that gross $500,000 or more per year.

While many small businesses might not think they are engaged in interstate commerce, the laws have been interpreted so broadly that nearly any use of the mails, interstate telephone service, or other interstate services, however minor, is enough to bring a business under the law. The authors of our Constitution clearly intended for most rights to be reserved to the states, but the *commerce clause* has been used to expand federal control to many unintended areas.

***Minimum wage.*** The federal wage and hour laws are contained in the Federal Fair Labor Standards Act. In 1996, Congress passed and President Clinton signed legislation raising the minimum wage to $5.15 an hour beginning September 1, 1997.

In certain circumstances, a wage of $3.62 may be paid to employees under twenty years of age for a ninety day training period.

For employees who regularly receive more than $30 a month in tips, the minimum wage is $2.13 per hour. But if the employee's tips do not bring him up to the full $5.15 minimum wage, then the employer must make up the difference.

**Overtime.** Workers who work over forty hours in a week must be paid time-and-a-half for the time worked over forty hours.

**Exempt employees.** While nearly all businesses are covered, certain employees are exempt from the FLSA. Exempt employees include employees that are considered executives, administrative and managerial, professionals, computer professionals, and outside salespeople.

Whether or not one of these exceptions applies to a particular employee is a complicated legal question. Thousands of court cases have been decided on this issue, but they have given no clear answers. In one case a person could be determined to be exempt because of his duties, but in another, a person with the same duties could be found not exempt.

One thing that is clear is that the determination is made on the employee's function, and not just the job title. You can't make a secretary exempt by calling her a manager if most of her duties are clerical. For more information contact:

Wage and Hour Division
U. S. Department of Labor
200 Constitution Ave., N.W. Room S-3325
Washington, DC 20210

Or call the Philadelphia office at 215-596-1193

On the internet you can obtain information on the Department of Labor's *Small Business Handbook* at:
**http://www.dol.gov/dol/asp/public/programs/handbook/main.htm**

PENNSYLVANIA
LAW

Pennsylvania has several laws that relate to the payment of wages, among these are the Equal Pay Law, the Prevailing Wage Act, the Wage Payment and Collection Law and the Seasonal Farm Labor Act.

The Equal Pay Law, Act 694 of 1959, prohibits discrimination of the rate of pay on the basis of sex by paying wages at a rate less than the rate at which wages are paid to a employees of the opposite sex for equal work, the performance of which requires equal skill, effort, and responsibility and are performed under equal working conditions *except* where payment is made subject to a seniority system, a merit system, a system that makes payment on the basis of quality or quantity of production or any factor other than gender. An agreement by the employee to accept less money for the same job as a member of the opposite sex is *not* a defense to a violation of this Act. Any employer subject to this act cannot lower the wages of the higher paid employee in order to comply with the act and a violation of this Act subjects the employer to liability for the amount of the unpaid wages *plus* an equal amount of the unpaid wages as liquidated damages. Records must be kept on the wages, wage rate, job classifications, and other terms and conditions of employment by the employer. Failure to maintain the records and to make them available to the Department of Labor and Industry upon request will result in the employer being fined $50 to $200 dollars. An abstract of this Act must be posted in a conspicuous place. A copy of the abstract may be obtained by calling the Labor Standards Office in your region, the numbers are listed in the government pages of your telephone book. The Equal Pay Law does not apply to anyone who is subject to Section 6 of the Federal Fair Labor Standards Act.

The Prevailing Wage Act, Act 442 of 1961, requires that contractors and subcontractors performing a public works contract must pay at least the minimum prevailing wage for the job performed. A public works contract is any contract exceeding $25,000 and paid for, in whole or in part, by the funds of the public body. A public works contract includes contracts for the construction, reconstruction, demolition, alteration and repair work other than maintenance work under contract. A worker subject to this Act is any laborer, mechanic, skilled and semi-skilled laborer and apprentices, whether or not their work is performed on the job site. It is the duty of the public body making the contract to determine the prevailing wage rate through the Secretary of the Department of Labor and Industry, but it is important to know of the existence of this law because contractors and subcontractors are required to post the prevailing wages for each craft and classification involved in the contract performance and to protect yourself in case of any protest in the payment of wages on the basis that they are in violation of this law.

There is also the Wage Payment and Collection Law, Act 329 of 1961, which requires that wages be paid on regular paydays designated in advance by the employer. The employer is required to notify the employee of the time and place of payment, the rate of pay and any benefits at the time of hiring.

The Seasonal Farm Labor Act, Act 93 of 1978, was intended to improve the conditions of seasonal farm workers by creating standards for their wages, hours, work conditions, housing, sanitation, food facilities, fire protection, and safety. It requires farm labor contractors to obtain certificates of registration, and forbids the isolation of workers from services to which they are entitled, and limits child labor. Seasonal farm labor camps are inspected by the Department of Environmental Protection and potable drinking water and adequate, sanitary toilet facilities must be provided.

# Pension and Benefit Laws

There are no laws requiring small businesses to provide any types of special benefits to employees. Such benefits are given to attract and keep good employees. With pension plans the main concern is if you do start one it must comply with federal tax laws.

HOLIDAYS    There are no federal or Pennsylvania laws which require that employees be given holidays off. You can require them to work Thanksgiving and Christmas and dock their pay or fire them for failing to show. Of course, you will not have much luck keeping employees with such a policy.

Most companies give full time employees a certain number of paid holidays, such as: New Year's Day (January 1); Memorial Day (last Monday in May); Fourth of July; Labor Day (first Monday in September); Thanksgiving (fourth Thursday in November); and Christmas (December 25). Some, but not many, employers include other holidays such as Martin Luther King, Jr.'s birthday (January 15); President's Day; and Columbus Day. If one of the holidays falls on a Saturday or Sunday, many employers give the preceding Friday or following Monday off.

Pennsylvania law says that legal holidays include all of those in the previous paragraph (except President's Day) as well as the following:

Abraham Lincoln's birthday (February 12)

George Washington's birthday (February 22)

Good Friday (varies)

Primary Election Day (varies—usually in May)

Columbus Day (second Monday in October)

Veterans' Day (November 11)

General Election Day (varies)

However, the fact that these are designated state holidays does not mean anything. In fact, not even the state government is closed on all of these days.

SICK DAYS    There is no federal or Pennsylvania law mandating that an employee be paid for time that he or she is home sick. In fact, the Pennsylvania Labor Law (43 PACS) states that all employers must only pay employees for hours worked. The situation seems to be that the larger the company, the more paid sick leave is allowed. Part time workers rarely get sick leave and small business sick leave is usually limited for the simple reason that they cannot afford to pay for time that employees do not work.

Some small companies have an official policy of no paid sick leave, but when an important employee misses a day because he or she is clearly sick, it is paid.

BREAKS     There are no federal or Pennsylvania laws requiring coffee breaks or lunch breaks. However, it is common sense that employees will be more productive if they have reasonable breaks for nourishment or to use the toilet facilities.

PENSION PLANS AND RETIREMENT ACCOUNTS     Few small new businesses can afford to provide pension plans for their employees. The first concern of a small business is usually how the owner can shelter income in a pension plan without having to set up a pension plan for an employee. Under most pension plans, this is not allowed.

*IRA.* Anyone with $2,000 of earnings can put up to that amount in an Individual Retirement Account. Unless the person or his or her spouse are covered by a company pension plan and have income over a certain amount, the amount put into the account is fully tax deductible.

*ROTH IRA.* Contributions to a Roth IRA are not tax deductible but then when the money is taken out it is not taxable. People who expect to still have taxable income when they withdraw from their IRA can benefit from these.

*SEP IRA, SAR-SEP IRA, SIMPLE IRA.* With these types of retirement accounts, a person can put a much greater amount into a retirement plan and deduct it from their taxable income. Employees must also be covered by such plans, but certain employees are exempt so it is sometimes possible to use these for the owners alone. The best source for more information is a mutual fund company (such as Vanguard, Fidelity, Dreyfus, etc.) or a local bank, which can set up the plan and provide you with all of the rules. These have an advantage over qualified plans (discussed below) since they do not have the high annual fees. One internet site which contains some

useful information on these accounts is:
**http://www.retirement-information.com/iraaccts.htm**.

***Qualified Retirement Plans.*** Qualified retirement plans are 401(k) plans, Keough plans, and corporate retirement plans. These are covered by ERISA, the Employee Retirement Income Security Act which is a complicated law meant to protect employee pension plans. Congress did not want employees who contributed to pension plans all their lives ending up with nothing when the plan goes bankrupt. The law is so complicated and the penalties so severe that some companies are cancelling their pension plans, and applications for new plans are a fraction of what they were previously. However, many banks and mutual funds have created "canned plans" which can be used instead of drafting one from scratch. Still the fees for administering them are steep. Check with a bank or mutual fund for details.

# FAMILY AND MEDICAL LEAVE LAW

FEDERAL LAW

Since Congress thinks business owners are not capable of deciding what type of leave to offer their employees, it passed the Family and Medical Leave Act of 1993. This law requires an employee to be given up to twelve weeks of unpaid leave when:

- ☞ The employee or employee's spouse has a child
- ☞ The employee adopts a child or takes in a foster child
- ☞ The employee needs to care for an ill spouse, child, or parent
- ☞ The employee becomes seriously ill

Fortunately, the law only applies to employers with fifty or more employees. Also, the top ten percent of an employer's salaried employees can be denied this leave because of the disruption in business their loss could cause.

PENNSYLVANIA
LAW

There is no Pennsylvania law requiring family or medical leave. Therefore, the federal act controls.

# CHILD LABOR LAWS

FEDERAL LAW

The Federal Fair Labor Standards Act also contains rules regarding the hiring of children. The basic rules are that children under sixteen years old may not be hired at all except in a few jobs such as acting and newspaper delivery, and those under eighteen may not be hired for dangerous jobs. Children may not work more than three hours a day/eighteen hours a week in a school week or more than eight hours a day/forty hours a week in a non-school week. If you plan to hire children, you should check the Federal Fair Labor Standards Act which is in Chapter 29, United States Code (29 USC) and also the related regulations which are in Chapter 29 of the Code of Federal Regulations (29 CFR).

PENNSYLVANIA LAW

Many immigrant children in Pennsylvania worked in deplorable conditions and died under horrifying circumstances in the coal mines, sweat shops, and factories at the turn of the century. Because of abuses of Child Labor Laws in other states, Pennsylvania created the rather long and complicated Child Labor Law, Act 177 of 1915 that is applicable in addition to the Federal Laws.

Generally, a minor under age fourteen may not be permitted to work in *any* occupation, except those employed on farms or in domestic service in private homes. The farmer is the only person permitted to hire a minor under age fourteen to work on a farm. Twelve to fourteen-year-olds may be employed as caddies if they carry no more than one golf bag at a time and for not more than eighteen holes in one day. Eleven-year-olds may be employed as newscarriers and seven-year-olds may be performers in the entertainment field. Other minor and infants may also be cast in motion pictures, but a special permit must be obtained from the Department of Labor and Industry and certain moral (a minor cannot be present during the filming of a nude scene) and educational requirements (a minimum number of instructional hours must be fulfilled) must be met.

Any working minor must have an employment certificate issued by the child's school and the certificates must be kept on file by the employer. There are three types of work permits that are issued by the child's school: general, vacation, and transferrable. The special permit, required for minors to perform in a theatrical or other performance, is obtained from the Department of Labor and Industry and is in addition to the school employment permits. The transferrable work permit may be issued to sixteen and seventeen-year-olds. A new permit is not required each time a child changes jobs but the employer must notify the school within five days that the child begins or terminates his or her employment. It is advisable for the employer to always keep a photocopy of the child's work permit in their personnel files just in case any questions about the child's employment ever arises. The photocopy will function as a legally recognizable record of employment but only if the employer records the occupation that the minor is engaged in on the photocopy.

Minors ages fourteen and fifteen may work during the school term for a maximum of four hours a school day and eight hours any other day. The minor may only work for a maximum of eighteen hours from Monday through Friday and a total of eight hours on Saturday and/or Sunday. During summer vacation, a minor may work a maximum of eight hours a day, forty-four hours per week. Minors age fourteen and fifteen may not work after 7 P.M. or before 7 A.M. with the exception of summer when they can work until 10 P.M. A minor hired to work on a farm by someone other than the farmer in the hatching, raising, or harvesting of poultry may work until 10 P.M. providing that the minor is not in an agricultural occupation deemed hazardous by the U.S. Secretary of Labor. A minor age eleven and up may work as a news carrier, or selling or distributing magazines or other publications between 5 A.M. and 8 P.M.

Minors aged sixteen and seventeen may work a maximum of twenty-eight hours a school week (Monday through Friday) if enrolled in a regular day school plus an additional eight hours on Saturday *and* an additional eight hours on Sunday, but they cannot exceed working hours a day. Minors aged sixteen and seventeen cannot work after midnight Sunday through Thursday or before 6 A.M. any day. On nights preceding a school holiday, sixteen and seventeen-year-olds may work until 1 A.M. On Friday and Saturday night, the minor may work until 1 A.M. There is no limit to night work that a sixteen and seventeen-year-old may work during summer vacation and there is no limit to night work for any minor legally excused from school attendance.

If a child is seventeen and has graduated from high school or has obtained their academic potential as determined by the Chief School Administrator, that child may be treated as an eighteen-year-old for purposes of the Child Labor Law. Also, there are special rules that apply to sixteen and seventeen-year-olds that work during the summer at summer resident camps, conferences or retreats operated by religious or scouting organizations.

A general rule of thumb for all minors is that they may only work six days a week and a thirty minute meal break must be provided either on or before five consecutive hours of work.

Any employer who violates or permits the Child Labor Law to be violated faces a fine of $100 to $300 for the first offense and $250 to $1000 and/or ten days in prison for any subsequent offense. While this may not seem terribly steep, if that illegally employed minor is injured while on the job, the employer will be required to pay an additional fifty percent of the worker's compensation that the child is awarded.

There are two special prohibitions that are not part of the Child Labor Law but that are very important and are applicable to the employment situation. According to the Vehicle Code, minors sixteen and over may operate a vehicle providing it is not in excess of 30,000 pounds registered gross weight and/or a vehicle towing a trailer that is in excess of 10,000 pounds gross weight. According to the Liquor Code, Section 493(13), any minor sixteen and over may be employed as a food waiter or waitress (that means they may *not* also carry alcoholic beverages) or as bus boys/girls at an establishment where alcoholic liquors are sold, dispensed or made. At age eighteen, a minor may then serve alcoholic beverages at a licensed establishment.

A child is prohibited from engaging in many occupations. Some are practical and obvious and some seem silly in our modern times. Rather than repeat this exhaustive list here, you are encouraged to obtain a copy of the Child Labor Law abstract that must be posted in a conspicuous place from the Bureau of Labor Standards in your region.

# IMMIGRATION LAWS

FEDERAL LAW

In 1986, a law was passed by Congress which imposes stiff penalties for any business which hires aliens who are not eligible to work. Under this law, you must verify both the identity and the employment eligibility of anyone you hire by using form I-9. Both you and the employee must fill out the form and you must check an employee's identification cards or papers. Fines for hiring illegal aliens range from $250 to $2,000 for the first offense and up to $10,000 for the third offense. Failure to maintain the proper paperwork may result in a fine of up to $1,000. The law does not apply to independent contractors with whom you may contract and it does not penalize you if the employee used fake identification.

There are also penalties which apply to employers of four or more persons for discriminating against eligible applicants because they appear foreign or because of their national origin or citizenship status.

The following pages include a list of acceptable documentation, a sample filled-in Form I-9, and instructions. A blank form is in the appendix. The blank form can also be downloaded from the following web site: **http://www.ins.usdoj.gov/forms/download/i-9.htm**

For more information call 1-202-514-2000 for the *Handbook for Employers and Instructions for Completing Form I-9*, check the INS web site (**http://www.ins.usdoj.gov**) or write to the following address:

U. S. Department of Justice
Immigration and Naturalization Service
425 I Street, NW
Washington, DC 20536

The Illegal Immigration Reform and Immigrant Responsibility Act of 1996 (IIRIRA) required changes in the rules but as of early 1999 the INS had not yet promulgated final versions of the rules. The interim rule made the following changes to the requirements:

☛ Remove documents 2, 3, 8 and 9 from column A

☛ Allow document 4 only for aliens authorized to work for a specific employer

☛ New rules for employees who do not have their original documents

However, no new forms or instructions have been made available and employers are not yet being prosecuted for violations of these changes. Employers can receive updates to these laws by fax. To receive them, send your name, address, and fax number to 202-305-2523.

PENNSYLVANIA LAW

There is no Pennsylvania law pertaining to hiring illegal aliens. Therefore, the federal act controls.

# HIRING "OFF THE BOOKS"

Because of the taxes, insurance, and red tape involved with hiring employees, some new businesses hire people "off the books." They pay them in cash and never admit they are employees. While the cash paid in wages would not be deductible, they consider this a smaller cost than compliance. Some even use "off the books" receipts to cover it.

Except in cases where your spouse or child is giving you some temporary help, this is a terrible idea. Hiring people off the books can result in civil fines, loss of insurance coverage, and even criminal penalties. When engaged in dangerous work like roofing or using power tools, you are risking millions of dollars in potential liability if a worker is killed or seriously injured.

It may be more costly and time consuming to comply with the employment laws, but if you are concerned with long term growth with less risk, it's the wiser way to go.

# FEDERAL CONTRACTS

Companies which do work for the federal government are subject to several laws.

DAVIS-BACON ACT

The Davis-Bacon Act requires contractors engaged in U.S. government construction projects to pay wages and benefits which are equal to or better than the prevailing wages in the area.

MCNAMARA-O'HARA SERVICE CONTRACT ACT

The McNamara-O'Hara Service Contract Act sets wages and other labor standards for contractors furnishing services to agencies of the U.S. government.

WALSH-HEALEY PUBLIC CONTRACTS ACT

The Walsh-Healey Public Contracts Act requires the Department of Labor to settle disputes regarding manufacturers supplying products to the U.S. government.

# MISCELLANEOUS LAWS

*Affirmative action.* In most cases, the federal government does not yet tell employers who they must hire. This would be especially true for small new businesses. The only situation where a small business would need to comply with affirmative action requirements would be if it accepted federal contracts or subcontracts. These requirements could include the hiring of minorities or of Vietnam veterans.

*Layoffs.* Companies with 100 or more full-time employees at one location are subject to the Worker Adjustment and Retraining

Notification Act. This law requires a sixty-day notification prior to certain lay-offs and has other strict provisions.

*Unions.* The National Labor Relations Act of 1935 (29 U.S.C. § 151 and following) gives employees the right to organize a union or to join one. There are things employers can do to protect themselves, but you should consult a labor attorney or a book on the subject before taking action which might be illegal and result in fines.

*Poster laws.* Yes, there are laws regarding what posters you may or may not display in the workplace. A previous edition of this book stated that nothing forbids Playboy or Playgirl-type posters, but a "politically correct" federal judge ruled in 1991 that Playboy posters in a workplace were sexual harassment. This ruling is being appealed by the American Civil Liberties Union (ACLU). However, there are other poster laws which require certain posters to be displayed to inform employees of their rights. Not all businesses are required to display all posters, but the following list should be of help.

☞ All employers must display the wage and hour poster available from:

> U. S. Department of Labor
> 200 Constitution Ave., NW
> Washington, DC 20210

☞ Employers with fifteen or more employees for twenty weeks of the year must display the sex, race, religion, and ethnic discrimination poster and the age discrimination poster available from:

> EEOC
> 2401 E Street NW
> Washington, DC 20506

☞ Employers with federal contracts or subcontracts of $10,000 or more must display the sex, race, etc. discrimination poster mentioned above plus a poster regarding Vietnam Era Veterans available from the local federal contracting office.

☞ Employers with government contracts subject to the Service Contract Act or the Public Contracts Act must display a notice to employees working on government contracts available from:

> Employment Standards Division
> U. S. Department of Labor
> 200 Constitution Ave., NW
> Washington, DC 20210

PENNSYLVANIA
LAW

*Veteran's Preference.* Pennsylvania has something called the Veteran's Preference Act, Act 92 of 1975. The VPA gives preference to *any* veteran over any other applicant for a position. Most recently, a school district in the state has been in litigation over this because they were compelled to hire a less qualified applicant over a better qualified applicant because of his status as a veteran. (*Brickhouse v. Springford School District* 656 A.2d. 483 (Pa. 1995)). The Supreme Court held that the school district was not compelled to hire the veteran when the veteran failed to meet the school districts other qualifications for the position (for example: pursuant to the VPA, a school district would be required to hire a non-certified veteran as a teacher over a certified non-veteran). The general rule of thumb for you to follow is that if you have two applicants of equal skill, qualifications, certifications, etc. (whatever your job requirements are) you are compelled to choose the veteran over the non-veteran. A lot of information regarding labor rules and regulations can be obtained through the Pennsylvanian Department of Labor and Industry's website: **http://www.LI. state.pa.us/**.

Please read instructions carefully before completing this form. The instructions must be available during completion of this form. **ANTI-DISCRIMINATION NOTICE.** It is illegal to discriminate against work eligible individuals. Employers **CANNOT** specify which document(s) they will accept from an employee. The refusal to hire an individual because of a future expiration date may also constitute illegal discrimination.

**Section 1. Employee Information and Verification.** To be completed and signed by employee at the time employment begins

| Print Name: Last | First | Middle Initial | Maiden Name |
|---|---|---|---|
| REDDENBACHER | MARY | J. | HASSENFUSS |

| Address (Street Name and Number) | Apt. # | Date of Birth (month/day/year) |
|---|---|---|
| 1234 LIBERTY LANE | | 1/26/69 |

| City | State | Zip Code | Social Security # |
|---|---|---|---|
| ALLENTOWN | PA | 17110 | 123-45-6789 |

I am aware that federal law provides for imprisonment and/or fines for false statements or use of false documents in connection with the completion of this form.

I attest, under penalty of perjury, that I am (check one of the following):
- [X] A citizen or national of the United States
- [ ] A Lawful Permanent Resident (Alien # A _____
- [ ] An alien authorized to work until ___/___/___
(Alien # or Admission # _____

| Employee's Signature *Mary Reddenbacher* | Date (month/day/year) 1/29/00 |
|---|---|

**Preparer and/or Translator Certification.** (To be completed and signed if Section 1 is prepared by a person other than the employee.) I attest, under penalty of perjury, that I have assisted in the completion of this form and that to the best of my knowledge the information is true and correct.

| Preparer's/Translator's Signature | Print Name |
|---|---|
| Address (Street Name and Number, City, State, Zip Code) | Date (month/day/year) |

**Section 2. Employer Review and Verification.** To be completed and signed by employer. **Examine one document from List A OR examine one document from List B and one from List C** as listed on the reverse of this form and record the title, number and expiration date, if any, of the document(s)

| | List A | OR | List B | AND | List C |
|---|---|---|---|---|---|
| Document title: | PASSPORT | | | | |
| Issuing authority: | PASSPORT AGENCY ALTN | | | | |
| Document #: | 123456789 | | | | |
| Expiration Date (if any): | 10/5/06 | | ___/___/___ | | ___/___/___ |
| Document #: | | | | | |
| Expiration Date (if any): | ___/___/___ | | | | |

**CERTIFICATION -** I attest, under penalty of perjury, that I have examined the document(s) presented by the above-named employee, that the above-listed document(s) appear to be genuine and to relate to the employee named, that the employee began employment on (month/day/year) 02/02/02 and that to the best of my knowledge the employee is eligible to work in the United States. (State employment agencies may omit the date the employee began employment).

| Signature of Employer or Authorized Representative *Darron Krebbs* | Print Name Darron Krebbs | Title owner |
|---|---|---|

| Business or Organization Name | Address (Street Name and Number, City, State, Zip Code) | Date (month/day/year) |
|---|---|---|
| Krebbs Company | 100 Maynard Dr., Allentown, PA 17110 | 2/2/02 |

**Section 3. Updating and Reverification.** To be completed and signed by employer

| A. New Name (if applicable) | B. Date of rehire (month/day/year) (if applicable) |
|---|---|

C. If employee's previous grant of work authorization has expired, provide the information below for the document that establishes current employment eligibility.

Document Title: _____ Document #: _____ Expiration Date (if any): ___/___/___

I attest, under penalty of perjury, that to the best of my knowledge, this employee is eligible to work in the United States, and if the employee presented document(s), the document(s) I have examined appear to be genuine and to relate to the individual.

| Signature of Employer or Authorized Representative | Date (month/day/year) |
|---|---|

Form I-9 (Rev. 11-21-91) N

# INSTRUCTIONS
### PLEASE READ ALL INSTRUCTIONS CAREFULLY BEFORE COMPLETING THIS FORM.

**Anti-Discrimination Notice.** It is illegal to discriminate against any individual (other than an alien not authorized to work in the U.S.) in hiring, discharging, or recruiting or referring for a fee because of that individual's national origin or citizenship status. It is illegal to discriminate against work eligible individuals. Employers **CANNOT** specify which document(s) they will accept from an employee. The refusal to hire an individual because of a future expiration date may also constitute illegal discrimination.

**Section 1 - Employee.** All employees, citizens and noncitizens, hired after November 6, 1986, must complete Section 1 of this form at the time of hire, which is the actual beginning of employment. **The employer is responsible for ensuring that Section 1 is timely and properly completed.**

**Preparer/Translator Certification.** The Preparer/Translator Certification must be completed if Section 1 is prepared by a person other than the employee. A preparer/translator may be used only when the employee is unable to complete Section 1 on his/her own. However, the employee must still sign Section 1 personally.

**Section 2 - Employer.** For the purpose of completing this form, the term "employer" includes those recruiters and referrers for a fee who are agricultural associations, agricultural employers, or farm labor contractors.

Employers must complete Section 2 by examining evidence of identity and employment eligibility within three (3) business days of the date employment begins. If employees are authorized to work, but are unable to present the required document(s) within three business days, they must present a receipt for the application of the document(s) within three business days and the actual document(s) within ninety (90) days. However, if employers hire individuals for a duration of less than three business days, Section 2 must be completed at the time employment begins. **Employers must record: 1)** document title; **2)** issuing authority; **3)** document number, **4)** expiration date, if any; and **5)** the date employment begins. Employers must sign and date the certification. Employees must present original documents. Employers may, but are not required to, photocopy the document(s) presented. These photocopies may only be used for the verification process and must be retained with the I-9. **However, employers are still responsible for completing the I-9.**

**Section 3 - Updating and Reverification.** Employers must complete Section 3 when updating and/or reverifying the I-9. Employers must reverify employment eligibility of their employees on or before the expiration date recorded in Section 1. Employers **CANNOT** specify which document(s) they will accept from an employee.

- If an employee's name has changed at the time this form is being updated/ reverified, complete Block A.

- If an employee is rehired within three (3) years of the date this form was originally completed and the employee is still eligible to be employed on the same basis as previously indicated on this form (updating), complete Block B and the signature block.

- If an employee is rehired within three (3) years of the date this form was originally completed and the employee's work authorization has expired or if a current employee's work authorization is about to expire (reverification), complete Block B and:
  - examine any document that reflects that the employee is authorized to work in the U.S. (see List A or C),
  - record the document title, document number and expiration date (if any) in Block C, and
  - complete the signature block.

**Photocopying and Retaining Form I-9.** A blank I-9 may be reproduced provided both sides are copied. The Instructions must be available to all employees completing this form. Employers must retain completed I-9s for three (3) years after the date of hire or one (1) year after the date employment ends, whichever is later.

**For more detailed information, you may refer to the INS Handbook for Employers, (Form M-274). You may obtain the handbook at your local INS office.**

**Privacy Act Notice.** The authority for collecting this information is the Immigration Reform and Control Act of 1986, Pub. L. 99-603 (8 U.S.C. 1324a).

This information is for employers to verify the eligibility of individuals for employment to preclude the unlawful hiring, or recruiting or referring for a fee, of aliens who are not authorized to work in the United States.

This information will be used by employers as a record of their basis for determining eligibility of an employee to work in the United States. The form will be kept by the employer and made available for inspection by officials of the U.S. Immigration and Naturalization Service, the Department of Labor, and the Office of Special Counsel for Immigration Related Unfair Employment Practices.

Submission of the information required in this form is voluntary. However, an individual may not begin employment unless this form is completed since employers are subject to civil or criminal penalties if they do not comply with the Immigration Reform and Control Act of 1986.

**Reporting Burden.** We try to create forms and instructions that are accurate, can be easily understood, and which impose the least possible burden on you to provide us with information. Often this is difficult because some immigration laws are very complex. Accordingly, the reporting burden for this collection of information is computed as follows: **1)** learning about this form, 5 minutes; **2)** completing the form, 5 minutes; and **3)** assembling and filing (recordkeeping) the form, 5 minutes, for an average of 15 minutes per response. If you have comments regarding the accuracy of this burden estimate, or suggestions for making this form simpler, you can write to both the Immigration and Naturalization Service, 425 I Street, N.W., Room 5304, Washington, D. C. 20536; and the Office of Management and Budget, Paperwork Reduction Project, OMB No. 1115-0136, Washington, D.C. 20503.

Form I-9 (Rev. 11-21-91) N

**EMPLOYERS MUST RETAIN COMPLETED I-9**
**PLEASE DO NOT MAIL COMPLETED I-9 TO INS**

# LISTS OF ACCEPTABLE DOCUMENTS

| LIST A | | LIST B | | LIST C |
|---|---|---|---|---|
| **Documents that Establish Both Identity and Employment Eligibility** | **OR** | **Documents that Establish Identity** | **AND** | **Documents that Establish Employment Eligibility** |

## LIST A — Documents that Establish Both Identity and Employment Eligibility

1. U.S. Passport (unexpired or expired)

2. Certificate of U.S. Citizenship (INS Form N-560 or N-561)

3. Certificate of Naturalization (INS Form N-550 or N-570)

4. Unexpired foreign passport, with I-551 stamp or attached INS Form I-94 indicating unexpired employment authorization

5. Alien Registration Receipt Card with photograph (INS Form I-151 or I-551)

6. Unexpired Temporary Resident Card (INS Form I-688)

7. Unexpired Employment Authorization Card (INS Form I-688A)

8. Unexpired Reentry Permit (INS Form I-327)

9. Unexpired Refugee Travel Document (INS Form I-571)

10. Unexpired Employment Authorization Document issued by the INS which contains a photograph (INS Form I-688B)

## LIST B — Documents that Establish Identity

1. Driver's license or ID card issued by a state or outlying possession of the United States provided it contains a photograph or information such as name, date of birth, sex, height, eye color, and address

2. ID card issued by federal, state, or local government agencies or entities provided it contains a photograph or information such as name, date of birth, sex, height, eye color, and address

3. School ID card with a photograph

4. Voter's registration card

5. U.S. Military card or draft record

6. Military dependent's ID card

7. U.S. Coast Guard Merchant Mariner Card

8. Native American tribal document

9. Driver's license issued by a Canadian government authority

**For persons under age 18 who are unable to present a document listed above:**

10. School record or report card

11. Clinic, doctor, or hospital record

12. Day-care or nursery school record

## LIST C — Documents that Establish Employment Eligibility

1. U.S. social security card issued by the Social Security Administration (other than a card stating it is not valid for employment)

2. Certification of Birth Abroad issued by the Department of State (Form FS-545 or Form DS-1350)

3. Original or certified copy of a birth certificate issued by a state, county, municipal authority or outlying possession of the United States bearing an official seal

4. Native American tribal document

5. U.S. Citizen ID Card (INS Form I-197)

6. ID Card for use of Resident Citizen in the United State (INS Form I-179)

7. Unexpired employment authorization document issued by the INS (other than those listed under List A)

**Illustrations of many of these documents appear in Part 8 of the Handbook for Employers (M-274)**

Form I-9 (Rev. 11-21-91) N

FPI-RBK

# ADVERTISING AND PROMOTION LAWS

# 11

## ADVERTISING LAWS AND RULES

FEDERAL LAW    The federal government regulates advertising through the Federal Trade Commission (FTC). The rules are contained in the Code of Federal Regulations (CFR). You can find these rules in most law libraries and many public libraries. If you plan any advertising that you think may be questionable, you might want to check the rules. If your advertising plans seem questionable, then most likely it is forbidden. As you read the rules below you will probably think of many violations you see every day.

Federal rules do not apply to every business; and small businesses that operate only within the state and do not use the postal service may be exempt. However, many of the federal rules have been adopted into law by the state of Pennsylvania. Therefore, a violation could be prosecuted by the state rather than the federal government.

Some of the important rules are summarized below. If you wish to learn more details about the rules you should obtain copies from your library.

***Deceptive Pricing*** (16 CFR Ch. I Part 233). When prices are being compared, it is required that actual and not inflated prices are used. For example, if an object would usually be sold for seven dollars, one should not first offer it for ten dollars and offer it at thirty percent off. It is considered misleading to suggest that a discount from list price is a bargain if the item is rarely sold at list price. If most surrounding stores sell an item for seven dollars, it is considered misleading to say it has a "retail value of ten dollars" even if there are some stores elsewhere selling it at that price.

*Bait advertising* (16 CFR Ch. I Part 238). Bait advertising is placing an ad when you don't really want the respondents to buy the product offered but to switch to another item. The factors used to determine if there was a violation are similar to those used by Pennsylvania.

*Use of "free," "half off," and similar words* (16 CFR Ch. I Part 251). Use of words such as "free," "1¢ sale" and the like must not be misleading. This means that the "regular price" must not include a mark-up to cover the "free" item. The seller must expect to sell the product without the free item at some time in the future. How many violations of this rule can you find in today's paper?

*Substantiation of claims* (16 CFR 3.40; 48 FR 10471, March 11, 1983). The FTC requires that advertisers be able to substantiate their claims. Some information on this policy is contained on the internet at **http://www.ftc.gov/bcp/guides/ad3subst.htm**.

*Endorsements* (16 CFR Ch. I Part 255). This rule forbids endorsements that are misleading. An example is a quote from a film review that is used in such a way as to change the substance of the review. It is not necessary to use the exact words of the person endorsing the product as long as the opinion is not distorted. If a product is changed, an endorsement that does not apply to the new version cannot be used. For some items, such as drugs, claims cannot be used without scientific proof. Endorsements by organizations cannot be used unless one is sure that the membership holds the same opinion.

*Unfairness* (15 USC 45). Any advertising practices which can be deemed to be "unfair" are forbidden by the FTC. An explanation of this policy is located on the internet at **http://www.ftc.gov/bcp/policy stmt/ad-unfair.htm**.

***Negative Option Plans*** (16 CFR Ch. 1 Part 425). When a seller uses a sales system in which the buyer must notify the seller if he does not want the goods, the seller must provide the buyer with a form to decline the sale and at least ten days in which to decline. Bonus merchandise must be shipped promptly and the seller must promptly terminate any who so request after completion of the contract.

***Laser eye surgery*** (15 USC §§ 45, 52-57). Under the laws governing deceptive advertising, the FTC and the FDA are regulating the advertising of laser eye surgery. Anyone involved in this area should obtain a copy of these rules. The are located on the internet at **http://www.ftc.gov/bcp/guides/eyecare2.htm**.

***Food and dietary supplements*** (21 USC § 343). Under the Nutritional Labeling Education Act of 1990, the FTC and the FDA regulate the packaging and advertising of food and dietary products. Anyone involved in this area should obtain a copy of these rules. The are located on the internet at **http://www.ftc.gov/bcp/guides/ad4diet.htm** and **http://www.ftc.gov/bcp/guides/ad-food.htm**.

***Jewelry and precious metals*** (61 CFR 27212). The FTC has numerous rules governing the sale and advertising of jewelry and precious metals. Anyone in this business should obtain a copy of these rules. The are located on the internet at **http://www.ftc.gov/bcp/guides/jewel-gd.htm**.

PENNSYLVANIA LAW

Most of Pennsylvania's advertising laws are included with the Unfair Trade Practices and Consumer Protection Act 387 of 1968.

***Misleading Advertising***. It is illegal to use advertising which is "misleading," or to use words like "wholesale" or "below cost" unless the goods are actually at or below the retailer's net cost. If demanded by a consumer, a retailer must provide to the Better Business Bureau, the Chamber of Commerce, or the State Attorney's office proof of his or her cost and must help that person figure out the net cost. Retailers may

**125**

not advertise items at a special price unless they have reasonable quantities or state in the ad the quantity available (unless they give rain checks). A customer may sue a business under this law and receive his or her attorney's fees, court costs, actual and punitive damages.

Under the Unfair Trade Practices and Consumer Protection Act 387 of 1968, it is forbidden to make any misrepresentations of goods or services to the public including any of the following:

- ☞ Misrepresenting the owner, manufacturer, distributor, source, or geographical origin of goods.

- ☞ Misrepresenting the age, model, grade, style, or standard of goods.

- ☞ Misrepresenting the sponsorship, endorsement, approval, or certification of goods or services.

- ☞ Misrepresenting the affiliation, connection, or association of any goods or services.

- ☞ Misrepresenting the nature, characteristics, standard ingredients, uses, benefits, warranties, guarantees, quantities, or qualities of goods or services.

- ☞ Misrepresenting used, altered, deteriorated, or repossessed goods as new; however, goods returned to a seller undamaged may be sold as new.

- ☞ Disparaging goods, services, or business of another by false or misleading representation.

- ☞ Advertising goods or services with intent not to sell them as advertised.

- ☞ Advertising goods or services with the intent not to supply reasonably expectable public demand, unless the advertisement discloses a limitation of quantity.

- ☞ Making false or misleading statements of fact concerning the reasons for, existence of, or amounts of price reductions.

☞ Promising or offering to give the buyer, any compensation or reward for the procurement of a contract for the purchase of goods or services with another when such payment or reward is contingent upon the occurrence of an event subsequent to the time of the signing of the contract to purchase.

☞ Promising or offering to give the buyer any compensation or reward for the referral of the name of another for the purpose of procuring a contract of purchase with such other person when such payment or reward is contingent upon the occurrence of an event subsequent to the time of the signing of the contract to purchase.

☞ Pyramid schemes are expressly forbidden by the Act. The Act forbids the promoting or engaging in any plan by which goods or services are sold to a person for a consideration. Upon the further consideration that the purchaser secure or attempt to secure one or more persons likewise to join the said plan, each purchaser is to be given the right to secure money; goods; or services depending upon the number of persons joining the plan. In addition, promoting or engaging in any plan, commonly known as or similar to the so-called "Chain Letter Plan" or "Pyramid Club." The terms Chain Letter Plan and Pyramid Club mean any scheme for the disposal or distribution of property, services, or anything of value whereby a participant pays valuable consideration, in whole or in part, for an opportunity to receive compensation for introducing or attempting to introduce one or more additional persons to participate in the scheme, or for the opportunity to receive compensation when a person introduced by the participant introduces a new participant. As used in this subclause the term consideration means an investment of cash or the purchase of goods, other property, training or services, but does not include payments made for sales demonstration equipment and materials for use in making sales and not for resale furnished at no profit to any person in the program or to the company or corporation, nor does the term apply to a minimal initial payment of twenty-five dollars or less.

☞ Failing to comply with the terms of any written guarantee or warranty given to the buyer at, prior to, or after a contract for the purchase of goods or services is made.

☞ Knowingly misrepresenting that services, replacements, or repairs are needed if they are not needed.

☞ Making repairs, improvements, or replacements on tangible, real, or personal property, of a nature or quality inferior to or below the standard of that agreed to in writing.

☞ Engaging in any other fraudulent conduct that creates a likelihood of confusion or misunderstanding.

Note especially that under the Act, if you publish an advertisement or broadcast an advertisement over the radio or on a television station, you are *not* liable if the ad copy that you are given does not comply with the Unfair Trade Practices and Consumer Protection Law and you are unaware that the copy does not comply.

***Assignment of Indebtedness***. Another rule to remember in a sales contract situation is that you may not transfer or assign the indebtedness to any third party prior to midnight of the fifth day the sales contract was signed. If the seller plans to repossess the goods delivered, he or she must do so within twenty days of the date of notice of cancellation or forfeit all rights to the delivered goods.

A consumer may not waive their rights under this Act unless the goods or services are needed to meet a "bona fide personal emergency" of the buyer, and the buyer furnishes the seller with a separate dated and signed personal statement in the buyer's handwriting describing the emergency and expressly acknowledging and waiving the right to cancel the sale within three business days. The Unfair Trade Practices and Consumer Protection Act does not apply to real estate and is applicable to the sale of any other goods in excess of twenty-five dollars.

Penalties for violation of this Act are fairly steep and the Office of Attorney General is extremely aggressive in enforcing the Act's provisions. An injunction may be issued against you, stopping you from continuing your business practices, and in some instances, preventing you from continuing your business at all until a hearing is held. You may also be required to forfeit your franchise or right to do business. Fines for violation of this Act range from $1,000 to $5,000. In addition, the court may assess punitive damages in the amount of up to three times the amount of damages sustained but not less than $100.

# INTERNET SALES LAWS

FEDERAL LAW

There are not yet specific laws governing internet transactions which are different from laws governing other transactions. The FTC feels that its current rules regarding deceptive advertising, substantiation, disclaimers, refunds, and related matters must be followed by internet businesses and that consumers are adequately protected by them. See the first three pages of this chapter for that information.

For some specific guidelines on internet advertising, see the FTC's site at **http://ftc.gov/bcp/conline/pubs/buspubs/ruleroad.htm.**

# HOME SOLICITATION LAWS

FEDERAL LAW

The Federal Trade Commission has rules governing door-to-door sales. It is a deceptive trade practice in any such sale to fail to furnish a receipt explaining the sale (in the language of the presentation) and giving notice that there is a right to back out of the contract within three days, known as a right of rescission. The notice must be supplied in duplicate, must be in at least 10-point type and must be captioned either "Notice of Right to Cancel" or "Notice of Cancellation." The notice must be worded as follows:

NOTICE OF CANCELLATION

_____
Date

YOU MAY CANCEL THIS TRANSACTION, WITHOUT ANY PENALTY OR OBLIGATION, WITHIN THREE BUSINESS DAYS FROM THE ABOVE DATE.

IF YOU CANCEL, ANY PROPERTY TRADED IN, ANY PAYMENTS MADE BY YOU UNDER THE CONTRACT OR SALE, AND ANY NEGOTIABLE INSTRUMENT EXECUTED BY YOU WILL BE RETURNED TO YOU WITHIN 10 BUSINESS DAYS FOLLOWING RECEIPT BY THE SELLER OF YOUR CANCELLATION NOTICE, AND ANY SECURITY INTEREST ARISING OUT OF THE TRANSACTION WILL BE CANCELLED.

IF YOU CANCEL, YOU MUST MAKE AVAILABLE TO THE SELLER AT YOUR RESIDENCE, IN SUBSTANTIALLY AS GOOD CONDITION AS WHEN RECEIVED, ANY GOODS DELIVERED TO YOU UNDER THIS CONTRACT OR SALE; OR YOU MAY IF YOU WISH, COMPLY WITH THE INSTRUCTIONS OF THE SELLER REGARDING THE RETURN SHIPMENT OF THE GOODS AT THE SELLER'S EXPENSE AND RISK.

IF YOU DO MAKE THE GOODS AVAILABLE TO THE SELLER AND THE SELLER DOES NOT PICK THEM UP WITHIN 20 DAYS OF THE DATE OF YOUR NOTICE OF CANCELLATION, YOU MAY RETAIN OR DISPOSE OF THE GOODS WITHOUT ANY FURTHER OBLIGATION. IF YOU FAIL TO MAKE THE GOODS AVAILABLE TO THE SELLER, OR IF YOU AGREE TO RETURN THE GOODS AND FAIL TO DO SO, THEN YOU REMAIN LIABLE FOR PERFORMANCE OF ALL OBLIGATIONS UNDER THE CONTRACT.

TO CANCEL THIS TRANSACTION, MAIL OR DELIVER A SIGNED AND DATED COPY OF THIS CANCELLATION NOTICE OR ANY OTHER WRITTEN NOTICE, OR SEND A TELEGRAM, TO [name of seller], AT [address of seller's place of business] NOT LATER THAN MIDNIGHT OF _____ (date).

I HEREBY CANCEL THIS TRANSACTION.

_____     _____
(Buyer's signature)                                              (Date)

The seller must complete the notice and orally inform the buyer of the right to cancel. He cannot misrepresent the right to cancel, assign the contract until the fifth business day, nor include a confession of judgment in the contract. For more specific details see the rules contained in 16 CFR Ch. I Part 429.

**PENNSYLVANIA LAW**

Home solicitation sales are also addressed by the Uniform Trade Practices and Consumer Protection Act. If you call on the buyer at his home and the sale you make to them is twenty-five dollars or more, the person to whom you sold the goods may cancel the sale or contract with you within three business days following the date of the sale if they do so in writing. The buyer must return the goods to you in their original condition and you must return the full sales price. Note that the "mail box rule" applies here: if the consumer drops the notice of cancellation to you in the mail and it is postmarked three business days after the date the contract was signed, even though you may not receive the notice for a week, the notice is deemed timely because of the date of the postmark.

All home solicitation sales contracts must be in the same principal language used in the sales presentation and in English as well. It must contain the date of the transaction and the name and address of the seller and as close as possible to the line upon which the seller must sign his or her name the following clause which must be in bold faced, ten-point type and must say:

---

**BUYER'S RIGHT TO CANCEL**

**This is a home solicitation sale, and if you do not want the goods or services, you may cancel this agreement by providing written notice to the Seller in person, by telegram, or by mail. This notice must indicate that you do not want the goods or services and must be delivered or postmarked before midnight of the third business day after you sign this agreement. If you cancel this agreement, the Seller may not keep all or part of any cash down payment.**

---

You must also include a duplicate form that is attached to the contract but easily detachable (any reputable printer will have the appropriate paper to do this) that will have in bold faced, ten-point type, in the same language as the rest of the contract the following:

> Both copies of the above notice must be completed by entering the name and address of the seller, the date of the transaction and the date by which the buyer may cancel the contract. The buyer must also be informed orally of his or her right to cancel the sale. The date on which the buyer is orally told of his or her right to cancel the contract and has been provided with his or her copy of the "Notice of Cancellation" is the date that controls when the buyer may legally cancel the sale.

Upon exercising his or her right to cancel the sales contract, the cancellation and refund must be honored by the seller within ten days, all goods must be returned to the seller within the same time period and any negotiable instrument must be returned and cancelled. Any action necessary to terminate any security interest must also be taken.

## TELEPHONE SOLICITATION LAWS

FEDERAL LAW

*Phone calls.* Telephone solicitations are governed by the Telephone Consumer Protection Act (47 USC 227) and the Federal Communications Commission rules implementing the act (47 CFR 64.1200). Violators of the act can be sued for $500 damages by consumers and can be fined $10,000 by the FCC. Some of the requirements under the law are:

☞ Calls can only be made between 8 A.M. and 9 P.M.

☞ Solicitors must keep a "do not call" list and honor requests to not call.

☞ There must be a written policy that the parties called are told the name of the caller, the caller's business name, and phone number or address. They must also be informed that the call is a sales call and the nature of the goods or services.

☞ Personnel must be trained in the policies.

☞ Recorded messages cannot be used to call residences.

*Faxes.* It is illegal under the act to send advertising faxes to anyone who has not consented to receiving such faxes or is an existing customer.

# PRICING, WEIGHTS, AND LABELING

FEDERAL LAW

*Food products.* Beginning in 1994, all food products were required to have labels with information on the product's nutritional values such as calories, fat, and protein. For most products, the label must be in the required format so that consumers can easily compare products. However, if such a format will not fit on the product label, the information may be in another format which is easily readable.

*Metric measures.* In 1994, federal rules requiring metric measurement of products took effect. Some federal agencies, such as the federal highway department, indefinitely postponed implementation of the rules, but the Federal Trade Commission (FTC) and the Food and Drug Administration intend to enforce the rules against businesses.

Under these rules, metric measures do not have to be the first measurement on the container, but they must be included. Food items that are packaged as they are sold (such as delicatessen items), do not have to contain metric labels.

PENNSYLVANIA
LAW

Under 76 PACS 10 Pa Code, § 1.1 et seq., it is a second degree misdemeanor (meaning a fine of up to $500 and up to sixty days in jail) to violate any of the following rules:

*Misrepresenting Quantity*. No person shall misrepresent the quantity of goods offered for sale or goods purchased by wrapping the goods in such a way to mislead a consumer.

*Misrepresenting Price.* No person shall misrepresent the price of any commodity or represent the price in any manner calculated to confuse. When a price includes a fraction of a cent, all elements of the fraction must be prominently displayed.

*Method of Price.* Generally, dairy products in liquid form must be sold by liquid measure or weight, as well as butter, margarine, flour, corn meal, grits, and potatoes.

*Information Required on Packages.* Generally, all packages of commodities for sale must bear a conspicuous statement of:

- ☛ Identity of commodity unless it can be identified through wrapper.

- ☛ Net quantity of contents in terms of weight, measure, or count.

- ☛ For goods sold other than where they are packed, the name and place of business of the manufacturer, packer, or distributor.

- ☛ The word "when packed" as a qualifier or the word "jumbo," "giant," "full," and "etc." cannot be used when describing the packaged quantity.

*Declaration of Unit Price on Random Packages.* In addition to the bulk sales requirements above, when goods are offered in packages of different weights, with the price stated on them, the price per single unit of weight must also be stated.

*Advertising Packages for Sale.* When a packaged commodity is advertised for sale with a price stated, the quantity must also be conspicuously stated.

# PAYMENT AND COLLECTIONS LAWS

# 12

Depending on the business you are in, you may be paid by cash, checks, credit cards, or some sort of financing arrangement such as a promissory note and mortgage. Both state and federal laws affect the type of payments you collect, and failure to follow the laws can cost you considerably.

## CASH

Cash is probably the easiest form of payment and it is subject to few restrictions. The most important one is that you keep an accurate accounting of your cash transactions and that you report all of your cash income on your tax return. Recent efforts to stop the drug trade have resulted in some serious penalties for failing to report cash transactions and for money laundering. The laws are so sweeping that even if you deal in cash in an ordinary business, you may violate the law and face huge fines and imprisonment.

The most important law to be concerned with is the one requiring the filing of IRS Form 8300 for cash transactions of $10,000 or more. A transaction does not have to happen in one day. If a person brings you smaller amounts of cash that add up to $10,000 and the government can construe them as one transaction, the form must be filed. For more information, obtain Form 8300 and instructions from the IRS.

PENNSYLVANIA
LAW

Pennsylvania has the Cash Consumer Protection Act, Act 132 of 1984. This Act prohibits a merchant from refusing to sell goods or services to individuals who do not possess credit cards. You are permitted to demand and receive security before goods or services are provided and that security can take the form of cash-on-account that is reasonably related to the value of the property (think of this as a "down payment" situation). Any violation of this Act carries with it a civil penalty of $1,000 for each violation. A person harmed by this can bring a private actions for $100 or actual harm suffered, whichever is greater, and the court may award up to three times the actual damages sustained as a punitive measure.

# CHECKS

It is important to accept checks in your business. While there is a small percentage which will be bad, most checks will be good, and you will be able to accommodate more customers. To avoid having problems with checks, you should comply with the following rules:

CREDIT CARD
INFORMATION
ACT

Act 36 of 1992, the Credit Card Information Act, forbids a business from requiring a customer to provide a credit card number or expiration date in order to pay by cash or check. The business can request to see a card to establish that the customer is credit-worthy or for additional identification and can record the type of credit card and issuing company. The business cannot record the number of the card. The penalty for a violation is a fine of $250 for the first violation and $1000 for each subsequent violation.

REFUNDS AFTER
CASHING A
CHECK

A popular scam is for a person to purchase something by using a check only to return the next day and demand a refund. After making the refund, the business discovers the initial payment check bounced. Do not make refunds until checks clear! Many large retailers do this already, Wal-Mart is one of the most notable.

# CREDIT CARDS

In our buy-now, pay-later society, charge cards can add greatly to your sales potential, especially with large, discretionary purchases. For MasterCard, Visa, and Discover, the merchant fees are about two percent, and this amount is easily paid for by the extra purchases that the cards allow. American Express charges four to five percent and you may decide this is not worth paying, since almost everyone who has an American Express card also has another card. You will find that affluent purchasers prefer to use American Express. (And, if ordering by phone, the insecure among them will mention to you if it is a gold card.)

For businesses that have a retail outlet, there is usually no problem getting merchant status. Most commercial banks can handle it. Discover can also set you up to accept their card as well as MasterCard and Visa, and they will wire the money into your bank account daily.

For mail order businesses, especially those operating out of the home, it is much harder to get merchant status. This is because of the number of scams in which large amounts are charged, no products are shipped and the company folds. At one point, even a business offering to post a large cash bond and let the bank hold the charges for six months was refused.

Today things are a little better. Some companies are even soliciting merchants. But beware of those that charge exorbitant fees (such as $5 or $10 per order for "processing"). One good thing about American Express is that they will accept mail order companies operating out of the home. However, not as many people have their cards as others.

Some companies open a small storefront (or share one) to get merchant status, then process mostly mail orders. The processors usually do not want to accept you if you will do more than fifty percent mail order;

but if you do not have many complaints, you may be allowed to process mostly mail orders. Whatever you do, keep your charge customers happy so that they do not complain!

You might be tempted to try to run your charges through another business. This may be okay if you actually sell your products through them, but if you run your business charges through their account the other business may lose its merchant status. People who bought a book by mail from you and then have a charge on their statement from a florist shop will probably call the credit card company saying that they never bought anything from the florist shop. Too many of these and the account will be closed.

## FINANCING LAWS

Some businesses can make sales more easily if they finance the purchases themselves. If the business has enough capital to do this, it can earn extra profits on the financing terms. However, because of abuses, many consumer protection laws have been passed by both the federal and state governments.

FEDERAL LAW
**Reg. Z.** Two important federal laws regarding financing are called the *Truth in Lending Act* and the *Fair Credit Billing Act*. These are implemented by what is called *Regulation Z* (commonly known as *Reg. Z*), issued by the Board of Governors of the Federal Reserve System. It is contained in Volume 12 of the Code of Federal Regulations, page 226 (cited by lawyers as 12 CFR 226). This is a very complicated law and some have said that no business can be sure to be in compliance with it.

The regulation covers all transactions in which four conditions are met:

☛ credit is offered

☛ the offering of credit is regularly done

☛ there is a finance charge for the credit or there is a written agreement with more than four payments

☛ the credit is for personal, family, or household purposes

It also covers credit card transactions where only the first two conditions are met. It applies to leases if the consumer ends up paying the full value and keeping the item leased. It does not apply to the following transactions:

☛ transactions with businesses or agricultural purposes

☛ transactions with organizations such as corporations or the government

☛ transactions of over $25,000 that are not secured by the consumer's dwelling

☛ credit involving public utilities

☛ credit involving securities or commodities

☛ home fuel budget plans

The way for a small business to avoid Reg. Z violations is to avoid transactions that meet the conditions or to make sure all transactions fall under the exceptions. This is easy for many businesses. Instead of extending credit to customers, accept credit cards and let the credit card company extend the credit. However, if your customers usually do not have credit cards or if you are in a business, such as used car sales, which often extends credit, you should consult a lawyer knowledgeable about Reg. Z or, if you dare, get a copy for yourself.

PENNSYLVANIA LAWS

Pennsylvania also has laws regarding financing arrangements. Anyone engaged in retail installment selling must be licensed by the Pennsylvania Department of Banking. The law specifies what size type must be used in printed contracts, what notices must be included in them, and many other details. Anyone engaged in installment sales in

Pennsylvania should carefully review the latest versions of the following statutes:

- ☞ Goods and Services Installment Sales Act, Act 7 Special Session #1 of 1966 and Act 1 of 1991

- ☞ Motor Vehicle Sales Finance, Act 476 of 1947 and Act 25 of 1990

- ☞ Home Improvement Sales and Finance, Act 464 of 1963 and Act 68 of 1994

- ☞ Insurance Premium Finance Co. Alt Act 224 of 1984

- ☞ Goods and Services Installment Sales Act, Act 7 of Special Session #1 of 1991

- ☞ Goods and Services Installment Sales Act—Amending Services Charges, Act 1 of 1991

- ☞ Goods and Services Installment Sales Act—Amending Late Fees and Interest Rates, Act 39 of 1994

- ☞ Motor Vehicle Sales Finance Act, Act 476 of 1947

- ☞ Motor Vehicle Sales Finance Act—Amending Contracts and Rates, Act 25 of 1990

- ☞ Motor Vehicle Sales Finance Act—Amending Installment Sales Contracts, Act 55 of 1992

- ☞ Home Improvement Finance Act, Act 464 of 1963

- ☞ Home Improvement Finance Act—Amendments, Act 68 of 1994

- ☞ Insurance Premium Finance Company Act, Act 224 of 1984

# Usury

*Usury* is the charging of an illegally high rate of interest on amounts of loans. In Pennsylvania, the usury laws are contained in the Loan Interest and Protection Law, Act 6 of 1974. According to the Act, the maximum lawful interest rate on the loan or use of money in an amount of $50,000 or less where there is no express contract for a lesser rate is capped at six percent. If a contract is silent as to the obligation to pay a sum of money "with interest" shall be construed to refer to a rate of interest of six percent. If the loan is in excess of $50,000, the maximum rate allowable is the amount of the monthly index of long term government bond yields. There are specific rules that apply when the rate changes and you are advised to read the Act regarding these changes. The only exception to this rule are residential mortgage interest rates, federally guaranteed loans and commitments to enter into residential mortgages.

The penalty for charging in excess of the legal rate is that the borrower does not have to pay any interest and the lender has to repay triple the amounts received but this is limited to a four year period of the contract.

# COLLECTIONS

FEDERAL LAW  The Fair Debt Collection Practices Act of 1977 bans the use of deception, harassment, and other unreasonable acts in the collection of debts.

The Federal Trade Commission has issued some rules that prohibit deceptive representations such as pretending to be in the motion picture industry, the government, or a credit bureau and/or using questionnaires that do not say that they are for the purpose of collecting a debt (16 CFR Ch I Part 237).

# BUSINESS RELATIONS LAWS 13

## THE UNIFORM COMMERCIAL CODE

The Uniform Commercial Code (UCC) is a set of laws regulating numerous aspects of doing business. To avoid having a patchwork of different laws around the fifty states, a national group drafted this set of uniform laws. Although some states modified some sections of the laws, the code is basically the same in most of the states. Each chapter is concerned with a different aspect of commercial relations such as sales, warranties, bank deposits, commercial paper, and bulk transfers.

Businesses that wish to know their rights in all types of transactions should obtain a copy of the UCC and become familiar with it. It is especially useful in transactions between merchants. However, the meaning is not always clear from a reading of the statutes. In law school, students usually spend a full semester studying each chapter of this law.

## COMMERCIAL DISCRIMINATION

FEDERAL LAW     The Robinson-Patman Act of 1936 prohibits businesses from injuring competition by offering the same goods at different prices to different buyers. It also requires that promotional allowances must be made on proportionally the same terms to all buyers.

As a small business you may be a victim of Robinson-Patman Act violations. A good place to look for information on the act is the following web site: **http://www.lawmall.com/rpa/**.

# RESTRAINING TRADE

FEDERAL LAW

One of the earliest federal laws affecting business is the Sherman Antitrust Act of 1890. The purpose of the law was to protect competition in the marketplace by prohibiting monopolies. For example, one large company might buy out all of its competitors and raise prices to astronomical levels. In recent years, this law was used to break-up AT&T.

Examples of some things that are prohibited are:

☞ agreements between competitors to sell at the same prices;

☞ agreements between competitors on how much will be sold or produced;

☞ agreements between competitors to divide up a market;

☞ refusing to sell one product without a second product; and

☞ exchanging information among competitors which results in similarity of prices.

As a new business, you probably won't be in a position to violate the act, but you should be aware of it in case a larger competitor tries to put you out of business. A good place to find information on the act is the following internet site: **http://www.lawmall.com/sherman.act/index.html**.

# INTELLECTUAL PROPERTY PROTECTION

As a business owner, you should know enough about intellectual property law to protect your own creations and to keep from violating the rights of others. Intellectual property is that which is the product of human creativity, such as writings, designs, inventions, melodies, and processes. They are things which can be stolen without being physically taken. For example, if you write a book, someone can steal the words from your book without stealing a physical copy of it.

As the internet grows, intellectual property is becoming more valuable. Smart business owners are those who will take the action necessary to protect their company's intellectual property. Additionally, business owners should know intellectual property law to be sure that they do not violate the rights of others. Even an unknowing violation of the law can result in stiff fines and penalties.

The following are the types of intellectual property and the ways to protect them.

PATENT   A patent is protection given to new and useful inventions, discoveries, and designs. To be entitled to a patent, a work must be completely new and "unobvious." A patent is granted to the first inventor who files for the patent. Once an invention is patented, no one else can make use of that invention, even if they discover it independently after a lifetime of research. A patent protects an invention for seventeen years; for designs it is 3-1/2, seven, or fourteen years. Patents cannot be renewed. The patent application must clearly explain how to make the invention so that when the patent expires, others will be able to freely make and use the invention. Patents are registered with the United States Patent and Trademark Office (USPTO). Examples of things which would be patentable would be mechanical devices or new drug formulas.

COPYRIGHT   A copyright is protection given to "original works of authorship," such as written works, musical works, visual works performance works or computer software programs. A copyright exists from the moment of creation, but one cannot register a copyright until it has been fixed in tangible form. Also, one cannot copyright titles, names, or slogans. A copyright currently gives the author and his heirs exclusive right to his work for the life of the author plus seventy years. Copyrights first registered before 1978 last for ninety-five years. This was previously seventy-five years but was extended twenty years to match the European system. (Perhaps because copyrights owned by Disney and Warner Brothers were due to expire?) Copyrights are registered with the Register of Copyrights at the Library of Congress. Examples of works which would be copyrightable are books, paintings, songs, poems, plays, drawings, and films.

TRADEMARK

A trademark is protection given to a name or symbol which is used to distinguish one person's goods or services from those of others. It can consist of letters, numerals, packaging, labeling, musical notes, colors, or a combination of these. If a trademark is used on services as opposed to goods, it is called service mark. A trademark lasts indefinitely if it is used continuously and renewed properly. Trademarks are registered with the United States Patent and Trademark Office and with individual states. This is explained further in chapter 3. Examples of trademarks are the "Chrysler" name on automobiles, the red border on TIME magazine, and the shape of the Coca-Cola bottle.

TRADE SECRET

A trade secret is some information or process that provides a commercial advantage which is protected by keeping it a secret. Examples of trade secrets may be a list of successful distributors, the formula for Coca-Cola, or some unique source code in a computer program. Trade secrets are not registered anywhere, they are protected by the fact that they are not disclosed They are protected only for as long as they are kept secret. If you independently discover the formula for Coca-Cola tomorrow, you can freely market it. (But you can't use the trademark "Coca-Cola" on your product to market it.)

UNPROTECTABLE

Some things are just unprotectable. Such things as ideas, systems, and discoveries are not allowed any protection under any law. If you have a great idea, such as selling packets of hangover medicine in bars, you can't stop others from doing the same thing. If you invent a new medicine, you can patent it; if you pick a distinctive name for it, you can register it as a trademark; if you create a unique picture or instructions for the package, you can copyright them. But you cannot stop others from using your basic business idea of marketing hangover medicine in bars.

Notice the subtle differences between the protective systems available. If you invent something two days after someone else does, you cannot even use it yourself if the other person has patented it. But if you write the same poem as someone else and neither of you copied the other, both of you can copyright the poem. If you patent something, you can have the exclusive rights to it for the term of the patent; but you must disclose how others can make it after the patent expires; however, if you keep it a trade secret, you have exclusive rights as long as no one learns the secret.

We are in a time of transition of the law of intellectual property. Every year new changes are made in the laws and new forms of creativity win protection. For more information, you should consult a new edition of a book on these types of property. Some are listed in the section of this book "FOR FURTHER READING."

# ENDLESS LAWS 14

The state of Pennsylvania and the federal government have numerous laws and rules which apply to every aspect of every type of business. There are laws governing even such things as fence posts, hosiery, rabbit raising, refund policies, frozen desserts, and advertising. Every business is affected by one or another of these laws.

Some activities are covered by both state and federal laws. In such cases, you must obey the stricter of the rules. In addition, more than one agency of the state or federal government may have rules governing your business. Each of these may have the power to investigate violations and impose fines or other penalties.

Penalties for violations of these laws can range from a warning to a criminal fine and even jail time. In some cases, employees can sue for damages. Recently, employees have been given awards of millions of dollars from employers who violated the law. Since "ignorance of the law is no excuse," it is your duty to learn which laws apply to your business or risk these penalties.

Very few people in business know the laws that apply to their businesses. If you take the time to learn them, you can become an expert in your field and avoid problems with regulators. You can also fight back if one of your competitors uses some illegal method to compete with you.

The laws and rules which affect the most businesses are explained in this section. Following that is a list of more specialized laws. You should read through this list and see which ones may apply to your business. Then go to your public library or law library and read them. Some may not apply to your phase of the business, but if any of them do apply, you should make copies to keep on hand.

No one could possibly know all the rules that affect business, much less comply with them all. The Interstate Commerce Commission alone has 40 trillion (that is 40 million million or 40,000,000,000,000) rates on its books telling the transportation industry what it should charge! But if you keep up with the important rules, you will stay out of trouble and have more chance of success.

# FEDERAL LAWS

The federal laws which are most likely to affect small businesses are rules of the Federal Trade Commission (FTC). The FTC has some rules which affect many businesses such as the rules about labeling, warranties, and mail order sales. Other rules affect only certain industries.

If you sell goods by mail you should send for their booklet, *A Business Guide to the Federal Trade Commission's Mail Order Rule*. You should ask for their latest information on the subject if you are going to be involved in a certain industry such as those listed below, or using warranties or your own labeling. The address is:

Federal Trade Commission
Washington, DC 20580

The rules of the FTC are contained in the Code of Federal Regulations (CFR) in Chapter 16. Some of the industries covered are:

| INDUSTRY | PART |
| --- | --- |
| Adhesive Compositions | 235 |
| Aerosol Products Used for Frosting Cocktail Glasses | 417 |

| | |
|---|---|
| Nursery | 18 |
| Ophthalmic Practices | 456 |
| Photographic Film and Film Processing | 242 |
| Private Vocational and Home Study Schools | 254 |
| Radiation Monitoring Instruments | 232 |
| Retail Food Stores (Advertising) | 424 |
| Shell Homes | 230 |
| Shoes | 231 |
| Sleeping Bags | 400 |
| Tablecloths and Related Products | 404 |
| Television Sets | 410 |
| Textile Wearing Apparel | 423 |
| Textiles | 236 |
| Tires | 228 |
| Used Automobile Parts | 20 |
| Used Lubricating Oil | 406 |
| Used Motor Vehicles | 455 |
| Waist Belts | 405 |
| Watches | 245 |
| Wigs and Hairpieces | 252 |

Some other federal laws which affect businesses are as follows:

☛ Alcohol Administration Act (27 U.S.C. §201 et seq.)

☛ Child Protection and Toy Safety Act (1969)

☛ Clean Water Act (U.S.C. Title 33)

☛ Comprehensive Smokeless Tobacco Health Education Act (1986). See also 16 CFR Ch. I, Part 307 for rules.

☛ Consumer Credit Protection Act (1968)

☛ Consumer Product Safety Act (1972)

☛ Energy Policy and Conservation Act. See also 16 CFR Ch. I, Part 305 for rules about energy cost labeling.

- Environmental Pesticide Control Act of 1972
- Fair Credit Reporting Act (1970)
- Fair Packaging and Labeling Act (1966). See also 16 CFR Ch. I, Parts 500-503 for rules.
- Flammable Fabrics Act (1953). See also 16 CFR Ch. II, Parts 1602-1632 for rules.
- Food, Drug, and Cosmetic Act (21 U.S.C. §301 et seq.)
- Fur Products Labeling Act (1951). See also 16 CFR Ch. I, Part 301 for rules.
- Hazardous Substances Act (1960)
- Hobby Protection Act. See also 16 CFR Ch. I, Part 304 for rules.
- Insecticide, Fungicide, and Rodenticide Act (7 U.S.C. §136 et seq.)
- Magnuson-Moss Warranty Act. See also 16 CFR Ch. I, Part 239 for rules.
- Poison Prevention Packaging Act of 1970. See also 16 CFR Ch. II, Parts 1700-1702 for rules.
- Solid Waste Disposal Act (42 U.S.C. §6901 et seq.)
- Textile Fiber Products Identification Act. See also 16 CFR Ch. I, Part 303 for rules.
- Toxic Substance Control Act (U.S.C. Title 15)
- Wool Products Labeling Act (1939). See also 16 CFR Ch. I, Part 300 for rules.
- Nutrition Labeling and Education Act of 1990. See also 21 CFR, Ch. 1, Subch. B
- Food Safety Enforcement Enhancement Act of 1997

# PENNSYLVANIA LAWS

Pennsylvania has numerous laws regulating specific types of businesses or certain activities of businesses. The following is a list of those laws which are most likely to affect small businesses.

LAWS REGULATING BUSINESS IN PENNSYLVANIA

Citations refer to Pennsylvania Consolidated Statutes (Pa.C.S.) or Pennsylvania Administrative Code (Pa. Code)

| | |
|---|---|
| Adoption agencies | 23 Pa.C.S. § 2101 et seq. |
| Adult congregate living facilities | Act 118 of 1990 |
| Adult day care facilities | Act 118 of 1990 |
| Adult foster home care | Act 118 of 1990 |
| Ambulance service contracts | Act 293 of 1927 |
| Animals | 3 Pa.C.S. |
| Auctions and Auctioneers | Act 85 of 1983 |
| Banking | 7 Pa.C.S. |
| | 10 Pa. Code |
| Boiler safety | Act 451 of 1929 |
| Boxing & fighting | 5 Pa.C.S. § 301 et seq. |
| Buildings, radon resistance stds. | Act 75 of 1992 |
| Burial contracts | 9 Pa.C.S. |
| Cemeteries | 9 Pa.C.S. |
| Charitable solicitation | 10 Pa.C.S |
| Commissions merchants | Act 675 of 1857 |
| Condominiums | Act 117 of 1963 |
| Construction | 1 Pa.C.S. § 1501 |
| Consumer finance | Act 66 of 1937 |
| | Act 387 of 1968 |

| | |
|---|---|
| Cooperatives | Act 21 of 1935 |
| Cooperatives, Agricultural | 15 Pa.C.S. § 7501 et seq. |
| Cooperatives, Electrical | 15 Pa.C.S. § 7301 et seq. |
| Cooperatives, Mortgage | Act 21 of 1935 |
| Cooperatives, Real Estate | 68 Pa.C.S. § 4101 et seq. |
| Cooperatives, Worker's Corporation | 15 Pa.C.S. § 7701 et seq. |
| Cosmetics | Act 86 of 1933 |
| Credit cards | Act 36 of 1992 |
| | Act 150 of 1992 |
| Credit service organizations | Act 150 of 1992 |
| Dairies | 3 Pa.C.S. |
| | Act 25 of 1885 |
| Desserts, frozen | Act 215 of 1965 |
| Drugs (Pharmaceuticals) | Act 699 of 1961 |
| Dry cleaning | Act 214 of 1990 |
| Eggs & poultry | Act 356 of 1919 |
| | 3 Pa.C.S. |
| Electrical | Act 75 of 1992 |
| Elevators | Act 99 of 1895 |
| Energy conservation standards | Act 222 of 1980 |
| Explosives | Act 537 of 1937 |
| | Act 362 of 1957 |
| Factory built housing | Act 192 of 1982 |
| Fiduciary funds | Act 3 of 1995 |
| Fireworks | Act 65 of 1939 |
| Food | 31 Pa.C.S. |
| Fruits & vegetables | Act 97 of 1929 |
| Fuels, liquid | 75 Pa.C.S. § 9401 et seq. |
| Gasoline & oil | 58 Pa.C.S. |

| | |
|---|---|
| Glass (Glazing) | Act 5 of 1971 |
| Hazardous substances | Act 165 of 1990 |
| Hazardous waste clean-up | Act 108 of 1988 |
| Health care | 35 Pa.C.S. |
| | 40 Pa.C.S. |
| Health clubs | Act 87 of 1989 |
| Home health agencies | Act 48 of 1979 |
| | Act 691 of 1961 |
| Home improvement sales & fin. | Act 62 of 1986 |
| Honey | Act 184 of 1971 |
| Horseracing | Act 135 of 1981 |
| | Act 18 of 1993 |
| Hospices | Act 19 of 1893 |
| Hotels | Act 318 of 1913 |
| | Act 509 of 1855 |
| Household waste products | Act 155 of 1994 |
| Housing codes, state minimum | Act 459 of 1949 |
| Insurance and service plans | 40 Pa.C.S. |
| | 31 Pa. Code |
| Land sales | Act 9 of 1980 |
| Legal services | 37 Pa. Code |
| Liquor | 47 Pa.C.S. |
| | 40 Pa. Code |
| Livestock | 3 Pa.C.S. |
| Lodging | 48 Pa.C.S. |
| Lotteries | Act 91 of 1971 |
| Meats | 3 Pa.C.S. |
| Mental health | 50 PaC.S. |
| Metal recyclers | Act 17 of 1984 |

| | |
|---|---|
| Milk & milk products | Act 105 of 1937 |
| Mining waste | Act 82 of 1955 |
| Mobile homes | Act 261 of 1976 |
| Money orders | Act 79 of 1996 |
| Motion pictures | Act 42 of 1937 |
| | Act 211 of 1935 |
| Motor vehicle lemon law | Act 28 of 1984 |
| Motor vehicles | 75 Pa.C.S. |
| Multi-level marketing | Act 387 of 1968 |
| Naval stores | Act 152 of 1925 |
| Non-Alcoholic beverages | Act 214 of 1937 |
| Newsprint | 45 Pa.C.S. §301 et seq. |
| Nursing homes | Act 691 of 1961 |
| Oil | 58 Pa.C.S. |
| Pest control | Act 251 of 1967 |
| Pigeons, Racing and Carrier | Act 100 of 1965 |
| Plumbing | Act 135 of 1895 |
| Pyramid schemes | Act 387 of 1968 |
| Radiation | Act 147 of 1984 |
| Radio & television repairs | Act 173 of 1961 |
| Real estate sales | Act 9 of 1980 |
| Rental housing | 66 Pa.C.S. |
| Restaurants | Act 35 of 1995 |
| Secondhand dealers | Act 67 of 1927 |
| Securities transactions | 70 Pa.C.S. |
| | 64 Pa. Code |
| Swimming & bathing places | Act 299 of 1931 |
| Syrup | Act 8 of 1925 |
| Television picture tubes | Act 173 of 1961 |

| | |
|---|---|
| Timber and Lumber | Act 174 of 1876 |
| Tobacco | 3 Pa.C.S. |
| Tourist camps | Act 285 of 1953 |
| Watches, used | Act 100 of 1945 |
| Weapons and firearms | 18 Pa.C.S. § 6101 et seq. |

# BOOKKEEPING AND ACCOUNTING 15

It is beyond the scope of this book to explain all the intricacies of setting up a business' bookkeeping and accounting systems. But the important thing is to realize that if you do not set up an understandable bookkeeping system, your business will undoubtedly fail.

Without accurate records of where your income is coming from and where it is going, you will be unable to increase your profits, lower your expenses, obtain needed financing or make the right decisions in all areas of your business. The time to decide how you will handle your bookkeeping is when you open your business, not a year later when it is tax time.

## INITIAL BOOKKEEPING

If you do not understand business taxation, you should pick up a good book on the subject as well as the IRS tax guide for your type of business (proprietorship, partnership, or corporation). A few good books on the subject are *The Small Business Survival Guide* by Robert Fleury (Sourcebooks), *Small Time Operator* by Bernard Kamoroff (Bell Springs), and *Tax Savvy for Small Business* by Frederick Daily (Nolo Press).

The IRS tax book for small businesses is Publication 334, *Tax Guide for Small Businesses*. There are also instruction booklets for each type of business form: Schedule C for proprietorships, Form 1120 or 1120S for C corporations and S corporations, and 1165 for partnerships and businesses which are taxed like partnerships (LLCs, LLPs).

Keep in mind that the IRS doesn't give you the best advice for saving on taxes and does not give you the other side of contested issues. For that you need a private tax guide or advisor.

The most important thing to do is to set up your bookkeeping so that you can easily fill out your monthly, quarterly, and annual tax returns.

The best way to do this is to get copies of the returns, note the categories that you will need to supply, and set up your bookkeeping system to arrive at those totals.

For example, for a sole proprietorship you will use "Schedule C" to report business income and expenses to the IRS at the end of the year. Use the categories on that form to sort your expenses. To make your job especially easy, every time you pay a bill, put the category number on the check.

# ACCOUNTANTS

In the beginning, your new business will most likely not be able to afford hiring an accountant to handle your books. That is good. Doing them yourself will force you to learn about business accounting and taxation. The worst way to run a business is to know nothing about the tax laws and turn everything over to an accountant at the end of the year to find out what is due.

You should know the basics of tax law before making decisions such as whether to buy or rent equipment or premises. You should understand accounting so you can time your financial affairs appropriately. If you were a boxer who only needed to win fights, you could turn everything over to an accountant. If your business needs to buy supplies, inventory, or equipment and provides goods or services throughout the year, you need to at least have a basic understanding of the system within which you are working.

Once you can afford an accountant, you should weigh the cost against your time and the risk that you will make an error. Even if you think you know enough to do your own corporate tax return, you should still take it to an accountant one year to see if you have been missing any deductions. You might decide that the money saved is worth the cost of the accountant's services.

# COMPUTER PROGRAMS

Today, every business should keep its books by computer. There are inexpensive programs such as Quicken which can instantly provide you with reports of your income and expenses and the right figures to plug into your tax returns.

Most programs even offer a tax program each year which will take all of your information and print it out on the current year's tax forms. It sure beats sorting through shoe boxes of receipts with an adding machine!

# TAX TIPS

Here are a few tax tips for small businesses which will help you save money:

☛ Usually when you buy equipment for a business, you must amortize the cost over several years. That is, you don't deduct it all when you buy it, you take, say, twenty-five percent of the cost off your taxes each year for four years. (The time is determined by the theoretical usefulness of the item.) However, small businesses are allowed to write off the entire cost of a limited amount of items under Internal Revenue Code § 179. If you have income to shelter, use it.

☞ Owners of S corporations do not have to pay social security or medicare taxes on the part of their profits that is not considered salary. As long as you pay yourself a reasonable salary, other money you take out is not subject to these taxes.

☞ You should not neglect to deposit withholding taxes for your own salary or profits. Besides being a large sum to come up with all at once in April, there are penalties which must be paid for failure to do so.

☞ Do not fail to keep track of and remit your employees' withholding. You will be personally liable for them even if you are a corporation.

☞ If you keep track of the use of your car for business, you can deduct 31.5¢ per mile (this may go up or down each year). If you use your car for business a considerable amount of time, you may be able to depreciate it.

☞ If your business is a corporation and if you designate the stock as "section 1244 stock;" then if the business fails, you are able to get a much better deduction for the loss.

☞ By setting up a retirement plan, you can exempt up to twenty percent of your salary from income tax. See chapter 10. But don't use money you might need later. There are penalties for taking it out of the retirement plan.

☞ When you buy things which will be resold or made into products which will be resold, you do not have to pay sales taxes on those purchases. See chapter 17.

# PAYING FEDERAL TAXES 16

## FEDERAL INCOME TAX

The manner in which each type of business pays taxes is as follows:

PROPRIETORSHIP

An individual reports profits and expenses on Schedule C attached to the usual Form 1040 and pays tax on all of the net income of the business. Each quarter Form ES-1040 must be filed along with payment of one-quarter of the amount of income tax and social security taxes estimated to be due for the year.

PARTNERSHIP

The partnership files a return showing the income and expenses but pays no tax. Each partner is given a form showing his or her share of the profits or losses and reports these on Schedule E of Form 1040. Each quarter, Form ES-1040 must be filed by each partner along with payment of one-quarter of the amount of income tax and social security taxes estimated to be due for the year.

C CORPORATION

A regular corporation is a separate taxpayer, and pays tax on its profits after deducting all expenses, including officers' salaries. If dividends are distributed, they are paid out of after-tax dollars, and the shareholders pay tax a second time when they receive the dividends. If a corporation needs to accumulate money for investment, it may be able to do so at lower tax rates than the shareholders. But if all profits will be distributed to shareholders, the double-taxation may be excessive unless all income is paid as salaries. A C corporation files Form 1120.

**S CORPORATION**

A small corporation has the option of being taxed like a partnership. If Form 2553 is filed by the Corporation and accepted by the Internal Revenue Service, the S corporation will only file an informational return listing profits and expenses. Each shareholder will be taxed on a proportional share of the profits (or be able to deduct a proportional share of the losses). Unless a corporation will make a large profit which will not be distributed, S-status is usually best in the beginning. An S corporation files Form 1120S and distributes Form K-1 to each shareholder. If any money is taken out by a shareholder that is not listed as wages subject to withholding, then the shareholder will usually have to file form ES-1040 each quarter along with payment of the estimated withholding on the withdrawals.

**LIMITED LIABILITY COMPANIES AND PARTNERSHIPS**

Limited liability companies and limited liability partnerships are allowed by the IRS to elect to be taxed either as a partnership or a corporation. To make this election you file Form 8832, Entity Classification Election with the IRS.

**TAX WORKSHOPS AND BOOKLETS**

The IRS conducts workshops to inform businesses about the tax laws. (Don't expect in-depth study of the loopholes.) For more information, call or write to the IRS at the following addresses:

Internal Revenue Service
Philadelphia, PA 19255
1-800-829-1040

For specific forms or questions the following services are also available. Their lines are often busy so you may have to keep trying:

| | |
|---|---|
| Federal Tax Inquiries | 1-800-829-1040 |
| Problem Resolution | 1-800-829-1040 |
| Tax Forms and Publications | 1-800-829-3676 |
| Tele-Tax Service and Refund Information | 1-800-829-4477 |
| Tele-TIN (Telephone EIN) | 215-574-2400 |

# Federal Withholding, Social Security, and Medicare Taxes

If you need basic information on business tax returns, the IRS publishes a rather large booklet that answers most questions and is available free of charge. Call or write them and ask for *Publication No. 334.* If you have any questions, look up their toll-free number in the phone book under United States Government/Internal Revenue Service. If you want more creative answers and tax saving information, you should find a good local accountant. But to get started you will need the following:

**Employer Identification Number**

If you are a sole proprietor with no employees, you can use your social security number for your business. If you are a corporation, a partnership or a proprietorship with employees, you must obtain an "Employer Identification Number." This is done by filing form SS-4. It usually takes a week or two to receive. You will need this number to open bank accounts for the business, so you should file this form a soon as you decide to go into business. A sample filled-in form and instructions are at the end of this chapter.

**Employee's Withholding Allowance Certificate**

You must have each employee fill out a W-4 form to calculate the amount of federal taxes to be deducted and to obtain their social security numbers. (The number of allowances on this form is used with IRS Circular E, Publication 15, to figure out the exact deductions.) A sample filled-in form is at the end of this chapter.

**Federal Tax Deposit Coupons**

After taking withholdings from employees' wages, you must deposit them at a bank which is authorized to accept such funds. If at the end of any month you have over $1000 in withheld taxes (including your contribution to FICA), you must make a deposit prior to the 15th of the following month. If on the 3rd, 7th, 11th, 15th, 19th, 22nd, or 25th of any month you have over $3,000 in withheld taxes, you must make a deposit within three banking days. The deposit is made using the coupons in the Form 8109 booklet. A sample 8109-B coupon, which you will use to order your booklet, is shown at the end of this chapter.

**ELECTRONIC FILING**
Businesses which make $50,000 or more a year in federal tax deposits are required to begin electronic filing by June 30, 1999. However, this deadline has been extended in the past and may be again. (It was originally scheduled for July 1, 1997, but faced strong business opposition.)

**ESTIMATED TAX PAYMENT VOUCHER**
Sole proprietors and partners usually take draws from their businesses without the formality of withholding. However, they are still required to make deposits of income and FICA taxes each quarter. If more than $500 is due in April on a person's 1040 form, not enough money was withheld each quarter and a penalty is assessed unless the person falls into an exception. The quarterly withholding is submitted on Form 1040-ES on April 15th, June 15th, September 15th, and January 15th each year. If these days fall on a weekend, the due date is the following Monday. The worksheet with Form 1040-ES can be used to determine the amount to pay. *Important Note*: One of the exceptions to the rule is that if you withhold the same amount as last year's tax bill, you do not have to pay a penalty. This is usually a lot easier than filling out the 1040-ES worksheet.

**EMPLOYER'S QUARTERLY TAX RETURN**
Each quarter you must file Form 941 reporting your federal withholding and FICA taxes. If you owe more than $1000 at the end of a quarter, you are required to make a deposit at the end of any month that you have $1000 in withholding. The deposits are made to the Federal Reserve Bank or an authorized financial institution on Form 501. Most banks are authorized to accept deposits. If you owe more than $3,000 for any month, you must make a deposit at any point in the month in which you owe $3,000. After you file form SS-4, the 941 forms will be sent to you automatically if you checked the box saying that you expect to have employees.

**WAGE AND TAX STATEMENT**
At the end of each year, you are required to issue a W-2 Form to each employee. This form shows the amount of wages paid to the employee during the year as well as the amounts withheld for taxes, social security, medicare, and other purposes. A sample W-2 is at the end of this chapter.

MISCELLANEOUS
INCOME

If you pay at least $600 to a person other than an employee (such as independent contractors), you are required to file a Form 1099 for that person. Along with the 1099s, you must file a form 1096, which is a summary sheet.

Many people are not aware of this law and fail to file these forms, but they are required for such things as services, royalties, rents, awards, and prizes which you pay to individuals (but not corporations). The rules for this are quite complicated so you should either obtain "Package 1099" from the IRS or consult your accountant. Sample forms 1099 and 1096 are at the end of this chapter.

EARNED INCOME
CREDIT

Persons who are not liable to pay income tax may have the right to a check from the government because of the "Earned Income Credit." You are required to notify your employees of this. You can satisfy this requirement with one of the following:

☛ a W-2 Form with the notice on the back;

☛ a substitute for the W-2 Form with the notice on it;

☛ a copy of Notice 797; or

☛ a written statement with the wording from Notice 797.

A Notice 797 can be obtained by calling 1-800-829-3676.

# FEDERAL EXCISE TAXES

Excise taxes are taxes on certain activities or items. Most federal excise taxes have been eliminated since World War II, but a few remain.

Some of the things which are subject to federal excise taxes are tobacco and alcohol, gasoline, tires and inner tubes, some trucks and trailers, firearms, ammunition, bows, arrows, fishing equipment, the use of highway vehicles of over 55,000 pounds, aircraft, wagering, telephone and teletype services, coal, hazardous wastes, and vaccines. If you are involved with any of these, you should obtain from the IRS publication No. 510, *Information on Excise Taxes.*

# UNEMPLOYMENT COMPENSATION TAXES

You must pay federal unemployment taxes if you paid wages of $1,500 in any quarter, or if you had at least one employee for twenty calendar weeks. The federal tax amount is 0.8% of the first $7,000 of wages paid each employee. If more than $100 is due by the end of any quarter (if you paid $12,500 in wages for the quarter), Form 508 must be filed with an authorized financial institution or the Federal Reserve Bank in your area. You will receive Form 508 when you obtain your employer identification number.

At the end of each year, you must file Form 940 or Form 940EZ. This is your annual report of federal unemployment taxes. You will receive an original form from the IRS.

| Form **SS-4**<br>(Rev. April 2000)<br>Department of the Treasury<br>Internal Revenue Service | **Application for Employer Identification Number**<br>(For use by employers, corporations, partnerships, trusts, estates, churches,<br>government agencies, certain individuals, and others. See instructions.)<br>▶ Keep a copy for your records. | EIN<br><br>OMB No. 1545-0003 |

Please type or print clearly.

**1** Name of applicant (legal name) (see instructions)
Doe Company

**2** Trade name of business (if different from name on line 1)

**3** Executor, trustee, "care of" name

**4a** Mailing address (street address) (room, apt., or suite no.)
123 Main Street

**5a** Business address (if different from address on lines 4a and 4b)

**4b** City, state, and ZIP code
Harrisburg, PA 17000

**5b** City, state, and ZIP code

**6** County and state where principal business is located
Dauphin, Pennsylvania

**7** Name of principal officer, general partner, grantor, owner, or trustor—SSN or ITIN may be required (see instructions) ▶
John Doe

**8a** Type of entity (Check only one box.) (see instructions)

**Caution:** *If applicant is a limited liability company, see the instructions for line 8a.*

- [ ] Sole proprietor (SSN) _____
- [X] Partnership
- [ ] REMIC
- [ ] State/local government
- [ ] Church or church-controlled organization
- [ ] Other nonprofit organization (specify) ▶ _____
- [ ] Other (specify) ▶
- [ ] Personal service corp.
- [ ] National Guard
- [ ] Farmers' cooperative
- [ ] Estate (SSN of decedent) _____
- [ ] Plan administrator (SSN) _____
- [ ] Other corporation (specify) ▶ _____
- [ ] Trust
- [ ] Federal government/military
- (enter GEN if applicable) _____

**8b** If a corporation, name the state or foreign country (if applicable) where incorporated

| State | Foreign country |
|---|---|

**9** Reason for applying (Check only one box.) (see instructions)
- [X] Started new business (specify type) ▶
  clothing manufacturing
- [ ] Hired employees (Check the box and see line 12.)
- [ ] Created a pension plan (specify type) ▶
- [ ] Banking purpose (specify purpose) ▶
- [ ] Changed type of organization (specify new type) ▶ _____
- [ ] Purchased going business
- [ ] Created a trust (specify type) ▶ _____
- [ ] Other (specify) ▶

**10** Date business started or acquired (month, day, year) (see instructions)
10-15-2000

**11** Closing month of accounting year (see instructions)
December

**12** First date wages or annuities were paid or will be paid (month, day, year). **Note:** *If applicant is a withholding agent, enter date income will first be paid to nonresident alien. (month, day, year)* . . . . . . . . . . . ▶ 10-22-2000

**13** Highest number of employees expected in the next 12 months. **Note:** *If the applicant does not expect to have any employees during the period, enter -0-. (see instructions)* . . . . ▶

| Nonagricultural | Agricultural | Household |
|---|---|---|
| 3 | | |

**14** Principal activity (see instructions) ▶ clothing manufacturing

**15** Is the principal business activity manufacturing? . . . . . . . . . . . . . . . . . . . . . [X] Yes [ ] No
If "Yes," principal product and raw material used ▶ fabric

**16** To whom are most of the products or services sold? Please check one box. . . [X] Business (wholesale)
- [ ] Public (retail)
- [ ] Other (specify) ▶
- [ ] N/A

**17a** Has the applicant ever applied for an employer identification number for this or any other business? . . . . [ ] Yes [ ] No
**Note:** *If "Yes," please complete lines 17b and 17c.*

**17b** If you checked "Yes" on line 17a, give applicant's legal name and trade name shown on prior application, if different from line 1 or 2 above.     X
Legal name ▶                              Trade name ▶

**17c** Approximate date when and city and state where the application was filed. Enter previous employer identification number if known.

| Approximate date when filed (mo., day, year) | City and state where filed | Previous EIN |
|---|---|---|

Under penalties of perjury, I declare that I have examined this application, and to the best of my knowledge and belief, it is true, correct, and complete.

Business telephone number (include area code)
( 717) 555-0000

Fax telephone number (include area code)
(       )

Name and title (Please type or print clearly.) ▶ John Doe, Partner

Signature ▶ *John Doe*     Date ▶ 10/15/2000

**Note:** *Do not write below this line. For official use only.*

| Please leave<br>blank ▶ | Geo. | Ind. | Class | Size | Reason for applying |
|---|---|---|---|---|---|

For Privacy Act and Paperwork Reduction Act Notice, see page 4.     Cat. No. 16055N     Form **SS-4** (Rev. 4-2000)

Form SS-4 (Rev. 4-2000)                                                                                    Page **2**

# General Instructions

*Section references are to the Internal Revenue Code unless otherwise noted.*

## Purpose of Form

Use Form SS-4 to apply for an employer identification number (EIN). An EIN is a nine-digit number (for example, 12-3456789) assigned to sole proprietors, corporations, partnerships, estates, trusts, and other entities for tax filing and reporting purposes. The information you provide on this form will establish your business tax account.

**Caution:** *An EIN is for use in connection with your business activities only. Do not use your EIN in place of your social security number (SSN).*

## Who Must File

You must file this form if you have not been assigned an EIN before and:

● You pay wages to one or more employees including household employees.

● You are required to have an EIN to use on any return, statement, or other document, even if you are not an employer.

● You are a withholding agent required to withhold taxes on income, other than wages, paid to a nonresident alien (individual, corporation, partnership, etc.). A withholding agent may be an agent, broker, fiduciary, manager, tenant, or spouse, and is required to file **Form 1042,** Annual Withholding Tax Return for U.S. Source Income of Foreign Persons.

● You file **Schedule C,** Profit or Loss From Business, **Schedule C-EZ,** Net Profit From Business, or **Schedule F,** Profit or Loss From Farming, of **Form 1040,** U.S. Individual Income Tax Return, **and** have a Keogh plan or are required to file excise, employment, or alcohol, tobacco, or firearms returns.

The following must use EINs even if they do not have any employees:

● State and local agencies who serve as tax reporting agents for public assistance recipients, under Rev. Proc. 80-4, 1980-1 C.B. 581, should obtain a separate EIN for this reporting. See **Household employer** on page 3.

● Trusts, except the following:

   **1.** Certain grantor-owned trusts. (See the **Instructions for Form 1041,** U.S. Income Tax Return for Estates and Trusts.)

   **2.** Individual retirement arrangement (IRA) trusts, unless the trust has to file **Form 990-T,** Exempt Organization Business Income Tax Return. (See the **Instructions for Form 990-T.**)

● Estates

● Partnerships

● REMICs (real estate mortgage investment conduits) (See the **Instructions for Form 1066,** U.S. Real Estate Mortgage Investment Conduit (REMIC) Income Tax Return.)

● Corporations

● Nonprofit organizations (churches, clubs, etc.)

● Farmers' cooperatives

● Plan administrators (A plan administrator is the person or group of persons specified as the administrator by the instrument under which the plan is operated.)

## When To Apply for a New EIN

**New Business.** If you become the new owner of an existing business, **do not** use the EIN of the former owner. **If you already have an EIN, use that number.** If you do not have an EIN, apply for one on this form. If you become the "owner" of a corporation by acquiring its stock, use the corporation's EIN.

**Changes in Organization or Ownership.** If you already have an EIN, you may need to get a new one if either the organization or ownership of your business changes. If you incorporate a sole proprietorship or form a partnership, you must get a new EIN. However, **do not** apply for a new EIN if:

● You change only the name of your business,

● You elected on **Form 8832,** Entity Classification Election, to change the way the entity is taxed, or

● A partnership terminates because at least 50% of the total interests in partnership capital and profits were sold or exchanged within a 12-month period. (See Regulations section 301.6109-1(d)(2)(iii).) The EIN for the terminated partnership should continue to be used.

**Note:** *If you are electing to be an "S corporation," be sure you file* **Form 2553,** *Election by a Small Business Corporation.*

**File Only One Form SS-4.** File only one Form SS-4, regardless of the number of businesses operated or trade names under which a business operates. However, each corporation in an affiliated group must file a separate application.

**EIN Applied for, But Not Received.** If you do not have an EIN by the time a return is due, write "Applied for" and the date you applied in the space shown for the number. **Do not** show your social security number (SSN) as an EIN on returns.

If you do not have an EIN by the time a tax deposit is due, send your payment to the Internal Revenue Service Center for your filing area. (See **Where To Apply** below.) Make your check or money order payable to "United States Treasury" and show your name (as shown on Form SS-4), address, type of tax, period covered, and date you applied for an EIN. Send an explanation with the deposit.

For more information about EINs, see **Pub. 583,** Starting a Business and Keeping Records, and **Pub. 1635,** Understanding Your EIN.

## How To Apply

You can apply for an EIN either by mail or by telephone. You can get an EIN immediately by calling the Tele-TIN number for the service center for your state, or you can send the completed Form SS-4 directly to the service center to receive your EIN by mail.

**Application by Tele-TIN.** Under the Tele-TIN program, you can receive your EIN by telephone and use it immediately to file a return or make a payment. To receive an EIN by telephone, complete Form SS-4, then call the Tele-TIN number listed for your state under **Where To Apply.** The person making the call must be authorized to sign the form. (See **Signature** on page 4.)

An IRS representative will use the information from the Form SS-4 to establish your account and assign you an EIN. Write the number you are given on the upper right corner of the form and sign and date it.

*Mail or fax (facsimile) the signed Form SS-4 within 24 hours to the Tele-TIN Unit at the service center address for your state.* The IRS representative will give you the fax number. The fax numbers are also listed in Pub. 1635.

Taxpayer representatives can receive their client's EIN by telephone if they first send a fax of a completed **Form 2848,** Power of Attorney and Declaration of Representative, or **Form 8821,** Tax Information Authorization, to the Tele-TIN unit. The Form 2848 or Form 8821 will be used solely to release the EIN to the representative authorized on the form.

**Application by Mail.** Complete Form SS-4 at least 4 to 5 weeks before you will need an EIN. Sign and date the application and mail it to the service center address for your state. You will receive your EIN in the mail in approximately 4 weeks.

## Where To Apply

The Tele-TIN numbers listed below will involve a long-distance charge to callers outside of the local calling area and can be used only to apply for an EIN. **The numbers may change without notice.** Call 1-800-829-1040 to verify a number or to ask about the status of an application by mail.

| If your principal business, office or agency, or legal residence in the case of an individual, is located in: | Call the Tele-TIN number shown or file with the Internal Revenue Service Center at: |
|---|---|
| Florida, Georgia, South Carolina | Attn: Entity Control Atlanta, GA 39901 770-455-2360 |
| New Jersey, New York (New York City and counties of Nassau, Rockland, Suffolk, and Westchester) | Attn: Entity Control Holtsville, NY 00501 516-447-4955 |
| New York (all other counties), Connecticut, Maine, Massachusetts, New Hampshire, Rhode Island, Vermont | Attn: Entity Control Andover, MA 05501 978-474-9717 |
| Illinois, Iowa, Minnesota, Missouri, Wisconsin | Attn: Entity Control Stop 6800 2306 E. Bannister Rd. Kansas City, MO 64999 816-926-5999 |
| Delaware, District of Columbia, Maryland, Pennsylvania, Virginia | Attn: Entity Control Philadelphia, PA 19255 215-516-6999 |
| Indiana, Kentucky, Michigan, Ohio, West Virginia | Attn: Entity Control Cincinnati, OH 45999 859-292-5467 |

| Kansas, New Mexico, Oklahoma, Texas | Attn: Entity Control<br>Austin, TX 73301<br>512-460-7843 |
| --- | --- |
| Alaska, Arizona, California (counties of Alpine, Amador, Butte, Calaveras, Colusa, Contra Costa, Del Norte, El Dorado, Glenn, Humboldt, Lake, Lassen, Marin, Mendocino, Modoc, Napa, Nevada, Placer, Plumas, Sacramento, San Joaquin, Shasta, Sierra, Siskiyou, Solano, Sonoma, Sutter, Tehama, Trinity, Yolo, and Yuba), Colorado, Idaho, Montana, Nebraska, Nevada, North Dakota, Oregon, South Dakota, Utah, Washington, Wyoming | Attn: Entity Control<br>Mail Stop 6271<br>P.O. Box 9941<br>Ogden, UT 84201<br>801-620-7645 |
| California (all other counties), Hawaii | Attn: Entity Control<br>Fresno, CA 93888<br>559-452-4010 |
| Alabama, Arkansas, Louisiana, Mississippi, North Carolina, Tennessee | Attn: Entity Control<br>Memphis, TN 37501<br>901-546-3920 |
| If you have no legal residence, principal place of business, or principal office or agency in any state | Attn: Entity Control<br>Philadelphia, PA 19255<br>215-516-6999 |

## Specific Instructions

The instructions that follow are for those items that are not self-explanatory. Enter N/A (nonapplicable) on the lines that do not apply.

**Line 1.** Enter the legal name of the entity applying for the EIN exactly as it appears on the social security card, charter, or other applicable legal document.

*Individuals.* Enter your first name, middle initial, and last name. If you are a sole proprietor, enter your individual name, not your business name. Enter your business name on line 2. Do not use abbreviations or nicknames on line 1.

*Trusts.* Enter the name of the trust.

*Estate of a decedent.* Enter the name of the estate.

*Partnerships.* Enter the legal name of the partnership as it appears in the partnership agreement. **Do not** list the names of the partners on line 1. See the specific instructions for line 7.

*Corporations.* Enter the corporate name as it appears in the corporation charter or other legal document creating it.

*Plan administrators.* Enter the name of the plan administrator. A plan administrator who already has an EIN should use that number.

**Line 2.** Enter the trade name of the business if different from the legal name. The trade name is the "doing business as" name.

**Note:** *Use the full legal name on line 1 on all tax returns filed for the entity. However, if you enter a trade name on line 2 and choose to use the trade name instead of the legal name, enter the trade name on all returns you file. To prevent processing delays and errors, **always** use either the legal name only or the trade name only on all tax returns.*

**Line 3.** Trusts enter the name of the trustee. Estates enter the name of the executor, administrator, or other fiduciary. If the entity applying has a designated person to receive tax information, enter that person's name as the "care of" person. Print or type the first name, middle initial, and last name.

**Line 7.** Enter the first name, middle initial, last name, and SSN of a principal officer if the business is a corporation; of a general partner if a partnership; of the owner of a single member entity that is disregarded as an entity separate from its owner; or of a grantor, owner, or trustor if a trust. If the person in question is an alien individual with a previously assigned individual taxpayer identification number (ITIN), enter the ITIN in the space provided, instead of an SSN. You are not required to enter an SSN or ITIN if the reason you are applying for an EIN is to make an entity classification election (see Regulations section 301.7701-1 through 301.7701-3), and you are a nonresident alien with no effectively connected income from sources within the United States.

**Line 8a.** Check the box that best describes the type of entity applying for the EIN. If you are an alien individual with an ITIN previously assigned to you, enter the ITIN in place of a requested SSN.

**Caution:** *This is not an election for a tax classification of an entity. See "Limited liability company (LLC)" below.*

If not specifically mentioned, check the "Other" box, enter the type of entity and the type of return that will be filed (for example, common trust fund, Form 1065). Do not enter N/A. If you are an alien individual applying for an EIN, see the **Line 7** instructions above.

*Sole proprietor.* Check this box if you file Schedule C, C-EZ, or F (Form 1040) and have a qualified plan, or are required to file excise, employment, or alcohol, tobacco, or firearms returns, or are a payer of gambling winnings. Enter your SSN (or ITIN) in the space provided. If you are a nonresident alien with are a nonresident alien with no effectively

connected income from sources within the United States, you do not need to enter an SSN or ITIN.

*REMIC.* Check this box if the entity has elected to be treated as a real estate mortgage investment conduit (REMIC). See the Instructions for Form 1066 for more information.

*Other nonprofit organization.* Check this box if the nonprofit organization is other than a church or church-controlled organization and specify the type of nonprofit organization (for example, an educational organization).

If the organization also seeks tax-exempt status, you must file either **Package 1023,** Application for Recognition of Exemption, or **Package 1024,** Application for Recognition of Exemption Under Section 501(a). Get **Pub. 557,** Tax Exempt Status for Your Organization, for more information.

*Group exemption number (GEN).* If the organization is covered by a group exemption letter, enter the four-digit GEN. (Do not confuse the GEN with the nine-digit EIN.) If you do not know the GEN, contact the parent organization. Get Pub. 557 for more information about group exemption numbers.

*Withholding agent.* If you are a withholding agent required to file Form 1042, check the "Other" box and enter "Withholding agent."

*Personal service corporation.* Check this box if the entity is a personal service corporation. An entity is a personal service corporation for a tax year only if:

- The principal activity of the entity during the testing period (prior tax year) for the tax year is the performance of personal services substantially by employee-owners, and

- The employee-owners own at least 10% of the fair market value of the outstanding stock in the entity on the last day of the testing period.

Personal services include performance of services in such fields as health, law, accounting, or consulting. For more information about personal service corporations, see the **Instructions for Forms 1120 and 1120-A,** and **Pub. 542,** Corporations.

*Limited liability company (LLC).* See the definition of limited liability company in the **Instructions for Form 1065,** U.S. Partnership Return of Income. An LLC with two or more members can be a partnership or an association taxable as a corporation. An LLC with a single owner can be an association taxable as a corporation or an entity disregarded as an entity separate from its owner. See Form 8832 for more details.

**Note:** *A domestic LLC with at least two members that does not file Form 8832 is classified as a partnership for Federal income tax purposes.*

- If the entity is classified as a partnership for Federal income tax purposes, check the "partnership" box.

- If the entity is classified as a corporation for Federal income tax purposes, check the "Other corporation" box and write "limited liability co." in the space provided.

- If the entity is disregarded as an entity separate from its owner, check the "Other" box and write in "disregarded entity" in the space provided.

*Plan administrator.* If the plan administrator is an individual, enter the plan administrator's SSN in the space provided.

*Other corporation.* This box is for any corporation other than a personal service corporation. If you check this box, enter the type of corporation (such as insurance company) in the space provided.

*Household employer.* If you are an individual, check the "Other" box and enter "Household employer" and your SSN. If you are a state or local agency serving as a tax reporting agent for public assistance recipients who become household employers, check the "Other" box and enter "Household employer agent." If you are a trust that qualifies as a household employer, you do not need a separate EIN for reporting tax information relating to household employees; use the EIN of the trust.

*QSub.* For a qualified subchapter S subsidiary (QSub) check the "Other" box and specify "QSub."

**Line 9.** Check only **one** box. Do not enter N/A.

*Started new business.* Check this box if you are starting a new business that requires an EIN. If you check this box, enter the type of business being started. **Do not** apply if you already have an EIN and are only adding another place of business.

*Hired employees.* Check this box if the existing business is requesting an EIN because it has hired or is hiring employees and is therefore required to file employment tax returns. **Do not** apply if you already have an EIN and are only hiring employees. For information on the applicable employment taxes for family members, see **Circular E,** Employer's Tax Guide (Publication 15).

*Created a pension plan.* Check this box if you have created a pension plan and need an EIN for reporting purposes. Also, enter the type of plan.

**Note:** *Check this box if you are applying for a trust EIN when a new pension plan is established.*

Form SS-4 (Rev. 4-2000)                                                                                          Page **4**

*Banking purpose.* Check this box if you are requesting an EIN for banking purposes only, and enter the banking purpose (for example, a bowling league for depositing dues or an investment club for dividend and interest reporting).

*Changed type of organization.* Check this box if the business is changing its type of organization, for example, if the business was a sole proprietorship and has been incorporated or has become a partnership. If you check this box, specify in the space provided the type of change made, for example, "from sole proprietorship to partnership."

*Purchased going business.* Check this box if you purchased an existing business. **Do not** use the former owner's EIN. **Do not** apply for a new EIN if you already have one. Use your own EIN.

*Created a trust.* Check this box if you created a trust, and enter the type of trust created. For example, indicate if the trust is a nonexempt charitable trust or a split-interest trust.

**Note:** *Do **not** check this box if you are applying for a trust EIN when a new pension plan is established. Check "Created a pension plan."*

**Exception.** Do **not** file this form for certain grantor-type trusts. The trustee does not need an EIN for the trust if the trustee furnishes the name and TIN of the grantor/owner and the address of the trust to all payors. See the Instructions for Form 1041 for more information.

*Other (specify).* Check this box if you are requesting an EIN for any other reason, and enter the reason.

**Line 10.** If you are starting a new business, enter the starting date of the business. If the business you acquired is already operating, enter the date you acquired the business. Trusts should enter the date the trust was legally created. Estates should enter the date of death of the decedent whose name appears on line 1 or the date when the estate was legally funded.

**Line 11.** Enter the last month of your accounting year or tax year. An accounting or tax year is usually 12 consecutive months, either a calendar year or a fiscal year (including a period of 52 or 53 weeks). A calendar year is 12 consecutive months ending on December 31. A fiscal year is either 12 consecutive months ending on the last day of any month other than December or a 52-53 week year. For more information on accounting periods, see Pub. 538, Accounting Periods and Methods.

*Individuals.* Your tax year generally will be a calendar year.

*Partnerships.* Partnerships generally must adopt one of the following tax years:
● The tax year of the majority of its partners,
● The tax year common to all of its principal partners,
● The tax year that results in the least aggregate deferral of income, or
● In certain cases, some other tax year.

See the Instructions for Form 1065 for more information.

*REMIC.* REMICs must have a calendar year as their tax year.

*Personal service corporations.* A personal service corporation generally must adopt a calendar year unless:
● It can establish a business purpose for having a different tax year, or
● It elects under section 444 to have a tax year other than a calendar year.

*Trusts.* Generally, a trust must adopt a calendar year except for the following:
● Tax-exempt trusts,
● Charitable trusts, and
● Grantor-owned trusts.

**Line 12.** If the business has or will have employees, enter the date on which the business began or will begin to pay wages. If the business does not plan to have employees, enter N/A.

*Withholding agent.* Enter the date you began or will begin to pay income to a nonresident alien. This also applies to individuals who are required to file Form 1042 to report alimony paid to a nonresident alien.

**Line 13.** For a definition of agricultural labor (farmwork), see **Circular A,** Agricultural Employer's Tax Guide (Publication 51).

**Line 14.** Generally, enter the exact type of business being operated (for example, advertising agency, farm, food or beverage establishment, labor union, real estate agency, steam laundry, rental of coin-operated vending machine, or investment club). Also state if the business will involve the sale or distribution of alcoholic beverages.

*Governmental.* Enter the type of organization (state, county, school district, municipality, etc.).

*Nonprofit organization (other than governmental).* Enter whether organized for religious, educational, or humane purposes, and the principal activity (for example, religious organization—hospital, charitable).

*Mining and quarrying.* Specify the process and the principal product (for example, mining bituminous coal, contract drilling for oil, or quarrying dimension stone).

*Contract construction.* Specify whether general contracting or special trade contracting. Also, show the type of work normally performed (for example, general contractor for residential buildings or electrical subcontractor).

*Food or beverage establishments.* Specify the type of establishment and state whether you employ workers who receive tips (for example, lounge—yes).

*Trade.* Specify the type of sales and the principal line of goods sold (for example, wholesale dairy products, manufacturer's representative for mining machinery, or retail hardware).

*Manufacturing.* Specify the type of establishment operated (for example, sawmill or vegetable cannery).

**Signature.** The application must be signed by (a) the individual, if the applicant is an individual, (b) the president, vice president, or other principal officer, if the applicant is a corporation, (c) a responsible and duly authorized member or officer having knowledge of its affairs, if the applicant is a partnership or other unincorporated organization, or (d) the fiduciary, if the applicant is a trust or an estate.

## How To Get Forms and Publications

**Phone.** You can order forms, instructions, and publications by phone 24 hours a day, 7 days a week. Just call 1-800-TAX-FORM (1-800-829-3676). You should receive your order or notification of its status within 10 workdays.

**Personal computer.** With your personal computer and modem, you can get the forms and information you need using IRS's Internet Web Site at www.irs.gov or File Transfer Protocol at ftp.irs.gov.

**CD-ROM.** For small businesses, return preparers, or others who may frequently need tax forms or publications, a CD-ROM containing over 2,000 tax products (including many prior year forms) can be purchased from the National Technical Information Service (NTIS).

To order Pub. 1796, Federal Tax Products on CD-ROM, call **1-877-CDFORMS** (1-877-233-6767) toll free or connect to **www.irs.gov/cdorders**

**Privacy Act and Paperwork Reduction Act Notice.** We ask for the information on this form to carry out the Internal Revenue laws of the United States. We need it to comply with section 6109 and the regulations thereunder which generally require the inclusion of an employer identification number (EIN) on certain returns, statements, or other documents filed with the Internal Revenue Service. Information on this form may be used to determine which Federal tax returns you are required to file and to provide you with related forms and publications. We disclose this form to the Social Security Administration for their use in determining compliance with applicable laws. We will be unable to issue an EIN to you unless you provide all of the requested information which applies to your entity.

You are not required to provide the information requested on a form that is subject to the Paperwork Reduction Act unless the form displays a valid OMB control number. Books or records relating to a form or its instructions must be retained as long as their contents may become material in the administration of any Internal Revenue law. Generally, tax returns/return information are confidential, as required by section 6103.

The time needed to complete and file this form will vary depending on individual circumstances. The estimated average time is:

**Recordkeeping** . . . . . . . . . . . . . . . . 7 min.

**Learning about the law or the form** . . . . . . . . 22 min.

**Preparing the form** . . . . . . . . . . . . . . 46 min.

**Copying, assembling, and sending the form to the IRS** . . 20 min.

If you have comments concerning the accuracy of these time estimates or suggestions for making this form simpler, we would be happy to hear from you. You can write to the Tax Forms Committee, Western Area Distribution Center, Rancho Cordova, CA 95743-0001. **Do not** send the form to this address. Instead, see **Where To Apply** on page 2.

# Form W-4 (2001)

**Purpose.** Complete Form W-4 so your employer can withhold the correct Federal income tax from your pay. Because your tax situation may change, you may want to refigure your withholding each year.

**Exemption from withholding.** If you are exempt, complete only lines 1, 2, 3, 4, and 7, and sign the form to validate it. Your exemption for 2001 expires February 18, 2002.

**Note:** *You cannot claim exemption from withholding if (1) your income exceeds $750 and includes more than $250 of unearned income (e.g., interest and dividends) and (2) another person can claim you as a dependent on their tax return.*

**Basic instructions.** If you are not exempt, complete the **Personal Allowances Worksheet** below. The worksheets on page 2 adjust your withholding allowances based on itemized deductions, certain credits, adjustments to

income, or two-earner/two-job situations. Complete all worksheets that apply. They will help you figure the number of withholding allowances you are entitled to claim. **However, you may claim fewer (or zero) allowances.**

**Head of household.** Generally, you may claim head of household filing status on your tax return only if you are unmarried and pay more than 50% of the costs of keeping up a home for yourself and your dependent(s) or other qualifying individuals. See line E below.

**Tax credits.** You can take projected tax credits into account in figuring your allowable number of withholding allowances. Credits for child or dependent care expenses and the child tax credit may be claimed using the **Personal Allowances Worksheet** below. See **Pub. 919,** How Do I Adjust My Tax Withholding? for information on converting your other credits into withholding allowances.

**Nonwage income.** If you have a large amount of nonwage income, such as interest or dividends,

consider making estimated tax payments using **Form 1040-ES,** Estimated Tax for Individuals. Otherwise, you may owe additional tax.

**Two earners/two jobs.** If you have a working spouse or more than one job, figure the total number of allowances you are entitled to claim on all jobs using worksheets from only one Form W-4. Your withholding usually will be most accurate when all allowances are claimed on the Form W-4 for the highest paying job and zero allowances are claimed on the others.

**Check your withholding.** After your Form W-4 takes effect, use Pub. 919 to see how the dollar amount you are having withheld compares to your projected total tax for 2001. Get Pub. 919 especially if you used the **Two-Earner/Two-Job Worksheet** on page 2 and your earnings exceed $150,000 (Single) or $200,000 (Married).

**Recent name change?** If your name on line 1 differs from that shown on your social security card, call 1-800-772-1213 for a new social security card.

---

**Personal Allowances Worksheet** (Keep for your records.)

**A** Enter "1" for **yourself** if no one else can claim you as a dependent . . . . . . . . . . . **A** __1__

**B** Enter "1" if:
- You are single and have only one job; or
- You are married, have only one job, and your spouse does not work; or
- Your wages from a second job or your spouse's wages (or the total of both) are $1,000 or less. } . . **B** __1__    1

**C** Enter "1" for your **spouse.** But, you may choose to enter -0- if you are married and have either a working spouse or more than one job. (Entering -0- may help you avoid having too little tax withheld.) . . . . . . . . . **C** __0__

**D** Enter number of **dependents** (other than your spouse or yourself) you will claim on your tax return . . . . . **D** __1__

**E** Enter "1" if you will file as **head of household** on your tax return (see conditions under **Head of household** above) . **E** _____

**F** Enter "1" if you have at least $1,500 of **child or dependent care expenses** for which you plan to claim a credit . . **F** _____
(Note: Do **not** include child support payments. See **Pub. 503,** Child and Dependent Care Expenses, for details.)

**G** **Child Tax Credit** (including additional child tax credit):
- If your total income will be between $18,000 and $50,000 ($23,000 and $63,000 if married), enter "1" for each eligible child.
- If your total income will be between $50,000 and $80,000 ($63,000 and $115,000 if married), enter "1" if you have two eligible children, enter "2" if you have three or four eligible children, or enter "3" if you have five or more eligible children. **G** _____   1

**H** Add lines A through G and enter total here. (Note: *This may be different from the number of exemptions you claim on your tax return.*) ▶ **H** __3__

For accuracy, complete all worksheets that apply.
- If you plan to **itemize or claim adjustments to income** and want to reduce your withholding, see the **Deductions and Adjustments Worksheet** on page 2.
- If you are **single,** have **more than one job** and your combined earnings from all jobs exceed $35,000, **or** if you are **married** and have a **working spouse or more than one job** and the combined earnings from all jobs exceed $60,000, see the **Two-Earner/Two-Job Worksheet** on page 2 to avoid having too little tax withheld.
- If **neither** of the above situations applies, **stop here** and enter the number from line H on line 5 of Form W-4 below.

---

............ **Cut here and give Form W-4 to your employer. Keep the top part for your records.** ............

**Form W-4**
Department of the Treasury
Internal Revenue Service

## Employee's Withholding Allowance Certificate

▶ **For Privacy Act and Paperwork Reduction Act Notice, see page 2.**

OMB No. 1545-0010

**2001**

**1** Type or print your first name and middle initial: George   H.    Last name: Smith   x

**2** Your social security number: 345 67 8900

**3** ☐ Single ☒ Married ☐ Married, but withhold at higher Single rate.
**Note:** *If married, but legally separated, or spouse is a nonresident alien, check the Single box.*

Home address (number and street or rural route): 4567 Paris Street

City or town, state, and ZIP code: Allentown, PA 17000

**4** If your last name differs from that on your social security card, check here. You must call 1-800-772-1213 for a new card. ▶ ☐

**5** Total number of allowances you are claiming (from line **H** above **or** from the applicable worksheet on page 2) **5** __3__ 0

**6** Additional amount, if any, you want withheld from each paycheck . . . . . . . . . . . **6** $ __0__

**7** I claim exemption from withholding for 2001, and I certify that I meet **both** of the following conditions for exemption:
- Last year I had a right to a refund of **all** Federal income tax withheld because I had **no** tax liability **and**
- This year I expect a refund of **all** Federal income tax withheld because I expect to have **no** tax liability.

If you meet both conditions, write "Exempt" here . . . . . . . . ▶ **7**

Under penalties of perjury, I certify that I am entitled to the number of withholding allowances claimed on this certificate, or I am entitled to claim exempt status.

**Employee's signature** (Form is not valid unless you sign it.) ▶ *George H. Smith*    Date ▶ *November 6 2000*

**8** Employer's name and address (Employer: Complete lines 8 and 10 only if sending to the IRS.)   **9** Office code (optional)   **10** Employer identification number

Cat. No. 10220Q

# Sample Form 8109-B: Federal Tax Deposit Coupons

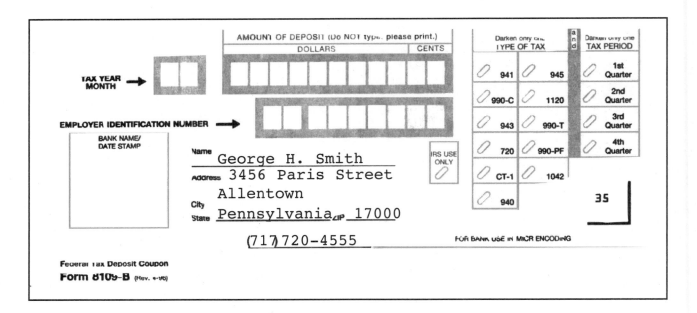

## Sample Form 1040-ES: Estimated Tax Payment Voucher

Cat. No. 61900V

OMB No. 1545-0087

Form 1040-ES (OCR)

Department of the Treasury
Internal Revenue Service

2000 Estimated Tax

Payment Voucher **4**

Calendar year—
Due Jan. 15, 2000

Cross out any errors and print the correct information. Get **Form 8822** to report a new address (see instructions). For Paperwork Reduction Act Notice, see instructions.

0746497

07 234-56-7890 DC 9712

234-56-7890 DC WARD 30 0 9712 430 07

JOHN DOE
123 MAIN STREET
HARRISBURG PA 17000

PHILADELPHIA PA 19255-001

**Enter the amount of your payment.**
File this voucher only if you are making a payment of **estimated** tax.

$

► Make your check or money order payable to **"Internal Revenue Service."**
► Write your social security number and "1999 Form 1040-ES" on your payment.
► Send your payment and payment voucher to the address above.
► Do not send cash. Do not staple your payment to the voucher.

# SAMPLE FORM W-2: WAGE AND TAX STATEMENT

| **a** Control number | 22222 | Void ☐ | For Official Use Only ▶ OMB No. 1545-0008 | |
|---|---|---|---|---|

| **b** Employer's identification number 59-123456 | **1** Wages, tips, other compensation 25,650.00 | **2** Federal income tax withheld 5,050.00 |
|---|---|---|

| **c** Employer's name, address, and ZIP code | **3** Social security wages 25,650.00 | **4** Social security tax withheld 1,590.30 |
|---|---|---|
| Doe Company | **5** Medicare wages and tips 25,650.00 | **6** Medicare tax withheld 371.93 |
| 123 Main Street | **7** Social security tips 0 | **8** Allocated tips 0 |
| Harrisburg, PA 17000 | | |

| **d** Employee's social security number 123-45-6789 | **9** Advance EIC payment 0 | **10** Dependent care benefits 0 |
|---|---|---|

| **e** Employee's name (first, middle initial, last) | **11** Nonqualified plans 0 | **12** Benefits included in box 1 0 |
|---|---|---|
| John A. Smith | | |
| 567 Wharf Boulevard | **13** See Instrs. for box 13 | **14** Other |
| Harrisburg, PA 17000 | | |

| 15 | Statutory employee ☐ | Deceased ☐ | Pension plan ☐ | Legal rep. ☐ | Hshld. emp. ☐ | Subtotal ☐ | Deferred compensation ☐ |
|---|---|---|---|---|---|---|---|

**f** Employee's address and ZIP code

| **16** State | Employer's state I.D. No. | **17** State wages, tips, etc. | **18** State income tax | **19** Locality name | **20** Local wages, tips, etc. | **21** Local income tax |
|---|---|---|---|---|---|---|
| PA | 98765432 | 25,650.00 | 565.00 | | | |
| | | | | | | |

Cat. No. 10134D

Department of the Treasury—Internal Revenue Service

**Form W-2 Wage and Tax Statement 2000**

For Paperwork Reduction Act Notice, see separate instructions.

Copy A For Social Security Administration

# SAMPLE FORMS 1099 AND 1096: MISCELLANEOUS INCOME

9595 ☐ VOID ☐ CORRECTED

| PAYER'S name, street address, city, state, and ZIP code | 1 Rents $ 12,000.00 | OMB No. 1545-0115 | |
|---|---|---|---|
| Doe Company<br>123 Main Street<br>Harrisburg, PA 17000 | 2 Royalties $ | **2000**<br>Form **1099-MISC** | **Miscellaneous Income** |
| | 3 Other income $ | | |

| PAYER'S Federal identification number | RECIPIENT'S identification number | 4 Federal income tax withheld | 5 Fishing boat proceeds | **Copy A** |
|---|---|---|---|---|
| 59-123456 | 9876532 | $ | $ | **For Internal Revenue Service Center** |
| RECIPIENT'S name<br>John A. Smith | | 6 Medical and health care payments $ | 7 Nonemployee compensation $ 21,000 | **File with Form 1096.** |
| Street address (including apt. no.)<br>567 Wharf Boulevard | | 8 Substitute payments in lieu of dividends or interest $ | 9 Payer made direct sales of $5,000 or more of consumer products to a buyer (recipient) for resale ▶ ☐ | For Paperwork Reduction Act Notice and instructions for completing this form, see **Instructions for Forms 1099, 1098, 5498, and W-2G.** |
| City, state, and ZIP code<br>Harrisburg, PA 17000 | | 10 Crop insurance proceeds $ | 11 State income tax withheld $ 00.00 | |
| Account number (optional) | 2nd TIN Not. ☐ | 12 State/Payer's state number 8884444 | | |

Form **1099-MISC**    Cat. No. 14425J    Department of the Treasury - Internal Revenue Service

**Do NOT Cut or Separate Forms on This Page**

DO NOT STAPLE 6969

| Form **1096**<br>Department of the Treasury<br>Internal Revenue Service | **Annual Summary and Transmittal of U.S. Information Returns** | OMB No. 1545-0108<br>**2000** |
|---|---|---|

FILER'S name

　Doe Company

Street address (including room or suite number)

　123 Main Street

City, state, and ZIP code
　Harrisburg, PA 17000

| If you are not using a preprinted label, enter in box 1 or 2 below the identification number you used as the filer on the information returns being transmitted. Do not fill in both boxes 1 and 2. | Name of person to contact if the IRS needs more information<br>John Doe<br>Telephone number<br>(717) 5550000 | **For Official Use Only** |
|---|---|---|

| 1 Employer identification number | 2 Social security number | 3 Total number of forms | 4 Federal income tax withheld | 5 Total amount reported with this Form 1096 |
|---|---|---|---|---|
| 59-123456 | | 3 | $ 0 | $ $63,000 |

Enter an "X" in only one box below to indicate the type of form being filed.    If this is your FINAL return, enter an "X" here . . ▶ ☒

| W-2G 32 | 1098 81 | 1099-A 80 | 1099-B 79 | 1099-C 85 | 1099-DIV 91 | 1099-G 86 | 1099-INT 92 | 1099-MISC 95 | 1099-OID 96 | 1099-PATR 97 | 1099-R 98 | 1099-S 75 | 5498 28 |
|---|---|---|---|---|---|---|---|---|---|---|---|---|---|
| ☐ | ☐ | ☐ | ☐ | ☐ | ☐ | ☐ | ☐ | ☒ | ☐ | ☐ | ☐ | ☐ | ☐ |

# PAYING PENNSYLVANIA TAXES 17

## SALES AND USE TAX

If you will be selling or renting goods or services at retail, you must collect Pennsylvania sales and use tax. Many items such as drugs, some wearing apparel, dental products, and sanitary products are exempt. For a list of exempt and non-exempt goods and services, obtain the pamphlet *Retailers' Information* from the Pennsylvania Department of Revenue. Call 717-787-8201.

First, you must obtain a tax number by filling out form PA-100. This is a multi-page form that covers registration of a business with various divisions of Pennsylvania government. A sample filled-in copy of the form is on page 182 and a blank form is contained in the appendix. (Sections 14-17 and 19-22 do not necessarily apply to new businesses and have not been filled in the sample.)

To order this form or any tax form twenty-four hours a day, call the Pennsylvania Department of Revenue at 800-362-2050 or if you are in the Harrisburg area or calling from out of state, dial 717-787-8094. You may also send written requests to the Pennsylvania Department of Revenue, Tax Forms Distribution Unit, 2850 Turnpike Industrial Drive, Middletown, PA 17057-5492. Forms may also be obtained from their Website at: **http://www.revenue.state.pa.us**.

You are also advised to contact your county government to determine if there are any local taxes for which you may be responsible.

The sales and use tax returns are due for each month on the twentieth of the following month. You are allowed to deduct one percent of the tax as your reimbursement for collecting the tax if your remit on time. Rest assured the amount will never be near enough to compensate for the work. In some cases, if your sales are very limited (under $100 a quarter) you may be allowed to file returns quarterly.

Once you file your Combined Registration Form, you will have to start filing monthly returns whether you have any sales or not. If you do not file the return, even if you had no sales, you must pay a penalty of five percent with a minimum or $2. If you do not expect to have any sales for the first few months while you are setting up your business, you probably should wait before sending in the registration. Otherwise, you may forget to file the returns marked with zeros and end up paying the penalties.

One reason to get a tax number early is to exempt your purchases from tax. When you buy a product which you will resell, or use as part of a product which you will sell, you are exempt from paying tax on it. To get the exemption, you need to submit a Pennsylvania Exemption Certificate to the seller. This form must contain your sales and use tax registration number.

If you will only be selling items wholesale or out of state, you might think that you would not need a tax number or to submit returns, but you will need to be registered to obtain the tax number to exempt your purchases.

If you have any sales before you get your monthly tax return forms, you should calculate the tax anyway and submit it. Otherwise, you will be charged a penalty even if it was not your fault that you did not have the forms.

SELLING TO TAX
EXEMPT
PURCHASERS

You are required to collect sales and use taxes for all sales you make unless you have documentation on file proving that a purchase was exempt from the tax. The form to use for this is the Pennsylvania Exemption Certificate, which is included in this book in the appendix.

In some cases, new businesses are required to post a bond to insure taxes are paid.

# MISCELLANEOUS BUSINESS TAXES

Although Pennsylvania taxes are some of the lowest in the nation, there are some additional taxes that must be paid that may or may not affect the type of business that you plan to open and where you plan to open it. For example, the City of Philadelphia and the County of Allegheny (including the City of Pittsburgh) must collect an additional one percent local sales and use tax. The Allegheny tax must be paid for any goods to be used in the county. This has caused much confusion and some merchants require a customer to produce their driver's licenses in order to determine whether the goods will be used in the county or not. Questions regarding the one percent local sales and use tax can be addressed by calling the Bureau of Business Trust Fund Tax at 717-783-5470. At this number, you may also obtain information regarding the Public Transportation Assistance Fund taxes. The Miscellaneous Tax Division covers the Cigarette Tax 717-783-9374, the Malt Beverage Tax 717-783-9354, the Small Games of Chance and Pari-Mutual Tax 717-787-8275. You may qualify for a sales tax exemption depending on your business, call 717-783-5473 to see if you may qualify.

Corporations also have several additional taxes placed upon them. The Bureau of Corporate Taxes at 717-783-6035 can help you with the Rate and Base Changes, the Capital Stock/Franchise Tax and the Corporate Loans Tax. Information about prepayment requirements can be found at 717-787-1808.

The Employer Withholding Division can help you with your withholding requirements for your employees. Contact them at 717-787-1586.

There are also several taxes relating to transportation: the Motor Carriers Road Tax, the Liquid Fuels Tax, the Diesel Fuels tax (for usage) and the Oil Franchise Tax. Contact the Bureau of Motor Fuels Tax at 717-783-9191.

## PERSONAL PROPERTY TAXES

Personal property taxes are levied against tangible and intangible property. Examples of intangible property are "holdings" such as stocks and bonds. The personal property tax is administered on the county level and varies from county to county across the state. You are encouraged to contact your county tax assessment office.

## UNEMPLOYMENT COMPENSATION TAXES

Employers in Pennsylvania are responsible for contributing to the Unemployment Compensation Fund. This fund provides benefits to employees who are separated from their service through no fault of their own. Situations where a discharged employee can receive their benefits include lay-offs due to decrease in work and natural disasters that prevent a business from operating. Situations where an employee may *not* collect unemployment compensation include being fired and voluntarily quitting their position. To determine how much an employer needs to contribute to the fund, the Assigned Contribution Rate (determined annually by the Department of Labor and Industry) is multiplied by the wages paid to an employee. The Assigned Contribution Rate is determined by the department by considering such factors as the number of employees and past employment history. The assigned contribution rate varies from employer to employer. You may be liable to contribute to the Unemployment Compensation Fund if you employ at least one other person. You may be liable for the unemployment compensation tax as well. Contact the Department of Labor and Industry, Bureau of

Employer Tax Operations at 717-787-2009 or the district or regional office nearest you which is located in the blue pages of your telephone directory.

# INCOME TAX

Yes, Pennsylvania does tax corporations. The type of business and its structure determine any taxes for which that business is obligated to pay. You are encouraged to seek information from the Pennsylvania Department of Revenue at 717-783-6035 or direct your inquiries to:

> Pennsylvania Department of Revenue
> 1131 Strawberry Square
> Harrisburg, PA 17128-1100

or by internet to:

> http://www.Revenue.State.PA.US

The Department of Revenue also publishes the *Pennsylvania Tax Update* to which you may subscribe. Inquiries may be emailed to parev@revenue.state.pa.us.

# PENNSYLVANIA ENTERPRISE REGISTRATION

The Pennsylvania Enterprise Registration Form (PA-100) must be completed by enterprises to register for certain taxes and services administered by the PA Department of Revenue and the PA Department of Labor & Industry. The form is also designed to be used by previously registered enterprises to register for additional taxes and services, reactivate a tax or service, or notify both Departments that additional establishment locations have been added. The form is also used to request the Unemployment Compensation Experience Record and Reserve Account Balance of a Predecessor.

For registration assistance, contact:

(717) 787-1064, 1-800-447-3020 (Services for Special Hearing and Speaking Needs Only) Monday through Friday 8:00 AM to 4:30 PM

## What is an enterprise?

An enterprise is any individual or organization, sole-proprietorship, partnership, corporation, government organization, business trust, association, etc., which is subject to the laws of the Commonwealth of Pennsylvania and performs at least one of the following:

- Pays wages to employees
- Offers products for sale to others
- Offers services for sale to others
- Collects donations
- Collects taxes
- Is allocated use of tax dollars
- Has a name which is intended for use and, by that name, is to be recognized as an organization engaged in economic activity.

## What is an establishment?

An establishment is an economic unit, generally at a single physical location where:

- Business is conducted inside PA
- Business is conducted outside PA with reporting requirements to PA
- PA residents are employed, inside or outside of PA.

The enterprise and the establishment may have the same physical location.

## Multiple establishments exist if the following apply:

- Business is conducted at multiple locations.
- Distinct and separate economic activities involving separate employees are performed at a single location. Each activity may be treated as a separate establishment as long as separate reports can be prepared for the number of employees, wages and salaries or sales and receipts.

## How to complete the registration form:

- **New registrants** must complete every item in Sections 1 through 10.
- **Registered enterprises** must complete every item in Sections 1 through 4 and additional sections as indicated.
- Section 5 has indicators to direct the registrant to additional sections.
- To determine the registration requirements for a specific tax service and/or license, see pages 2 and 3.
- Type or print legibly using black ink.
- Retain a copy of the completed registration form for your records.

## How to avoid delays in processing:

- Review the registration form and accompanying sections to be sure that every item is complete. The preparer will be contacted to supply information if required sections are not completed.
- Enclose payment for license or registration fees, payable to **PA Department of Revenue.**
- If a quarterly UC Report/payment is submitted, attach a separate check payable to **PA Unemployment Compensation Fund.**
- Sign the registration form.
- Remove completed pages from the booklet, arrange in sequential order and mail to the PA Department of Revenue.

It is your responsibility to **notify the Bureau of Business Trust Fund Taxes** in writing within 30 days of any change to the information provided on the registration form.

**Completing this form will NOT fulfill the requirement to register for corporate taxes. Registering corporations must also contact the PA Department of State to secure corporate name clearance and register for corporation tax purposes. Contact the PA Department of State at (717) 787-1057.**

## TABLE OF CONTENTS

1

## THE FOLLOWING CHART WILL HELP DETERMINE THE SECTIONS OF THIS BOOKLET THAT SHOULD BE COMPLETED FOR VARIOUS TAX TYPES.
### COMPLETE THE SECTIONS THAT APPLY TO YOUR ENTERPRISE.

- New registrants should complete sections 1 through 10 plus the sections indicated.
- Previous registrants should complete sections 1 through 4 plus the additional sections indicated.

| TAXES AND SERVICES | REQUIREMENTS | SECTIONS TO COMPLETE |
|---|---|---|
| **CIGARETTE TAX** IS AN EXCISE TAX IMPOSED ON THE SALE OR POSSESSION OF CIGARETTES. ADEALER IS ANY CIGARETTE STAMPING AGENT, WHOLESALER OR RETAILER. | • CIGARETTE DEALER'S LICENSE<br><br>• SALES TAX LICENSE (RETAILER) | • SECTION 19<br><br>• SECTION 18 |
| **CORPORATION TAXES** ARE IMPOSED ON DOMESTIC AND FOREIGN CORPORATIONS, CERTAIN BUSINESS TRUSTS, AND LIMITED LIABILITY COMPANIES WHICH ARE REGISTERED AND/OR TRANSACTING BUSINESS WITHIN THE COMMONWEALTH OF PENNSYLVANIA. SUBJECTIVITYTO SPECIFIC CORPORATION TAXES IS DETERMINED BY THE TYPE OF CORPORATE ORGANIZATION AND THE ACTIVITY CONDUCTED.<br><br>• **FINANCIAL INSTITUTIONS TAXES:** THE BANK AND TRUSTCOMPANYSHARES TAX IS IMPOSED ON EVERY BANK AND TRUST COMPANY HAVING CAPITAL STOCK AND CONDUCTING BUSINESS IN PENNSYLVANIA. DOMESTIC TITLE INSURANCE COMPANIES ARE SUBJECTTO THE TITLE INSURANCE COMPANY SHARES TAX. THE MUTUAL THRIFT INSTITUTIONS TAX IS IMPOSED ON SAVINGS INSTITUTIONS, SAVINGS BANKS, SAVINGS AND LOAN ASSOCIATIONS AND BUILDING AND LOAN ASSOCIATIONS CONDUCTING BUSINESS IN PENNSYLVANIA. CREDIT UNIONS ARE NOT SUBJECT TO TAX.<br><br>• **GROSS PREMIUMS TAX** IS LEVIED ON DOMESTIC AND FOREIGN INSURANCE COMPANIES. THE YEARLY GROSS PREMIUMS RECEIVED FORM THE TAX BASE. GROSS PREMIUMS ARE PREMIUMS, PREMIUM DEPOSITS OR ASSESSMENTS AND, ANNUITY CONSIDERATIONS FOR BUSINESS TRANSACTED IN PENNSYLVANIA.<br><br>• **GROSS RECEIPTS TAX** IS LEVIED ON PIPELINE, CONDUIT, WATER NAVIGATION AND TRANSPORTATION COMPANIES; TELEPHONE AND TELEGRAPH COMPANIES; ELECTRIC LIGHT, WATER POWER AND HYDROELECTRIC COMPANIES; GAS COMPANIES; MOTOR VEHICLE CARRIERS; AND FREIGHT AND OIL TRANSPORTATION COMPANIES.<br><br>THE TAX IS BASED ON GROSS RECEIPTS FROM PASSENGERS, BAGGAGE AND FREIGHT TRANSPORTED WITHIN PENNSYLVANIA; TELEGRAPH AND TELEPHONE MESSAGES TRANSMITTED WITHIN PENNSYLVANIA; AND SALES OF ELECTRICITYAND GAS IN PENNSYLVANIA.<br><br>• **PUBLIC UTILITY REALTY TAX** IS LEVIED AGAINST CERTAIN ENTITIES FURNISHING UTILITY SERVICES. PENNSYLVANIA IMPOSES THIS TAX ON PUBLIC UTILITY REALTY IN LIEU OF LOCAL REAL ESTATE TAXES AND DISTRIBUTES THE LOCAL REALTY TAX EQUIVALENT TO LOCALTAXING AUTHORITIES.<br><br>• **OTHER CORPORATION TAXES:** THIS GROUP IS COMPOSED PRIMARILY OF THE CORPORATE LOANS TAX, THE COOPERATIVE AGRICULTURALASSOCIATION AND ELECTRIC COOPERATIVE CORPORATION TAXES. | • REGISTRATION WITH PA DEPARTMENT OF STATE<br>• FORMS MUSTBE OBTAINED FROM PA DEPARTMENT OF STATE<br><br><br><br>• REGISTRATION WITH FEDERALOR STATE AUTHORITY THAT GRANTED CHARTER<br><br><br><br>• REGISTRATION WITH PA DEPARTMENT OF INSURANCE<br><br><br>• REGISTRATION WITH PA PUBLIC UTILITY COMMISSION<br><br><br><br>• REGISTRATION WITH PA PUBLIC UTILITYCOMMISSION<br><br>• REGISTRATION WITH PA DEPARTMENTOF STATE | • SECTION 11 |
| **EMPLOYER WITHHOLDING** IS THE WITHHOLDING OF PENNSYLVANIA PERSONAL INCOME TAX BY EMPLOYERS FROM COMPENSATION PAID TO PENNSYLVANIA RESIDENT EMPLOYEES FOR WORK PERFORMED INSIDE OR OUTSIDE OF PENNSYLVANIA AND NON-RESIDENT EMPLOYEES FOR WORK PERFORMED INSIDE PENNSYLVANIA. (SEE UNEMPLOYMENT COMPENSATION DEFINITION) | | • SECTION 9 |
| **LIQUID FUELS AND FUELS TAX** IS AN EXCISE TAX IMPOSED ON ALL LIQUID FUELS AND FUELS USED OR SOLD AND DELIVERED BY DISTRIBUTORS WITHIN PENNSYLVANIA, EXCEPTTHOSE DELIVERED TO EXEMPTPURCHASERS. LIQUID FUELS INCLUDE GASOLINE, GASOHOL, JET FUEL AND AVIATION GASOLINE. FUELS INCLUDE CLEAR DIESEL FUEL AND KEROSENE. ADDITIONALLY, THE LIQUID FUELS AND FUELS TAX ACT TAXES ALTERNATIVE FUELS (i.e. HIGHWAY FUELS OTHER THAN LIQUID FUELS OR FUELS) ATA RETAIL/USE TAX LEVEL. | • LIQUID FUELS AND FUELS TAX PERMIT | • SECTION 21 |
| **MOTOR CARRIERS ROAD TAX** IS IMPOSED ON MOTOR CARRIERS ENGAGED IN OPERATIONS ON PENNSYLVANIAHIGHWAYS. A MOTOR CARRIER IS ANY PERSON OR ENTERPRISE OPERATING A QUALIFIED MOTOR VEHICLE USED, DESIGNED OR MAINTAINED FOR THE TRANSPORTATION OF PERSONS OR PROPERTY WHERE (A) THE POWER UNIT HAS TWO AXLES AND A GROSS OR REGISTERED GROSS WEIGHT GREATER THAN 26,000 POUNDS, (B) THE POWER UNIT HAS THREE AXLES OR MORE REGARDLESS OF WEIGHT OR (C) VEHICLES ARE USED IN COMBINATION AND THE DECLARED COMBINATION WEIGHT EXCEEDS 26,000 POUNDS OR THE GROSS WEIGHT OF THE VEHICLES EXCEEDS 26,000 POUNDS. | • IFTA LICENSE AND IFTA DECALS<br><br>• PA NON-IFTA VEHICLE REGISTRATION AND PA NON-IFTA DECALS | • SECTION 21 |

2

| | | |
|---|---|---|
| **PROMOTER** IS ANY ENTERPRISE ENGAGED IN RENTING, LEASING OR GRANTING PERMISSION TO ANY PERSON TO USE SPACE AT A SHOW FOR THE DISPLAY OR FOR THE SALE OF TANGIBLE PERSONAL PROPERTY OR SERVICES. | • PROMOTER LICENSE | • SECTION 18 |
| **PUBLIC TRANSPORTATION ASSISTANCE TAX** IS A TAX OR FEE IMPOSED ON EACH SALE IN PENNSYLVANIA OF NEW TIRES FOR HIGHWAY USE, ON THE LEASE OF MOTOR VEHICLES, AND ON THE RENTAL OF MOTOR VEHICLES. THE TAX IS ALSO LEVIED ON THE STATE TAXABLE VALUE OF UTILITY REALTY OF ENTERPRISES SUBJECT TO THE PUBLIC UTILITY REALTY TAX AND ON PETROLEUM REVENUE OF OIL COMPANIES. | • SALES USE AND HOTEL OCCUPANCY TAX LICENSE<br><br>• PUBLIC TRANSPORTATION ASSISTANCE TAX LICENSE | • SECTION 18 |
| **REPORTING AND PAYMENT METHODS** OFFER THE TAXPAYER THE ABILITY TO FILE CERTAIN TAXES THROUGH ELECTRONIC DATA INTERCHANGE (EDI) AND TO MAKE PAYMENT THROUGH ELECTRONIC FUNDS TRANSFER (EFT). UNEMPLOYMENT COMPENSATION (UC) WAGES MAY BE REPORTED VIA A MAGNETIC MEDIUM. IN CERTAIN INSTANCES, AN ENTERPRISE MAY ELECT TO FINANCE UC COSTS UNDER A REIMBURSEMENT METHOD RATHER THAN THE CONTRIBUTORY METHOD. | • AUTHORIZATION AGREEMENT | • SECTION 12 |
| **SALES TAX** IS AN EXCISE TAX IMPOSED ON THE RETAIL SALE OR LEASE OF TAX-ABLE, TANGIBLE PERSONAL PROPERTY AND ON SPECIFIED SERVICES.<br><br>• **HOTEL OCCUPANCY TAX** IS AN EXCISE TAX IMPOSED ON EVERY HOTEL OR MOTEL ROOM OCCUPANCY LESS THAN THIRTY (30) CONSECUTIVE DAYS.<br><br>• **LOCAL SALES TAX** MAY BE IMPOSED, IN ADDITION TO THE STATE SALES AND USE TAX, ON THE RETAIL SALE OR USE OF TANGIBLE PERSONAL PROPERTY AND SERVICES AND ON HOTEL/MOTEL OCCUPANCIES IN COUNTIES THAT HAVE ENACTED SUCH ORDINANCES. | • SALES USE AND HOTEL OCCUPANCY TAX LICENSE<br><br>• SALES USE AND HOTEL OCCUPANCY TAX LICENSE<br><br>• SALES USE AND HOTEL OCCUPANCY TAX LICENSE | • SECTION 18<br><br>• SECTION 18<br><br>• SECTION 18 |
| **SALES TAX EXEMPT STATUS FOR CHARITABLE AND RELIGIOUS ORGANIZATIONS** IS THE QUALIFICATION OF AN INSTITUTION OF PURELY PUBLIC CHARITY TO BE EXEMPT FROM SALES AND USE TAX ON THE PURCHASE OF TANGIBLE PERSONAL PROPERTY OR SERVICES FOR USE IN CHARITABLE ACTIVITY. | • CERTIFICATE OF EXEMPT SALES TAX STATUS | • SECTION 22 |
| **SMALL GAMES OF CHANCE** IS THE REGULATION OF LIMITED GAMES OF CHANCE THAT QUALIFIED CHARITABLE AND NON-PROFIT ORGANIZATIONS CAN OPERATE IN PENNSYLVANIA. | • SMALL GAMES OF CHANCE DISTRIBUTOR LICENSE AND/OR<br>• MANUFACTURER REGISTRATION CERTIFICATE | • SECTION 20 |
| **TRANSIENT VENDOR** IS ANY ENTERPRISE, NOT HAVING A PERMANENT PHYSICAL BUSINESS LOCATION IN PENNSYLVANIA, WHICH SELLS TAXABLE, TANGIBLE PER-SONAL PROPERTY OR PERFORMS TAXABLE SERVICES IN PENNSYLVANIA. | • TRANSIENT VENDOR CERTIFICATE<br>• SALES TAX LICENSE | • SECTION 18 |
| **UNEMPLOYMENT COMPENSATION (UC)** PROVIDES A FUND FROM WHICH COM-PENSATION IS PAID TO WORKERS WHO HAVE BECOME UNEMPLOYED THROUGH NO FAULT OF THEIR OWN. CONTRIBUTIONS ARE REQUIRED TO BE MADE BY ALL EMPLOYERS WHO PAY WAGES TO INDIVIDUALS WORKING IN PA AND WHOSE SER-VICES ARE COVERED UNDER THE UC LAW. THIS TAX MAY INCLUDE EMPLOYEE CONTRIBUTIONS WITHHELD BY EMPLOYERS FROM EACH EMPLOYEE'S GROSS WAGES. (SEE EMPLOYER WITHHOLDING DEFINITION)<br><br>• **APPLICATION FOR PA UC EXPERIENCE RECORD AND RESERVE ACCOUNT BALANCE** ENABLES THE REGISTERING ENTERPRISE TO BENEFIT FROM A PREDECESSOR'S REPORTING HISTORY. REFER TO THE INSTRUCTIONS TO DETERMINE IF THIS IS ADVANTAGEOUS. | • APPLICATION FOR EXPERIENCE RECORD AND RESERVE ACCOUNT BALANCE OF PREDECESSOR | • SECTIONS 7, 9 IF APPLICABLE, 10 AND 14<br><br>• SECTIONS 14, 15 IF APPLICABLE, 16 |
| **USE TAX** IS AN EXCISE TAX IMPOSED ON PROPERTY USED IN PENNSYLVANIA ON WHICH SALES TAX HAS NOT BEEN PAID. | • USE TAX ACCOUNT | • SECTION 18 |
| **VEHICLE RENTAL TAX** IS IMPOSED ON RENTAL CONTRACTS BY ENTERPRISES HAVING AVAILABLE FOR RENTAL: (1) 5 OR MORE MOTOR VEHICLES DESIGNED TO CARRY 15 OR LESS PASSENGERS OR (2) TRUCKS, TRAILERS, OR SEMI-TRAILERS USED IN THE TRANSPORTATION OF PROPERTY. A RENTAL CONTRACT IS FOR A PERIOD OF 29 DAYS OR LESS. | • SALES USE AND HOTEL OCCUPANCY TAX LICENSE<br><br>• PTA LICENSE | • SECTION 18 |

## DETACH AND MAIL COMPLETED REGISTRATION FORM TO:

COMMONWEALTH OF PA
DEPARTMENT OF REVENUE
BUREAU OF BUSINESS TRUST FUND TAXES
DEPT. 280901
HARRISBURG, PA 17128-0901

## ORDERING FORMS

You may order any Pennsylvania tax form(s) or schedule(s) by calling the 24-hour answering service number: Nationwide (1-800) 362-2050. Address written requests to: PA Department of Revenue, Tax Forms Service Unit, 711 Gibson Boulevard, Harrisburg, PA 17104-3200. All mate-rial will be mailed directly to you. Please allow two to three weeks for delivery.

The PA Department of Revenue maintains a toll free service to assist taxpayers with general information, tax forms and schedules. For assis-tance call 1-888-PATAXES. Information and forms are also available on the Internet at **http://www.revenue.state.pa.us**. Or you may contact the Department at our E-Mail address: **parev@revenue.state.pa.us**.

PA-100 (1) 2-98

MAIL COMPLETED APPLICATION TO:
DEPARTMENT OF REVENUE
BUREAU OF BUSINESS TRUST FUND TAXES
DEPT. 280901
HARRISBURG, PA 17128-0901
TELEPHONE (717) 772-2340

**COMMONWEALTH OF PENNSYLVANIA**

# PA ENTERPRISE REGISTRATION FORM

**DEPARTMENT USE ONLY**

**RECEIVED DATE**

DEPARTMENT OF REVENUE &
DEPARTMENT OF LABOR AND INDUSTRY

**TYPE OR PRINT LEGIBLY, USE BLACK INK**

## SECTION 1 - REASON FOR THIS REGISTRATION

REFER TO THE INSTRUCTIONS (PAGE 18) AND CHECK THE APPLICABLE BOX(ES) TO INDICATE THE REASON(S) FOR THIS REGISTRATION.

1. ☒ NEW REGISTRATION
2. ☐ ADDING TAX(ES) & SERVICE(S)
3. ☐ REACTIVATING TAX(ES) & SERVICE(S)
4. ☐ ADDING ESTABLISHMENT(S)

5. ☐ ACQUISITION OF ALL OR PART OF AN EXISTING ENTERPRISE
   WAS THERE A PRIOR OWNER?  ☐ YES  ☐ NO
6. ☐ APPLICATION FOR PAUC EXPERIENCE RECORD AND
   RESERVE ACCOUNT BALANCE OF PREDECESSOR
7. ☐ INFORMATION UPDATE

## SECTION 2 - ENTERPRISE INFORMATION

| 1. DATE OF FIRST OPERATIONS | 2. DATE OF FIRST OPERATIONS IN PA | 3. ENTERPRISE FISCAL YEAR END |
|---|---|---|
| 1-1-98 | 1-1-01 | 12-31-01 |

| 4. ENTERPRISE LEGAL NAME | 5. FEDERAL EMPLOYER IDENTIFICATION NUMBER (EIN) |
|---|---|
| Superior Flooring, Inc. | 00-0000 |

| 6. ENTERPRISE TRADE NAME (if different than legal name) | 7. ENTERPRISE TELEPHONE NUMBER |
|---|---|
| Superior Flooring, Inc. | (789)  555-4321 |

| 8. ENTERPRISE STREET ADDRESS (do not use PO Box) | CITY/TOWN | COUNTY | STATE | ZIP CODE + 4 |
|---|---|---|---|---|
| 123 Main Street | Anytown | Capitol | PA | 10000-1234 |

| 9. ENTERPRISE MAILING ADDRESS (if different than street address) | CITY/TOWN | STATE | ZIP CODE + 4 |
|---|---|---|---|
| same | same | same | same |

| 10. LOCATION OF ENTERPRISE RECORDS (street address) | CITY/TOWN | STATE | ZIP CODE + 4 |
|---|---|---|---|
| 123 Main St. | Anytown | PA | 10000-1234 |

| 11. ESTABLISHMENT NAME (doing business as) | 12. NUMBER OF ESTABLISHMENTS * | 13. SCHOOL DISTRICT | 14. MUNICIPALITY |
|---|---|---|---|
| | | same | |

* Enterprises with more than one establishment as defined in the general instructions must complete Section 17.

## SECTION 3 - TAXES AND SERVICES

ALL REGISTRANTS MUST CHECK THE APPLICABLE BOX(ES) TO INDICATE THE TAX(ES) AND SERVICE(S) REQUESTED FOR THIS REGISTRATION AND COMPLETE THE CORRESPONDING SECTIONS INDICATED ON PAGES 2 AND 3. IF REACTIVATING ANY PREVIOUS ACCOUNT(S), LIST THE ACCOUNT NUMBER(S) IN THE SPACE PROVIDED.

| | PREVIOUS ACCOUNT NBR. | | PREVIOUS ACCOUNT NBR. |
|---|---|---|---|
| ☐ CIGARETTE DEALER'S LICENSE | _____ | ☐ PUBLIC TRANSPORTATION ASSISTANCE TAX LICENSE | _____ |
| ☐ CORPORATION TAXES | _____ | ☐ SALES TAX EXEMPT STATUS | _____ |
| ☐ EMPLOYER WITHHOLDING TAX | _____ | ☒ SALES, USE, HOTEL OCCUPANCY TAX LICENSE | _____ |
| ☐ FUELS TAX PERMIT | _____ | ☐ SMALL GAMES OF CHANCE LIC./CERT. | _____ |
| ☐ LIQUID FUELS TAX PERMIT | _____ | ☐ TRANSIENT VENDOR CERTIFICATE | _____ |
| ☐ LOCAL SALES, USE, HOTEL OCCUPANCY TAX | _____ | ☐ UNEMPLOYMENT COMPENSATION | _____ |
| ☐ MOTOR CARRIERS ROAD TAX/IFTA | _____ | ☐ USE TAX | _____ |
| ☐ PROMOTER LICENSE | _____ | ☐ VEHICLE RENTAL TAX | _____ |

## SECTION 4 - AUTHORIZED SIGNATURE

I, (WE) THE UNDERSIGNED, DECLARE UNDER THE PENALTIES OF PERJURY THAT THE STATEMENTS CONTAINED HEREIN ARE TRUE, CORRECT AND COMPLETE.

| AUTHORIZED SIGNATURE (ATTACH POWER OF ATTORNEY IF APPLICABLE) | TITLE Chief Executive Officer |
|---|---|
| *Janet A. Doe* | |
| **TYPE OR PRINT NAME**  Janet A. Doe | DATE 1-1-01 |

| PREPARER'S SIGNATURE (IF OTHER THAN OWNER, PARTNER OR CORPORATE OFFICER) | TITLE Accountant |
|---|---|
| *Michael B. Roe* | |

| TYPE OR PRINT NAME  Michael B. Roe | DAYTIME TELEPHONE NUMBER (717) 555 1212 | DATE 1-1-01 |
|---|---|---|

4

PA-100 2-98

| ENTERPRISE NAME | DEPARTMENT USE ONLY |
|---|---|
| Superior Flooring, Inc. | |

## SECTION 5 - FORM OF ORGANIZATION

CHECK THE APPROPRIATE BOXES. IN ADDITION TO SECTIONS 1 THROUGH 10, COMPLETE THE SECTION(S) INDICATED.

1. ☐ SOLE PROPRIETORSHIP(INDIVIDUAL)  ☐ CORPORATION (Sec. 11)  ☐ ASSOCIATION  ☐ BUSINESS TRUST  ☐ GOVERNMENT (Sec. 13)

☐ PARTNERSHIP: ☒ GENERAL  COMPANY: ☐ LIMITED LIABILITY  ☐ ESTATE  ☐ TRUST
☐ LIMITED  STATE WHERE CHARTERED N/A
☐ LIMITED LIABILITY  ☐ RESTRICTED PROFESSIONAL  ☐ OTHER, EXPLAIN N/A
☐ JOINT VENTURE  STATE WHERE CHARTERED_____

2. ☒ PROFIT  ☐ NON-PROFIT  IS THE ENTERPRISE ORGANIZED FOR PROFITOR NON-PROFIT?

3. ☐ YES  ☒ NO  IS THE ENTERPRISE EXEMPTFROM TAXATION UNDER INTERNALREVENUE CODE SECTION 501(C)(3)? IF YES, PROVIDE A COPY OF THE ENTERPRISE'S EXEMPTION AUTHORIZATION LETTER FROM THE INTERNALREVENUE SERVICE.

## SECTION 6 - OWNERS, PARTNERS, SHAREHOLDERS, OFFICERS, RESPONSIBLE PARTY INFORMATION

PROVIDE THE FOLLOWING FOR **ALL** INDIVIDUAL AND/OR ENTERPRISE OWNERS, PARTNERS, SHAREHOLDERS, OFFICERS AND RESPONSIBLE PARTIES. IF STOCK IS PUBLICLY TRADED, PROVIDE THE FOLLOWING FOR ANY SHAREHOLDER WITH AN EQUITYPOSITION OF 5% OR MORE. *ADDITIONAL SPACE IS AVAILABLE IN SECTION 6A.*

| 1. NAME Janet Doe | 2. SOCIAL SECURITYNUMBER 123-45-6789 | 3. DATE OF BIRTH * 1-2-34 | 4. FEDERAL EIN 00-00000 |
|---|---|---|---|
| 5. ☒ OWNER ☐ OFFICER ☐ PARTNER ☐ SHAREHOLDER ☐ RESPONSIBLE PARTY | 6. TITLE | 7. EFFECTIVE DATE OF TITLE | 8. PERCENTAGE OF OWNERSHIP 51% | 9. EFFECTIVE DATE OF OWNERSHIP 1-1-98 |

| 10. HOME ADDRESS (street) 345 First Ave | CITY/TOWN Anytown | COUNTY Capitol | STATE PA | ZIP CODE + 4 10001-1234 |
|---|---|---|---|---|

11. PERSON RESPONSIBLE TO REMIT:  ☒ SALES TAX  ☐ EMPLOYER WITHHOLDING  ☐ MOTOR FUELTAXES

SIGNATURE *Janet Doe*

\* DATE OF BIRTH REQUIRED ONLY IF APPLYING FOR ACIGARETTE WHOLESALE DEALER'S LICENSE, A SMALL GAMES OF CHANCE DISTRIBUTOR LICENSE OR A SMALLGAMES OF CHANCE MANUFACTURER CERTIFICATE.

## SECTION 7 - ESTABLISHMENT BUSINESS ACTIVITY INFORMATION

**REFER TO THE INSTRUCTIONS TO COMPLETE THIS SECTION.** COMPLETE SECTION 17 FOR MULTIPLE ESTABLISHMENTS.

1. ENTER THE PERCENTAGE THAT EACH **PA** BUSINESS ACTIVITY REPRESENTS OF THE TOTAL RECEIPTS OR REVENUES ATTHIS ESTABLISHMENT. LIST ALL PRODUCTS OR SERVICES ASSOCIATED WITH EACH BUSINESS ACTIVITY. ENTER THE PERCENTAGE THAT THE PRODUCTS OR SERVICES REPRESENT OF THE TOTAL RECEIPTS OR REVENUES ATTHIS ESTABLISHMENT.

| PA BUSINESS ACTIVITY | % | PRODUCTS OR SERVICES | % | ADDITIONAL PRODUCTS OR SERVICES | % |
|---|---|---|---|---|---|
| Construction | | | | | |
| Manufacturing | | | | | |
| Retail Trade | 70 | flooring/paneling | | | |
| Wholesale Trade | 30 | flooring/paneling | | | |
| Finance | | | | | |
| Insurance | | | | | |
| Real Estate | | | | | |
| Transportation | | | | | |
| Warehousing | | | | | |
| Communications | | | | | |
| Agriculture, Forestry, Fishing | | | | | |
| Mining, Quarrying, Oil/Gas Extraction | | | | | |
| Utility or Sanitary Service | | | | | |
| Services (Personal or Business) | | | | | |
| Domestic | | | | | |
| TOTAL | 100% | | | | |

2. ENTER THE PERCENTAGE THATTHIS ESTABLISHMENT'S RECEIPTS OR REVENUES REPRESENTOF THE TOTAL PARECEIPTS OR REVENUES OF THE ENTERPRISE.
_____80_%

3. ESTABLISHMENTS ENGAGED IN CONSTRUCTION **MUST** ENTER THE PERCENTAGE OF CONSTRUCTION ACTIVITYTHATIS NEW AND/OR RENOVATIVE.
_____ % NEW  _____ % RENOVATIVE

4. ☐ YES  ☒ NO  IS THIS ESTABLISHMENT **SOLELY** ENGAGED IN THE PERFORMANCE OF SUPPORTACTIVITIES FOR OTHER ESTABLISHMENTS OF THE SAME ENTERPRISE? IF YES, LISTTHE NAME(S) OF THE SUPPORTED ESTABLISHMENT(S) AND CHECK THE APPROPRIATE BOX TO DESCRIBE THE SUPPORT ACTIVITY._____

☐ ADMINISTRATION  ☐ RESEARCH/DEVELOPMENT  ☐ STORAGE/WAREHOUSE  ☐ OTHER (SPECIFY)_____

5

PA-100 2-98

| ENTERPRISE NAME | DEPARTMENT USE ONLY |
|---|---|
| Superior Flooring, Inc. | |

## SECTION 8 – ESTABLISHMENT SALES INFORMATION

1. ☒ YES ☐ NO    IS THIS ESTABLISHMENT SELLING TAXABLE PRODUCTS OR OFFERING TAXABLE SERVICES TO CONSUMERS FROM A LOCATION **IN PENNSYLVANIA**? IF YES, COMPLETE SECTION 18.

2. ☐ YES ☒ NO    IS THIS ESTABLISHMENT SELLING CIGARETTES **IN PENNSYLVANIA**? IF YES, COMPLETE SECTIONS 18 AND 19.

3. LIST EACH COUNTY **IN PENNSYLVANIA** WHERE THIS ESTABLISHMENT IS CONDUCTING TAXABLE SALES ACTIVITY(IES).

COUNTY Capitol    COUNTY _____    COUNTY _____

COUNTY _____    COUNTY _____    COUNTY _____

ATTACH ADDITIONAL 8 1/2" x 11" SHEETS IF NECESSARY.

## SECTION 9 – ESTABLISHMENT EMPLOYMENT INFORMATION

### PART 1

1. ☒ YES ☐ NO    DOES THIS ESTABLISHMENT EMPLOY INDIVIDUALS WHO WORK **IN PENNSYLVANIA?** IF YES, INDICATE:
   a. DATE WAGES FIRST **PAID** .................................................. 1-1-01
   b. DATE WAGES RESUMED WHEN FOLLOWING A BREAK IN EMPLOYMENT ............... _____
   c. TOTAL NUMBER OF EMPLOYEES ......................................... 3
   d. NUMBER OF EMPLOYEES PRIMARILY WORKING IN NEW CONSTRUCTION ............... 0
   e. NUMBER OF EMPLOYEES PRIMARILY WORKING IN RENOVATIVE CONSTRUCTION ......... 0
   f. ESTIMATED GROSS WAGES PER QUARTER ..................... $ 3,000 .00

2. ☐ YES ☒ NO    DOES THIS ESTABLISHMENT EMPLOY PA RESIDENTS WHO WORK **OUTSIDE OF PENNSYLVANIA?**
   IF YES, INDICATE:
   a. DATE WAGES FIRST **PAID** .................................................. _____
   b. DATE WAGES RESUMED WHEN FOLLOWING A BREAK IN EMPLOYMENT ............... _____
   c. ESTIMATED GROSS WAGES PER QUARTER. ..................... $ _____ .00

3. ☐ YES ☐ NO    DOES THIS ESTABLISHMENT PAY REMUNERATION FOR SERVICES TO PERSONS YOU DO NOT CONSIDER EMPLOYEES?
   IF YES, EXPLAIN THE SERVICES PERFORMED _____

### PART 2

1. ☐ YES ☒ NO    IS THIS REGISTRATION A RESULT OF A TAXABLE DISTRIBUTION FROM A BENEFIT TRUST, DEFERRED PAYMENT OR RETIREMENT PLAN FOR PA RESIDENTS?
   IF YES, INDICATE:
   a. DATE BENEFITS FIRST **PAID** .................................................. _____
   b. ESTIMATED BENEFITS PAID PER QUARTER ..................... $ _____ .00

## SECTION 10 – BULK SALE/TRANSFER INFORMATION

IF ASSETS WERE ACQUIRED IN BULK FROM MORE THAN ONE ENTERPRISE, PHOTOCOPY THIS SECTION AND PROVIDE THE FOLLOWING INFORMATION ABOUT EACH SELLER/TRANSFEROR.

1. ☐ YES ☒ NO    DID THE ENTERPRISE ACQUIRE 51% OR MORE OF **ANY CLASS** OF THE **PA ASSETS** OF ANOTHER ENTERPRISE?
   SEE THE CLASS OF ASSETS LISTED BELOW.

2. ☐ YES ☒ NO    DID THE ENTERPRISE ACQUIRE 51% OR MORE OF THE **TOTAL ASSETS** OF ANOTHER ENTERPRISE?

IF THE ANSWER TO EITHER QUESTION IS YES, PROVIDE THE FOLLOWING INFORMATION ABOUT THE **SELLER/TRANSFEROR.**

| 3. SELLER/TRANSFEROR NAME   N/A | 4. FEDERAL EIN   N/A |
|---|---|

| 5. SELLER/TRANSFEROR STREET ADDRESS   N/A | CITY/TOWN   N/A | STATE   N/A | ZIP CODE + 4   N/A |
|---|---|---|---|

| 6. DATE ASSETS ACQUIRED | 7. ASSETS ACQUIRED: | | |
|---|---|---|---|
| N/A | ☐ ACCOUNTS RECEIVABLE | ☐ FIXTURES | ☐ MACHINERY |
| | ☐ CONTRACTS | ☐ FURNITURE | ☐ NAME AND/OR GOODWILL |
| | ☐ CUSTOMERS/CLIENTS | ☐ INVENTORY | ☐ REAL ESTATE |
| | ☐ EQUIPMENT | ☐ LEASES | ☐ OTHER N/A |

**IMPORTANT:** IF, IN ADDITION TO ACQUIRING ASSETS IN BULK, THE ENTERPRISE ALSO ACQUIRED ALL OR PART OF A PREDECESSOR'S BUSINESS, **SECTION 14** MUST BE COMPLETED.

6

PA-100 2-98

| ENTERPRISE NAME | Superior Flooring, Inc. | DEPARTMENT USE ONLY |
|---|---|---|

## SECTION 11 - CORPORATION INFORMATION

| 1. DATE OF INCORPORATION | 2. STATE OF INCORPORATION | 3. CERTIFICATE OF AUTHORITYDATE (NON-PA CORP.) | 4. COUNTRYOF INCORPORATION |
|---|---|---|---|
| 1-1-01 | PA | N/A | USA |

5. ☐ YES    ☒ NO    IS THIS CORPORATION'S STOCK PUBLICLY TRADED?

6. CHECK THE APPROPRIATE BOX(ES) TO DESCRIBE THIS CORPORATION:

CORPORATION: ☐ STOCK    ☒ PROFESSIONAL    BANK: ☐ STATE    MUTUALTHRIFT: ☐ STATE    INSURANCE ☐ PA

☒ NON-STOCK    ☐ COOPERATIVE    ☐ FEDERAL    ☐ FEDERAL    COMPANY: ☐ NON-PA

☐ MANAGEMENT    ☐ STATUTORY CLOSE

6. S-CORPORATION: ☐ FEDERAL    ☒ PENNSYLVANIA    (REV-1640 MUSTBE FILED TO ELECT PENNSYLVANIA S STATUS.)

## SECTION 12 - REPORTING & PAYMENT METHODS

1. ☒ YES    ☐ NO    DOES THIS ENTERPRISE MEET THE DEPARTMENT OF REVENUE'S REQUIREMENTS FOR ELECTRONIC FUNDS TRANSFERS (EFT) FILING? THE REQUIREMENTOF PAYMENTVIAEFT APPLIES TO PAYMENTS OF $20,000 OR MORE.

2. ☒ YES    ☐ NO    DOES THIS ENTERPRISE WANT TO PARTICIPATE IN THE DEPARTMENT OF REVENUE'S EFT PROGRAM EVEN THOUGH ITDOES NOT MEET THE $20,000 PAYMENTTHRESHOLD?

3. ☒ YES    ☐ NO    IS THIS ENTERPRISE INTERESTED IN RECEIVING INFORMATION ABOUT THE DEPARTMENT OF REVENUE'S ELECTRONIC DATA INTERCHANGE (EDI) PROGRAM?

4. ☐ YES    ☒ NO    DOES THIS ENTERPRISE MEETTHE DEPARTMENT OF LABOR & INDUSTRY'S REQUIREMENT FOR REPORTING WAGE INFORMATION ON MAGNETIC MEDIA? THE REQUIREMENT OF REPORTING VIA MAGNETIC MEDIAAPPLIES TO 250 OR MORE WAGE ENTRIES PER QUARTERLY REPORT.

5. ☐ YES    ☒ NO    IS THIS ENTERPRISE INTERESTED IN RECEIVING INFORMATION ABOUT THE DEPARTMENT OF LABOR & INDUSTRY'S MAGNETIC MEDIA REPORTING METHODS? THIS INCLUDES A PERSONAL COMPUTER PROGRAM TO ASSIST IN PAYROLL PREPARATION, TAX WITHHOLDING AND UC REPORTING AND FILING PREPARATION.

6. ☐ YES    ☒ NO    IS THIS ENTERPRISE INTERESTED IN RECEIVING INFORMATION ABOUT THE DEPARTMENT OF LABOR & INDUSTRY'S OPTION TO ELECT TO FINANCE UC COSTS UNDER THE REIMBURSEMENTMETHOD IN LIEU OF THE CONTRIBUTORY METHOD?

## SECTION 13 - GOVERNMENT FORM OF ORGANIZATION

1. IS THE ENTERPRISE A:

☐ GOVERNMENTBODY    ☐ GOVERNMENT OWNED ENTERPRISE    ☐ GOVERNMENT & PRIVATE SECTOR OWNED ENTERPRISE

2. IS THE GOVERNMENT:

☒ DOMESTIC/USA    ☐ FOREIGN/NON USA    ☐ MULTI-NATIONAL

3. IF DOMESTIC, IS THE GOVERNMENT:

☐ FEDERAL    LOCAL: ☒ COUNTY    ☐ BOROUGH

☐ STATE GOVERNOR'S JURISDICTION    ☐ CITY    ☐ SCHOOLDISTRICT

☐ STATE NON-GOVERNOR'S JURISDICTION    ☐ TOWN    ☐ OTHER _____

☐ TOWNSHIP

7

PA-100 2-98

| ENTERPRISE NAME | DEPARTMENT USE ONLY |
|---|---|
| Superior Flooring, Inc. | |

## SECTION 14 – PREDECESSOR/SUCCESSOR INFORMATION

COMPLETE THIS SECTION IF THE REGISTERING ENTERPRISE IS WHOLLY OR PARTIALLY SUCCEEDING A PREDECESSOR.
FOR ASSISTANCE, CONTACT THE NEAREST LABOR AND INDUSTRY FIELD ACCOUNTING SERVICE OFFICE.

IF THE ENTERPRISE HAS MORE THAN ONE PREDECESSOR, PHOTOCOPY THIS PAGE TO PROVIDE THE FOLLOWING INFORMATION ABOUT EACH.

| 1. PREDECESSOR LEGAL NAME | 2. PREDECESSOR PAUC ACCOUNT NUMBER |
|---|---|
| 3. PREDECESSOR TRADE NAME | 4. PREDECESSOR FEDERAL EIN |

| 5. PREDECESSOR STREET ADDRESS | CITY/TOWN | STATE | ZIP CODE + 4 |
|---|---|---|---|

6. SPECIFY HOW THE BUSINESS OPERATION WAS ACQUIRED: ☐ ACQUISITION OF EXISTING OPERATION ☐ CHANGE IN LEGAL STRUCTURE
☐ CONSOLIDATION ☐ GIFT ☐ MERGER ☐ IRC SEC. 338 ELECTION ☐ OTHER (SPECIFY) _____

7. ☐ ACQUISITION DATE _____

8. PERCENTAGE OF THE PREDECESSOR'S TOTAL BUSINESS OPERATION (PA AND NON-PA) ACQUIRED _____ %

9. PERCENTAGE OF THE PREDECESSOR'S **PA** BUSINESS OPERATION ACQUIRED _____ %
IF LESS THAN 100%, PROVIDE THE NAME(S) AND ADDRESS(ES) OF THE ESTABLISHMENT(S) THAT CONDUCTED OPERATIONS IN PA OR EMPLOYED PA RESIDENTS.
ATTACH ADDITIONAL 8 1/2 X 11 SHEETS IF NECESSARY.

NAME OF ESTABLISHMENT(S)                    ADDRESS(ES)

10. WHAT WAS THE PREDECESSOR'S BUSINESS ACTIVITY IN THE **PA** BUSINESS OPERATION THAT WAS ACQUIRED?

11. ASSETS ACQUIRED:  ☐ ACCOUNTS RECEIVABLE  ☐ FIXTURES  ☐ MACHINERY
    ☐ CONTRACTS  ☐ FURNITURE  ☐ NAME AND/OR GOODWILL
    ☐ CUSTOMERS/CLIENTS  ☐ INVENTORY  ☐ REAL ESTATE
    ☐ EQUIPMENT  ☐ LEASES  ☐ OTHER) _____

12. ☐ YES ☐ NO    HAS THE PREDECESSOR CEASED PAYING WAGES IN PA? IF YES, ENTER THE DATE PA WAGES CEASED,
    IF KNOWN. _____

13. ☐ YES ☐ NO    HAS THE PREDECESSOR CEASED OPERATIONS IN PA? IF YES, ENTER THE DATE PA OPERATIONS CEASED,
    IF KNOWN. _____
    IF NO, DESCRIBE THE PREDECESSOR'S PRESENT PA BUSINESS ACTIVITY, IF KNOWN. _____

14. AT THE TIME OF TRANSFER FROM THE PREDECESSOR ENTERPRISE TO THE REGISTERING ENTERPRISE:

a. ☐ YES ☐ NO    WERE ANY OF THE OWNERS, SHAREHOLDERS (5% OR GREATER), PARTNERS, OFFICERS OR DIRECTORS OF THE PREDECESSOR
    OR OF ANY AFFILIATE, SUBSIDIARY OR PARENT CORPORATION OF THE PREDECESSOR ALSO OWNERS, SHAREHOLDERS (5% OR
    GREATER), PARTNERS, OFFICERS OR DIRECTORS OF THE REGISTERING ENTERPRISE OR OF ANY AFFILIATE, SUBSIDIARY OR
    PARENT CORPORATION OF THE REGISTERING ENTERPRISE?

b. ☐ YES ☐ NO    WAS THE PREDECESSOR, OR ANY AFFILIATE, SUBSIDIARY OR PARENT CORPORATION OF THE PREDECESSOR, AN OWNER,
    SHAREHOLDER (5% OR GREATER) OR PARTNER IN THE REGISTERING ENTERPRISE?

c. ☐ YES ☐ NO    WAS THE REGISTERING ENTERPRISE, OR ANY AFFILIATE, SUBSIDIARY OR PARENT CORPORATION OF THE REGISTERING
    ENTERPRISE, AN OWNER, SHAREHOLDER (5% OR GREATER) OR PARTNER IN THE PREDECESSOR?

IF THE ANSWER TO ANY OF THE QUESTIONS IN 14 IS YES, PROVIDE THE FOLLOWING INFORMATION. ATTACH ADDITIONAL 8 1/2 X 11 SHEETS IF NECESSARY.

• IDENTIFY THOSE PERSONS AND ENTITIES BY THEIR FULL NAME;

• DESCRIBE THEIR RELATIONSHIP TO THE PREDECESSOR AND ANY AFFILIATE, SUBSIDIARY AND PARENT CORPORATION OF THE PREDECESSOR; AND

• DESCRIBE THEIR RELATIONSHIP TO THE REGISTERING ENTERPRISE AND ANY AFFILIATE, SUBSIDIARY AND PARENT CORPORATION OF THE REGISTERING ENTERPRISE.

THE REGISTERING ENTERPRISE MAY APPLY FOR A TRANSFER IN WHOLE OR IN PART OF THE PREDECESSOR'S UNEMPLOYMENT COMPENSATION (UC)
EXPERIENCE RECORD AND RESERVE ACCOUNT BALANCE, IF THE REGISTERING ENTERPRISE IS CONTINUING ESSENTIALLY THE SAME BUSINESS
ACTIVITY AS THE PREDECESSOR AND BOTH PROVIDED PA COVERED EMPLOYMENT. COMPLETE SECTION 15 AND, IF APPLICABLE, SECTION 16.

NOTE: A REGISTERING ENTERPRISE MAY APPLY THE UC TAXABLE WAGES PAID BY A PREDECESSOR TOWARD THE REGISTERING ENTERPRISE'S UC TAXABLE WAGE BASE FOR THE CALENDAR YEAR OF
    ACQUISITION WITHOUT TRANSFERRING THE PREDECESSOR'S EXPERIENCE RECORD AND RESERVE ACCOUNT BALANCE.

PA-100 2-98

| ENTERPRISE NAME | DEPARTMENT USE ONLY |
|---|---|
| Superior Flooring, Inc. | |

## SECTION 15 – APPLICATION FOR PA UC EXPERIENCE RECORD AND RESERVE ACCOUNT BALANCE OF PREDECESSOR

A REGISTERING ENTERPRISE MAY APPLY THE UNEMPLOYMENT COMPENSATION (UC) TAXABLE WAGES PAID BY A PREDECESSOR TOWARD THE REGISTERING ENTERPRISE'S UC TAXABLE WAGE BASE FOR THE CALENDAR YEAR OF ACQUISITION WITHOUT TRANSFERRING THE PREDECESSOR'S EXPERIENCE RECORD AND RESERVE ACCOUNT BALANCE.

REFER TO THE INSTRUCTIONS TO DETERMINE IF IT IS ADVANTAGEOUS TO APPLY FOR A PREDECESSOR'S UC EXPERIENCE RECORD AND RESERVE ACCOUNT BALANCE.

**IMPORTANT:** THIS APPLICATION CANNOT BE CONSIDERED UNLESS IT IS SIGNED BY AN AUTHORIZED SIGNATORY OF BOTH THE PREDECESSOR AND THE REGISTERING ENTERPRISE. THE TRANSFER IN WHOLE OR IN PART OF THE EXPERIENCE RECORD AND RESERVE ACCOUNT BALANCE IS BINDING AND IRREVOCABLE ONCE IT HAS BEEN APPROVED BY THE DEPARTMENT OF LABOR AND INDUSTRY.

APPLICATION IS HEREBY MADE BY THE PREDECESSOR AND THE REGISTERING ENTERPRISE FOR A TRANSFER TO THE REGISTERING ENTERPRISE OF THE PENNSYLVANIA UNEMPLOYMENT COMPENSATION EXPERIENCE RECORD AND RESERVE ACCOUNT BALANCE OF THE PREDECESSOR WITH RESPECT TO THE TRANSFER.

WE HEREBY CERTIFY THAT THE TRANSFER REFERENCED IN SECTION 14 HAS OCCURRED AS DESCRIBED THEREIN AND THAT THE REGISTERING ENTERPRISE IS CONTINUING ESSENTIALLY THE SAME BUSINESS ACTIVITY AS THE PREDECESSOR.

COMPLETE THIS SECTION <u>ONLY</u> IF YOU WANT TO APPLY FOR THE PREDECESSOR'S EXPERIENCE RECORD AND RESERVE ACCOUNT BALANCE.

| 1. PREDECESSOR NAME | | DATE |
|---|---|---|
| AUTHORIZED SIGNATURE | TYPE OR PRINT NAME | TITLE |

| 2. REGISTERING ENTERPRISE NAME | | DATE |
|---|---|---|
| AUTHORIZED SIGNATURE | TYPE OR PRINT NAME | TITLE |

## SECTION 16 – UNEMPLOYMENT COMPENSATION PARTIAL TRANSFER INFORMATION

COMPLETE THIS SECTION IF THE REGISTERING ENTERPRISE ACQUIRED ONLY PART OF THE PREDECESSOR'S PENNSYLVANIA (PA) BUSINESS OPERATION AND IS MAKING APPLICATION FOR THE TRANSFER OF A PORTION OF THE PREDECESSOR'S EXPERIENCE RECORD AND RESERVE ACCOUNT BALANCE.

**COMPLETE REPLACEMENT UC-2A FOR PARTIAL TRANSFER (FORM UC-252).** THE PREDECESSOR'S PA PAYROLL RECORDS FOR THE TWO YEARS PRIOR TO THE QUARTER OF THE TRANSFER AND/OR ACQUISITION MUST REMAIN AVAILABLE TO THE REGISTERING ENTERPRISE TO ENABLE THE REGISTERING ENTERPRISE TO PROVIDE REQUIRED INFORMATION REGARDING SEPARATED AND/OR TRANSFERRED EMPLOYEES.

**UNEMPLOYMENT COMPENSATION (UC) TAXABLE WAGES** ARE THOSE WAGES THAT DO NOT EXCEED THE UC TAXABLE WAGE BASE APPLICABLE TO A GIVEN CALENDAR YEAR.

1. NUMBER OF EMPLOYEES WHO WORKED IN THE PART OF THE PREDECESSOR'S PA BUSINESS OPERATION THAT WAS TRANSFERRED TO OR ACQUIRED BY THE REGISTERING ENTERPRISE:

2. DATE WAGES FIRST PAID BY PREDECESSOR OR PRE-PREDECESSOR(S) IN THE PART OF THE PA BUSINESS OPERATION TRANSFERRED (ACQUIRED) FOR WHICH CONTRIBUTIONS WERE PAID UNDER THE PROVISIONS OF THE PA UC LAW.

   DATE:

3. CHECKMARK THE CALENDAR QUARTERS IN THE YEAR OF TRANSFER AND IN THE PRECEDING FIVE CALENDAR YEARS IN WHICH PA UC CONTRIBUTIONS WERE **PAID IN THE PART OF THE PA BUSINESS OPERATION THAT WAS TRANSFERRED.** ENTER A ZERO IN EACH QUARTER WHEN NO CONTRIBUTION WAS DUE AND PAYABLE IN THE PART TRANSFERRED.

| YEAR____ | | | | YEAR____ | | | | YEAR____ | | | | YEAR____ | | | | YEAR____ | | | | YEAR____ OF TRANSFER | | | |
|---|---|---|---|---|---|---|---|---|---|---|---|---|---|---|---|---|---|---|---|---|---|---|---|
| QUARTERS | | | | QUARTERS | | | | QUARTERS | | | | QUARTERS | | | | QUARTERS | | | | QUARTERS | | | |
| 1 | 2 | 3 | 4 | 1 | 2 | 3 | 4 | 1 | 2 | 3 | 4 | 1 | 2 | 3 | 4 | 1 | 2 | 3 | 4 | 1 | 2 | 3 | 4 |
| | | | | | | | | | | | | | | | | | | | | | | | |

4. CHECKMARK THE CALENDAR QUARTERS IN THE YEAR OF TRANSFER AND IN THE PRECEDING FIVE CALENDAR YEARS IN WHICH PA UC CONTRIBUTIONS WERE PAID IN THE **PART OF THE PA BUSINESS OPERATION THAT WAS <u>NOT</u> TRANSFERRED.** ENTER A ZERO IN EACH QUARTER WHEN NO CONTRIBUTION WAS DUE AND PAYABLE IN THE PART RETAINED.

| YEAR____ | | | | YEAR____ | | | | YEAR____ | | | | YEAR____ | | | | YEAR____ | | | | YEAR____ OF TRANSFER | | | |
|---|---|---|---|---|---|---|---|---|---|---|---|---|---|---|---|---|---|---|---|---|---|---|---|
| QUARTERS | | | | QUARTERS | | | | QUARTERS | | | | QUARTERS | | | | QUARTERS | | | | QUARTERS | | | |
| 1 | 2 | 3 | 4 | 1 | 2 | 3 | 4 | 1 | 2 | 3 | 4 | 1 | 2 | 3 | 4 | 1 | 2 | 3 | 4 | 1 | 2 | 3 | 4 |
| | | | | | | | | | | | | | | | | | | | | | | | |

5a. PREDECESSOR'S PA UC **TAXABLE PAYROLL IN THE PART OF THE PA BUSINESS OPERATION TRANSFERRED FOR THE PERIOD OF THREE CALENDAR YEARS PRIOR TO THE YEAR OF TRANSFER (ACQUISITION).**

5b. IF THE **PART OF THE PA BUSINESS OPERATION TRANSFERRED** WAS NOT IN EXISTENCE FOR THREE CALENDAR YEARS PRIOR TO THE YEAR OF THE TRANSFER, ENTER THE PA **TAXABLE PAYROLL FOR THE PERIOD OF ITS EXISTENCE TO DATE OF TRANSFER** .

OR

$____

$____

6. PREDECESSOR'S ENTIRE PA UC **TAXABLE** PAYROLL FOR SAME PERIOD INDICATED IN ITEMS 5a OR 5b.

7. PREDECESSOR'S ENTIRE PA UC **TAXABLE** PAYROLL FOR THE PERIOD FROM THE BEGINNING OF THE QUARTER OF TRANSFER TO THE DATE OF TRANSFER

$____

$____

PA-100 2-98

| ENTERPRISE NAME | Superior Flooring, Inc. | DEPARTMENT USE ONLY |
|---|---|---|

## SECTION 17 – MULTIPLE ESTABLISHMENT INFORMATION

### PART 1 ESTABLISHMENT INFORMATION

COMPLETE THIS SECTION FOR EACH ADDITIONAL ESTABLISHMENT CONDUCTING BUSINESS IN PA OR EMPLOYING PA RESIDENTS. PHOTOCOPY THIS SECTION AS NECESSARY.

| 1. ESTABLISHMENT NAME (doing business as) | | 2. DATE OF FIRST OPERATIONS | 3. TELEPHONE NUMBER ( ) |
|---|---|---|---|
| 4. STREET ADDRESS | CITY/TOWN | COUNTY | STATE ZIP CODE + 4 |
| 5. SCHOOL DISTRICT | | 6. MUNICIPALITY | |

### PART 2 ESTABLISHMENT BUSINESS ACTIVITY INFORMATION

*REFER TO THE INSTRUCTIONS TO COMPLETE THIS SECTION.*

1. ENTER THE PERCENTAGE THAT EACH PA BUSINESS ACTIVITY REPRESENTS OF THE TOTAL RECEIPTS OR REVENUES AT THIS ESTABLISHMENT. LIST ALL PRODUCTS OR SERVICES ASSOCIATED WITH EACH BUSINESS ACTIVITY. ENTER THE PERCENTAGE THAT THE PRODUCTS OR SERVICES REPRESENT OF THE TOTAL RECEIPTS OR REVENUES AT THIS ESTABLISHMENT.

| PA BUSINESS ACTIVITY | % | PRODUCTS OR SERVICES | % | ADDITIONAL PRODUCTS OR SERVICES | % |
|---|---|---|---|---|---|
| Construction | | | | | |
| Manufacturing | | | | | |
| Retail Trade | | | | | |
| Wholesale Trade | | | | | |
| Finance | | | | | |
| Insurance | | | | | |
| Real Estate | | | | | |
| Transportation | | | | | |
| Warehousing | | | | | |
| Communications | | | | | |
| Agriculture, Forestry, Fishing | | | | | |
| Mining, Quarrying Oil/Gas Extraction | | | | | |
| Utility or Sanitary Service | | | | | |
| Services (Personal or Business) | | | | | |
| Domestic | | | | | |
| TOTAL | 100% | | | | |

2. ENTER THE PERCENTAGE THAT THIS ESTABLISHMENT'S RECEIPTS OR REVENUES REPRESENT OF THE TOTAL PA RECEIPTS OR REVENUES OF THE ENTERPRISE.

_____%

3. ESTABLISHMENTS ENGAGED IN CONSTRUCTION MUST ENTER THE PERCENTAGE OF CONSTRUCTION ACTIVITY THAT IS NEW AND/OR RENOVATIVE.

_____% NEW  _____% RENOVATIVE

4.. ☐ YES  ☐ NO  IS THIS ESTABLISHMENT SOLELY ENGAGED IN THE PERFORMANCE OF SUPPORT ACTIVITIES FOR OTHER ESTABLISHMENTS OF THE SAME ENTERPRISE? IF YES, LIST THE NAME(S) OF THE SUPPORTED ESTABLISHMENT(S) AND CHECK THE APPROPRIATE BOX TO DESCRIBE THE SUPPORT ACTIVITY.

_____

_____

☐ ADMINISTRATION  ☐ RESEARCH/DEVELOPMENT  ☐ STORAGE/WAREHOUSE  ☐ OTHER (SPECIFY) _____

PA-100 2-98

| ENTERPRISE NAME | Superior Flooring, Inc. |
|---|---|

DEPARTMENT USE ONLY

## PART 3  ESTABLISHMENT SALES INFORMATION

1. ☐ YES  ☐ NO  IS THIS ESTABLISHMENT SELLING TAXABLE PRODUCTS OR OFFERING TAXABLE SERVICES TO CONSUMERS FROM A LOCATION **IN PENNSYLVANIA?** IF YES, COMPLETE SECTION 18.

2. ☐ YES  ☐ NO  IS THIS ESTABLISHMENT SELLING CIGARETTES **IN PENNSYLVANIA?** IF YES, COMPLETE SECTIONS 18 AND 19.

3. LIST EACH COUNTY **IN PENNSYLVANIA** WHERE THIS ESTABLISHMENT IS CONDUCTING TAXABLE SALES ACTIVITY(IES).

COUNTY _____  COUNTY _____  COUNTY _____

COUNTY _____  COUNTY _____  COUNTY _____

ATTACH ADDITIONAL 8 1/2" x 11" SHEETS IF NECESSARY.

## PART 4a  ESTABLISHMENT EMPLOYMENT INFORMATION

1. ☐ YES  ☐ NO  DOES THIS ESTABLISHMENT EMPLOY INDIVIDUALS WHO WORK **IN PENNSYLVANIA?** IF YES, INDICATE:
   a. DATE WAGES FIRST **PAID** ................................................. _____
   b. DATE WAGES RESUMED WHEN FOLLOWING A BREAK IN EMPLOYMENT .............. _____
   c. TOTAL NUMBER OF EMPLOYEES ................................................ _____
   d. NUMBER OF EMPLOYEES PRIMARILY WORKING IN NEW CONSTRUCTION ............ _____
   e. NUMBER OF EMPLOYEES PRIMARILY WORKING IN RENOVATIVE CONSTRUCTION ..... _____
   f. ESTIMATED GROSS WAGES PER QUARTER ................................. $ _____ .00

2. ☐ YES  ☐ NO  DOES THIS ESTABLISHMENT EMPLOY PA RESIDENTS WHO WORK **OUTSIDE OF PENNSYLVANIA?** IF YES, INDICATE:
   a. DATE WAGES FIRST **PAID** ................................................. _____
   b. DATE WAGES RESUMED WHEN FOLLOWING A BREAK IN EMPLOYMENT .............. _____
   c. ESTIMATED GROSS WAGES PER QUARTER ................................. $ _____ .00

3. ☐ YES  ☐ NO  DOES THIS ESTABLISHMENT PAY REMUNERATION FOR SERVICES TO PERSONS YOU DO NOT CONSIDER EMPLOYEES?
   IF YES, EXPLAIN THE SERVICES PERFORMED _____

## PART 4b

1. ☐ YES  ☐ NO  IS THIS REGISTRATION A RESULT OF A TAXABLE DISTRIBUTION FROM A BENEFIT TRUST, DEFERRED PAYMENT OR RETIREMENT PLAN FOR PA RESIDENTS? IF YES, INDICATE:
   a. DATE BENEFITS FIRST **PAID** ............................................. _____
   b. ESTIMATED BENEFITS PAID PER QUARTER ................................. $ _____ .00

## SECTION 6A – ADDITIONAL OWNERS, PARTNERS, SHAREHOLDERS, OFFICERS, RESPONSIBLE PARTY INFORMATION

PROVIDE THE FOLLOWING FOR **ALL** INDIVIDUAL AND/OR ENTERPRISE OWNERS, PARTNERS, SHAREHOLDERS, OFFICERS AND RESPONSIBLE PARTIES. IF STOCK IS PUBLICLY TRADED, PROVIDE THE FOLLOWING FOR ANY SHAREHOLDER WITH AN EQUITY POSITION OF 5% OR MORE. *PHOTOCOPY IF ADDITIONAL SPACE IS NEEDED.*

| 1. NAME | | 2. SOCIAL SECURITY NUMBER | 3. DATE OF BIRTH * | 4. FEDERAL EIN |
|---|---|---|---|---|
| 5. ☐ OWNER ☐ OFFICER ☐ PARTNER ☐ SHAREHOLDER ☐ RESPONSIBLE PARTY | 6. TITLE | 7. EFFECTIVE DATE OF TITLE | 8. PERCENTAGE OF OWNERSHIP % | 9. EFFECTIVE DATE OF OWNERSHIP |
| 10. HOME ADDRESS (street) | CITY/TOWN | COUNTY | STATE | ZIP CODE + 4 |

11. PERSON RESPONSIBLE TO REMIT:  ☐ SALES TAX  ☐ EMPLOYER WITHHOLDING  ☐ MOTOR FUEL TAXES

SIGNATURE _____

| 1. NAME | | 2. SOCIAL SECURITY NUMBER | 3. DATE OF BIRTH * | 4. FEDERAL EIN |
|---|---|---|---|---|
| 5. ☐ OWNER ☐ OFFICER ☐ PARTNER ☐ SHAREHOLDER ☐ RESPONSIBLE PARTY | 6. TITLE | 7. EFFECTIVE DATE OF TITLE | 8. PERCENTAGE OF OWNERSHIP % | 9. EFFECTIVE DATE OF OWNERSHIP |
| 10. HOME ADDRESS (street) | CITY/TOWN | COUNTY | STATE | ZIP CODE + 4 |

11. PERSON RESPONSIBLE TO REMIT:  ☐ SALES TAX  ☐ EMPLOYER WITHHOLDING  ☐ MOTOR FUEL TAXES

SIGNATURE _____

* DATE OF BIRTH REQUIRED ONLY IF APPLYING FOR A CIGARETTE WHOLESALE DEALER'S LICENSE, A SMALL GAMES OF CHANCE DISTRIBUTOR LICENSE OR A SMALL GAMES OF CHANCE MANUFACTURER CERTIFICATE.

11

PA-100 2-98

**ENTERPRISE NAME** Superior Flooring, Inc.

DEPARTMENT USE ONLY

**SECTION 18 –** SALES USE AND HOTEL OCCUPANCY TAX LICENSE, PUBLIC TRANSPORTATION ASSISTANCE TAX LICENSE, VEHICLE RENTAL TAX, TRANSIENT VENDOR CERTIFICATE OR PROMOTER LICENSE

**PART 1** SALES USE AND HOTEL OCCUPANCY TAX, PUBLIC TRANSPORTATION ASSISTANCE TAX OR VEHICLE RENTAL TAX

ENTERPRISES APPLYING FOR A SALES, USE AND HOTEL OCCUPANCY TAX LICENSE, PUBLIC TRANSPORTATION ASSISTANCE TAX LICENSE AND/OR VEHICLE RENTAL TAX, COMPLETE PART 1.

**IF THE ENTERPRISE IS:**

- SELLING TAXABLE PRODUCTS OR SERVICES TO CONSUMERS **IN PENNSYLVANIA**, ENTER DATE OF FIRST TAXABLE SALE ___1-1-01___

- PURCHASING TAXABLE PRODUCTS OR SERVICES FOR ITS OWN USE **IN PENNSYLVANIA** AND INCURRING NO SALES TAX, ENTER DATE OF FIRST PURCHASE ___1-1-01___

- SELLING NEW TIRES TO CONSUMERS **IN PENNSYLVANIA**, ENTER DATE OF FIRST SALE _____

- LEASING OR RENTING MOTOR VEHICLES, ENTER DATE OF FIRST LEASE OR RENTAL _____

- RENTING FIVE OR MORE MOTOR VEHICLES, ENTER DATE OF FIRST RENTAL _____

- CONDUCTING RETAIL SALES IN PENNSYLVANIA AND NOT MAINTAINING A PERMANENT LOCATION IN PA, ENTER DATE OF FIRST TAXABLE SALE _____ (COMPLETE PART 2)

- ACTIVELY PROMOTING SHOWS IN PENNSYLVANIA WHERE TAXABLE PRODUCTS WILL BE OFFERED FOR RETAIL SALE, ENTER DATE OF FIRST SHOW _____ . (COMPLETE PART 3)

SALES TAX COLLECTED MUST BE SEGREGATED FROM OTHER FUNDS AND MUST REMAIN IN THE COMMONWEALTH OF PENNSYLVANIA UNTIL REMITTED TO THE DEPARTMENT OF REVENUE. (COMPLETE PART 4)

**PART 2** TRANSIENT VENDOR CERTIFICATE

IF THE ENTERPRISE PARTICIPATES IN ANY SHOWS OTHER THAN THOSE LISTED, PROVIDE THE NAME(S) OF THE SHOW(S) AND INFORMATION ABOUT THE SHOW(S) TO THE DEPARTMENT OF REVENUE AT LEAST 10 DAYS PRIOR TO THE SHOW.

IF THE ENTERPRISE IS NOT ASSOCIATED WITH A PA LICENSED PROMOTER FOR EACH SHOW, A $500 SECURITY DEPOSIT MUST BE SUBMITTED WITH THIS FORM.

PROVIDE THE FOLLOWING INFORMATION FOR **EACH SHOW:**

| 1. PROMOTER NUMBER . | 2. SHOW NAME | 3. COUNTY | |
|---|---|---|---|
| N/A | | | |
| 4. SHOW ADDRESS (STREET, CITY, STATE, ZIP) | | 5. START DATE | 6. END DATE |
| 1. PROMOTER NUMBER | 2. SHOW NAME | 3. COUNTY | |
| 4. SHOW ADDRESS (STREET, CITY, STATE, ZIP) | | 5. START DATE | 6. END DATE |

**ATTACH ADDITIONAL 8 1/2 X 11 SHEETS IF NECESSARY.**

**PART 3** PROMOTER LICENSE

PROVIDE THE FOLLOWING INFORMATION FOR **EACH SHOW:**

| 1. SHOW NAME N/A | 2. TYPE OF SHOW | 3. START DATE | 4. END DATE |
|---|---|---|---|
| 5. SHOW ADDRESS (STREET, CITY, STATE, ZIP) | 6. COUNTY | 7. NBR OF VENDORS | |
| 1. SHOW NAME | 2. TYPE OF SHOW | 3. START DATE | 4. END DATE |
| 5. SHOW ADDRESS (STREET, CITY, STATE, ZIP) | 6. COUNTY | 7. NBR OF VENDORS | |

**ATTACH ADDITIONAL 8 1/2 X 11 SHEETS IF NECESSARY.**

**PART 4** LOCATION OF SALES TAX COLLECTED

PROVIDE THE FOLLOWING INFORMATION ABOUT THE PENNSYLVANIA FINANCIAL INSTITUTION OR OTHER LOCATION WHERE SALES TAX FUNDS WILL BE PLACED PENDING REMISSION TO THE DEPARTMENT OF REVENUE.

| 1. NAME OF FINANCIAL INSTITUTION | 2. ACCOUNT NAME | 3. ACCOUNT NUMBER | | |
|---|---|---|---|---|
| USA Bank | Superior Flooring, Inc. | 777888090 | | |

| 4. TYPE OF ACCOUNT: | ☐ SAVINGS | ☒ CHECKING | ☐ CD | ☐ ESCROW |
|---|---|---|---|---|

| 5. FINANCIAL INSTITUTION STREET ADDRESS | CITY/TOWN | COUNTY | STATE | ZIP CODE + 4 |
|---|---|---|---|---|
| 444 2nd St. | Anytown | Capitol | PA | 10000-1234 |
| 6. OTHER LOCATION N/A | CITY/TOWN | COUNTY | STATE | ZIP CODE + 4 |

12

PA-100 2-98

| ENTERPRISE NAME | Superior Flooring, Inc. | DEPARTMENT USE ONLY |
|---|---|---|

## SECTION 19 – CIGARETTE DEALER'S LICENSE

### PART 1   LICENSE TYPE

CHECK THE APPROPRIATE BOX(ES) TO INDICATE LICENSE TYPE REQUESTED. A SEPARATE LICENSE MUST BE OBTAINED FOR EACH ESTABLISHMENT THAT SELLS RETAIL, OVER-THE-COUNTER CIGARETTES. A SEPARATE DECAL MUST BE PURCHASED FOR EACH VENDING MACHINE LOCATION. A CHECK OR MONEY ORDER MUST BE SUBMITTED WITH THIS APPLICATION.

| LICENSE TYPE | NUMBER | FEE | AMOUNT REMITTED |
|---|---|---|---|
| ☐ RETAIL OVER-THE-COUNTER | _____ | @ $  25  EACH LOCATION | $ _____ |
| ☐ VENDING MACHINE (ATTACH A LISTING OF LOCATIONS) | _____ | @ $  25  EACH DECAL | $ _____ |
| ☐ WHOLESALER | | @ $  500 | $ _____ |
| ☐ CIGARETTE STAMPING AGENT AND WHOLESALER | | @ $  1,500 | $ _____ |
| | | TOTAL AMOUNT REMITTED | $ _____ |

### MAKE CHECKS PAYABLE TO PA DEPARTMENT OF REVENUE

### PART 2   CIGARETTE WHOLESALER

LIST CIGARETTE STORAGE LOCATION(S) (P.O. BOXES ARE NOT ACCEPTABLE).

1. STREET ADDRESS

| CITY/TOWN | COUNTY | STATE | ZIP CODE + 4 |
|---|---|---|---|
| | | | |

2. ☐ YES   ☐ NO   HAS ANY OWNER, PARTNER, OFFICER, DIRECTOR OR MAJOR STOCKHOLDER BEEN CONVICTED OF ANY VIOLATION OF THE PENNSYLVANIA CIGARETTE TAX ACT OR ANY MISDEMEANOR OR FELONY?

IF YES, LIST ALL CONVICTIONS WITHIN THE PREVIOUS 10 YEAR PERIOD. ATTACH ADDITIONAL 8 1/2 X 11 SHEETS IF NECESSARY

3. THE APPLICANT HAS COMPLIED WITH ARTICLE II-A OF THE CIGARETTE SALES AND LICENSING ACT. UNDER PENALTY OF PERJURY, OF ADHERENCE TO STATE PRESUMPTIVE MINIMUM PRICES OR APPROVAL TO SELL AT A DIFFERENT PRICE, IN ACCORDANCE WITH THE ACT:

☐ CIGARETTES WILL BE SOLD AT OR ABOVE THE PRESUMPTIVE MINIMUM PRICE.

☐ CIGARETTES WILL BE SOLD AT AN APPROVED MINIMUM PRICE.

### PART 3   CIGARETTE STAMPING AGENT

1. ☐ YES   ☐ NO   DOES THE ENTERPRISE PURCHASE OR SELL ANY CIGARETTES WHICH ARE NOT PA STAMPED?

IF YES, LIST STATES: _____  _____  _____  _____  _____

PA-100 2-98

| ENTERPRISE NAME Superior Flooring, Inc. | DEPARTMENT USE ONLY |
|---|---|

## SECTION 20 – SMALL GAMES OF CHANCE LICENSE/CERTIFICATE

### PART 1   DISTRIBUTOR AND/OR MANUFACTURER

TO BE COMPLETED BY ALL APPLICANTS (DISTRIBUTOR AND/OR MANUFACTURER)

APPLICANTS MUST SUBMIT A COPY OF THE CERTIFICATE OF INCORPORATION, ARTICLES OF INCORPORATION, CERTIFICATE OF AUTHORITY(NON-PA CORPORATIONS), BY-LAWS, CONSTITUTION OR FICTITIOUS NAME REGISTRATION.

APPLICANTS FOR A MANUFACTURER CERTIFICATE MUST SUBMIT A COPY OF THE COMPANYLOGO(S).

1.   CHECK APPROPRIATE BOX(ES) TO INDICATE TYPE OF LICENSE/CERTIFICATE REQUESTED

| LICENSE/CERTIFICATE TYPE | FEE | AMOUNT REMITTED |
|---|---|---|
| ☐ DISTRIBUTOR LICENSE | $ 1,000 | $_____ |
| ☐ MANUFACTURER REGISTRATION CERTIFICATE | $ 2,000 | $_____ |
| ☐ REPLACEMENTLICENSE | $ 100 | $_____ |
| ☐ REPLACEMENTCERTIFICATE | $ 100 | $_____ |
| NUMBER OF BACKGROUND INVESTIGATIONS FOR OWNERS/OFFICERS, ETC. _____ @ | $ 10 | $_____ |
| | TOTALAMOUNTREMITTED | $_____ |

### MAKE CHECKS PAYABLE TO PA DEPARTMENT OF REVENUE

IF THE DEPARTMENT DENIES AN APPLICATION, A$100 APPLICATION PROCESSING FEE SHALLBE RETAINED BYTHE DEPARTMENT. NO PART OF THE REGISTRATION OR LICENSE FEE SHALLBE SUBJECT TO PRORATION. NO INVESTIGATION FEE SHALLBE REFUNDED.

2.   MANUFACTURERS AND DISTRIBUTORS LIST ALL INDIVIDUALS RESPONSIBLE FOR TAKING ORDERS AND MAKING SALES OF SMALL GAMES OF CHANCE MERCHANDISE. IF AN INDIVIDUALRESIDES IN PENNSYLVANIA, INDICATE IF COMMISSION OR NONCOMMISSION.

| NAME | TITLE | ☐ SELLS FOR DISTRIBUTOR | ☐ COMMISSION | |
|---|---|---|---|---|
| | | ☐ SELLS FOR MANUFACTURER | ☐ NONCOMMISSION | |
| HOME ADDRESS (STREET) | CITY/TOWN | STATE | ZIP CODE + 4 | TELEPHONE NBR. ( ) |
| NAME | TITLE | ☐ SELLS FOR DISTRIBUTOR | ☐ COMMISSION | |
| | | ☐ SELLS FOR MANUFACTURER | ☐ NONCOMMISSION | |
| HOME ADDRESS (STREET) | CITY/TOWN | STATE | ZIP CODE + 4 | TELEPHONE NBR. ( ) |

#### ATTACH ADDITIONAL 8 1/2 X 11 SHEETS IF NECESSARY

MANUFACTURERS ONLY MUST SUBMIT A CATALOG OF THE SMALLGAMES CHECKED BELOW.  IF CATALOG IS UNAVAILABLE, PROVIDE NAME OF GAME(S) AND FORM NUMBER(S), NUMBER OF TICKETS PER DEAL, HIGHEST INDIVIDUAL PRIZE VALUE AND PERCENTAGE OF PAYOUT.

3.   CHECK THE APPROPRIATE BOX(ES) TO INDICATE THE TYPES OF SMALLGAMES DISTRIBUTED OR MANUFACTURED.

☐ DAILY DRAWINGS        ☐ PULL-TABS        ☐ PUNCHBOARDS        ☐ RAFFLES        ☐ DISPENSING MACHINES

### PART 2   DISTRIBUTOR

LISTALLSMALL GAMES OF CHANCE MANUFACTURERS WITH WHOM THE DISTRIBUTOR DOES BUSINESS.

| MANUFACTURER'S LEGAL NAME | MANUFACTURER'S CERTIFICATE NBR. M- | TELEPHONE NBR. ( ) | |
|---|---|---|---|
| STREETADDRESS | CITY/TOWN | STATE | ZIP CODE +4 |
| MANUFACTURER'S LEGAL NAME | MANUFACTURER'S CERTIFICATE NBR. M- | TELEPHONE NBR. ( ) | |
| STREETADDRESS | CITY/TOWN | STATE | ZIP CODE +4 |

#### ATTACH ADDITIONAL 8 1/2X 11 SHEETS IF NECESSARY

14

---

**PART 3**   SMALL GAMES OF CHANCE CERTIFICATION

**MUST BE COMPLETED BY ALL SMALL GAMES OF CHANCE APPLICANTS.**

I CERTIFY THAT THE FOLLOWING TAX STATEMENTS ARE TRUE AND CORRECT

- ALL PA STATE TAX REPORTS AND RETURNS HAVE BEEN FILED, AND

- ALL PA STATE TAXES HAVE BEEN PAID, OR

- ANY PA STATE TAXES OWNED ARE SUBJECT TO TIMELY ADMINISTRATIVE OR JUDICIAL APPEAL; OR ANY DELINQUENT PA TAXES ARE SUBJECT TO DULY APPROVED DEFERRED PAYMENT PLAN (COPY ENCLOSED).

---

I CERTIFY THAT NO OWNER, PARTNER, OFFICER, DIRECTOR, OR OTHER PERSON IN A SUPERVISORY OR MANAGEMENT POSITION OR EMPLOYEE ELIGIBLE TO MAKE SALES ON BEHALF OF THIS BUSINESS:

- HAS BEEN CONVICTED OF A FELONY IN A STATE OR FEDERAL COURT WITHIN THE PAST FIVE YEARS; OR

- HAS BEEN CONVICTED WITHIN TEN YEARS OF THE DATE OF APPLICATION IN A STATE OR FEDERAL COURT OF A VIOLATION OF THE BINGO LAW OR OF THE LOCAL OPTION SMALL GAMES OF CHANCE ACT OR A GAMBLING-RELATED OFFENSE UNDER TITLE 18 OF THE PENNSYLVANIA CONSOLIDATED STATUTES OR OTHER COMPARABLE STATE OR FEDERAL LAW; OR

- HAS NOT BEEN REJECTED IN ANY STATE FOR A DISTRIBUTOR LICENSE OR MANUFACTURER REGISTRATION CERTIFICATE, OR EQUIVALENT THERETO.

---

I DECLARE THAT I HAVE EXAMINED THIS APPLICATION, INCLUDING ALL ACCOMPANYING STATEMENTS, AND TO THE BEST OF MY KNOWLEDGE AND BELIEF IT IS TRUE, CORRECT AND COMPLETE.

| NOTARY | AUTHORIZATION | |
|---|---|---|
| SWORN AND SUBSCRIBED TO BEFORE ME THIS | | |
| DAY OF , 19 | | |
| | SIGNATURE OF AN OWNER, PARTNER, OFFICER OR DIRECTOR | SOCIAL SECURITY NUMBER |
| NOTARY PUBLIC | PRINT NAME | DATE |
| MY COMMISSION EXPIRES _____ | TITLE | |
| | (  ) TELEPHONE NUMBER | |
| NOTARY SEAL | | CORPORATE SEAL |

PA-100 2-98

| ENTERPRISE NAME  Superior Flooring, Inc. | DEPARTMENT USE ONLY |
|---|---|

## SECTION 21 – MOTOR CARRIER REGISTRATION & DECAL/MOTOR FUELS LICENSE & PERMIT

### PART 1   VEHICLE OPERATIONS

A DECAL IS REQUIRED IF AN ENTERPRISE IS OPERATING A QUALIFIED MOTOR VEHICLE, SEE PAGE 25, PART 1 - VEHICLE OPERATIONS.

CHECK THE APPROPRIATE BOX(ES) TO DESCRIBE THE ENTERPRISE OPERATIONS:

☐ COMMON CARRIER          ☐ CONTRACT CARRIER          ☐ FOR HIRE CARRIER          ☐ PRIVATE CARRIER

INDICATE THE FUEL TYPES FOR PENNSYLVANIA BASED QUALIFIED MOTOR VEHICLES:

☐ DIESEL          ☐ GASOLINE          ☐ ETHANOL/GASOHOL          ☐ LPGAS          ☐ CNG/LNG

### MOTOR CARRIER ROAD TAX/IFTA VEHICLE DECAL REQUESTS

COMPLETE THE FOLLOWING FOR EACH QUALIFIED MOTOR VEHICLE YOU INTEND TO OPERATE IN PENNSYLVANIA DURING THE ENSUING CALENDAR YEAR.

**NOTE: DECALS ARE $5.00 PER SET OF TWO.**

1.  **IFTA** DECALS (NUMBER OF VEHICLES THAT TRAVEL IN PA AND OUT OF STATE)   _____

2.  **NON IFTA** DECALS (NUMBER OF VEHICLES THAT TRAVEL IN PA EXCLUSIVELY)   _____

3.  TOTAL DECALS REQUESTED (ADD LINES 1 AND 2)   _____

4.  TOTAL AMOUNT DUE (MULTIPLY LINE 3 BY **$5**)   $_____

**REMITTANCE SUBMITTED:**

5.  AUTHORIZED ADJUSTMENT (ATTACH ORIGINAL CREDIT NOTICE)   $_____

6.  CHECK OR MONEY ORDER AMOUNT   $_____

### MAKE CHECKS PAYABLE TO PA DEPARTMENT OF REVENUE

CHECK THE APPROPRIATE BOX(ES) TO INDICATE THE JURISDICTION(S) WHERE:

**COLUMN A** – QUALIFIED MOTOR VEHICLES ARE OPERATED           **COLUMN C** – BULK STORAGE FOR GASOLINE IS MAINTAINED
**COLUMN B** – BULK STORAGE OF DIESEL FUEL IS MAINTAINED       **COLUMN D** – BULK STORAGE OF ANY OTHER MOTOR FUEL IS MAINTAINED

| A B C D | | A B C D | | A B C D | | A B C D | |
|---|---|---|---|---|---|---|---|
| ☐ ☐ ☐ ☐ | AK – ALASKA | ☐ ☐ ☐ ☐ | ID – IDAHO | ☐ ☐ ☐ ☐ | MT – MONTANA | ☐ ☐ ☐ ☐ | RI – RHODE ISLAND |
| ☐ ☐ ☐ ☐ | AL – ALABAMA | ☐ ☐ ☐ ☐ | IL – ILLINOIS | ☐ ☐ ☐ ☐ | NC – NORTH CAROLINA | ☐ ☐ ☐ ☐ | SC – SOUTH CAROLINA |
| ☐ ☐ ☐ ☐ | AR – ARKANSAS | ☐ ☐ ☐ ☐ | IN – INDIANA | ☐ ☐ ☐ ☐ | ND – NORTH DAKOTA | ☐ ☐ ☐ ☐ | SD – SOUTH DAKOTA |
| ☐ ☐ ☐ ☐ | AZ – ARIZONA | ☐ ☐ ☐ ☐ | KS – KANSAS | ☐ ☐ ☐ ☐ | NE – NEBRASKA | ☐ ☐ ☐ ☐ | TN – TENNESSEE |
| ☐ ☐ ☐ ☐ | CA – CALIFORNIA | ☐ ☐ ☐ ☐ | KY – KENTUCKY | ☐ ☐ ☐ ☐ | NH – NEW HAMPSHIRE | ☐ ☐ ☐ ☐ | TX – TEXAS |
| ☐ ☐ ☐ ☐ | CO – COLORADO | ☐ ☐ ☐ ☐ | LA – LOUISIANA | ☐ ☐ ☐ ☐ | NJ – NEW JERSEY | ☐ ☐ ☐ ☐ | UT – UTAH |
| ☐ ☐ ☐ ☐ | CT – CONNECTICUT | ☐ ☐ ☐ ☐ | MA – MASSACHUSETTS | ☐ ☐ ☐ ☐ | NM – NEW MEXICO | ☐ ☐ ☐ ☐ | VA – VIRGINIA |
| ☐ ☐ ☐ ☐ | DC – DIST. OF COLUMBIA | ☐ ☐ ☐ ☐ | MD – MARYLAND | ☐ ☐ ☐ ☐ | NV – NEVADA | ☐ ☐ ☐ ☐ | VT – VERMONT |
| ☐ ☐ ☐ ☐ | DE – DELAWARE | ☐ ☐ ☐ ☐ | ME – MAINE | ☐ ☐ ☐ ☐ | NY – NEW YORK | ☐ ☐ ☐ ☐ | WA – WASHINGTON |
| ☐ ☐ ☐ ☐ | FL – FLORIDA | ☐ ☐ ☐ ☐ | MI – MICHIGAN | ☐ ☐ ☐ ☐ | OH – OHIO | ☐ ☐ ☐ ☐ | WI – WISCONSIN |
| ☐ ☐ ☐ ☐ | GA – GEORGIA | ☐ ☐ ☐ ☐ | MN – MINNESOTA | ☐ ☐ ☐ ☐ | OK – OKLAHOMA | ☐ ☐ ☐ ☐ | WV – WEST VIRGINIA |
| ☐ ☐ ☐ ☐ | HI – HAWAII | ☐ ☐ ☐ ☐ | MO – MISSOURI | ☐ ☐ ☐ ☐ | OR – OREGON | ☐ ☐ ☐ ☐ | WY – WYOMING |
| ☐ ☐ ☐ ☐ | IA – IOWA | ☐ ☐ ☐ ☐ | MS – MISSISSIPPI | ☐ ☐ ☐ ☐ | PA – PENNSYLVANIA | | |

| A B C D | | A B C D | | A B C D | | A B C D | |
|---|---|---|---|---|---|---|---|
| ☐ ☐ ☐ ☐ | AB – ALBERTA | ☐ ☐ ☐ ☐ | NB – NEW BRUNSWICK | ☐ ☐ ☐ ☐ | NT – N W TERRITORY | ☐ ☐ ☐ ☐ | PQ – QUEBEC |
| ☐ ☐ ☐ ☐ | BC – BRITISH COLUMBIA | ☐ ☐ ☐ ☐ | NF – NEWFOUNDLAND | ☐ ☐ ☐ ☐ | ON – ONTARIO | ☐ ☐ ☐ ☐ | SK – SASKATCHEWAN |
| ☐ ☐ ☐ ☐ | MB – MANITOBA | ☐ ☐ ☐ ☐ | NS – NOVA SCOTIA | ☐ ☐ ☐ ☐ | PE – PRINCE EDWARD IS. | ☐ ☐ ☐ ☐ | YT – YUKON TERRITORY |

### PART 2   FUELS

CHECK THE APPROPRIATE BOX(ES) IF THE ENTERPRISE WILL SELL, USE OR TRANSPORT ANY FUELS IN PENNSYLVANIA.

☐ LIQUID FUELS AND FUELS TAX - YEARLY PERMIT REQUIRED BY WHOLESALE DISTRIBUTORS (i.e. ONE LICENSED TO HANDLE TAX FREE LIQUID FUELS OR FUELS IN PA) OR AN IMPORTER OR EXPORTER OF LIQUID FUELS OR FUELS.
ESTIMATED DATE OF FIRST TAX-FREE LIQUID FUELS PURCHASE OR SALE _____

☐ ALTERNATIVE FUELS TAX - YEARLY PERMIT REQUIRED BY ALTERNATIVE FUEL DEALER-USERS FOR THE REMISSION OF TAX ON ALTERNATIVE FUELS (HIGHWAY FUELS OTHER THAN LIQUID FUELS OR FUELS) PLACED INTO THE SUPPLY TANK OF A MOTOR VEHICLE FOR USE ON PA HIGHWAYS.
ESTIMATED DATE OF FIRST FUELING OF VEHICLES _____

PROVIDE A LIST OF ALL PA LOCATIONS WHERE LIQUID FUELS OR FUELS WILL BE SOLD.

| STREET ADDRESS | CITY/TOWN | COUNTY | STATE | ZIP CODE + 4 |
|---|---|---|---|---|
| STREET ADDRESS | CITY/TOWN | COUNTY | STATE | ZIP CODE + 4 |

ATTACH ADDITIONAL 8 1/2 x 11 SHEETS IF NECESSARY

16

PA-100 2-98

| ENTERPRISE NAME Superior Flooring, Inc. | DEPARTMENT USE ONLY |
|---|---|

## SECTION 22 – SALES TAX EXEMPT STATUS FOR CHARITABLE AND RELIGIOUS ORGANIZATIONS

### PART 1

ACT 55 OF 1997, KNOWN AS THE INSTITUTIONS OF PURELY PUBLIC CHARITY ACT, WAS SIGNED INTO LAW ON NOVEMBER 26, 1997. THIS LAW HAS CODIFIED THE REQUIREMENTS AN INSTITUTION MUST MEET IN ORDER TO QUALIFY FOR EXEMPTION, OUTLINING FIVE CRITERIA THAT MUST BE MET. EACH INSTITUTION MUST: (1) ADVANCE A CHARITABLE PURPOSE; (2) DONATE OR RENDER GRATUITOUSLY A SUBSTANTIAL PORTION OF ITS SERVICES; (3) BENEFIT A SUBSTANTIAL AND INDEFINITE CLASS OF PERSONS WHO ARE LEGITIMATE SUBJECTS OF CHARITY; (4) RELIEVE THE GOVERNMENT OF SOME BURDEN; (5) OPERATE ENTIRELY FREE FROM PRIVATE PROFIT MOTIVE.

**ORGANIZATIONS OF THE FOLLOWING TYPE DO NOT QUALIFY FOR EXEMPTION STATUS:**

- AN ASSOCIATION OF EMPLOYEES, THE MEMBERSHIP OF WHICH IS LIMITED TO THE EMPLOYEES OF A DESIGNATED ENTERPRISE

- A LABOR ORGANIZATION

- AN AGRICULTURAL OR HORTICULTURAL ORGANIZATION

- A BUSINESS LEAGUE, CHAMBER OF COMMERCE, REAL ESTATE BOARD, BOARD OF TRADE OR PROFESSIONAL SPORT LEAGUE

- A CLUB ORGANIZED FOR PLEASURE OR RECREATION

- A FRATERNAL BENEFICIARY SOCIETY, ORDER OR ASSOCIATION.

TO APPLY OR RENEW SALES TAX EXEMPTION STATUS A REV-72 APPLICATION **MUST** BE COMPLETED. THIS APPLICATION MAY BE OBTAINED BY COMPLETING THE BELOW FORM OR CALL (717) 783-5473, TTD# (717) 772-2252 (HEARING IMPAIRED ONLY).

IF THE ORGANIZATION CONDUCTS SALES ACTIVITIES AND IS NOT REGISTERED FOR COLLECTION OF PA SALES TAX, REFER TO SECTION 18 OF THIS BOOKLET.

### PART 2    REQUEST FOR SALES TAX EXEMPT STATUS APPLICATION

NAME

| MAILING ADDRESS | CITY/TOWN | STATE | ZIP CODE + 4 |
|---|---|---|---|

## RETURN COMPLETED FORM TO:

PA DEPARTMENT OF REVENUE
BUREAU OF BUSINESS TRUST FUND TAXES
DEPT. 280909
HARRISBURG, PA 17128-0909

PA-100 2-98

## SECTION 1 – REASON FOR THIS REGISTRATION

An enterprise may select more than one reason for registration.

- New registrants must complete Sections 1 through 10 and additional sections as appropriate.

- Registered enterprises must complete Sections 1 through 4 and additional sections as indicated. Complete Sections 5 through 7 to update information.

1. **New Registration:** An enterprise never registered with the PA Department of Revenue or the PA Department of Labor & Industry must complete Sections 1 through 10 and additional sections as appropriate.

2. **Adding Tax(es) and Service(s):** A registered enterprise adding tax(es) and service(s) must complete Sections 1 through 4 and additional sections as appropriate.

3. **Reactivating Tax(es) and Service(s):** A registered enterprise reactivating tax(es) and service(s) must complete Sections 1 through 4 and additional sections as appropriate.

4. **Adding Establishment(s):** A registered enterprise adding establishment location(s) must complete Sections 1 through 4 and Section 17, Multiple Establishment Information.

5. **Acquisition of All or Part of an Existing Enterprise:** An enterprise acquiring the business operation of another enterprise in whole or in part must complete Section 14, Predecessor/Successor Information. The business operation can be acquired by consolidation, merger, gift or change in legal structure. A stock acquisition *alone* does not constitute a transfer of the business operation.

   - A newly formed enterprise must complete Sections 1 through 10 and additional sections as appropriate.

   - A previously registered enterprise must complete Sections 1 through 4, 10 and additional sections as appropriate.

6. **Application for PA UC Experience Record and Reserve Account Balance of Predecessor:** An enterprise requesting the PA Unemployment Compensation (UC) experience record and reserve account balance of a predecessor (prior owner) must complete Section 15, Application for PA UC Experience Record and Reserve Account Balance of Predecessor.

   - A newly formed enterprise must complete Sections 1 through 10, 14 and additional sections as appropriate.

   - A previously registered enterprise must complete Sections 1 through 4, 10, 14 and additional sections as appropriate.

7. **Information Update:** A registered enterprise providing changes in demographic or other information must complete Sections 1 through 4 and additional sections as appropriate.

## SECTION 2 – ENTERPRISE INFORMATION

1. **Date of First Operations:** Enter the first date the enterprise conducted any activity. This includes start-up operations prior to opening for business.

2. **Date of First Operations in PA:** Enter the first date the enterprise conducted any activity in PA or employed PA residents. This includes start-up operations prior to opening for business.

3. **Enterprise Fiscal Year End:** Enter the month (January, February, etc.) used by the enterprise to designate the end of its accounting period.

4. **Enterprise Legal Name:** Enter the legal name of the enterprise.

| IF THE FORM OF ORGANIZATION IS: | USE THE: |
|---|---|
| SOLE PROPRIETORSHIP | INDIVIDUAL OWNER'S NAME. |
| CORPORATION | NAME AS SHOWN IN THE ARTICLES OF INCORPORATION. |
| PARTNERSHIP | NAME AS SHOWN IN THE PARTNERSHIP AGREEMENT. |
| ASSOCIATION | NAME AS SHOWN IN THE ASSOCIATION AGREEMENT. |
| BUSINESS TRUST | NAME AS SHOWN IN THE TRUST AGREEMENT. |
| ESTATE | LEGAL NAME OF THE ESTATE. |
| TRUST | NAME AS SHOWN IN THE TRUST AGREEMENT. |
| LIMITED LIABILITY COMPANY | NAME AS SHOWN IN THE ARTICLES OF ORGANIZATION. |
| RESTRICTED PROFESSIONAL COMPANY | NAME AS SHOWN IN THE ARTICLES OF ORGANIZATION. |
| GOVERNMENT | OFFICIAL/LEGAL NAME OF THE ORGANIZATION. |
| OTHER | LEGAL NAME OF THE ENTERPRISE. |

5. **Federal EIN:** Enter the federal Employer Identification Number (EIN) assigned to the enterprise by the Internal Revenue Service. If the enterprise does not have an EIN, enter "N/A". If the enterprise has made application for an EIN, enter "Applied For".

6. **Enterprise Trade Name:** Enter the name by which the enterprise is commonly known (doing business as, trading as, also known as), if it is a name other than the legal name. If the enterprise has a fictitious name registered with the PA Department of State, enter it here. If the trade name is the same as the legal name, enter "Same".

7. **Enterprise Telephone Number:** Enter the telephone number for the enterprise.

8. **Enterprise Street Address:** Enter the physical location of the enterprise. **A post office box is not acceptable.**

9. **Enterprise Mailing Address:** Enter the address where the enterprise prefers to receive mail if at an address other than the enterprise street address. A post office box is acceptable. If the mailing address is the same as the enterprise street address, enter "Same".

   To indicate multiple mailing addresses and the purposes, attach a separate 8 1/2" X 11" sheet and identify the purpose of each.

   For example, an enterprise may want tax forms or licenses mailed to the enterprise address, but payroll-related forms such as Employer Withholding and Unemployment Compensation Returns mailed to the address of a particular payroll service.

10. **Location of Enterprise Records:** Enter the street address where the enterprise records are kept. A post office box is not acceptable. If the records are kept at the enterprise street address, enter "Same".

11. **Establishment Name:** Enter the name by which the establishment is known to the public; for example, the name on the front of the store. If the same as the enterprise legal name, enter "Same".

12. **Number of Establishments:** Enter the number of establishments. If the enterprise has more than one establishment conducting business in PA or employing PA residents, refer to the instructions and complete Section 17, Multiple Establishment Information.

13. **School District:** Enter the school district where the establishment is located. If not a PA school district, enter "N/A".

14. **Municipality:** Enter the municipality (borough, city, town or township) where the establishment is located. The municipality may be different from the city/town used for postal delivery. If not a PA municipality, enter "N/A".

## SECTION 3 – TAXES AND SERVICES

Indicate the tax(es) and service(s) requested. Descriptions, additional requirements and sections to complete are on page(s) 2 and 3. Enter the previous account number(s) when reactivating tax(es) and service(s).

## SECTION 4 – AUTHORIZED SIGNATURE

**Authorized Signature:** Owner, general partner, officer or agent signature is required. Enter the title of the person who signed the form. Attach Power of Attorney document, if applicable.

**Type or Print Name:** Type or print the name of the person who signed the document and enter the date it was signed.

**Preparer's Signature:** Enter the signature and title of the person who prepared the form, if other than the owner, partner or officer.

**Type or Print Name:** Type or print the name of the preparer. Enter the preparer's daytime telephone number and the date the form was signed.

## SECTION 5 – FORM OF ORGANIZATION

1. Check the box to select the form of organization that applies to the enterprise.
   - A sole proprietor is one individual owner and indicates 100 percent ownership.
   - Two or more individuals listed as owners constitute a partnership and will be registered as one. Registrants for Unemployment Compensation should attach a copy of the partnership agreement, if available.
   - Limited liability companies and restricted professional companies must enter the state/province where chartered.

   The following forms of organization require the completion of additional sections:
   - Corporation - Complete Section 11, Corporation Information.
   - Government - Complete Section 13, Government Information.

2. Check the box to indicate if the enterprise is profit or non-profit.

3. If an enterprise is exempt under Section 501(c)(3) of the Internal Revenue Code, and is also subject to the contribution provisions of the Pennsylvania Unemployment Compensation (UC) Law, it has the option to elect to finance UC costs under the reimbursement method in lieu of the contributory method.

See page 22 of the instructions for further explanations regarding contributory and reimbursement methods of making payments to the Unemployment Compensation Fund.

## SECTION 6 – OWNERS, PARTNERS, SHAREHOLDERS, OFFICERS AND RESPONSIBLE PARTY INFORMATION

Identify and provide information on the following:
- The sole proprietor who is 100 percent owner. A sole proprietor must be one individual.

- All general partners and all limited partners who are involved in the daily operation of the business.
- All shareholders (both individuals and enterprises) owning stock. If the stock is publicly traded, identify any shareholder with an equity position of 5 percent or more.
- All officers of the corporation, association or business trust.
- All individuals responsible for remitting trust fund taxes to the Department of Revenue.

1. **Name:** Enter the name(s) of the owner, partner, shareholder, officer, or responsible party of the enterprise. If the owner is another enterprise, enter the legal name of the enterprise.

2. **Social Security Number:** Enter the Social Security Number of the owner, partner, shareholder, officer or responsible party.

3. **Date of Birth:** Enter the individual's date of birth if applying for a Cigarette Wholesale Dealer's License or a Small Games of Chance Distributor License or Manufacturer Certificate.

4. **Federal EIN:** Enter the federal Employer Identification Number (EIN) if the owner, partner or shareholder is another enterprise.

5. **Type of Ownership/Position:** Check the box(es) to designate if an owner, partner, officer or shareholder.

6-9. **Title, Effective Dates, Percentage of Ownership:** Enter the title, effective dates, and percentage of ownership as indicated.

10. **Home Address:** Enter the home street address of the owner, partner, shareholder, officer or responsible party. If the owner, partner or shareholder is another enterprise, enter the street address of the enterprise. **A post office box is not acceptable**.

11. **Person Responsible to Remit:** Signature of individual responsible for remitting trust fund taxes to the Department of Revenue is required.

**Department of Revenue Responsible Party:**

Responsible parties (Sales Tax, Employer Withholding and Motor Fuel Taxes): Please identify the person(s) responsible for remitting trust fund taxes to the Department of Revenue. Under Pennsylvania law, a proprietor, a general partner, or a corporation's chief operating officers and chief financial officer is responsible for ensuring that collected Sales Tax, Employer Withholding Tax, Liquid Fuels and Fuels Tax (trust funds) is remitted to the Department on a timely basis. Other individuals may also be responsible, if their duties, position or authority over financial matters and decision-making put them in a position to influence the payment of these taxes. Failure to remit these taxes in a timely manner may result in the personal assessment of a responsible party for the amount of tax together with the possibility of criminal sanctions, if warranted.

An individual who signs the application for an enterprise's or organization's state trust fund tax license or who signs a Pennsylvania trust fund tax return for an enterprise or organization will be presumed to be a responsible party in the absence of any contradicting evidence.

Space for additional information of owners, partners, shareholders, officers and/or responsible parties can be found on page 11. Attach additional 8 1/2 X 11 sheets if necessary.

**SECTION 7 – ESTABLISHMENT BUSINESS ACTIVITY INFORMATION**

ENTER THE PERCENTAGE THE PA BUSINESS ACTIVITY REPRESENTS OF THE TOTAL RECEIPTS OR REVENUES AT THIS ESTABLISHMENT. SPECIFY THE PRODUCTS AND/OR SERVICES PROVIDED AT THIS ESTABLISHMENT AND ENTER THE PERCENTAGE EACH REPRESENTS OF THE TOTAL RECEIPTS OR REVENUES AT THIS ESTABLISHMENT.

## EXAMPLE

| PA BUSINESS ACTIVITY | % | PRODUCTS OR SERVICES | % | ADDITIONAL PRODUCTS OR SERVICES | % |
|---|---|---|---|---|---|
| CONSTRUCTION | 70 | BUILDING SINGLE FAMILY HOMES | 40 | BUILDING APARTMENT BUILDINGS | 30 |
| MANUFACTURING | | | | | |
| RETAIL TRADE | | | | | |
| WHOLESALE TRADE | 30 | WOOD PANELING | 30 | | |

### PA BUSINESS ACTIVITIES AND TYPICAL PRODUCTS OR SERVICES EXAMPLES
**THIS SECTION IS NOT FOR DETERMINING THE TAXABILITY OF PRODUCTS OR SERVICES, ONLY THE CLASSIFICATION OF PRODUCTS AND SERVICES.**

| PA BUSINESS ACTIVITY | TYPICAL PRODUCTS OR SERVICES |
|---|---|
| **CONSTRUCTION** - ESTABLISHMENTS ENGAGED IN NEW CONSTRUCTION WORK, RENOVATIVE CONSTRUCTION WORK, ADDITIONS, ALTERATIONS, INSTALLATIONS AND REPAIRS.<br>**CATEGORY INCLUDES**<br>GENERAL CONTRACTORS, SUBCONTRACTORS, SPECIAL TRADE CONTRACTORS, BUILDING CONSTRUCTION, HEAVY CONSTRUCTION.<br>**CATEGORY EXCLUDES**<br>FORCE ACCOUNT CONSTRUCTION, INSTALLATION WORK INCIDENTAL TO SALE. | SPECIFY THE TYPES OF STRUCTURES OR PROJECTS. *FOR EXAMPLE:*<br>BRIDGES • FARM BUILDING • PAINTING<br>CARPENTRY • HIGHWAYS • PLUMBING<br>COMMERCIAL BUILDING • INDUSTRIAL BUILDING • SEWER<br>ELECTRICAL • INSTALLATION OF BUILDING EQPT. • SIDING<br>EXCAVATION • LAND CLEARING • SINGLE FAMILY HOUSING<br>FACTORY BUILDING • MASONRY • STREETS |
| **MANUFACTURING** - ESTABLISHMENTS ENGAGED IN MECHANICAL OR CHEMICAL TRANSFORMATION OF MATERIALS INTO NEW PRODUCTS, ASSEMBLING COMPONENT PARTS, BLENDING OF MATERIALS.<br>**CATEGORY INCLUDES**<br>FOOD & TOBACCO PRODUCTS, TEXTILES & APPAREL, WOOD PRODUCTS, FURNITURE & FIXTURES, PRINTING & PUBLISHING, CHEMICALS & PETROLEUM REFINING, RUBBER & PLASTIC, LEATHER PRODUCTS, STONE, CLAY, GLASS & CONCRETE PRODUCTS, PRIMARY & FABRICATED METAL, MACHINERY & EQUIPMENT, ELECTRICAL & ELECTRONIC EQUIPMENT.<br>**CATEGORY EXCLUDES**<br>PROCESSING ON FARMS, CONSTRUCTION FABRICATION ON SITE, BREAKING OF BULK AND REDISTRIBUTION, MOST REPAIR ACTIVITIES. | SPECIFY THE PRODUCTS MANUFACTURED AND/OR TYPE OF PLANT & PRINCIPAL PROCESS USED. *FOR EXAMPLE:*<br>AIRCRAFT ENGINES • LOGGING • PRECIOUS METAL/JEWELRY<br>CANNED FRUITS • MEATPACKING PLANT • SOLID FIBER BOXES<br>CARPETS • METAL HEAT TREATING • STEEL PIPE<br>COTTON FABRIC • METAL OFFICE FURNITURE • STRUCTURAL STEEL<br>ELECTRONIC COMPUTERS • NAVIGATIONAL INSTRUMENTS • TELEPHONE SETS<br>ELEVATORS • NEWSPAPERS • TIRES<br>FARM MACHINERY • OFFSET PRINTING • WOMEN'S BLOUSES<br>FLAT GLASS • PLASTIC FILM • WOOD PALLETS<br>INDUSTRIAL GASES • POULTRY SLAUGHTERING |
| **MINING, QUARRYING, OIL / GAS EXTRACTION** - ESTABLISHMENTS ENGAGED IN THE EXTRACTION OF MINERALS OCCURRING NATURALLY AND PREPARATION DONE AT A MINE SITE.<br>**CATEGORY INCLUDES**<br>METAL MINING, COAL MINING, NATURAL GAS PROD., NON-METALLIC MINERALS.<br>**CATEGORY EXCLUDES**<br>PRODUCING PRIMARY MAGNESIUM METAL, PRODUCING PACKAGED FUEL, PIPELINE TRANS. OF GASOLINE (EXCEPT CRUDE), CUTTING AND FINISHING STONE PRODUCTS | SPECIFY EACH MINERAL OR PRODUCT EXTRACTED. IF SERVICES, DESCRIBE SERVICE AND MINERAL INVOLVED. *FOR EXAMPLE:*<br>BITUMINOUS COAL SURFACE MINING • CLAY QUARRYING • IRON ORE<br> • CRUSHED MARBLE • LOGGING ON A CONTRACT BASIS<br>BITUMINOUS COAL UNDERGROUND MINING • DIMENSION STONE • SILVER ORE<br>BROKEN LIMESTONE • INDUSTRIAL DIAMOND MINING • STRIPPING SERVICES |
| **RETAIL TRADE** - ESTABLISHMENTS ENGAGED IN SELLING MERCHANDISE TO THE GENERAL PUBLIC FOR PERSONAL OR HOUSEHOLD CONSUMPTION.<br>**CATEGORY INCLUDES**<br>BUILDING MATERIALS, GENERAL MERCHANDISE STORES, FOOD STORES, AUTOMOBILE DEALERS, SERVICE STATIONS, APPAREL STORES, FURNITURE STORES, EATING PLACES.<br>**CATEGORY EXCLUDES**<br>FARM EQUIPMENT, USED VEHICLE PARTS, COMMERCIAL EQUIPMENT.. | SPECIFY SEPARATELY THE DIFFERENT TYPES OF GOODS SOLD, WHETHER THE GOODS ARE NEW OR USED, OR SPECIFY THE TYPE OF STORE OR RETAIL ACTIVITY. *FOR EXAMPLE:*<br>BRIDAL SHOP • LUMBER • RETAIL MAIL ORDER HOUSE<br>CUSTOM TAILOR • LUNCH WAGON • TAVERN<br>DEPARTMENT STORE • NEW AUTO PARTS • USED HOUSEHOLD APPLIANCES<br>GASOLINE STATION • PETS<br>GIFTS • RESTAURANT<br>GROCERY STORE • RETAIL BAKERY • WALLPAPER |
| **WHOLESALE TRADE** - ESTABLISHMENTS ENGAGED IN SELLING MERCHANDISE TO RETAILERS, PROFESSIONAL BUYERS & WHOLESALERS, AND AGENTS & BROKERS.<br>**CATEGORY INCLUDES**<br>DURABLE GOODS, NON-DURABLE GOODS.<br>**CATEGORY EXCLUDES**<br>SELLING CONSTRUCTION MATERIALS TO THE GENERAL PUBLIC, INSTALLING ELECTRICAL & PLUMBING EQUIPMENT, WHOLESALE OF GOODS MANUFACTURED AT THE SAME ESTABLISHMENT. | SPECIFY SEPARATELY THE DIFFERENT TYPES OF GOODS SOLD. *FOR EXAMPLE:*<br>ADVERTISING SPECIALTIES • INDUSTRIAL SUPPLIES • PLASTICS FILM<br>BUSES • MEDICAL EQUIPMENT • SERVICE STATION EQUIPMENT<br>CANNED GOODS • MILK DEPOT • SHIPPING SUPPLIES<br>FARM EQUIPMENT • NEW AND/OR USED AUTO PARTS • STRAW<br>FARM SUPPLIES • • TELEPHONE EQUIPMENT<br>HAY • PETROLEUM BULK STATION • WASTE MATERIALS |
| **FINANCE** - ESTABLISHMENTS ENGAGED IN FINANCIAL SERVICES<br>**CATEGORY INCLUDES**<br>DEPOSITORY INSTITUTIONS, NON-DEPOSITORY INSTITUTIONS, SECURITY BROKERS & DEALERS, HOLDING COMPANIES.<br>**CATEGORY EXCLUDES**<br>INSURANCE, SHORT-TERM OR EXTENDED-TERM LEASING OF VEHICLES. | SPECIFY THE TYPE OF FINANCIAL INSTITUTION, CHARTER AND TYPE OF FINANCIAL PRODUCTS AND SERVICES OFFERED. *FOR EXAMPLE:*<br>AGRICULTURAL LOAN COMPANY • STATE SAVINGS BANK • MORTGAGE BANKER<br>BANKS FOR COOPERATIVES • FINANCIAL LEASING OF VEHICLES OR EQUIPMENT • PATENT LEASING<br>CHECK CASHING AGENCY • INVESTMENT ADVISORY SERVICE • PERSONAL CREDIT INSTITUTION<br>COMMODITY CONTRACT BROKER • INVESTMENT BANKER<br>FEDERAL RESERVE BANK • MANAGEMENT OF EDUCATIONAL TRUSTS • STATE COMMERCIAL BANK TRUSTS |
| **INSURANCE** - ESTABLISHMENTS ENGAGED IN INSURANCE SERVICES.<br>**CATEGORY INCLUDES**<br>INSURANCE CARRIERS, INSURANCE AGENTS, INSURANCE BROKERS, INSURANCE SERVICE.<br>**CATEGORY EXCLUDES**<br>FINANCE AND SEARCHING REAL ESTATE TITLES. | SPECIFY EACH TYPE OF INSURANCE SOLD AND SPECIFY IF THE INSURANCE IS UNDERWRITTEN BY THE SAME ENTERPRISE. *FOR EXAMPLE:*<br>ACCIDENT INSURANCE UNDERWRITING • HOSPITAL & MEDICAL SERVICE PLANS • MANAGING PENSION FUNDS<br>BONDING • INSURANCE • SURETY INSURANCE<br>FIRE INSURANCE UNDERWRITING • LIFE INSURANCE AGENT • TITLE INSURANCE UNDERWRITING<br>HEALTH INSURANCE FOR PETS • LIFE INSURANCE UNDERWRITING • WORKERS COMPENSATION |

| PA BUSINESS ACTIVITY | TYPICAL PRODUCTS OR SERVICES | | |
|---|---|---|---|
| **REAL ESTATE** – ESTABLISHMENTS ENGAGED IN REAL ESTATE SERVICES.<br><br>**CATEGORY INCLUDES**<br>REAL ESTATE OPERATORS, OWNERS AND LESSORS OF REAL PROPERTY, REAL ESTATE AGENTS, REAL ESTATE BROKERS.<br><br>**CATEGORY EXCLUDES**<br>OPERATORS OF HOTELS OR CAMPS, OR DEVELOPING LOTS FOR OTHERS | SPECIFY EACH TYPE OF REAL ESTATE ACTIVITY. FOR OPERATORS OR MANAGERS OF RESIDENTIAL PROPERTIES, SPECIFY THE NUMBER OF HOUSING UNITS AND WHETHER THIS ENTERPRISE OWNS THE PROPERTY OR OPERATES IT FOR OTHERS. *FOR EXAMPLE:*<br><br>CEMETERY ASSOCIATION<br><br>LESSORS OF RAILROAD PROPERTY | REAL ESTATE AGENTS FOR OTHERS<br><br>REAL ESTATE MANAGERS FOR OTHERS | OWNER-OPERATOR OF APARTMENT BUILDING<br>OWNER-OPERATOR OF NON-RESIDENTIAL BUILDING<br>TITLE ABSTRACT COMPANY |
| **TRANSPORTATION** - ESTABLISHMENTS ENGAGED IN PROVIDING PASSENGER OR FREIGHT TRANSPORTATION.<br><br>**CATEGORY INCLUDES**<br>RAILROADS, LOCAL & SUBURBAN TRANSIT, MOTOR FREIGHT TRANSPORTATION, USPS, WATER TRANSPORTATION, AIR TRANSPORTATION, PIPELINE TRANSPORTATION.<br><br>**CATEGORY EXCLUDES**<br>LESSORS OF RAILROAD PROPERTY OR ARMORED CAR SERVICE. | SPECIFY SEPARATELY EACH TRANSPORTATION MODE. IF SERVICES SPECIFY THE TYPE OF SERVICE. FOR EXAMPLE: *FOR EXAMPLE:*<br><br>BOAT CLEANING<br>CRUDE PETROLEUM PIPELINES<br>FERRIES<br>FREIGHT FORWARDING SERVICE<br>INTERURBAN RAILWAYS | LOADING VESSELS<br>LOCAL BUS CHARTER SERVICE<br>LOCAL BUS LINE OPERATION<br>LOCAL TRUCKING<br>LONG-DISTANCE TRUCKING<br>PRIVATE PACKAGE DELIVERY | ROAD AMBULANCE SERVICE<br>SCHEDULED AIR CARGO-CARRIER<br>SCHOOL BUSES<br>TAXICABS<br>TRAVEL AGENCIES |
| **WAREHOUSING** – ESTABLISHMENTS ENGAGED IN THE STORAGE OF GOODS FOR OTHERS.<br><br>**CATEGORY INCLUDES**<br>REFRIGERATED WAREHOUSES, GENERAL WAREHOUSES, SPECIALIZED WAREHOUSES.<br><br>CATEGORY EXCLUDES<br>WAREHOUSING FOR OTHER ESTABLISHMENTS OF THE SAME ENTERPRISE, FIELD WAREHOUSING. | SPECIFY THE TYPE OF STORAGE AND/OR THE TYPE OF GOODS STORED. *FOR EXAMPLE:*<br><br>FROZEN FOOD LOCKER RENTAL<br><br>FUR STORAGE FOR THE TRADE | POTATO CELLARS<br><br>SELF-STORAGE WAREHOUSING | WAREHOUSING FARM PRODUCTS<br><br>WHISKEY WAREHOUSING |
| **COMMUNICATIONS** – ESTABLISHMENTS ENGAGED IN FURNISHING POINT-TO-POINT COMMUNICATION SERVICES.<br><br>**CATEGORY INCLUDES**<br>TELEPHONE COMMUNICATION, TELEGRAPH COMMUNICATIONS, RADIO & TELEVISION.<br><br>**CATEGORY EXCLUDES**<br>TELEPHONE ANSWERING SERVICE, PRODUCING TAPED TELEVISION PROGRAM MATERIALS | SPECIFY TYPES OF SERVICES. *FOR EXAMPLE:*<br><br>CABLE TV SERVICES<br><br>LOCAL & LONG DISTANCE TELEPHONE SERVICES<br><br>PAGING SERVICES | RADIO BROADCASTING<br><br>TELEVISION BROADCASTING<br><br>TELEX SERVICES | |
| **AGRICULTURE, FORESTRY, FISHING** – ESTABLISHMENTS ENGAGED IN AGRICULTURAL PRODUCTION, COMMERCIAL FISHING AND HUNTING.<br><br>**CATEGORY INCLUDES**<br>AGRICULTURAL CROPS, AGRICULTURAL LIVESTOCK, AGRICULTURAL SERVICES, FORESTRY, FISHING, HUNTING, TRAPPING.<br><br>**CATEGORY EXCLUDES**<br>SALES OF PRODUCTS ONLY, TRAINING RACEHORSES, INSTALLATION OF ARTIFICIAL TURF, OR LOGGING. | SPECIFY EACH TYPE OF CROP GROWN, LIVESTOCK RAISED, FISH CAUGHT AND FORESTRY WORK. ALSO SPECIFY WHERE GROWN OR PURPOSE FOR WHICH RAISED. *FOR EXAMPLE:*<br><br>BOARDING KENNELS<br>CATTLE RANCH<br>CATTLE SPRAYING<br>CHICKEN HATCHERY<br>CORN FARM<br>DAIRY FARM<br>FISH HATCHERY | GAME PRESERVE<br>GENERAL LANDSCAPING SERVICES<br>GROWING OF NURSERY STOCK<br>LAWN & GARDEN SERVICES | SOIL PREPARATION SERVICES<br>TIMBER VALUATION<br>TOMATOES GROWN UNDER-COVER<br>TREE TRIMMING<br>VETERINARY SERVICES FOR PETS |
| **UTILITY, SANITARY SERVICE** – ESTABLISHMENTS ENGAGED IN PROVIDING ELECTRIC, GAS, AND SANITARY SERVICES.<br><br>**CATEGORY INCLUDES**<br>ELECTRIC SERVICES, GAS TRANSMISSION, WATER SUPPLY, SANITARY SERVICES.<br><br>**CATEGORY EXCLUDES**<br>DISTRIBUTION OF LP GAS IN STEEL CONTAINERS, COLLECTING AND TRANSPORTING REFUSE. | SPECIFY SEPARATELY EACH TYPE OF SERVICE. *FOR EXAMPLE:*<br><br>DISTRIBUTION OF COOLED AIR<br><br>IRRIGATION SYSTEM OPERATOR<br><br>LANDFILL OPERATIONS | NATURAL GAS DISTRIBUTION<br><br>NATURAL GAS PIPELINE<br><br>OIL SPILL CLEANUP | PROVIDING ELECTRIC SERVICE<br><br>SEWAGE SYSTEMS<br><br>WATER SUPPLY SYSTEMS |
| **SERVICES** – ESTABLISHMENTS ENGAGED IN PROVIDING A WIDE VARIETY OF SERVICES FOR INDIVIDUALS, BUSINESS AND GOVERNMENT ESTABLISHMENTS.<br><br>**CATEGORY INCLUDES**<br>LODGING PLACES, PERSONAL SERVICES, BUSINESS SERVICES, AUTOMOTIVE SERVICES, REPAIR SERVICES, MOTION PICTURES, AMUSEMENT & RECREATION SERVICES, HEALTH SERVICES, LEGAL SERVICES, EDUCATIONAL SERVICES, SOCIAL SERVICES, MUSEUMS, MEMBERSHIP ORGANIZATIONS, ENGINEERING, ACCOUNTING, EMPLOYEE LEASING, PAYROLL SERVICES, SHORT-TERM OR EXTENDED-TERM LEASING OF VEHICLES.<br><br>**CATEGORY EXCLUDES**<br>PAINTING CONTRACTORS, ELECTRICAL CONTRACTORS, APARTMENT HOTELS, INSTALLATION ONLY OF SECURITY DEVICES, WELDING ON-SITE, LANDSCAPE ARCHITECTURAL SERVICES. | SPECIFY SEPARATELY THE PRINCIPAL TYPES OF SERVICES PERFORMED. ALSO DESCRIBE THE DISTINCTIVE FEATURES OF THESE SERVICES. *FOR EXAMPLE:*<br><br>AERIAL ADVERTISING<br>ARCHITECTURAL SERVICES<br>ATTORNEY<br>AUTOMOTIVE BODY SHOP<br>BEAUTY SHOP<br>BOOKKEEPING SERVICES<br>CHILD DAY CARE<br>CIVIL ENGINEERS<br>COIN-OPERATED LAUNDRY<br>COMMERCIAL MARKET RESEARCH<br>COMPUTER CONSULTANTS | CUSTOM SOFTWARE PROGRAMMING<br>EMPLOYEE LEASING SERVICE<br>FURNITURE RENTAL & LEASING<br>GROUP FOSTER HOMES<br>HEALTH SERVICES (SPECIFY MD, DO, DDS, DP, ETC.). (SKILLED NURSING HOMES, INTERMEDIATE CARE FACILITIES, GENERAL HOSPITALS, CANCER HOSPITALS)<br>HIGH SCHOOLS<br>HOTEL / MOTEL | JANITORIAL SERVICE<br>PASSENGER CAR RENTAL OR LEASING<br>PORTRAIT PHOTOGRAPHER<br>PUBLIC GOLF COURSE<br>RADIO REPAIR SHOP<br>TELEMARKETING SERVICE<br>TELEVISION FILM PRODUCTION<br>TEMPORARY HELP SERVICE<br>TRADE ASSOCIATIONS<br>VIDEO TAPE RENTAL |
| **DOMESTIC** – PRIVATE HOUSEHOLDS WHO EMPLOY WORKERS TO SERVE ON OR ABOUT THE PREMISES.<br><br>**CATEGORY INCLUDES**<br>PRIVATE HOUSEHOLDS EMPLOYING DOMESTIC SERVICES.<br><br>**CATEGORY EXCLUDES**<br>PRIVATE DUTY NURSES EMPLOYED AND PAID THROUGH AN AGENCY | SPECIFY TYPES OF SERVICES. *FOR EXAMPLE:*<br><br>CARETAKING AND OTHER MAINTENANCE<br><br>COOK | MAID<br><br>NANNY<br><br>PERSONAL AFFAIRS MANAGER | |

2. **Percentage:** Enter the percentage that this establishment's receipts or revenues represent of the total PA receipts or revenues of the enterprise.

3. **New and/or Renovative:** Establishments involved in construction activity must enter the percentage of new construction activity and/or renovative construction activity. The percentage should equal 100 percent of the construction activity at this establishment.

4. **Support Activities:** Check the appropriate box to indicate if this establishment is solely engaged in the performance of support activities for other establishments of the same enterprise. If "yes", list the name(s) of the supported establishment(s), and check the appropriate box to describe the support activity.

21

## SECTION 8 – ESTABLISHMENT SALES INFORMATION

1. Check the appropriate box to indicate if the establishment is selling products or services subject to Sales Tax **In PA**. Products and services include the sale and/or repair to tangible personal property, prepared food, rental and leasing of motor vehicles and rental and leasing of equipment. Complete Section 18 to apply for a Sales Tax License.

2. Check the appropriate box to indicate if cigarettes are sold "over-the-counter" or at vending machine locations. Complete Section 18 to apply for a Sales Tax License and Section 19 to apply for a Cigarette Tax License.

3. List each county **In PA** where taxable sales and/or services are offered or supplied.

## SECTION 9 – ESTABLISHMENT EMPLOYMENT INFORMATION

### PART 1

1. **a – f** Complete if the establishment employs individuals working **In PA**. If the principal business activity is not construction, enter "N/A" in items D and E.

2. **a – c** Complete if the establishment employs **PA residents working outside of PA**.

3. Check the appropriate box. If yes, explain the services performed and why you do not consider the individual(s) to be employee(s).

### PART 2

1. **a – b** Complete if registering for withholding on **taxable benefits paid from a benefit trust, deferred payment or retirement plan for PA residents.**

## SECTION 10 – BULK SALE/TRANSFER INFORMATION

A separate copy of Section 10 must be completed for each transferor from which assets were acquired.

Assets include, but are not limited to, any stock of goods, wares or merchandise of any kind, fixtures, machinery, equipment, buildings or real estate, name and/or goodwill. Refer to the form for the class of assets.

1. Indicate if the enterprise has acquired "IN BULK" 51 percent or more of **any class of PA assets** of another enterprise.

2. Indicate if the enterprise has acquired "IN BULK" 51 percent or more of the **total assets** of another enterprise.

3-7. Complete if the answer to question 1 or 2 is "Yes".

## SECTION 11 – CORPORATION INFORMATION

**All corporations must register with the PA Department of State to secure corporate name clearance and register for Corporation Tax purposes. Call the PA Department of State at (717) 787-1057.**

1-6. Describe the corporation.

7. Check the appropriate box if the corporation is a federal "S" corporation. If so, check the box to indicate if the corporation is also a PA "S" corporation. **Note:** This does **not** constitute a PA "S" election. To elect PA "S" status, a REV-1640, Election and Shareholder's Consent Form must be submitted. This form can be obtained by calling the Department of Revenue at (717) 783-6050, or the forms ordering numbers listed on page 3.

## SECTION 12 – REPORTING & PAYMENT METHODS

1. Payments equal to or greater than $20,000 to the Department of Revenue must be remitted via an approved EFT method. If a payment of $20,000 or more is not made via an approved EFT method, the account is subject to a 3 percent penalty on the tax due up to $1,000. Taxpayers must register with the PA Department of Revenue to remit payments via EFT.

2. The enterprise may participate voluntarily in the Department of Revenue's EFT Program.

3. The Department of Revenue's EDI Program utilizes state-of-the-art technology for the computer-to-computer filing of tax return information. EDI reduces the costs and delays associated with processing paper tax returns.

4. Enterprises with 250 or more wage entries are required to report quarterly Unemployment Compensation (UC) wages to the Department of Labor & Industry via magnetic media. Noncompliance may result in penalty charges. Contact the Magnetic Media Reporting Unit at (717) 783-5802 for more information.

5. Enterprises with less than 250 wage entries may voluntarily report individuals' wages to the Department of Labor & Industry via magnetic media.

6. The Unemployment Compensation Contribution Methods are:

**Contributory Method:** Under the contributory method, the amount of employer contributions due is based on a specified percentage of taxable wages. The maximum amount of taxable wages subject to the employer contribution may change from year to year.

**Reimbursement Method:** Non-profit enterprises exempt under Section 501(c)(3) of the Internal Revenue Code and political subdivisions of PA who elect the reimbursement method are required to reimburse the UC Fund for all regular benefits paid which are attributable to service with the enterprise. Non-profit enterprises must pay for one-half of any extended benefits, while political subdivisions must pay the full amount of any extended benefits.

An enterprise will be assigned the contributory method of payment unless they file an election for reimbursement coverage with the PA Department of Labor & Industry.

**UC Employee Withholding Contributions:** Enterprises are required to report gross wages paid to employees, regardless of the method used to finance UC costs (contributory or reimbursement). Enterprises may be required to withhold and remit employee contributions according to Section 301.4(a) of the PAUC Law. The amount of employee contributions due is based on a specified percentage of gross wages. Employee contributions are not credited to an enterprise's reserve account balance, nor are they considered to be contributions for federal certification purposes under the Federal Unemployment Tax Act.

Payments for UC should be made payable to the PA Unemployment Compensation Fund.

Additional information is available by contacting the nearest Labor & Industry Field Accounting Service Office.

## SECTION 13 – GOVERNMENT FORM OF ORGANIZATION

Complete this section if the enterprise is a political subdivision of the Commonwealth of PA, or if the enterprise exercises political authority as a Government organization.

1. Check the appropriate box to describe the enterprise.

2. Check the appropriate box to further describe the type of government.

3. If the enterprise is a Domestic/USA form of government, check the appropriate box.

If an enterprise is a political subdivision of the Commonwealth of PA and is also subject to the contribution provisions of the PA Unemployment Compensation (UC) Law, it has the option to elect to finance UC costs under the reimbursement method in lieu of the contributory method. A state government organization will be assigned the reimbursement method.

See page 22 of the instructions for further explanations regarding contributory and reimbursement methods of making payments to the Unemployment Compensation Fund.

22

## SECTION 14 – PREDECESSOR/SUCCESSOR INFORMATION

Complete this section if the registering enterprise is succeeding a predecessor (prior owner) in whole or in part. For assistance in completing Sections 14, 15 and 16, contact the nearest Labor & Industry Field Accounting Service Office.

**Predecessor:** An enterprise that transfers all or part of its organization, trade or business to another enterprise.

**Successor:** An enterprise that acquires by transfer all or part of the organization, trade or business from another enterprise.

The registering enterprise may apply for the Unemployment Compensation (UC) experience record and reserve account balance of the predecessor by completing Section 15, Application for PA UC Experience Record & Reserve Account Balance of Predecessor.

The Department of Labor & Industry may determine that a transfer of experience from a predecessor to the registering enterprise will be mandatory provided there is common ownership or control, either directly or indirectly between the predecessor and the registering enterprise.

1-5. Provide predecessor information as requested on the form.

6. Check the appropriate box to indicate how the predecessor's business operation was acquired.

   **Acquisition of an Existing Enterprise:** Occurs when operations are continued by a new owner; for example, a purchase of all or part of the enterprise.

   **Change in Legal Structure:** Occurs when the form of organization changes; for example, when a sole proprietorship incorporates, or forms a partnership.

   **Consolidation:** Occurs when a new corporation is formed by combining two or more corporations which then cease to exist.

   **Gift:** Occurs when the title to the property is transferred without consideration.

   **Merger:** Occurs when one corporation is absorbed by another. One corporation preserves its original charter or identity and continues to exist and the other corporate existence terminates.

   **IRC Section 338 Election:** Occurs when a stock purchase is treated as an asset purchase under the Internal Revenue Code Section 338.

7. Enter the date the business operation was acquired.

8. Enter the percentage of the predecessor's total business operation acquired. Total business operation is defined as all activities reportable under a single federal Employer Identification Number (EIN) including any activities occurring outside of PA.

9. Enter the percentage of the predecessor's PA business operation acquired. If less than 100 percent, provide the additional information as requested on the form.

10. Describe the PA business activity(ies) that the registering enterprise acquired from the predecessor.

11. Check the appropriate box(es) to indicate the type(s) of assets acquired from the predecessor.

12. Enter the date the predecessor last paid wages in PA, if applicable.

13. Enter the date the predecessor ceased operations in PA, if applicable. If operations have not ceased, describe the predecessor's ongoing business activity in PA.

14. Check the appropriate box(es). If "Yes", provide the information requested on the form. Attach additional sheets if necessary.

## SECTION 15 – APPLICATION FOR PA UC EXPERIENCE RECORD & RESERVE ACCOUNT BALANCE OF PREDECESSOR

If the registering enterprise is continuing essentially the same business activity as the predecessor, the registering enterprise may apply for a transfer in whole or in part of the predecessor's Unemployment Compensation (UC) experience record and reserve account balance, provided that:

● The registering enterprise is continuing essentially the same business activity as the predecessor; *and*

● The registering enterprise's risk of unemployment is related to the employment experience of the predecessor based upon the following factors:

   ● Nature of the business activity of each enterprise

   ● Number of individuals employed by each enterprise

   ● Wages paid to the employees by each enterprise.

To determine if it is advantageous to apply for a predecessor's UC experience record and reserve account balance, the registering enterprise should compare the predecessor's rate for the year the transfer occurred to the applicable newly liable rate. The registering enterprise must also consider if a transfer of the predecessor's experience record and reserve account balance and any potential benefit charges attributable to the predecessor and/or the registering enterprise would have an adverse effect on future years rate calculations.

The basic contribution rate for a newly liable non-construction employer is 3.5 percent (.0350). The basic contribution rate for newly liable employers involved in the performance of a contract or subcontract for the construction of new roads, bridges, highways, buildings, factories, housing developments, or other construction projects is 9.7 percent (.0970).

For any given calendar year, newly liable contribution rates are subject to a positive or negative surcharge according to Sections 301.5 and 301.7 of the PA UC Law.

To be considered timely, an Application for the Transfer of the Experience Record & Reserve Account Balance of a Predecessor must be filed prior to the end of the calendar year immediately following the year in which the transfer occurred.

1-2. Complete only to apply for the predecessor's experience record and reserve account balance. The authorized signature should be that of the owner, general partner, or officer of the predecessor and the registering enterprise. Attach Power of Attorney document, if applicable. If the predecessor's signature is unavailable, contact the nearest Labor & Industry Field Accounting Service Office for additional information.

## SECTION 16 – UNEMPLOYMENT COMPENSATION PARTIAL TRANSFER INFORMATION

Complete this section if the registering enterprise acquired only part of the predecessor's PA business operation and is making application for the transfer of a portion of the predecessor's experience record and reserve account balance.

Contact the nearest Labor & Industry Field Accounting Service Office for Replacement UC-2A for Partial Transfer (Form UC-252) or for more information on the Unemployment Compensation (UC) taxable wage base for a specific year. Refer to page 27 for a list of offices.

If the Department of Labor & Industry determines that a transfer of experience is mandatory, the registering enterprise will be required to complete this section and Form UC-252.

1. Enter the number of employees who worked in the part of the predecessor's PA business operation that was transferred (acquired).

2. Enter the exact date wages were first paid in the part of the predecessor's PA business operation that was transferred. This date must include any wages paid by known pre-predecessors; that is, any previous owners of the part transferred who had transferred their experience and reserve account balance to any successors, the last of which would be the current predecessor.

23

3. Identify the year(s) and calendar quarters in which contributions were payable to the PA UC Fund for **taxable wages** applicable to the part of the predecessor's PA business operation that was transferred. Include any quarters applicable to known pre-predecessors.

4. Identify the year(s) and calendar quarters in which contributions were payable to the PA UC Fund for **taxable wages** applicable to any part of the predecessor's PA business operation that was retained. Include any quarters applicable to known pre-predecessors.

5. For the three calendar year period prior to the year of transfer (5a) or for a lesser period (5b) from the date wages were first paid to the actual date of transfer (acquisition), enter the total amount of **taxable wages** applicable to the part of the predecessor's PA business operation that was transferred.

6. Enter the total amount of **taxable wages** applicable to the predecessor's entire PA business operation for the period that directly corresponds to the same period in item 5a or 5b.

7. Enter the total amount of **taxable wages** applicable to the predecessor's entire PA business operation for the period from the beginning of the quarter the transfer occurred to the actual date of transfer.

### SECTION 17 – MULTIPLE ESTABLISHMENT INFORMATION

When an enterprise has more than one establishment conducting business in PA or employing PA residents, Section 17, Parts 1 through 4 must be completed. Photocopy this section as necessary.

### PART 1 - ESTABLISHMENT INFORMATION

1. **Establishment Name:** Enter the name by which this establishment is known to the public; for example, the name on the front of the store.

2. **Date of First Operations:** Enter the first date this establishment conducted any activity in PA or employed PA residents. This includes start-up operations prior to opening for business.

3. **Telephone Number:** Enter the telephone number for this establishment.

4. **Street Address:** Enter the physical location of this establishment. **A post office box is not acceptable.**

5. **School District:** Enter the school district where this establishment is located. If not a PA school district enter "N/A".

6. **Municipality:** Enter the municipality (borough, city, town or township) where this establishment is located. The municipality may be different from the city/town used for postal delivery. If not a PA municipality, enter "N/A".

### PART 2 - ESTABLISHMENT BUSINESS ACTIVITY INFORMATION

Refer to the instructions for Establishment Business Activity Information (Section 7).

### PART 3 - ESTABLISHMENT SALES INFORMATION

Refer to the instructions for Establishment Sales Information (Section 8).

### PART 4a & b - ESTABLISHMENT EMPLOYMENT INFORMATION

Refer to the instructions for Establishment Employment Information (Section 9).

### SECTION 6A – ADDITIONAL OWNERS. PARTNERS. SHAREHOLDERS OFFICERS, RESPONSIBLE PARTY INFORMATION

Refer to the instructions for Owners, Partners, Shareholders, Officers and Responsible Party Information (Section 6).

### SECTION 18 – SALES USE AND HOTEL OCCUPANCY TAX LICENSE PUBLIC TRANSPORTATION ASSISTANCE TAX LICENSE. VEHICLE RENTAL TAX. TRANSIENT VENDOR CERTIFICATE OR PROMOTER LICENSE

### PART 1 - SALES USE AND HOTEL OCCUPANCY TAX, PUBLIC TRANSPORTATION ASSISTANCE TAX OR VEHICLE RENTAL TAX

Complete Part 1 to apply for a Sales and Use Tax License and/or a Public Transportation Assistance Tax License which will authorize the enterprise to:

● Collect State and Local **Sales Tax** on taxable sales made within PA. Local Sales and Use Tax is collected in those counties where required by statute.

● Remit State and Local **Use Tax** incurred on property or services used within Pennsylvania where no Sales Tax has been paid to a vendor.

● Collect taxes and fees on leases of motor vehicles, sales of new tires and rentals of motor vehicles.

### PART 2 - TRANSIENT VENDOR CERTIFICATE

Complete Parts 1 and 2 to apply for a Transient Vendor Certificate. The certificate will authorize the enterprise to collect and remit Sales Tax on taxable sales made within PA.

**A Transient Vendor Certificate is needed if the enterprise:**

● Brings into PA, by automobile, truck or other means of transportation, or purchases in PA, tangible personal property that is subject to Sales Tax, or comes into PA to perform services that are subject to Sales Tax.

● Offers or intends to offer tangible personal property for retail sale in PA.

● Does not maintain an established office, distribution house, sales house, warehouse, service enterprise or residence where business is conducted in PA.

The term "transient vendor" does not include an enterprise that does one of the following:

● Delivers tangible personal property solicited or placed by mail or telephone order.

● Makes handcrafted items for sale at special events (e.g. fairs, carnivals, festivals, art and craft shows, and other celebrations within Pennsylvania).

If the applicant is not associated with a PA licensed promoter for each show, a $500 security deposit must be submitted with this form. The security deposit may be in the form of check, letter of credit or surety bond. Checks should be made payable to **PA Department of Revenue.**

**Show** is any event that involves the display or exhibition of any tangible personal property or services for sale. It may include, but is not limited to, a flea market, antique show, coin show, stamp show, comic book show, hobby show, automobile show, fair, or any similar show, if held regularly or temporarily, where more than one vendor displays for sale or sells tangible personal property or services subject to Sales Tax.

24

If the applicant participates once or twice a year in promoter-sponsored events in PA, a temporary Sales Tax License may be obtained from the district office in the county where the event is held. If retail sales or services in PA will occur more than twice a year, a permanent Sales Tax License should be obtained.

The Transient Vendor Certificate is renewable on a yearly basis beginning February 1 of each year.

## PART 3 - PROMOTER LICENSE

Complete Parts 1 and 3 to apply for a Promoter License. A Promoter is a person or enterprise who either directly or indirectly rents, leases, or otherwise operates or grants permission to any person to use space at a show for the display for sale or for the sale of tangible personal property or services subject to tax.

The Promoter 's License is renewable on a yearly basis beginning February 1 of each year.

This application must be completed and returned to the Department of Revenue at least 30 days prior to the opening of the first show.

## PART 4 - LOCATION OF SALES TAX COLLECTED

Complete Part 4 to identify the Pennsylvania financial institution and account number or other location where collected sales tax funds will be held until those funds are remitted to the Department of Revenue.

## SECTION 19 – CIGARETTE DEALER'S LICENSE

### PART 1 - LICENSE TYPE

Complete Section 19, Part 1 to apply for a Cigarette Dealer's License. A separate license must be obtained for each location where retail sale of cigarettes, cigarette wholesale activity, or cigarette tax stamping will occur.

A Cigarette Dealer's License is **not** transferable.

If the enterprise is applying for a Cigarette Vending Machine License, a list of machine locations must be attached to the registration form. Provide the name of the establishment, street address, city and county where each machine is located.

Note: The Department of Revenue will allow the purchase of extra vending machine decals for machines to be placed at new locations (up to 10 percent or 10 extra decals, whichever is greater) without submitting actual locations. Within 30 days, licensees must advise the Department of the date an additional vending machine decal is affixed and the location of the machine.

All Cigarette Dealer's Licenses expire on the last day of February and are renewable on a yearly basis. License fees are not prorated.

### PART 2 - CIGARETTE WHOLESALER

Complete Parts 1 and 2 to apply for a Cigarette Wholesaler License.

All applicants for a Cigarette Wholesaler or Cigarette Stamping Agent License will be subject to a criminal background investigation prior to the issuance of a license. This investigation will be completed within 60 days of receipt of the completed application.

### PART 3 - CIGARETTE STAMPING AGENT

Complete Parts 1, 2 and 3 to apply for a Cigarette Stamping Agent License.

All applicants for a Cigarette Stamping Agent License must submit written commitments from at least two cigarette manufacturers whose aggregate share is at least 40 percent of the Commonwealth's cigarette market.

## SECTION 20 – SMALL GAMES OF CHANCE LICENSE/CERTIFICATE

Complete Parts 1, 2 and 3 to apply for a Distributor License .

Complete Parts 1 and 3 to apply for a Manufacturer Registration Certificate.

Questions may be directed to (717) 787-8275.

### PART 1 - DISTRIBUTOR AND/OR MANUFACTURER

The following items must be enclosed with the registration form.

● Corporations must submit a copy of the Certificate of Incorporation, Articles of Incorporation, Certificate of Authority (non-PA corporations), By-laws or Constitution. If doing business using a fictitious name, submit a copy of the fictitious name registration.

● The logo(s) used by the Manufacturer.

● The fee for the Distributor License or the Manufacturer Registration Certificate as listed on the registration form.

● A $10 nonrefundable background investigation fee for each owner, partner, officer, director and shareholder controlling 10 percent or more of outstanding stock.

A Distributor License expires on April 30 and is renewable on a yearly basis.

A Manufacturer Registration Certificate expires on March 31 and is renewable on a yearly basis.

### PART 2 - DISTRIBUTOR

Complete this section to apply for a Distributor License only.

### PART 3 - SMALL GAMES OF CHANCE CERTIFICATION

Certification must be **signed and notarized** by all Small Games of Chance applicants.

## SECTION 21 – MOTOR CARRIER REGISTRATION & DECAL/MOTOR FUELS LICENSE & PERMIT

All enterprises applying for a Motor Carrier Road Tax (MCRT)/ International Fuel Tax Agreement (IFTA) Decal must complete Part 1.

Authorized signature in Section 4 indicates applicant agrees to comply with the reporting, payment, record keeping, and license display requirements as specified in MCRT and/or the IFTA.

### PART 1 - VEHICLE OPERATIONS

A qualified motor vehicle is a motor vehicle used, designed or maintained for the transportation of persons or property which has: (a) two axles and a gross or registered gross weight greater than 26,000 pounds, (b) three axles or more regardless of weight, or (c) a combination weight greater than 26,000 pounds.

#### MOTOR CARRIER ROAD TAX

**Common Carrier:** Any motor carrier which holds itself out of the general public to engage in the transportation by motor vehicle of passengers or property for compensation.

**Contract Carrier:** Any motor carrier transporting persons or property for compensation or hire under contract to a particular person, firm or corporation.

**For-Hire Carrier:** An enterprise providing transportation of passengers or property by motor vehicle using the public utility commission rights of another carrier.

**Private Carrier:** A person, firm, or corporation which utilizes its own trucks to transport its own freight.

**Truck:** Every motor vehicle designed, used or maintained primarily for the transportation of property.

**Truck Tractor:** A motor vehicle designed and used primarily for drawing other vehicles but so constructed as to carry a load other than a part of the weight of the vehicle and load so drawn.

**Combination:** A power unit used in combination with trailers and semi-trailers.

**Exemptions Include:** Vehicles operated by the U.S. Government, the Commonwealth of PA and its political subdivisions, other states publicly-owned vehicles, volunteer fire, rescue and ambulance associations, farm vehicle, implements of husbandry, tow truck (not roll-backs), special mobile equipment, unladen vehicle being operated with a repair facility certificate from a PA repair facility, carriers who obtain permission from the PA State Police for emergency repair and carriers operating on dealer or similar tags and operating vehicle incidental to their sale, demonstration or repossession.

**IFTA Decals:** Request IFTA Decals for PA-qualified vehicles that travel in and outside of PA. An IFTA License must be carried in each vehicle and the vehicle must display decals on both sides of the cab.

Carriers Purchasing IFTA credentials must file IFTA Quarterly Fuel Tax reports.

**Non-IFTA Decals:** For PA-qualified vehicles that travel exclusively in PA, request non-IFTA Decals. Carriers from non-IFTA states operating qualified motor vehicles in PA must likewise display non-IFTA Decals. A Road Tax Cab Card must be carried in each vehicle and the vehicle must display decals on both sides of the cab. As of January 1, 1998, the only U.S. and Canadian jurisdictions not participating in IFTA are: Alaska, Hawaii, District of Columbia, Northwest Territories and the Yukon Territory.

Carriers purchasing Non-IFTA credentials must maintain operational records; however, quarterly Motor Carrier Road Tax reports are **not required.**

If a carrier is based in a non-IFTA jurisdiction and intends to operate qualified motor vehicles based in that state and travel in PA, use this application to order non-IFTA Decals.

### ALL DECALS ARE VALID FOR ONE CALENDAR YEAR.

Make checks or money orders payable to the PA Department of Revenue. Allow two or three weeks for delivery of the decals requested. **Do not send cash.** If a decal is purchased, quarterly tax reports will be required.

For IFTA, decal and tax information, contact the PA Department of Revenue, Bureau of Motor Fuel Taxes at (1-800) 482-IFTA (4382) or (717) 787-5355, TDD# (717) 772-2252 (hearing impaired only).

**PART 2 - FUELS**

Before the issuance of a Liquid Fuels and Fuel Tax Permit, an on-site inspection contact will be made by the PA Department of Revenue, Enforcement Division.

A surety bond is required for Liquid Fuels and Fuel Tax. The enterprise will be contacted by the Bureau of Motor Fuel Taxes, Enforcement Division regarding the surety bond requirements.

**SECTION 22** – SALES TAX EXEMPT STATUS FOR CHARITABLE AND RELIGIOUS ORGANIZATIONS

Charitable, religious, non-profit educational institutions, and volunteer fire companies may be eligible for Sales Tax exempt status.

Act 55 of 1997, known as the Institutions of Purely Public Charity Act, changes the procedure and filing requirements for organizations seeking to qualify or renew Sales and Use Tax exemption status.

To apply, a separate application (REV-72) must be completed. See Section 22, page 17 for more details. In addition to completing the REV-72, the following documents are required and must be attached to the application:

- A copy of the Articles of Incorporation, By-laws, Constitution, or other governing legal document specifically including:

  * Aims and purpose of the institution;

  * A provision that expressly prohibits the use of any surplus funds for private inurement to any person in the event of a sale or dissolution of the institution.

- The most current financial statement (new organizations may substitute a proposed budget) including:

  * All income and expenses listed by source and category:

  * A list of the beneficiaries (individual, general public, other organizations, etc.) of the institution's activities and how those beneficiaries are selected; and

  * A list of sales activities (gift shop, bookstore, social club, etc.) used to raise funds. The institution must apply for a Sales Tax License if engaging in sales activities.

- If the institution has tax exempt status with the Internal Revenue Service, a copy of the approval letter must be submitted.

- If the institution has voluntary agreements with political subdivisions, enclose copy of same.

- If the institution files Form 990, provide a copy of the most recently completed form.

The location of these offices may change.
To verify the location of an office, please call Monday through Friday 8:30 AM to 5:00 PM (EST) at the number listed for that office.

## REVENUE DISTRICT OFFICES

**Altoona**
(Blair, Centre, Fulton,
Huntingdon, and Mifflin)
Cricket Field Plaza
615 Howard Avenue
Altoona, PA 16601-4867
(814) 946-7310

**Bethlehem**
(Lehigh and Northampton)
44 East Broad Street
Bethlehem, PA 18018-5998
(610) 861-2000

**Bradford**
(Cameron, Elk, Forest,
McKean, Potter, and Warren)
Second Floor
86 Boylston Street
Bradford, PA 16701-2011
(814) 368-7113

**Doylestown**
(Bucks)
Suite 104
600 Louis Drive
Warminster, PA 18974-2847
(215) 443-2990

**Erie**
(Erie and Crawford)
448 West 11th Street
Erie, PA 16501-1501
(814) 871-4491

**Greensburg**
(Westmoreland)
Second Floor
15 West Third Street
Greensburg, PA 15601-3003
(724) 832-5386

**Harrisburg**
(Cumberland, Dauphin, and Perry)
Lobby
Strawberry Square
Harrisburg, PA 17128-0101
(717) 783-1405

**Indiana**
(Armstrong, Clarion, Indiana,
and Jefferson)
Canterbury Office Suites
2263 Philadelphia Street
Indiana, PA 15701-1595
(724) 357-7600

**Johnstown**
(Bedford, Cambria, Clearfield, and
Somerset)
Third Floor
345 Main Street
Johnstown, PA 15901-1614
(814) 533-2495

**Lancaster**
(Lancaster and Lebanon)
Suite 201
315 West James Street
Lancaster, PA 17603-2911
(717) 299-7581

**New Castle**
(Beaver, Butler, Lawrence,
Mercer, and Venango)
Room 201
101 South Mercer Street
New Castle, PA 16101-3837
(724) 656-3203

**Newtown Square**
(Chester and Delaware)
Suite 1
90 South Newtown Street Road
(Route 252)
Newtown Square, PA 19073-4090
(610) 353-4051

**Norristown**
(Montgomery)
Second Floor
Stoney Creek Office Center
151 West Marshall Street
Norristown, PA 19401-4739
(610) 270-1780

**Philadelphia**
(Philadelphia)
Room 201
State Office Building
1400 West Spring Garden Street
Philadelphia, PA 19130-4088
(215) 560-2056

**Pittsburgh**
(Allegheny)
Suite 104
State Office Building
300 Liberty Avenue
Pittsburgh, PA 15222-1210
(412) 565-7540

**Pottsville**
(Carbon and Schuylkill)
115 South Centre Street
Pottsville, PA 17901-3047
(570) 621-3175

**Reading**
(Berks)
Room 239
625 Cherry Street
Reading, PA 19602-1186
(610) 378-4401

**Scranton**
(Lackawanna, Monroe, Pike,
Susquehanna, and Wayne)
Room 305
Samters Building
101 Penn Avenue
Scranton, PA 18503-1970
(570) 963-4585

**Sunbury**
(Columbia, Juniata, Montour,
Northumberland, Snyder, and Union)
330 Market Street
Sunbury, PA 17801-3404
(570) 988-5520

**Washington**
(Fayette, Greene, and
Washington)
Room 204
Landmark Building
75 East Maiden Street
Washington, PA 15301-4963
(724) 223-4550

**Wilkes-Barre**
(Luzerne and Wyoming)
Suite 201
Thomas C. Thomas Building
100 East Union Street
Wilkes-Barre, PA 18701-3200
(570) 826-2466

**Williamsport**
(Bradford, Clinton, Lycoming,
Sullivan, and Tioga)
440 Little League Blvd.
Williamsport, PA 17701-5055
(570) 327-3475

**York**
(Adams, Franklin, and York)
140 North Duke Street
York, PA 17401-1110
(717) 845-6661

## LABOR & INDUSTRY FIELD ACCOUNTING SERVICE OFFICES
### LOCATIONS AND COUNTIES SERVED

**Allentown**
1 S. Second St. Ste. 400 — Lehigh, Northampton
Allentown, PA 18102-4901
(610) 821-6559

**Altoona**
1101 Green Ave. Rm. 169 — Bedford, Blair, Huntingdon
Altoona, PA 16601-3474
(814) 946-6991

**Beaver Falls**
2103 Ninth Ave. — Beaver, Lawrence
Beaver Falls, PA 15010-3957
(724) 846-8803

**Bradford**
42 Davis St. — Forest, McKean, Warren
Bradford, PA 16701-2016
(814) 362-6992

**Butler**
227 W. Cunningham St. — Armstrong, Butler
P.O. Box 951
Butler, PA 16003-0951
(724) 284-8170

**Carlisle**
1 Alexandra Ct. — Cumberland
Carlisle, PA 17013-7667
(717) 249-8211

**Chambersburg**
600 Norland Ave. — Franklin, Fulton
P.O. Box 190
Chambersburg, PA 17201-0190
(717) 264-7192

**Chester**
2nd Fl. Ste. D — Delaware
701 Crosby St.
Chester, PA 19013-6089
(610) 447-3290

**Clearfield**
211 E. Locust St. — Cameron, Clearfield, Elk, Jefferson
Clearfield, PA 16830-2490
(814) 765-0572

**Doylestown**
70 W. Oakland Ave. — Bucks
Doylestown, PA 18901-4299
(215) 345-7104

**Erie**
1316 State St. — Crawford, Erie
Erie, PA 16501-1978
(814) 871-4381

**Greensburg**
593 Sells Ln. — Westmoreland
Greensburg, PA 15601-4496
(724) 832-5275

**Harrisburg**
1171 S. Cameron St. Rm. 311 — Dauphin, Juniata, Lebanon, Mifflin, Perry
Harrisburg, PA 17104-2591
(717) 787-1700

**Johnstown**
200 Lincoln St. — Cambria, Indiana, Somerset
Johnstown, PA 15901-1592
(814) 533-2371

**Lancaster**
70 W. Walnut St. — Lancaster
P.O. Box 1563
Lancaster, PA 17608-1563
(717) 299-7606

**Malvern**
Century Plz. 2nd Fl. — Chester
72 Lancaster Ave.
Malvern, PA 19355-2160
(610) 647-3799

**Mercer**
114 W. South St. — Clarion, Mercer, Venango
Mercer, PA 16137-1549
(724) 983-5709

**Norristown East/West**
1931 New Hope St. — Montgomery
Norristown, PA 19401-3143
(610) 270-1316 - East
(610) 270-3450 - West

**Philadelphia**
444 N. Third St. 3rd Fl. — Philadelphia
Philadelphia, PA 19123-4190
(215) 560-3136/1828

**Pittsburgh**
933 Penn Ave. 2nd Fl. — Allegheny
Pittsburgh, PA 15222-3815
(412) 565-2400

**Reading**
625 Cherry St. Rm. 250 — Berks
Reading, PA 19602-1184
(610) 378-4395

**Scranton**
1 Westside Dr. — Bradford, Lackawanna, Susquehanna, Wayne, Wyoming
Carbondale, PA 18407-2294
(717) 963-4686

**State College**
456 E. Beaver Ave. Ste. 104 — Centre
State College, PA 16801-5600
(814) 863-1828

**Sunbury**
535 Chestnut St. — Columbia, Montour, Northumberland, Schuylkill, Snyder, Union
Sunbury, PA 17801-2865
(717) 988-5542

**Tannersville**
Rt. 611 Merchants Plz. — Monroe, Pike
P.O. Box 789
Tannersville, PA 18372-0789
(717) 620-2870

**Uniontown**
32 Iowa St. — Fayette, Greene
Uniontown, PA 15401-3513
(724) 439-7230

**Washington**
75 E. Maiden St. Rm. 203 — Washington
Washington, PA 15301-4907
(724) 223-4530

**Wilkes-Barre**
32 E. Union St. 2nd Fl. — Carbon, Luzerne, Sullivan
Wilkes-Barre, PA 18711-0651
(717) 826-2426

**Williamsport**
208 W. Third St. Ste. 301 — Clinton, Lycoming, Potter, Tioga
Williamsport, PA 17701-6477
(717) 327-3525

**York**
841 Vogelsong Rd. — Adams, York
P.O. Box 14008
York, PA 17404-0868
(717) 767-7620

**Out-of-State**
L & I Bldg. Rm. 700 — Those enterprises not having a PA location.
Seventh & Forster Sts.
Harrisburg, PA 17121-0001
(717) 787-5939

For the hearing impaired only
(717) 783-3545

27

# Out-of-State Taxes 18

## State Sales Taxes

In 1992, the United States Supreme Court struck a blow for the rights of small businesses by ruling that state tax authorities cannot force them to collect sales taxes on interstate mail orders (*Quill Corporation v. North Dakota*).

Unfortunately, the court left open the possibility that Congress could allow interstate taxation of mail order sales, and since then several bills have been introduced which would do so. One, introduced by Arkansas senator Dale Bumpers was given the Orwellian "newspeak" title, *The Consumer and Main Street Protection Act*.

At present, companies are only required to collect sales taxes for states in which they *do business*. Exactly what business is enough to trigger taxation is a legal question and some states try to define it as broadly as possible.

If you have an office in a state, you are doing business there and any goods shipped to consumers in that state are subject to sales taxes. If you have a full time employee working in the state most of the year, many states will consider you doing business there. In some states, attending a two-day trade show is enough business to trigger taxation for the entire year for every order shipped to the state. One loophole that often works is to be represented at shows by persons who are not your employees.

Because the laws are different in each state, you will have to do some research on a state-by-state basis to find out how much business you can do in a state without being subject to their taxation. You can request a state's rules from its department of revenue, but keep in mind that what a department of revenue wants the law to be is not always what the courts will rule that it is.

# Business Taxes

Even worse than being subject to a state's sales taxes is to be subject to their income or other business taxes. For example, California charges every company doing business in the state a minimum $800 a year fee and charges income tax on a portion of the company's worldwide income. Doing a small amount of business in the state is clearly not worth getting mired in California taxation.

For this reason, some trade shows have been moved from the state and this has resulted in a review of the tax policies and some "safe-harbor" guidelines to advise companies on what they can do without becoming subject to taxation.

Write to the department of revenue of any state with which you have business contacts to see what might trigger your taxation.

# Internet Taxes

State revenue departments are drooling at the prospect of taxing commerce on the internet. Theories have already been proposed that web sites available to state residents mean a company is doing business in a state.

Fortunately, Congress has passed a moratorium on taxation of the internet. This will be extended, hopefully, and will give us a new tax-free world, but don't count on it. A government has never let a new source of revenue go untapped. It would take a tremendous outcry to keep the internet tax-free. Keep an eye out for any news stories on proposals to tax the internet and petition your representatives against them.

## CANADIAN TAXES

Apparently oblivious to the logic of the U.S. Supreme Court, the Canadian government expects American companies, which sell goods by mail order to Canadians, to collect taxes for them and file returns with Revenue Canada, their tax department.

Those that receive an occasional unsolicited order are not expected to register and Canadian customers, who order things from the U.S., pay the tax plus a $5 fee upon receipt of the goods. But companies that solicit Canadian orders are expected to be registered if their worldwide income is $30,000 or more per year. In some cases, a company may be required to post a bond and to pay for the cost of Canadian auditors visiting its premises and auditing its books! For these reasons, you may notice that some companies decline to accept orders from Canada. So much for the benefits of NAFTA.

# THE END... AND THE BEGINNING 19

If you have read through this whole book, you know more about the rules and laws for operating a Pennsylvania business than most people in business today. But after learning about all the governmental regulations, you may become discouraged. You are probably wondering how you can keep track of all the laws and how you will have any time left to make money after complying with the laws. But its not that bad. People are starting businesses every day and they are making money, lots of money. At least we don't have laws like some countries that have marginal tax rates as high as 105%!

The regulations that exist right now are enough to strangle some businesses. The laws and regulations and especially the registration fees can seem confusing, conflicting, and outrageous. At times, the laws and regulations can seem down-right senseless. Remember this: prior to reading this book, you faced an uphill struggle against an unknown, sometimes adversarial bureaucracy, but now you have all the knowledge to proceed with your dream of starting your own business and succeeding! There is a system in place that you must go through to start your business and two things can happen: the system can work you or *you can work the system* and you can make it work for you! By reading this book, there is no reason why you can't make the system work for you, so—*go for it!* No doubt, you will encounter some problems along the way even though you are empowered with the knowledge in this book. If you feel you are treated unfairly or differently or do not understand an explanation given to you—speak up! You are entitled to know all the answers to all your questions and you are entitled to be treated with respect and dignity. If you are ever dissatisfied, seek help "up the ladder" and contact your legislator! Most legislators have knowledgeable staffs that can assist you in any registration or certification requirement that you must fulfill. Your taxes and your vote support your legislator, so do not be afraid to make use of their services.

In a pure democracy, fifty-one percent of the voters can decide that all left-handed people must wear green shirts and that everyone must go to church three days a week. It is the Bill of Rights in our Constitution that protects us from the tyrannical whims of the majority.

In America today, there are no laws regarding left-handed people or going to church, but there are laws controlling minute aspects of our personal and business lives. Does a majority have the right to decide what hours you can work, what you can sell, or where you can sell it? You must decide for yourself and act accordingly.

One way to avoid problems with the government is to keep a low profile and avoid open confrontation. For a lawyer, it can be fun going to appeals court over an unfair parking ticket or making a federal case out of a $25 fine. But for most people the expenses of a fight with the government are unbearable. If you start a mass protest against the IRS or OSHA, they will have to make an example of you so that no one else gets any ideas.

The important thing is that you know the laws and the penalties for violations before making your decision. Knowing the laws will also allow you to use the loopholes in the laws to avoid violations.

Congratulations on deciding to start a business in Pennsylvania! I hope you get rich in record time. If you have any unusual experiences along the way, drop us a line at the following address. The information may be useful for a future book.

Sphinx Publishing
P.O. Box 4410
Naperville, Illinois 60567-4410

# FOR FURTHER READING

The following books will provide valuable information to new businesses:

For inspiration to give you the drive to succeed:

> Karbo, Joe. *The Lazy Man's Way to Riches*

> Schwartz, David J. *The Magic of Thinking Big*

> Hill, Napoleon. *Think and Grow Rich*

For hints on how to be successful:

> Ringer, Robert J. *Looking Out for #1*

> Ringer, Robert J. *Million Dollar Habits*

> Ringer, Robert J. *Winning Through Intimidation*

For advice on bookkeeping and organization:

> Kamoroff, Bernard. *Small Time Operator*

For good investment advice:

> Tobias, Andrew. *The Only Other Investment Guide You'll Ever Need*

For government bureaucracy information:

> Simon, William E. *A Time For Truth*

For advice on how to avoid governmental problems:

Browne, Harry. *How I Found Freedom in an Unfree World*

Sourcebooks, Inc. publishes the following self-help law books (formerly from Sphinx Publishing) which may be helpful to your business. They are available from your local bookstore or by mail from the publisher.

Warda, Mark. *How to Negotiate Real Estate Contracts*

Warda, Mark. *How to Negotiate Real Estate Leases*

Warda, Mark. *How to Register Your Own Copyright*

Warda, Mark. *How to Register Your Own Trademark*

Herskowitz, Suzan. *Legal Research Made Easy*

Ray, James C. *The Most Valuable Business Forms You'll Ever Need*

Ray, James C. *The Most Valuable Corporate Forms You'll Ever Need*

Bonamer, Charles S. *Successful Real Estate Brokerage Management*

# Appendix: Tax Timetable & Ready-to-use Forms

The following forms may be photocopied or removed from this book and used immediately. Some of the tax forms explained in this book are not included here because you should use original returns provided by the IRS (940, 941) or the Pennsylvania Department of Revenue (quarterly unemployment compensation form).

These forms are included on the following pages:

# Tax Timetable

| | Pennsylvania | | | Federal | | | |
|---|---|---|---|---|---|---|---|
| | Sales | Unemployment | Corp. Income | Est. Payment | Annual Return | Form 941* | Misc. |
| JAN. | 20th | 6th | 15th | 15th | | 31st | 31st 940 W-2 508 1099 |
| FEB. | 20th | 3rd | 15th | | | | |
| MAR. | 20th | 3rd | 15th | | 15th Corp. & Partnership | | |
| APR. | 20th | 5th | 15th | 15th | 15th Personal | 30th | 30th 508 |
| MAY | 20th | 5th | 15th | | | | |
| JUN. | 20th | 3rd | 15th | 15th | | | |
| JUL. | 20th | 6th | 15th | | | 31st | 31st 508 |
| AUG. | 20th | 4th | 15th | | | | |
| SEPT. | 20th | 3rd | 15th | 15th | | | |
| OCT. | 20th | 5th | 15th | | | 31st | 31st 508 |
| NOV. | 20th | 3rd | 15th | | | | |
| DEC. | 20th | 3rd | 15th | | | | |

*In addition to form 941, deposits must be made regularly if withholding exceeds $500 in any month

_____
**Secretary of the Commonwealth**

# APPLICATION FOR REGISTRATION OF FICTITIOUS NAME
DCB:54-311 (Rev 90)

In compliance with the requirements of 54 Pa.C.S. § 311 (relating to registration), the undersigned entity(ies) desiring to register a fictitious name under 54 Pa.C.S. Ch. 3 (relating to fictitious names), hereby state(s) that:

1. Then fictitious **name** is: _____

2. A brief statement of the character or nature of the business or other activity to be carried on under or through the fictitious name is:

   _____

3. The **address**, including number and street, if any, of the principal place of business of the business or other activity to be carried on under or through the fictitious name is (P.O. Box alone is **not** acceptable):

   _____

   Number and Street       City      State      Zip      County

4. The **name** and **address**, including number and street, if any, of each individual interested in the business is:

   Name      Number and Street      City      State

   _____

   _____

   _____

   _____

5. Each **entity**, other than an individual, interested in such business is (are):

   Name      Form of Organization      Organizing Jurisdiction      Principal Office Address      Pa. Registered Office, if any

   _____

   _____

6. The applicant is familiar with the provisions of 54 Pa.C.S. §332 (relating to effect of registration) and understands that filing under the Fictitious Name Act does not create any exclusive or other right in the fictitious name.

7. **(Optional):** The **name(s)** of the agent(s), if any, any one of whom is authorized to execute amendments to, withdrawals from or cancellation of this registration in behalf of all then existing parties to the registration, is (are):

   _____

IN TESTIMONY WHEREOF, the undersigned have caused this Application for Registration of Fictitious Name to be executed this _____ day of _____, 19 _____.

_____
(Individual Signature)

_____
(Individual Signature)

_____
(Name of Entity)

BY: _____

TITLE: _____

_____
(Individual Signature)

_____
(Individual Signature)

_____
(Name of Entity)

BY: _____

TITLE: _____

## COUNTER - CORPORATE CERTIFICATION & SEARCH REQUEST FORM

ENTITY NAME: _____

_____

_____

_____

_____

DOCUMENT REQUESTED:

_____ Good Standing (Subsistence) Certificate

_____ Certified Copy of Corporate Index

_____ Great Seal Certificate attesting to _____

_____

_____ Certified Copy of _____

_____ Plain Copy of _____

_____ Corporate Record Search or Plain Copy of Index

_____ Name Reservation

COMMENTS:

REQUESTOR NAME: _____

REQUESTOR ADDRESS: _____

_____

Mail this order when complete. _____

**The undersigned agrees to pay all statutory fees with respect to this request in advance.**

**SIGNATURE OF REQUESTING PARTY:** _____

_____ Will pay by check.

_____ Deduct fees from Account# _____.

Total Due: $_____

*This page intentionally left blank.*

Microfilm Number _____ Filed with the Department of State on _____

Entity Number _____

_____

**Secretary of the Commonwealth**

# APPLICATION FOR REGISTRATION OF MARK
DSCB:54-1112 (REV 90)

In compliance with the requirements of 54 Pa.C.S. §1112 (relating to application for registration), the under-signed, having adopted and used a trade mark or service mark in this Commonwealth and desiring to register such mark, hereby states that:

1. The **name** of the applicant is (if a corporation, also give jurisdiction of incorporation): _____

_____

2. The **residence, location** or **place of business** of the applicant is:

_____

Number and Street          City          State      Zip      County

3. The **name and description of the mark** is (A facsimile of the mark to be registered accompanies this application as Exhibit A and is incorporated herein by reference):

_____

_____

4. The general **class** in which such goods or services fall is (use only one of the classifications as set forth in 54 Pa.C.S. §1103 (relating to classification)):_____

5. The **goods and services** in connection with which the mark is used and the mode and manner in which the mark is used in connection with such goods or services are:

_____

6. The **date** when the mark was first used anywhere is: _____

7. The **date** when the mark was first used in this Commonwealth by the applicant or the predecessor in title of the applicant is: _____ .

8. Applicant is the owner of the mark and no other person has the right to use such mark in this Commonwealth, either in the identical form thereof or in any such near resemblance thereto as might be calculated to deceive or to be mistaken therefore.

IN TESTIMONY WHEREOF, the undersigned person has caused this Application for Registration of Mark to be executed this _____ day of _____, 19 _____ .

_____
(Name of Applicant)

BY: _____
(Signature)

TITLE: _____

223

*This page intentionally left blank.*

## U.S. Department of Justice
Immigration and Naturalization Service

OMB No. 1115-0136
### Employment Eligibility Verification

Please read instructions carefully before completing this form. The instructions must be available during completion of this form. **ANTI-DISCRIMINATION NOTICE.** It is illegal to discriminate against work eligible individuals. Employers CANNOT specify which document(s) they will accept from an employee. The refusal to hire an individual because of a future expiration date may also constitute illegal discrimination.

### Section 1. Employee Information and Verification. To be completed and signed by employee at the time employment begins

| Print Name:    Last | First | Middle Initial | Maiden Name |
|---|---|---|---|

Address (Street Name and Number) | Apt. # | Date of Birth (month/day/year)

City | State | Zip Code | Social Security #

I am aware that federal law provides for imprisonment and/or fines for false statements or use of false documents in connection with the completion of this form.

I attest, under penalty of perjury, that I am (check one of the following):
- ☐ A citizen or national of the United States
- ☐ A Lawful Permanent Resident (Alien # A_____)
- ☐ An alien authorized to work until____/____/____
  (Alien # or Admission #_____)

Employee's Signature | Date (month/day/year)

**Preparer and/or Translator Certification.** (To be completed and signed if Section 1 is prepared by a person other than the employee.) I attest, under penalty of perjury, that I have assisted in the completion of this form and that to the best of my knowledge the information is true and correct.

Preparer's/Translator's Signature | Print Name

Address (Street Name and Number, City, State, Zip Code) | Date (month/day/year)

### Section 2. Employer Review and Verification. To be completed and signed by employer. Examine one document from List A OR examine one document from List B and one from List C as listed on the reverse of this form and record the title, number and expiration date, if any, of the document(s)

| List A | OR | List B | AND | List C |
|---|---|---|---|---|

Document title: _____

Issuing authority: _____

Document #: _____

Expiration Date (if any): ___/___/___

Document #: _____

Expiration Date (if any): ___/___/___

**CERTIFICATION - I attest, under penalty of perjury, that I have examined the document(s) presented by the above-named employee, that the above-listed document(s) appear to be genuine and to relate to the employee named, that the** employee began employment on (month/day/year) ___/___/___ **and that to the best of my knowledge the employee is eligible to work in the United States.** (State employment agencies may omit the date the employee began employment).

Signature of Employer or Authorized Representative | Print Name | Title

Business or Organization Name | Address (Street Name and Number, City, State, Zip Code) | Date (month/day/year)

### Section 3. Updating and Reverification. To be completed and signed by employer

A. New Name (if applicable) | B. Date of rehire (month/day/year) (if applicable)

C. If employee's previous grant of work authorization has expired, provide the information below for the document that establishes current employment eligibility.

Document Title:_____ Document #:_____ Expiration Date (if any):___/___/___

I attest, under penalty of perjury, that to the best of my knowledge, this employee is eligible to work in the United States, and if the employee presented document(s), the document(s) I have examined appear to be genuine and to relate to the individual.

Signature of Employer or Authorized Representative | Date (month/day/year)

Form I-9 (Rev. 11-21-91) N

225

# INSTRUCTIONS
## PLEASE READ ALL INSTRUCTIONS CAREFULLY BEFORE COMPLETING THIS FORM.

**Anti-Discrimination Notice.** It is illegal to discriminate against any individual (other than an alien not authorized to work in the U.S.) in hiring, discharging, or recruiting or referring for a fee because of that individual's national origin or citizenship status. It is illegal to discriminate against work eligible individuals. Employers **CANNOT** specify which document(s) they will accept from an employee. The refusal to hire an individual because of a future expiration date may also constitute illegal discrimination.

**Section 1 - Employee.** All employees, citizens and noncitizens, hired after November 6, 1986, must complete Section 1 of this form at the time of hire, which is the actual beginning of employment. **The employer is responsible for ensuring that Section 1 is timely and properly completed.**

**Preparer/Translator Certification.** The Preparer/Translator Certification must be completed if Section 1 is prepared by a person other than the employee. A preparer/translator may be used only when the employee is unable to complete Section 1 on his/her own. However, the employee must still sign Section 1 personally.

**Section 2 - Employer.** For the purpose of completing this form, the term "employer" includes those recruiters and referrers for a fee who are agricultural associations, agricultural employers, or farm labor contractors.

Employers must complete Section 2 by examining evidence of identity and employment eligibility within three (3) business days of the date employment begins. If employees are authorized to work, but are unable to present the required document(s) within three business days, they must present a receipt for the application of the document(s) within three business days and the actual document(s) within ninety (90) days. However, if employers hire individuals for a duration of less than three business days, Section 2 must be completed at the time employment begins. **Employers must record: 1)** document title; **2)** issuing authority; **3)** document number, **4)** expiration date, if any; and **5)** the date employment begins. Employers must sign and date the certification. Employees must present original documents. Employers may, but are not required to, photocopy the document(s) presented. These photocopies may only be used for the verification process and must be retained with the I-9. **However, employers are still responsible for completing the I-9.**

**Section 3 - Updating and Reverification.** Employers must complete Section 3 when updating and/or reverifying the I-9. Employers must reverify employment eligibility of their employees on or before the expiration date recorded in Section 1. Employers **CANNOT** specify which document(s) they will accept from an employee.

- If an employee's name has changed at the time this form is being updated/ reverified, complete Block A.

- If an employee is rehired within three (3) years of the date this form was originally completed and the employee is still eligible to be employed on the same basis as previously indicated on this form (updating), complete Block B and the signature block.

- If an employee is rehired within three (3) years of the date this form was originally completed and the employee's work authorization has expired **or** if a current employee's work authorization is about to expire (reverification), complete Block B and:
  - examine any document that reflects that the employee is authorized to work in the U.S. (see List A **or** C),
  - record the document title, document number and expiration date (if any) in Block C, and
  - complete the signature block.

**Photocopying and Retaining Form I-9.** A blank I-9 may be reproduced provided both sides are copied. The Instructions must be available to all employees completing this form. Employers must retain completed I-9s for three (3) years after the date of hire **or** one (1) year after the date employment ends, whichever is later.

**For more detailed information, you may refer to the INS Handbook for Employers, (Form M-274). You may obtain the handbook at your local INS office.**

**Privacy Act Notice.** The authority for collecting this information is the Immigration Reform and Control Act of 1986, Pub. L. 99-603 (8 U.S.C. 1324a).

This information is for employers to verify the eligibility of individuals for employment to preclude the unlawful hiring, or recruiting or referring for a fee, of aliens who are not authorized to work in the United States.

This information will be used by employers as a record of their basis for determining eligibility of an employee to work in the United States. The form will be kept by the employer and made available for inspection by officials of the U.S. Immigration and Naturalization Service, the Department of Labor, and the Office of Special Counsel for Immigration Related Unfair Employment Practices.

Submission of the information required in this form is voluntary. However, an individual may not begin employment unless this form is completed since employers are subject to civil or criminal penalties if they do not comply with the Immigration Reform and Control Act of 1986.

**Reporting Burden.** We try to create forms and instructions that are accurate, can be easily understood, and which impose the least possible burden on you to provide us with information. Often this is difficult because some immigration laws are very complex. Accordingly, the reporting burden for this collection of information is computed as follows: 1) learning about this form, 5 minutes; 2) completing the form, 5 minutes; and 3) assembling and filing (recordkeeping) the form, 5 minutes, for an average of 15 minutes per response. If you have comments regarding the accuracy of this burden estimate, or suggestions for making this form simpler, you can write to both the Immigration and Naturalization Service, 425 I Street, N.W., Room 5304, Washington, D. C. 20536; and the Office of Management and Budget, Paperwork Reduction Project, OMB No. 1115-0136, Washington, D.C. 20503.

Form I-9 (Rev. 11-21-91) N

**EMPLOYERS MUST RETAIN COMPLETED I-9**
**PLEASE DO NOT MAIL COMPLETED I-9 TO INS**

# LISTS OF ACCEPTABLE DOCUMENTS

| LIST A | | LIST B | | LIST C |
|---|---|---|---|---|
| **Documents that Establish Both Identity and Employment Eligibility** | **OR** | **Documents that Establish Identity** | **AND** | **Documents that Establish Employment Eligibility** |

**LIST A — Documents that Establish Both Identity and Employment Eligibility**

1. U.S. Passport (unexpired or expired)

2. Certificate of U.S. Citizenship (INS Form N-560 or N-561)

3. Certificate of Naturalization (INS Form N-550 or N-570)

4. Unexpired foreign passport, with I-551 stamp or attached INS Form I-94 indicating unexpired employment authorization

5. Alien Registration Receipt Card with photograph (INS Form I-151 or I-551)

6. Unexpired Temporary Resident Card (INS Form I-688)

7. Unexpired Employment Authorization Card (INS Form I-688A)

8. Unexpired Reentry Permit (INS Form I-327)

9. Unexpired Refugee Travel Document (INS Form I-571)

10. Unexpired Employment Authorization Document issued by the INS which contains a photograph (INS Form I-688B)

**OR**

**LIST B — Documents that Establish Identity**

1. Driver's license or ID card issued by a state or outlying possession of the United States provided it contains a photograph or information such as name, date of birth, sex, height, eye color, and address

2. ID card issued by federal, state, or local government agencies or entities provided it contains a photograph or information such as name, date of birth, sex, height, eye color, and address

3. School ID card with a photograph

4. Voter's registration card

5. U.S. Military card or draft record

6. Military dependent's ID card

7. U.S. Coast Guard Merchant Mariner Card

8. Native American tribal document

9. Driver's license issued by a Canadian government authority

**For persons under age 18 who are unable to present a document listed above:**

10. School record or report card

11. Clinic, doctor, or hospital record

12. Day-care or nursery school record

**AND**

**LIST C — Documents that Establish Employment Eligibility**

1. U.S. social security card issued by the Social Security Administration (other than a card stating it is not valid for employment)

2. Certification of Birth Abroad issued by the Department of State (Form FS-545 or Form DS-1350)

3. Original or certified copy of a birth certificate issued by a state, county, municipal authority or outlying possession of the United States bearing an official seal

4. Native American tribal document

5. U.S. Citizen ID Card (INS Form I-197)

6. ID Card for use of Resident Citizen in the United States (INS Form I-179)

7. Unexpired employment authorization document issued by the INS (other than those listed under List A)

**Illustrations of many of these documents appear in Part 8 of the Handbook for Employers (M-274)**

Form I-9 (Rev. 11-21-91) N

FPI-RBK

*This page intentionally left blank.*

# Application for Employer Identification Number

**(For use by employers, corporations, partnerships, trusts, estates, churches, government agencies, certain individuals, and others. See instructions.)**

▶ **Keep a copy for your records.**

EIN

OMB No. 1545-0003

**Please type or print clearly.**

| 1 | Name of applicant (legal name) (see instructions) |
|---|---|

| 2 Trade name of business (if different from name on line 1) | 3 Executor, trustee, "care of" name |
|---|---|

| 4a Mailing address (street address) (room, apt., or suite no.) | 5a Business address (if different from address on lines 4a and 4b) |
|---|---|

| 4b City, state, and ZIP code | 5b City, state, and ZIP code |
|---|---|

**6** County and state where principal business is located

**7** Name of principal officer, general partner, grantor, owner, or trustor—SSN or ITIN may be required (see instructions) ▶

**8a** Type of entity (Check only one box.) (see instructions)

**Caution:** *If applicant is a limited liability company, see the instructions for line 8a.*

☐ Sole proprietor (SSN) _____  ☐ Estate (SSN of decedent) _____

☐ Partnership   ☐ Personal service corp.   ☐ Plan administrator (SSN) _____

☐ REMIC   ☐ National Guard   ☐ Other corporation (specify) ▶ _____

☐ State/local government   ☐ Farmers' cooperative   ☐ Trust

☐ Church or church-controlled organization   ☐ Federal government/military

☐ Other nonprofit organization (specify) ▶ _____ (enter GEN if applicable) _____

☐ Other (specify) ▶

**8b** If a corporation, name the state or foreign country (if applicable) where incorporated

| State | Foreign country |
|---|---|

**9** Reason for applying (Check only one box.) (see instructions)   ☐ Banking purpose (specify purpose) ▶ _____

☐ Started new business (specify type) ▶_____   ☐ Changed type of organization (specify new type) ▶ _____

☐ Purchased going business

☐ Hired employees (Check the box and see line 12.)   ☐ Created a trust (specify type) ▶ _____

☐ Created a pension plan (specify type) ▶ _____   ☐ Other (specify) ▶

**10** Date business started or acquired (month, day, year) (see instructions)

**11** Closing month of accounting year (see instructions)

**12** First date wages or annuities were paid or will be paid (month, day, year). **Note:** *If applicant is a withholding agent, enter date income will first be paid to nonresident alien. (month, day, year)* . . . . . . . . . . . ▶

| 13 Highest number of employees expected in the next 12 months. **Note:** *If the applicant does not expect to have any employees during the period, enter -0-. (see instructions)* . . . . ▶ | Nonagricultural | Agricultural | Household |
|---|---|---|---|

**14** Principal activity (see instructions) ▶

**15** Is the principal business activity manufacturing? . . . . . . . . . . . . . . . . . ☐ Yes ☐ No
If "Yes," principal product and raw material used ▶

**16** To whom are most of the products or services sold? Please check one box.   ☐ Business (wholesale)
☐ Public (retail)   ☐ Other (specify) ▶   ☐ N/A

**17a** Has the applicant ever applied for an employer identification number for this or any other business? . . . . ☐ Yes ☐ No
**Note:** *If "Yes," please complete lines 17b and 17c.*

**17b** If you checked "Yes" on line 17a, give applicant's legal name and trade name shown on prior application, if different from line 1 or 2 above.
Legal name ▶   Trade name ▶

**17c** Approximate date when and city and state where the application was filed. Enter previous employer identification number if known.

| Approximate date when filed (mo., day, year) | City and state where filed | Previous EIN |
|---|---|---|

Under penalties of perjury, I declare that I have examined this application, and to the best of my knowledge and belief, it is true, correct, and complete.

| | Business telephone number (include area code) ( ) |
|---|---|
| Name and title (Please type or print clearly.) ▶ | Fax telephone number (include area code) ( ) |

Signature ▶   Date ▶

**Note:** *Do not write below this line. For official use only.*

| Please leave blank ▶ | Geo. | Ind. | Class | Size | Reason for applying |
|---|---|---|---|---|---|

**For Privacy Act and Paperwork Reduction Act Notice, see page 4.**   Cat. No. 16055N   Form **SS-4** (Rev. 4-2000)

# General Instructions

*Section references are to the Internal Revenue Code unless otherwise noted.*

## Purpose of Form

Use Form SS-4 to apply for an employer identification number (EIN). An EIN is a nine-digit number (for example, 12-3456789) assigned to sole proprietors, corporations, partnerships, estates, trusts, and other entities for tax filing and reporting purposes. The information you provide on this form will establish your business tax account.

**Caution:** *An EIN is for use in connection with your business activities only. Do **not** use your EIN in place of your social security number (SSN).*

## Who Must File

You must file this form if you have not been assigned an EIN before and:

● You pay wages to one or more employees including household employees.

● You are required to have an EIN to use on any return, statement, or other document, even if you are not an employer.

● You are a withholding agent required to withhold taxes on income, other than wages, paid to a nonresident alien (individual, corporation, partnership, etc.). A withholding agent may be an agent, broker, fiduciary, manager, tenant, or spouse, and is required to file **Form 1042,** Annual Withholding Tax Return for U.S. Source Income of Foreign Persons.

● You file **Schedule C,** Profit or Loss From Business, **Schedule C-EZ,** Net Profit From Business, or **Schedule F,** Profit or Loss From Farming, of **Form 1040,** U.S. Individual Income Tax Return, **and** have a Keogh plan or are required to file excise, employment, or alcohol, tobacco, or firearms returns.

The following must use EINs even if they do not have any employees:

● State and local agencies who serve as tax reporting agents for public assistance recipients, under Rev. Proc. 80-4, 1980-1 C.B. 581, should obtain a separate EIN for this reporting. See **Household employer** on page 3.

● Trusts, except the following:

   **1.** Certain grantor-owned trusts. (See the **Instructions for Form 1041,** U.S. Income Tax Return for Estates and Trusts.)

   **2.** Individual retirement arrangement (IRA) trusts, unless the trust has to file **Form 990-T,** Exempt Organization Business Income Tax Return. (See the **Instructions for Form 990-T.**)

● Estates

● Partnerships

● REMICs (real estate mortgage investment conduits) (See the **Instructions for Form 1066,** U.S. Real Estate Mortgage Investment Conduit (REMIC) Income Tax Return.)

● Corporations

● Nonprofit organizations (churches, clubs, etc.)

● Farmers' cooperatives

● Plan administrators (A plan administrator is the person or group of persons specified as the administrator by the instrument under which the plan is operated.)

## When To Apply for a New EIN

**New Business.** If you become the new owner of an existing business, **do not** use the EIN of the former owner. **If you already have an EIN, use that number.** If you do not have an EIN, apply for one on this form. If you become the "owner" of a corporation by acquiring its stock, use the corporation's EIN.

**Changes in Organization or Ownership.** If you already have an EIN, you may need to get a new one if either the organization or ownership of your business changes. If you incorporate a sole proprietorship or form a partnership, you must get a new EIN. However, **do not** apply for a new EIN if:

● You change only the name of your business,

● You elected on **Form 8832,** Entity Classification Election, to change the way the entity is taxed, or

● A partnership terminates because at least 50% of the total interests in partnership capital and profits were sold or exchanged within a 12-month period. (See Regulations section 301.6109-1(d)(2)(iii).) The EIN for the terminated partnership should continue to be used.

**Note:** *If you are electing to be an "S corporation," be sure you file* **Form 2553,** *Election by a Small Business Corporation.*

**File Only One Form SS-4.** File only one Form SS-4, regardless of the number of businesses operated or trade names under which a business operates. However, each corporation in an affiliated group must file a separate application.

**EIN Applied for, But Not Received.** If you do not have an EIN by the time a return is due, write "Applied for" and the date you applied in the space shown for the number. **Do not** show your social security number (SSN) as an EIN on returns.

If you do not have an EIN by the time a tax deposit is due, send your payment to the Internal Revenue Service Center for your filing area. (See **Where To Apply** below.) Make your check or money order payable to "United States Treasury" and show your name (as shown on Form SS-4), address, type of tax, period covered, and date you applied for an EIN. Send an explanation with the deposit.

For more information about EINs, see **Pub. 583,** Starting a Business and Keeping Records, and **Pub. 1635,** Understanding Your EIN.

## How To Apply

You can apply for an EIN either by mail or by telephone. You can get an EIN immediately by calling the Tele-TIN number for the service center for your state, or you can send the completed Form SS-4 directly to the service center to receive your EIN by mail.

**Application by Tele-TIN.** Under the Tele-TIN program, you can receive your EIN by telephone and use it immediately to file a return or make a payment. To receive an EIN by telephone, complete Form SS-4, then call the Tele-TIN number listed for your state under **Where To Apply.** The person making the call must be authorized to sign the form. (See **Signature** on page 4.)

An IRS representative will use the information from the Form SS-4 to establish your account and assign you an EIN. Write the number you are given on the upper right corner of the form and sign and date it.

*Mail or fax (facsimile) the signed Form SS-4* **within 24 hours** *to the Tele-TIN Unit at the service center address for your state.* The IRS representative will give you the fax number. The fax numbers are also listed in Pub. 1635.

Taxpayer representatives can receive their client's EIN by telephone if they first send a fax of a completed **Form 2848,** Power of Attorney and Declaration of Representative, or **Form 8821,** Tax Information Authorization, to the Tele-TIN unit. The Form 2848 or Form 8821 will be used solely to release the EIN to the representative authorized on the form.

**Application by Mail.** Complete Form SS-4 at least 4 to 5 weeks before you will need an EIN. Sign and date the application and mail it to the service center address for your state. You will receive your EIN in the mail in approximately 4 weeks.

## Where To Apply

The Tele-TIN numbers listed below will involve a long-distance charge to callers outside of the local calling area and can be used only to apply for an EIN. **The numbers may change without notice.** Call 1-800-829-1040 to verify a number or to ask about the status of an application by mail.

| If your principal business, office or agency, or legal residence in the case of an individual, is located in: | Call the Tele-TIN number shown or file with the Internal Revenue Service Center at: |
|---|---|
| Florida, Georgia, South Carolina | Attn: Entity Control Atlanta, GA 39901 770-455-2360 |
| New Jersey, New York (New York City and counties of Nassau, Rockland, Suffolk, and Westchester) | Attn: Entity Control Holtsville, NY 00501 516-447-4955 |
| New York (all other counties), Connecticut, Maine, Massachusetts, New Hampshire, Rhode Island, Vermont | Attn: Entity Control Andover, MA 05501 978-474-9717 |
| Illinois, Iowa, Minnesota, Missouri, Wisconsin | Attn: Entity Control Stop 6800 2306 E. Bannister Rd. Kansas City, MO 64999 816-926-5999 |
| Delaware, District of Columbia, Maryland, Pennsylvania, Virginia | Attn: Entity Control Philadelphia, PA 19255 215-516-6999 |
| Indiana, Kentucky, Michigan, Ohio, West Virginia | Attn: Entity Control Cincinnati, OH 45999 859-292-5467 |

Form **SS-8**

(Rev. June 1997)

Department of the Treasury
Internal Revenue Service

## Determination of Employee Work Status
## for Purposes of Federal Employment Taxes
## and Income Tax Withholding

OMB No. 1545-0004

## Paperwork Reduction Act Notice

We ask for the information on this form to carry out the Internal Revenue laws of the United States. You are required to give us the information. We need it to ensure that you are complying with these laws and to allow us to figure and collect the right amount of tax.

You are not required to provide the information requested on a form that is subject to the Paperwork Reduction Act unless the form displays a valid OMB control number. Books or records relating to a form or its instructions must be retained as long as their contents may become material in the administration of any Internal Revenue law. Generally, tax returns and return information are confidential, as required by Code section 6103.

The time needed to complete and file this form will vary depending on individual circumstances. The estimated average time is: **Recordkeeping, 34 hr., 55 min.; Learning about the law or the form, 12 min.;** and **Preparing and sending the form to the IRS, 46 min.** If you have comments concerning the accuracy of these time estimates or suggestions for making this form simpler, we would be happy to hear from you. You can write to the Tax Forms Committee, Western Area Distribution Center, Rancho Cordova, CA 95743-0001. **DO NOT** send the tax form to this address. Instead, see **General Information** for where to file.

## Purpose

Employers and workers file Form SS-8 to get a determination as to whether a worker is an employee for purposes of Federal employment taxes and income tax withholding.

## General Information

Complete this form carefully. If the firm is completing the form, complete it for **ONE** individual who is representative of the class of workers whose status is in question. If you want a written determination for more than one class of workers, complete a separate Form SS-8 for one worker

from each class whose status is typical of that class. A written determination for any worker will apply to other workers of the same class if the facts are not materially different from those of the worker whose status was ruled upon.

*Caution: Form SS-8 is not a claim for refund of social security and Medicare taxes or Federal income tax withholding. Also, a determination that an individual is an employee does not necessarily reduce any current or prior tax liability. A worker must file his or her income tax return even if a determination has not been made by the due date of the return.*

**Where to file.**—In the list below, find the state where your legal residence, principal place of business, office, or agency is located. Send Form SS-8 to the address listed for your location.

| Location: | Send to: |
|---|---|
| Alaska, Arizona, Arkansas, California, Colorado, Hawaii, Idaho, Illinois, Iowa, Kansas, Minnesota, Missouri, Montana, Nebraska, Nevada, New Mexico, North Dakota, Oklahoma, Oregon, South Dakota, Texas, Utah, Washington, Wisconsin, Wyoming | Internal Revenue Service SS-8 Determinations P.O. Box 1231, Stop 4106 AUSC Austin, TX 78767 |
| Alabama, Connecticut, Delaware, District of Columbia, Florida, Georgia, Indiana, Kentucky, Louisiana, Maine, Maryland, Massachusetts, Michigan, Mississippi, New Hampshire, New Jersey, New York, North Carolina, Ohio, Pennsylvania, Rhode Island, South Carolina, Tennessee, Vermont, Virginia, West Virginia, All other locations not listed | Internal Revenue Service SS-8 Determinations Two Lakemont Road Newport, VT 05855-1555 |
| American Samoa, Guam, Puerto Rico, U.S. Virgin Islands | Internal Revenue Service Mercantile Plaza 2 Avenue Ponce de Leon San Juan, Puerto Rico 00918 |

---

Name of firm (or person) for whom the worker performed services

Name of worker

---

Address of firm (include street address, apt. or suite no., city, state, and ZIP code)

Address of worker (include street address, apt. or suite no., city, state, and ZIP code)

---

Trade name

Telephone number (include area code)
( )

Worker's social security number

---

Telephone number (include area code)
( )

Firm's employer identification number

---

**Check type of firm for which the work relationship is in question:**

☐ Individual ☐ Partnership ☐ Corporation ☐ Other (specify) ▶ ........................................

---

### Important Information Needed To Process Your Request

---

This form is being completed by: ☐ Firm ☐ Worker

If this form is being completed by the worker, the IRS **must** have your permission to disclose your name to the firm.

**Do you object to disclosing your name and the information on this form to the firm?** . . . . . . . . ☐ Yes ☐ No

If you answer "Yes," the IRS cannot act on your request. **Do not complete the rest of this form unless the IRS asks for it.**

---

Under section 6110 of the Internal Revenue Code, the information on this form and related file documents will be open to the public if any ruling or determination is made. However, names, addresses, and taxpayer identification numbers will be removed before the information is made public.

**Is there any other information you want removed?** . . . . . . . . . . . . . . . . . . . . . ☐ Yes ☐ No

If you check "Yes," we cannot process your request unless you submit a copy of this form and copies of all supporting documents showing, in brackets, the information you want removed. Attach a separate statement showing which specific exemption of section 6110(c) applies to each bracketed part.

---

Cat. No. 16106T

Form **SS-8** (Rev. 6-97)

*This form is designed to cover many work activities, so some of the questions may not apply to you. **You must answer ALL items or mark them "Unknown" or "Does not apply."** If you need more space, attach another sheet.*

Total number of workers in this class. (Attach names and addresses. If more than 10 workers, list only 10.) ▶ _____

This information is about services performed by the worker from _____ to _____
                                                                            (month, day, year)                    (month, day, year)

Is the worker still performing services for the firm? . . . . . . . . . . . . . . . . . . . . . . . ☐ Yes ☐ No

● If "No," what was the date of termination? ▶ _____
                                                      (month, day, year)

**1a** Describe the firm's business ....................................................................................

  **b** Describe the work done by the worker ........................................................................
  ..................................................................................................................

**2a** If the work is done under a written agreement between the firm and the worker, attach a copy.

  **b** If the agreement is not in writing, describe the terms and conditions of the work arrangement .................
  ..................................................................................................................

  **c** If the actual working arrangement differs in any way from the agreement, explain the differences and why they occur .......
  ..................................................................................................................

**3a** Is the worker given training by the firm? . . . . . . . . . . . . . . . . . . . . . . . . ☐ Yes ☐ No
  ● If "Yes," what kind? ...........................................................................................
  ● How often? ....................................................................................................

  **b** Is the worker given instructions in the way the work is to be done (exclusive of actual training in 3a)? . ☐ Yes ☐ No
  ● If "Yes," give specific examples ..............................................................................

  **c** Attach samples of any written instructions or procedures.

  **d** Does the firm have the right to change the methods used by the worker or direct that person on how to
  do the work? . . . . . . . . . . . . . . . . . . . . . . . . . . . . . . . . . . . ☐ Yes ☐ No
  ● Explain your answer ...........................................................................................
  ..................................................................................................................

  **e** Does the operation of the firm's business require that the worker be supervised or controlled in the
  performance of the service? . . . . . . . . . . . . . . . . . . . . . . . . . . . . ☐ Yes ☐ No
  ● Explain your answer ...........................................................................................
  ..................................................................................................................

**4a** The firm engages the worker:
  ☐ To perform and complete a particular job only
  ☐ To work at a job for an indefinite period of time
  ☐ Other (explain)

  **b** Is the worker required to follow a routine or a schedule established by the firm? . . . . . . . . . ☐ Yes ☐ No
  ● If "Yes," what is the routine or schedule? ...................................................................
  ..................................................................................................................

  **c** Does the worker report to the firm or its representative?. . . . . . . . . . . . . . . . . . . ☐ Yes ☐ No
  ● If "Yes," how often? .........................................................................................
  ● For what purpose? ...........................................................................................
  ● In what manner (in person, in writing, by telephone, etc.)? .................................................
  ● Attach copies of any report forms used in reporting to the firm.

  **d** Does the worker furnish a time record to the firm? . . . . . . . . . . . . . . . . . ☐ Yes ☐ No
  ● If "Yes," attach copies of time records.

**5a** State the kind and value of tools, equipment, supplies, and materials furnished by:
  ● The firm ......................................................................................................
  ..................................................................................................................
  ● The worker ...................................................................................................
  ..................................................................................................................

  **b** What expenses are incurred by the worker in the performance of services for the firm? .......................
  ..................................................................................................................

  **c** Does the firm reimburse the worker for any expenses? . . . . . . . . . . . . . . . . . ☐ Yes ☐ No
  ● If "Yes," specify the reimbursed expenses ...................................................................

**6a** Will the worker perform the services personally? . . . . . . . . . . . . . . . . . ☐ Yes  ☐ No

  **b** Does the worker have helpers? . . . . . . . . . . . . . . . . . . . . . ☐ Yes  ☐ No

    ● If "Yes," who hires the helpers? ☐ Firm  ☐ Worker

    ● If the helpers are hired by the worker, is the firm's approval necessary? . . . . . . . . . ☐ Yes  ☐ No

    ● Who pays the helpers?    ☐ Firm  ☐ Worker

    ● If the worker pays the helpers, does the firm repay the worker? . . . . . . . . . . ☐ Yes  ☐ No

    ● Are social security and Medicare taxes and Federal income tax withheld from the helpers' pay? . . ☐ Yes  ☐ No

    ● If "Yes," who reports and pays these taxes?    ☐ Firm    ☐ Worker

    ● Who reports the helpers' earnings to the Internal Revenue Service? ☐ Firm  ☐ Worker

    ● What services do the helpers perform? _____

**7** At what location are the services performed? ☐ Firm's  ☐ Worker's  ☐ Other (specify) _____

**8a** Type of pay worker receives:

    ☐ Salary    ☐ Commission  ☐ Hourly wage    ☐ Piecework  ☐ Lump sum  ☐ Other (specify) _____

  **b** Does the firm guarantee a minimum amount of pay to the worker? . . . . . . . . . . ☐ Yes  ☐ No

  **c** Does the firm allow the worker a drawing account or advances against pay? . . . . . . . . ☐ Yes  ☐ No

    ● If "Yes," is the worker paid such advances on a regular basis? . . . . . . . . . ☐ Yes  ☐ No

  **d** How does the worker repay such advances? _____

**9a** Is the worker eligible for a pension, bonus, paid vacations, sick pay, etc.? . . . . . . . . ☐ Yes  ☐ No

    ● If "Yes," specify _____

  **b** Does the firm carry worker's compensation insurance on the worker? . . . . . . . . ☐ Yes  ☐ No

  **c** Does the firm withhold social security and Medicare taxes from amounts paid the worker? . . . . ☐ Yes  ☐ No

  **d** Does the firm withhold Federal income tax from amounts paid the worker? . . . . . . . ☐ Yes  ☐ No

  **e** How does the firm report the worker's earnings to the Internal Revenue Service?

    ☐ Form W-2  ☐ Form 1099-MISC    ☐ Does not report  ☐ Other (specify) _____

    ● Attach a copy.

  **f** Does the firm bond the worker? . . . . . . . . . . . . . . . . . . . ☐ Yes  ☐ No

**10a** Approximately how many hours a day does the worker perform services for the firm? _____

  **b** Does the firm set hours of work for the worker? . . . . . . . . . . . . . . . ☐ Yes  ☐ No

    ● If "Yes," what are the worker's set hours? _____ a.m./p.m. to _____ a.m./p.m. (Circle whether a.m. or p.m.)

  **c** Does the worker perform similar services for others? . . . . . . . . . . ☐ Yes  ☐ No  ☐ Unknown

    ● If "Yes," are these services performed on a daily basis for other firms? . . . . . ☐ Yes  ☐ No  ☐ Unknown

    ● Percentage of time spent in performing these services for:

    This firm ......... % Other firms ................. %    ☐ Unknown

    ● Does the firm have priority on the worker's time? . . . . . . . . . . . . . ☐ Yes  ☐ No

    ● If "No," explain _____

  **d** Is the worker prohibited from competing with the firm either while performing services or during any later period? . . . . . . . . . . . . . . . . . . . . . . . ☐ Yes  ☐ No

**11a** Can the firm discharge the worker at any time without incurring a liability? . . . . . . . . ☐ Yes  ☐ No

    ● If "No," explain _____

  **b** Can the worker terminate the services at any time without incurring a liability? . . . . . . . ☐ Yes  ☐ No

    ● If "No," explain _____

**12a** Does the worker perform services for the firm under:

    ☐ The firm's business name    ☐ The worker's own business name    ☐ Other (specify) _____

  **b** Does the worker advertise or maintain a business listing in the telephone directory, a trade journal, etc.? . . . . . . . . . . . . . . . . . . . . ☐ Yes  ☐ No  ☐ Unknown

    ● If "Yes," specify _____

  **c** Does the worker represent himself or herself to the public as being in business to perform the same or similar services? . . . . . . . . . . . . . . . ☐ Yes  ☐ No  ☐ Unknown

    ● If "Yes," how? _____

  **d** Does the worker have his or her own shop or office? . . . . . . . . . . ☐ Yes  ☐ No  ☐ Unknown

    ● If "Yes," where? _____

  **e** Does the firm represent the worker as an employee of the firm to its customers? . . . . . . . ☐ Yes  ☐ No

    ● If "No," how is the worker represented? _____

  **f** How did the firm learn of the worker's services? _____

**13** Is a license necessary for the work? . . . . . . . . . . . . . . . ☐ Yes  ☐ No  ☐ Unknown

    ● If "Yes," what kind of license is required? _____

    ● Who issues the license? _____

    ● Who pays the license fee?

**14** Does the worker have a financial investment in a business related to the services performed? . . . . . . . . . . . . . . . . . . . . . . . . . . . . . . . . ☐ **Yes** ☐ **No** ☐ **Unknown**
- If "Yes," specify and give amount of the investment .........................................................

**15** Can the worker incur a loss in the performance of the service for the firm? . . . . . . . . . . ☐ **Yes** ☐ **No**
- If "Yes," how? .........................................................

**16a** Has any other government agency ruled on the status of the firm's workers? . . . . . . . . . . ☐ **Yes** ☐ **No**
- If "Yes," attach a copy of the ruling.

  **b** Is the same issue being considered by any IRS office in connection with the audit of the worker's tax return or the firm's tax return, or has it been considered recently? . . . . . . . . . . . ☐ **Yes** ☐ **No**
- If "Yes," for which year(s)? .........................................................

**17** Does the worker assemble or process a product at home or away from the firm's place of business? ☐ **Yes** ☐ **No**
- If "Yes," who furnishes materials or goods used by the worker? ☐ Firm      ☐ Worker      ☐ Other
- Is the worker furnished a pattern or given instructions to follow in making the product? . . . . ☐ **Yes** ☐ **No**
- Is the worker required to return the finished product to the firm or to someone designated by the firm? ☐ **Yes** ☐ **No**

**18** Attach a detailed explanation of any other reason why you believe the worker is an employee or an independent contractor.

**Answer items 19a through o only if the worker is a salesperson or provides a service directly to customers.**

**19a** Are leads to prospective customers furnished by the firm? . . . . . . . . . ☐ **Yes** ☐ **No** ☐ **Does not apply**
  **b** Is the worker required to pursue or report on leads? . . . . . . . . . . . ☐ **Yes** ☐ **No** ☐ **Does not apply**
  **c** Is the worker required to adhere to prices, terms, and conditions of sale established by the firm? . . ☐ **Yes** ☐ **No**
  **d** Are orders submitted to and subject to approval by the firm? . . . . . . . . . . . . ☐ **Yes** ☐ **No**
  **e** Is the worker expected to attend sales meetings? . . . . . . . . . . . . . . ☐ **Yes** ☐ **No**
- If "Yes," is the worker subject to any kind of penalty for failing to attend? . . . . . . . . ☐ **Yes** ☐ **No**
  **f** Does the firm assign a specific territory to the worker? . . . . . . . . . . . . . ☐ **Yes** ☐ **No**
  **g** Whom does the customer pay?      ☐ Firm      ☐ Worker
- If worker, does the worker remit the total amount to the firm? . . . . . . . . . . . ☐ **Yes** ☐ **No**
  **h** Does the worker sell a consumer product in a home or establishment other than a permanent retail establishment? . . . . . . . . . . . . . . . . . . . . . . . . . . . . . . . ☐ **Yes** ☐ **No**
  **i** List the products and/or services distributed by the worker, such as meat, vegetables, fruit, bakery products, beverages (other than milk), or laundry or dry cleaning services. If more than one type of product and/or service is distributed, specify the principal one .........................................................
  **j** Did the firm or another person assign the route or territory and a list of customers to the worker? . . ☐ **Yes** ☐ **No**
- If "Yes," enter the name and job title of the person who made the assignment .........................................................
  **k** Did the worker pay the firm or person for the privilege of serving customers on the route or in the territory? ☐ **Yes** ☐ **No**
- If "Yes," how much did the worker pay (not including any amount paid for a truck or racks, etc.)? $ .........................................................
- What factors were considered in determining the value of the route or territory? .........................................................
  **l** How are new customers obtained by the worker? Explain fully, showing whether the new customers called the firm for service, were solicited by the worker, or both .........................................................
  **m** Does the worker sell life insurance? . . . . . . . . . . . . . . . . . . . ☐ **Yes** ☐ **No**
- If "Yes," is the selling of life insurance or annuity contracts for the firm the worker's entire business activity? . . . . . . . . . . . . . . . . . . . . . . . . . . . . . . . . ☐ **Yes** ☐ **No**
- If "No," list the other business activities and the amount of time spent on them .........................................................
  **n** Does the worker sell other types of insurance for the firm? . . . . . . . . . . . . ☐ **Yes** ☐ **No**
- If "Yes," state the percentage of the worker's total working time spent in selling other types of insurance ............. %
- At the time the contract was entered into between the firm and the worker, was it their intention that the worker sell life insurance for the firm:      ☐ on a full-time basis      ☐ on a part-time basis
- State the manner in which the intention was expressed .........................................................
  **o** Is the worker a traveling or city salesperson? . . . . . . . . . . . . . . . . ☐ **Yes** ☐ **No**
- If "Yes," from whom does the worker principally solicit orders for the firm? .........................................................
- If the worker solicits orders from wholesalers, retailers, contractors, or operators of hotels, restaurants, or other similar establishments, specify the percentage of the worker's time spent in the solicitation ............. %
- Is the merchandise purchased by the customers for resale or for use in their business operations? If used by the customers in their business operations, describe the merchandise and state whether it is equipment installed on their premises or a consumable supply

Under penalties of perjury, I declare that I have examined this request, including accompanying documents, and to the best of my knowledge and belief, the facts presented are true, correct, and complete.

Signature ▶ _____     Title ▶ _____     Date ▶ _____

If the firm is completing this form, an officer or member of the firm must sign it. If the worker is completing this form, the worker must sign it. If the worker wants a written determination about services performed for two or more firms, a separate form must be completed and signed for each firm. Additional copies of this form may be obtained by calling 1-800-TAX-FORM (1-800-829-3676).

✹

# Form W-4 (2001)

**Purpose.** Complete Form W-4 so your employer can withhold the correct Federal income tax from your pay. Because your tax situation may change, you may want to refigure your withholding each year.

**Exemption from withholding.** If you are exempt, complete only lines 1, 2, 3, 4, and 7, and sign the form to validate it. Your exemption for 2001 expires February 18, 2002.

**Note:** You cannot claim exemption from withholding if (1) your income exceeds $750 and includes more than $250 of unearned income (e.g., interest and dividends) and (2) another person can claim you as a dependent on their tax return.

**Basic instructions.** If you are not exempt, complete the **Personal Allowances Worksheet** below. The worksheets on page 2 adjust your withholding allowances based on itemized deductions, certain credits, adjustments to

income, or two-earner/two-job situations. Complete all worksheets that apply. They will help you figure the number of withholding allowances you are entitled to claim. **However, you may claim fewer (or zero) allowances.**

**Head of household.** Generally, you may claim head of household filing status on your tax return only if you are unmarried and pay more than 50% of the costs of keeping up a home for yourself and your dependent(s) or other qualifying individuals. See line E below.

**Tax credits.** You can take projected tax credits into account in figuring your allowable number of withholding allowances. Credits for child or dependent care expenses and the child tax credit may be claimed using the **Personal Allowances Worksheet** below. See **Pub. 919,** How Do I Adjust My Tax Withholding? for information on converting your other credits into withholding allowances.

**Nonwage income.** If you have a large amount of nonwage income, such as interest or dividends,

consider making estimated tax payments using **Form 1040-ES,** Estimated Tax for Individuals. Otherwise, you may owe additional tax.

**Two earners/two jobs.** If you have a working spouse or more than one job, figure the total number of allowances you are entitled to claim on all jobs using worksheets from only one Form W-4. Your withholding usually will be most accurate when all allowances are claimed on the Form W-4 for the highest paying job and zero allowances are claimed on the others.

**Check your withholding.** After your Form W-4 takes effect, use Pub. 919 to see how the dollar amount you are having withheld compares to your projected total tax for 2001. Get Pub. 919 especially if you used the **Two-Earner/Two-Job Worksheet** on page 2 and your earnings exceed $150,000 (Single) or $200,000 (Married).

**Recent name change?** If your name on line 1 differs from that shown on your social security card, call 1-800-772-1213 for a new social security card.

---

**Personal Allowances Worksheet** (Keep for your records.)

A   Enter "1" for **yourself** if no one else can claim you as a dependent . . . . . . . . . . . . . **A** _____

B   Enter "1" if:
- You are single and have only one job; or
- You are married, have only one job, and your spouse does not work; or
- Your wages from a second job or your spouse's wages (or the total of both) are $1,000 or less.     . . **B** _____

C   Enter "1" for your **spouse.** But, you may choose to enter -0- if you are married and have either a working spouse or more than one job. (Entering -0- may help you avoid having too little tax withheld.) . . . . . . . . . **C** _____

D   Enter number of **dependents** (other than your spouse or yourself) you will claim on your tax return . . . . . . **D** _____

E   Enter "1" if you will file as **head of household** on your tax return (see conditions under **Head of household** above) . **E** _____

F   Enter "1" if you have at least $1,500 of **child or dependent care expenses** for which you plan to claim a credit . . **F** _____

   (**Note:** Do not include child support payments. See **Pub. 503,** Child and Dependent Care Expenses, for details.)

G   **Child Tax Credit** (including additional child tax credit):
- If your total income will be between $18,000 and $50,000 ($23,000 and $63,000 if married), enter "1" for each eligible child.
- If your total income will be between $50,000 and $80,000 ($63,000 and $115,000 if married), enter "1" if you have two eligible children, enter "2" if you have three or four eligible children, or enter "3" if you have five or more eligible children. **G** _____

H   Add lines A through G and enter total here. (**Note:** This may be different from the number of exemptions you claim on your tax return.) ▶ **H** _____

| For accuracy, complete all worksheets that apply. | • If you plan to **itemize or claim adjustments to income** and want to reduce your withholding, see the **Deductions and Adjustments Worksheet** on page 2. |
|---|---|
| | • If you are **single,** have **more than one job** and your combined earnings from all jobs exceed $35,000, **or** if you are **married** and have a **working spouse or more than one job** and the combined earnings from all jobs exceed $60,000, see the **Two-Earner/Two-Job Worksheet** on page 2 to avoid having too little tax withheld. |
| | • If **neither** of the above situations applies, **stop here** and enter the number from line H on line 5 of Form W-4 below. |

---

····················· **Cut here and give Form W-4 to your employer. Keep the top part for your records.** ·····················

Form **W-4**
Department of the Treasury
Internal Revenue Service

## Employee's Withholding Allowance Certificate

▶ **For Privacy Act and Paperwork Reduction Act Notice, see page 2.**

OMB No. 1545-0010

**2001**

| 1   Type or print your first name and middle initial | Last name | | 2   Your social security number |
|---|---|---|---|

| Home address (number and street or rural route) | 3   ☐ Single  ☐ Married  ☐ Married, but withhold at higher Single rate. |
|---|---|
| | **Note:** If married, but legally separated, or spouse is a nonresident alien, check the Single box. |
| City or town, state, and ZIP code | 4   If your last name differs from that on your social security card, check here. You must call 1-800-772-1213 for a new card. ▶ ☐ |

5   Total number of allowances you are claiming (from line **H** above **or** from the applicable worksheet on page 2)   **5** |_____

6   Additional amount, if any, you want withheld from each paycheck . . . . . . . . . . . .   **6** $ |_____

7   I claim exemption from withholding for 2001, and I certify that I meet **both** of the following conditions for exemption:
- Last year I had a right to a refund of **all** Federal income tax withheld because I had **no** tax liability **and**
- This year I expect a refund of **all** Federal income tax withheld because I expect to have **no** tax liability.

   If you meet both conditions, write "Exempt" here . . . . . . . . . . . . . . . ▶   **7** |_____

Under penalties of perjury, I certify that I am entitled to the number of withholding allowances claimed on this certificate, or I am entitled to claim exempt status.

**Employee's signature**
(Form is not valid unless you sign it.) ▶ _____     Date ▶ _____

| 8   Employer's name and address (Employer: Complete lines 8 and 10 only if sending to the IRS.) | 9   Office code (optional) | 10   Employer identification number |
|---|---|---|

Cat. No. 10220Q

## Deductions and Adjustments Worksheet

**Note:** *Use this worksheet only if you plan to itemize deductions, claim certain credits, or claim adjustments to income on your 2001 tax return.*

| | | |
|---|---|---|
| 1 | Enter an estimate of your 2001 itemized deductions. These include qualifying home mortgage interest, charitable contributions, state and local taxes, medical expenses in excess of 7.5% of your income, and miscellaneous deductions. (For 2001, you may have to reduce your itemized deductions if your income is over $132,950 ($66,475 if married filing separately). See **Worksheet 3** in Pub. 919 for details.) . . . | **1** $ _____ |
| 2 | Enter: $\left\{\begin{array}{l}\$7,600 \text{ if married filing jointly or qualifying widow(er)} \\ \$6,650 \text{ if head of household} \\ \$4,550 \text{ if single} \\ \$3,800 \text{ if married filing separately}\end{array}\right\}$ . . . . . . | **2** $ _____ |
| 3 | **Subtract** line 2 from line 1. If line 2 is greater than line 1, enter -0- . . . . . . | **3** $ _____ |
| 4 | Enter an estimate of your 2001 adjustments to income, including alimony, deductible IRA contributions, and student loan interest | **4** $ _____ |
| 5 | **Add** lines 3 and 4 and enter the total (Include any amount for credits from **Worksheet 7** in Pub. 919.) | **5** $ _____ |
| 6 | Enter an estimate of your 2001 nonwage income (such as dividends or interest) . . . . . | **6** $ _____ |
| 7 | **Subtract** line 6 from line 5. Enter the result, but not less than -0- . . . . . | **7** $ _____ |
| 8 | **Divide** the amount on line 7 by $3,000 and enter the result here. Drop any fraction . . . . . | **8** _____ |
| 9 | Enter the number from the **Personal Allowances Worksheet,** line H, page 1 . . . . . | **9** _____ |
| 10 | **Add** lines 8 and 9 and enter the total here. If you plan to use the **Two-Earner/Two-Job Worksheet,** also enter this total on line 1 below. Otherwise, **stop here** and enter this total on Form W-4, line 5, page 1 . | **10** _____ |

## Two-Earner/Two-Job Worksheet

**Note:** *Use this worksheet only if the instructions under line H on page 1 direct you here.*

| | | |
|---|---|---|
| 1 | Enter the number from line H, page 1 (or from line 10 above if you used the **Deductions and Adjustments Worksheet**) | **1** _____ |
| 2 | Find the number in **Table 1** below that applies to the **lowest** paying job and enter it here . . . . | **2** _____ |
| 3 | If line 1 is **more than or equal to** line 2, subtract line 2 from line 1. Enter the result here (if zero, enter -0-) and on Form W-4, line 5, page 1. **Do not** use the rest of this worksheet . . . . . . . . | **3** _____ |

**Note:** *If line 1 is **less than** line 2, enter -0- on Form W-4, line 5, page 1. Complete lines 4–9 below to calculate the additional withholding amount necessary to avoid a year end tax bill.*

| | | | |
|---|---|---|---|
| 4 | Enter the number from line 2 of this worksheet . . . . . . . . . | **4** _____ | |
| 5 | Enter the number from line 1 of this worksheet . . . . . . . . . | **5** _____ | |
| 6 | **Subtract** line 5 from line 4 . . . . . . . . . . . . . . | | **6** _____ |
| 7 | Find the amount in **Table 2** below that applies to the **highest** paying job and enter it here . . . . | | **7** $ _____ |
| 8 | **Multiply** line 7 by line 6 and enter the result here. This is the additional annual withholding needed . . | | **8** $ _____ |
| 9 | Divide line 8 by the number of pay periods remaining in 2001. For example, divide by 26 if you are paid every two weeks and you complete this form in December 2000. Enter the result here and on Form W-4, line 6, page 1. This is the additional amount to be withheld from each paycheck . . . . . . . . | | **9** $ _____ |

### Table 1: Two-Earner/Two-Job Worksheet

| Married Filing Jointly | | | | All Others | | | |
|---|---|---|---|---|---|---|---|
| If wages from **LOWEST** paying job are— | Enter on line 2 above | If wages from **LOWEST** paying job are— | Enter on line 2 above | If wages from **LOWEST** paying job are— | Enter on line 2 above | If wages from **LOWEST** paying job are— | Enter on line 2 above |
| $0 - $4,000 | 0 | 42,001 - 47,000 | 8 | $0 - $6,000 | 0 | 65,001 - 80,000 | 8 |
| 4,001 - 8,000 | 1 | 47,001 - 55,000 | 9 | 6,001 - 12,000 | 1 | 80,001 - 105,000 | 9 |
| 8,001 - 14,000 | 2 | 55,001 - 65,000 | 10 | 12,001 - 17,000 | 2 | 105,001 and over | 10 |
| 14,001 - 19,000 | 3 | 65,001 - 70,000 | 11 | 17,001 - 22,000 | 3 | | |
| 19,001 - 25,000 | 4 | 70,001 - 90,000 | 12 | 22,001 - 28,000 | 4 | | |
| 25,001 - 32,000 | 5 | 90,001 - 105,000 | 13 | 28,001 - 40,000 | 5 | | |
| 32,001 - 38,000 | 6 | 105,001 - 115,000 | 14 | 40,001 - 50,000 | 6 | | |
| 38,001 - 42,000 | 7 | 115,001 and over | 15 | 50,001 - 65,000 | 7 | | |

### Table 2: Two-Earner/Two-Job Worksheet

| Married Filing Jointly | | All Others | |
|---|---|---|---|
| If wages from **HIGHEST** paying job are— | Enter on line 7 above | If wages from **HIGHEST** paying job are— | Enter on line 7 above |
| $0 - $50,000 | $440 | $0 - $30,000 | $440 |
| 50,001 - 100,000 | 800 | 30,001 - 60,000 | 800 |
| 100,001 - 130,000 | 900 | 60,001 - 120,000 | 900 |
| 130,001 - 250,000 | 1,000 | 120,001 - 270,000 | 1,000 |
| 250,001 and over | 1,100 | 270,001 and over | 1,100 |

**Privacy Act and Paperwork Reduction Act Notice.** We ask for the information on this form to carry out the Internal Revenue laws of the United States. The Internal Revenue Code requires this information under sections 3402(f)(2)(A) and 6109 and their regulations. **Failure to provide a properly completed form will result in your being treated as a single person who claims no withholding allowances; providing fraudulent information may also subject you to penalties.** Routine uses of this information include giving it to the Department of Justice for civil and criminal litigation, to cities, states, and the District of Columbia for use in administering their tax laws, and using it in the National Directory of New Hires.

You are not required to provide the information requested on a form that is subject to the Paperwork Reduction Act unless the form displays a valid OMB control number. Books or records relating to a form or its instructions must be retained as long as their contents may become material in the administration of any Internal Revenue law. Generally, tax returns and return information are confidential, as required by Code section 6103.

The time needed to complete this form will vary depending on individual circumstances. The estimated average time is: **Recordkeeping,** 46 min.; **Learning about the law or the form,** 13 min.; **Preparing the form,** 59 min. If you have comments concerning the accuracy of these time estimates or suggestions for making this form simpler, we would be happy to hear from you. You can write to the Tax Forms Committee, Western Area Distribution Center, Rancho Cordova, CA 95743-0001. **DO NOT** send the tax form to this address. Instead, give it to your employer.

PA-100 (1) 2-98

## COMMONWEALTH OF PENNSYLVANIA
# PA ENTERPRISE REGISTRATION FORM

DEPARTMENT USE ONLY

**RECEIVED DATE**

DEPARTMENT OF REVENUE &
DEPARTMENT OF LABOR AND INDUSTRY

**TYPE OR PRINT LEGIBLY, USE BLACK INK**

## SECTION 1 – REASON FOR THIS REGISTRATION

REFER TO THE INSTRUCTIONS (PAGE 18) AND CHECK THE APPLICABLE BOX(ES) TO INDICATE THE REASON(S) FOR THIS REGISTRATION.

1. ☐ NEW REGISTRATION
2. ☐ ADDING TAX(ES) & SERVICE(S)
3. ☐ REACTIVATING TAX(ES) & SERVICE(S)
4. ☐ ADDING ESTABLISHMENT(S)

5. ☐ ACQUISITION OF ALL OR PART OF AN EXISTING ENTERPRISE
   WAS THERE A PRIOR OWNER?   ☐ YES   ☐ NO
6. ☐ APPLICATION FOR PAUC EXPERIENCE RECORD AND
   RESERVE ACCOUNT BALANCE OF PREDECESSOR
7. ☐ INFORMATION UPDATE

## SECTION 2 – ENTERPRISE INFORMATION

| 1. DATE OF FIRST OPERATIONS | 2. DATE OF FIRST OPERATIONS IN PA | 3. ENTERPRISE FISCAL YEAR END |
|---|---|---|

| 4. ENTERPRISE LEGAL NAME | 5. FEDERAL EMPLOYER IDENTIFICATION NUMBER (EIN) |
|---|---|

| 6. ENTERPRISE TRADE NAME (if different than legal name) | 7. ENTERPRISE TELEPHONE NUMBER ( ) |
|---|---|

| 8. ENTERPRISE STREET ADDRESS (do not use PO Box) | CITY/TOWN | COUNTY | STATE | ZIP CODE + 4 |
|---|---|---|---|---|

| 9. ENTERPRISE MAILING ADDRESS (if different than street address) | CITY/TOWN | STATE | ZIP CODE + 4 |
|---|---|---|---|

| 10. LOCATION OF ENTERPRISE RECORDS (street address) | CITY/TOWN | STATE | ZIP CODE + 4 |
|---|---|---|---|

| 11. ESTABLISHMENT NAME (doing business as) | 12. NUMBER OF ESTABLISHMENTS * | 13. SCHOOL DISTRICT | 14. MUNICIPALITY |
|---|---|---|---|

* Enterprises with more than one establishment as defined in the general instructions must complete Section 17.

## SECTION 3 – TAXES AND SERVICES

ALL REGISTRANTS MUST CHECK THE APPLICABLE BOX(ES) TO INDICATE THE TAX(ES) AND SERVICE(S) REQUESTED FOR THIS REGISTRATION AND COMPLETE THE CORRESPONDING SECTIONS INDICATED ON PAGES 2 AND 3. IF REACTIVATING ANY PREVIOUS ACCOUNT(S), LIST THE ACCOUNT NUMBER(S) IN THE SPACE PROVIDED.

|   |   | PREVIOUS ACCOUNT NBR. |   |   | PREVIOUS ACCOUNT NBR. |
|---|---|---|---|---|---|
| ☐ | CIGARETTE DEALER'S LICENSE | _____ | ☐ | PUBLIC TRANSPORTATION ASSISTANCE TAX LICENSE | _____ |
| ☐ | CORPORATION TAXES | _____ | ☐ | SALES TAX EXEMPT STATUS | _____ |
| ☐ | EMPLOYER WITHHOLDING TAX | _____ | ☐ | SALES, USE, HOTEL OCCUPANCY TAX LICENSE | _____ |
| ☐ | FUELS TAX PERMIT | _____ | ☐ | SMALL GAMES OF CHANCE LIC./CERT. | _____ |
| ☐ | LIQUID FUELS TAX PERMIT | _____ | ☐ | TRANSIENT VENDOR CERTIFICATE | _____ |
| ☐ | LOCAL SALES, USE, HOTEL OCCUPANCY TAX | _____ | ☐ | UNEMPLOYMENT COMPENSATION | _____ |
| ☐ | MOTOR CARRIERS ROAD TAX/IFTA | _____ | ☐ | USE TAX | _____ |
| ☐ | PROMOTER LICENSE | _____ | ☐ | VEHICLE RENTAL TAX | _____ |

## SECTION 4 – AUTHORIZED SIGNATURE

I, (WE) THE UNDERSIGNED, DECLARE UNDER THE PENALTIES OF PERJURY THAT THE STATEMENTS CONTAINED HEREIN ARE TRUE, CORRECT AND COMPLETE.

| AUTHORIZED SIGNATURE (ATTACH POWER OF ATTORNEY IF APPLICABLE) | | TITLE |
|---|---|---|
| TYPE OR PRINT NAME | | DATE |
| PREPARER'S SIGNATURE (IF OTHER THAN OWNER, PARTNER OR CORPORATE OFFICER) | | TITLE |
| TYPE OR PRINT NAME | DAYTIME TELEPHONE NUMBER ( ) | DATE |

4

| ENTERPRISE NAME | DEPARTMENT USE ONLY |
|---|---|
|  |  |

## SECTION 5 - FORM OF ORGANIZATION

CHECK THE APPROPRIATE BOXES. IN ADDITION TO SECTIONS 1 THROUGH 10, COMPLETE THE SECTION(S) INDICATED.

1. ☐ SOLE PROPRIETORSHIP(INDIVIDUAL)  ☐ CORPORATION (Sec. 11)  ☐ ASSOCIATION  ☐ BUSINESS TRUST  ☐ GOVERNMENT (Sec. 13)

☐ PARTNERSHIP: ☐ GENERAL  COMPANY: ☐ LIMITED LIABILITY  ☐ ESTATE  ☐ TRUST
        ☐ LIMITED         *STATE WHERE CHARTERED* _____
        ☐ LIMITED LIABILITY  ☐ RESTRICTED PROFESSIONAL  ☐ OTHER, EXPLAIN _____
        ☐ JOINT VENTURE     *STATE WHERE CHARTERED* _____

2. ☐ PROFIT  ☐ NON-PROFIT  IS THE ENTERPRISE ORGANIZED FOR PROFIT OR NON-PROFIT?

3. ☐ YES  ☐ NO  IS THE ENTERPRISE EXEMPT FROM TAXATION UNDER INTERNAL REVENUE CODE SECTION 501(C)(3)? IF YES, PROVIDE A COPY OF THE ENTERPRISE'S EXEMPTION AUTHORIZATION LETTER FROM THE INTERNAL REVENUE SERVICE.

## SECTION 6 - OWNERS, PARTNERS, SHAREHOLDERS, OFFICERS, RESPONSIBLE PARTY INFORMATION

PROVIDE THE FOLLOWING FOR **ALL** INDIVIDUAL AND/OR ENTERPRISE OWNERS, PARTNERS, SHAREHOLDERS, OFFICERS AND RESPONSIBLE PARTIES. IF STOCK IS PUBLICLY TRADED, PROVIDE THE FOLLOWING FOR ANY SHAREHOLDER WITH AN EQUITY POSITION OF 5% OR MORE. *ADDITIONAL SPACE IS AVAILABLE IN SECTION 6A.*

| 1. NAME | 2. SOCIAL SECURITY NUMBER | 3. DATE OF BIRTH * | 4. FEDERAL EIN |
|---|---|---|---|
| 5. ☐ OWNER  ☐ OFFICER  ☐ PARTNER  ☐ SHAREHOLDER  ☐ RESPONSIBLE PARTY | 6. TITLE | 7. EFFECTIVE DATE OF TITLE | 8. PERCENTAGE OF OWNERSHIP  % | 9. EFFECTIVE DATE OF OWNERSHIP |
| 10. HOME ADDRESS (street) | CITY/TOWN | COUNTY | STATE | ZIP CODE + 4 |

11. PERSON RESPONSIBLE TO REMIT: ☐ SALES TAX  ☐ EMPLOYER WITHHOLDING  ☐ MOTOR FUEL TAXES

SIGNATURE _____

* DATE OF BIRTH REQUIRED ONLY IF APPLYING FOR A CIGARETTE WHOLESALE DEALER'S LICENSE, A SMALL GAMES OF CHANCE DISTRIBUTOR LICENSE OR A SMALL GAMES OF CHANCE MANUFACTURER CERTIFICATE.

## SECTION 7 - ESTABLISHMENT BUSINESS ACTIVITY INFORMATION

*REFER TO THE INSTRUCTIONS TO COMPLETE THIS SECTION.* COMPLETE SECTION 17 FOR MULTIPLE ESTABLISHMENTS.

1. ENTER THE PERCENTAGE THAT EACH **PA** BUSINESS ACTIVITY REPRESENTS OF THE TOTAL RECEIPTS OR REVENUES AT THIS ESTABLISHMENT. LIST ALL PRODUCTS OR SERVICES ASSOCIATED WITH EACH BUSINESS ACTIVITY. ENTER THE PERCENTAGE THAT THE PRODUCTS OR SERVICES REPRESENT OF THE TOTAL RECEIPTS OR REVENUES AT THIS ESTABLISHMENT.

| PA BUSINESS ACTIVITY | % | PRODUCTS OR SERVICES | % | ADDITIONAL PRODUCTS OR SERVICES | % |
|---|---|---|---|---|---|
| Construction |  |  |  |  |  |
| Manufacturing |  |  |  |  |  |
| Retail Trade |  |  |  |  |  |
| Wholesale Trade |  |  |  |  |  |
| Finance |  |  |  |  |  |
| Insurance |  |  |  |  |  |
| Real Estate |  |  |  |  |  |
| Transportation |  |  |  |  |  |
| Warehousing |  |  |  |  |  |
| Communications |  |  |  |  |  |
| Agriculture, Forestry, Fishing |  |  |  |  |  |
| Mining, Quarrying, Oil/Gas Extraction |  |  |  |  |  |
| Utility or Sanitary Service |  |  |  |  |  |
| Services (Personal or Business) |  |  |  |  |  |
| Domestic |  |  |  |  |  |
| TOTAL | 100% |  |  |  |  |

2. ENTER THE PERCENTAGE THAT THIS ESTABLISHMENT'S RECEIPTS OR REVENUES REPRESENT OF THE TOTAL PA RECEIPTS OR REVENUES OF THE ENTERPRISE.
_____ %

3. ESTABLISHMENTS ENGAGED IN CONSTRUCTION *MUST* ENTER THE PERCENTAGE OF CONSTRUCTION ACTIVITY THAT IS NEW AND/OR RENOVATIVE.
_____ % NEW  _____ % RENOVATIVE

4. ☐ YES  ☐ NO  IS THIS ESTABLISHMENT *SOLELY* ENGAGED IN THE PERFORMANCE OF SUPPORT ACTIVITIES FOR OTHER ESTABLISHMENTS OF THE SAME ENTERPRISE? IF YES, LIST THE NAME(S) OF THE SUPPORTED ESTABLISHMENT(S) AND CHECK THE APPROPRIATE BOX TO DESCRIBE THE SUPPORT ACTIVITY. _____

☐ ADMINISTRATION  ☐ RESEARCH/DEVELOPMENT  ☐ STORAGE/WAREHOUSE  ☐ OTHER (SPECIFY) _____

5

| ENTERPRISE NAME | DEPARTMENT USE ONLY |
|---|---|
| | |

## SECTION 8 – ESTABLISHMENT SALES INFORMATION

1. ☐ YES ☐ NO IS THIS ESTABLISHMENT SELLING TAXABLE PRODUCTS OR OFFERING TAXABLE SERVICES TO CONSUMERS FROM A LOCATION **IN PENNSYLVANIA?** IF YES, COMPLETE SECTION 18.

2. ☐ YES ☐ NO IS THIS ESTABLISHMENT SELLING CIGARETTES **IN PENNSYLVANIA?** IF YES, COMPLETE SECTIONS 18 AND 19.

3. LIST EACH COUNTY **IN PENNSYLVANIA** WHERE THIS ESTABLISHMENT IS CONDUCTING TAXABLE SALES ACTIVITY(IES).

COUNTY _____ COUNTY _____ COUNTY _____

COUNTY _____ COUNTY _____ COUNTY _____

ATTACH ADDITIONAL 8 1/2" x 11" SHEETS IF NECESSARY.

## SECTION 9 – ESTABLISHMENT EMPLOYMENT INFORMATION

### PART 1

1. ☐ YES ☐ NO DOES THIS ESTABLISHMENT EMPLOY INDIVIDUALS WHO WORK **IN PENNSYLVANIA?** IF YES, INDICATE:
   a. DATE WAGES FIRST **PAID** .......... _____
   b. DATE WAGES RESUMED WHEN FOLLOWING A BREAK IN EMPLOYMENT .......... _____
   c. TOTAL NUMBER OF EMPLOYEES .......... _____
   d. NUMBER OF EMPLOYEES PRIMARILY WORKING IN NEW CONSTRUCTION .......... _____
   e. NUMBER OF EMPLOYEES PRIMARILY WORKING IN RENOVATIVE CONSTRUCTION .......... _____
   f. ESTIMATED GROSS WAGES PER QUARTER .......... $ _____ .00

2. ☐ YES ☐ NO DOES THIS ESTABLISHMENT EMPLOY PA RESIDENTS WHO WORK **OUTSIDE OF PENNSYLVANIA?**
   IF YES, INDICATE:
   a. DATE WAGES FIRST **PAID** .......... _____
   b. DATE WAGES RESUMED WHEN FOLLOWING A BREAK IN EMPLOYMENT .......... _____
   c. ESTIMATED GROSS WAGES PER QUARTER .......... $ _____ .00

3. ☐ YES ☐ NO DOES THIS ESTABLISHMENT PAY REMUNERATION FOR SERVICES TO PERSONS YOU DO NOT CONSIDER EMPLOYEES?
   IF YES, EXPLAIN THE SERVICES PERFORMED _____

### PART 2

1. ☐ YES ☐ NO IS THIS REGISTRATION A RESULT OF A TAXABLE DISTRIBUTION FROM A BENEFIT TRUST, DEFERRED PAYMENT OR RETIREMENT PLAN FOR PA RESIDENTS?
   IF YES, INDICATE:
   a. DATE BENEFITS FIRST **PAID** .......... _____
   b. ESTIMATED BENEFITS PAID PER QUARTER .......... $ _____ .00

## SECTION 10 – BULK SALE/TRANSFER INFORMATION

IF ASSETS WERE ACQUIRED IN BULK FROM MORE THAN ONE ENTERPRISE, PHOTOCOPY THIS SECTION AND PROVIDE THE FOLLOWING INFORMATION ABOUT EACH SELLER/TRANSFEROR.

1. ☐ YES ☐ NO DID THE ENTERPRISE ACQUIRE 51% OR MORE OF **ANY CLASS** OF THE **PA ASSETS** OF ANOTHER ENTERPRISE? SEE THE CLASS OF ASSETS LISTED BELOW.

2. ☐ YES ☐ NO DID THE ENTERPRISE ACQUIRE 51% OR MORE OF THE **TOTAL ASSETS** OF ANOTHER ENTERPRISE?

**IF THE ANSWER TO EITHER QUESTION IS YES, PROVIDE THE FOLLOWING INFORMATION ABOUT THE SELLER/TRANSFEROR.**

| 3. SELLER/TRANSFEROR NAME | | 4. FEDERAL EIN | |
|---|---|---|---|
| 5. SELLER/TRANSFEROR STREET ADDRESS | CITY/TOWN | STATE | ZIP CODE + 4 |

| 6. DATE ASSETS ACQUIRED | 7. ASSETS ACQUIRED: | | |
|---|---|---|---|
| | ☐ ACCOUNTS RECEIVABLE | ☐ FIXTURES | ☐ MACHINERY |
| | ☐ CONTRACTS | ☐ FURNITURE | ☐ NAME AND/OR GOODWILL |
| | ☐ CUSTOMERS/CLIENTS | ☐ INVENTORY | ☐ REAL ESTATE |
| | ☐ EQUIPMENT | ☐ LEASES | ☐ OTHER_____ |

**IMPORTANT:** IF, IN ADDITION TO ACQUIRING ASSETS IN BULK, THE ENTERPRISE ALSO ACQUIRED ALL OR PART OF A PREDECESSOR'S BUSINESS, **SECTION 14** MUST BE COMPLETED.

6

| ENTERPRISE NAME | DEPARTMENT USE ONLY |
|---|---|
|  |  |

## SECTION 11 – CORPORATION INFORMATION

| 1. DATE OF INCORPORATION | 2. STATE OF INCORPORATION | 3. CERTIFICATE OF AUTHORITYDATE (NON-PA CORP.) | 4. COUNTRYOF INCORPORATION |
|---|---|---|---|
|  |  |  |  |

5. ☐ YES  ☐ NO    IS THIS CORPORATION'S STOCK PUBLICLY TRADED?

6. CHECK THE APPROPRIATE BOX(ES) TO DESCRIBE THIS CORPORATION:

| CORPORATION: ☐ STOCK | ☐ PROFESSIONAL | BANK: ☐ STATE | MUTUALTHRIFT: ☐ STATE | INSURANCE ☐ PA |
|---|---|---|---|---|
| ☐ NON-STOCK | ☐ COOPERATIVE | ☐ FEDERAL | ☐ FEDERAL | COMPANY: ☐ NON-PA |
| ☐ MANAGEMENT | ☐ STATUTORY CLOSE |  |  |  |

6. S-CORPORATION:  ☐ FEDERAL    ☐ PENNSYLVANIA    (REV-1640 MUSTBE FILED TO ELECT PENNSYLVANIA S STATUS.)

## SECTION 12 – REPORTING & PAYMENT METHODS

1. ☐ YES  ☐ NO    DOES THIS ENTERPRISE MEET THE DEPARTMENT OF REVENUE'S REQUIREMENTS FOR ELECTRONIC FUNDS TRANSFERS (EFT) FILING? THE REQUIREMENTOF PAYMENTVIAEFT APPLIES TO PAYMENTS OF $20,000 OR MORE.

2. ☐ YES  ☐ NO    DOES THIS ENTERPRISE WANT TO PARTICIPATE IN THE DEPARTMENT OF REVENUE'S EFT PROGRAM EVEN THOUGH ITDOES NOT MEET THE $20,000 PAYMENTTHRESHOLD?

3. ☐ YES  ☐ NO    IS THIS ENTERPRISE INTERESTED IN RECEIVING INFORMATION ABOUT THE DEPARTMENT OF REVENUE'S ELECTRONIC DATA INTERCHANGE (EDI) PROGRAM?

4. ☐ YES  ☐ NO    DOES THIS ENTERPRISE MEETTHE DEPARTMENT OF LABOR & INDUSTRY'S REQUIREMENT FOR REPORTING WAGE INFORMATION ON MAGNETIC MEDIA? THE REQUIREMENT OF REPORTING VIA MAGNETIC MEDIAAPPLIES TO 250 OR MORE WAGE ENTRIES PER QUARTERLY REPORT.

5. ☐ YES  ☐ NO    IS THIS ENTERPRISE INTERESTED IN RECEIVING INFORMATION ABOUT THE DEPARTMENT OF LABOR & INDUSTRY'S MAGNETIC MEDIA REPORTING METHODS? THIS INCLUDES A PERSONAL COMPUTER PROGRAM TO ASSIST IN PAYROLL PREPARATION, TAX WITHHOLDING AND UC REPORTING AND FILING PREPARATION.

6. ☐ YES  ☐ NO    IS THIS ENTERPRISE INTERESTED IN RECEIVING INFORMATION ABOUT THE DEPARTMENT OF LABOR & INDUSTRY'S OPTION TO ELECT TO FINANCE UC COSTS UNDER THE REIMBURSEMENTMETHOD IN LIEU OF THE CONTRIBUTORY METHOD?

## SECTION 13 – GOVERNMENT FORM OF ORGANIZATION

1. IS THE ENTERPRISE A:

☐ GOVERNMENTBODY    ☐ GOVERNMENT OWNED ENTERPRISE    ☐ GOVERNMENT & PRIVATE SECTOR OWNED ENTERPRISE

2. IS THE GOVERNMENT:

☐ DOMESTIC/USA    ☐ FOREIGN/NON USA    ☐ MULTI-NATIONAL

3. IF DOMESTIC, IS THE GOVERNMENT:

| ☐ FEDERAL | LOCAL: ☐ COUNTY | ☐ BOROUGH |
|---|---|---|
| ☐ STATE GOVERNOR'S JURISDICTION | ☐ CITY | ☐ SCHOOLDISTRICT |
| ☐ STATE NON-GOVERNOR'S JURISDICTION | ☐ TOWN | ☐ OTHER _____ |
|  | ☐ TOWNSHIP |  |

7

ENTERPRISE NAME

DEPARTMENT USE ONLY

## SECTION 14 – PREDECESSOR/SUCCESSOR INFORMATION

COMPLETE THIS SECTION IF THE REGISTERING ENTERPRISE IS WHOLLY OR PARTIALLY SUCCEEDING A PREDECESSOR.
FOR ASSISTANCE, CONTACT THE NEAREST LABOR AND INDUSTRY FIELD ACCOUNTING SERVICE OFFICE.

IF THE ENTERPRISE HAS MORE THAN ONE PREDECESSOR, PHOTOCOPY THIS PAGE TO PROVIDE THE FOLLOWING INFORMATION ABOUT EACH.

1. PREDECESSOR LEGAL NAME

2. PREDECESSOR PAUC ACCOUNT NUMBER

3. PREDECESSOR TRADE NAME

4. PREDECESSOR FEDERAL EIN

5. PREDECESSOR STREET ADDRESS | CITY/TOWN | STATE | ZIP CODE + 4

6. SPECIFY HOW THE BUSINESS OPERATION WAS ACQUIRED: ☐ ACQUISITION OF EXISTING OPERATION ☐ CHANGE IN LEGAL STRUCTURE
☐ CONSOLIDATION ☐ GIFT ☐ MERGER ☐ IRC SEC. 338 ELECTION ☐ OTHER (SPECIFY) _____

7. ☐ ACQUISITION DATE _____

8. PERCENTAGE OF THE PREDECESSOR'S TOTAL BUSINESS OPERATION (PA AND NON-PA) ACQUIRED _____ %

9. PERCENTAGE OF THE PREDECESSOR'S **PA** BUSINESS OPERATION ACQUIRED _____ %
IF LESS THAN 100%, PROVIDE THE NAME(S) AND ADDRESS(ES) OF THE ESTABLISHMENT(S) THAT CONDUCTED OPERATIONS IN PA OR EMPLOYED PA RESIDENTS.
ATTACH ADDITIONAL 8 1/2 X 11 SHEETS IF NECESSARY.

NAME OF ESTABLISHMENT(S)          ADDRESS(ES)

10. WHAT WAS THE PREDECESSOR'S BUSINESS ACTIVITY IN THE **PA** BUSINESS OPERATION THAT WAS ACQUIRED?

11. ASSETS ACQUIRED: ☐ ACCOUNTS RECEIVABLE    ☐ FIXTURES    ☐ MACHINERY
☐ CONTRACTS    ☐ FURNITURE    ☐ NAME AND/OR GOODWILL
☐ CUSTOMERS/CLIENTS    ☐ INVENTORY    ☐ REAL ESTATE
☐ EQUIPMENT    ☐ LEASES    ☐ OTHER) _____

12. ☐ YES    ☐ NO    HAS THE PREDECESSOR CEASED PAYING WAGES IN PA? IF YES, ENTER THE DATE PA WAGES CEASED,
IF KNOWN. _____

13. ☐ YES    ☐ NO    HAS THE PREDECESSOR CEASED OPERATIONS IN PA? IF YES, ENTER THE DATE PA OPERATIONS CEASED,
IF KNOWN. _____
IF NO, DESCRIBE THE PREDECESSOR'S PRESENT PA BUSINESS ACTIVITY, IF KNOWN. _____

14. AT THE TIME OF TRANSFER FROM THE PREDECESSOR ENTERPRISE TO THE REGISTERING ENTERPRISE:

a. ☐ YES    ☐ NO    WERE ANY OF THE OWNERS, SHAREHOLDERS (5% OR GREATER), PARTNERS, OFFICERS OR DIRECTORS OF THE PREDECESSO
OR OF ANY AFFILIATE, SUBSIDIARY OR PARENT CORPORATION OF THE PREDECESSOR ALSO OWNERS, SHAREHOLDERS (5% O
GREATER), PARTNERS, OFFICERS OR DIRECTORS OF THE REGISTERING ENTERPRISE  OR OF ANY AFFILIATE, SUBSIDIARY (
PARENT CORPORATION OF THE REGISTERING ENTERPRISE?

b. ☐ YES    ☐ NO    WAS THE PREDECESSOR, OR ANY AFFILIATE, SUBSIDIARY OR PARENT CORPORATION OF THE PREDECESSOR, AN OWNE
SHAREHOLDER (5% OR GREATER) OR PARTNER IN THE REGISTERING ENTERPRISE?

c. ☐ YES    ☐ NO    WAS THE REGISTERING ENTERPRISE, OR ANY AFFILIATE, SUBSIDIARY OR PARENT CORPORATION OF THE REGISTERIN
ENTERPRISE, AN OWNER, SHAREHOLDER (5% OR GREATER) OR PARTNER IN THE PREDECESSOR?

IF THE ANSWER TO ANY OF THE QUESTIONS IN 14 IS YES, PROVIDE THE FOLLOWING INFORMATION. ATTACH ADDITIONAL 8 1/2 X 11 SHEETS IF NECESSARY.

● IDENTIFY THOSE PERSONS AND ENTITIES BY THEIR FULL NAME;

● DESCRIBE THEIR RELATIONSHIP TO THE PREDECESSOR AND ANY AFFILIATE, SUBSIDIARY AND PARENT CORPORATION OF THE PREDECESSOR; AND

● DESCRIBE THEIR RELATIONSHIP TO THE REGISTERING ENTERPRISE AND ANY AFFILIATE, SUBSIDIARY AND PARENT CORPORATION OF THE REGISTERING ENTERPRISE.

THE REGISTERING ENTERPRISE MAY APPLY FOR A TRANSFER IN WHOLE OR IN PART OF THE PREDECESSOR'S UNEMPLOYMENT COMPENSATION (U
EXPERIENCE RECORD AND RESERVE ACCOUNT BALANCE, IF THE REGISTERING ENTERPRISE IS CONTINUING ESSENTIALLY THE SAME BUSINESS
ACTIVITY AS THE PREDECESSOR AND BOTH PROVIDED PA COVERED EMPLOYMENT. COMPLETE SECTION 15 AND, IF APPLICABLE, SECTION 16.

NOTE:    A REGISTERING ENTERPRISE MAY APPLY THE UC TAXABLE WAGES PAID BY A PREDECESSOR TOWARD THE REGISTERING ENTERPRISE'S UC TAXABLE WAGE BASE FOR THE CALENDAR YEAR
ACQUISITION WITHOUT TRANSFERRING THE PREDECESSOR'S EXPERIENCE RECORD AND RESERVE ACCOUNT BALANCE.

ENTERPRISE NAME

## SECTION 15 - APPLICATION FOR PA UC EXPERIENCE RECORD AND RESERVE ACCOUNT BALANCE OF PREDECESSOR

A REGISTERING ENTERPRISE MAY APPLY THE UNEMPLOYMENT COMPENSATION (UC) TAXABLE WAGES PAID BY A PREDECESSOR TOWARD THE REGISTERING ENTERPRISE'S UC TAXABLE WAGE BASE FOR THE CALENDAR YEAR OF ACQUISITION WITHOUT TRANSFERRING THE PREDECESSOR'S EXPERIENCE RECORD AND RESERVE ACCOUNTBALANCE.

REFER TO THE INSTRUCTIONS TO DETERMINE IF IT IS ADVANTAGEOUS TO APPLY FOR A PREDECESSOR'S UC EXPERIENCE RECORD AND RESERVE ACCOUNTBALANCE.

IMPORTANT: THIS APPLICATION CANNOT BE CONSIDERED UNLESS IT IS SIGNED BY AN AUTHORIZED SIGNATORY OF BOTH THE PREDECESSOR AND THE REGISTERING ENTERPRISE. THE TRANSFER IN WHOLE OR IN PART OF THE EXPERIENCE RECORD AND RESERVE ACCOUNT BALANCE IS BINDING AND IRREVOCABLE ONCE IT HAS BEEN APPROVED BY THE DEPARTMENT OF LABOR AND INDUSTRY.

APPLICATION IS HEREBY MADE BY THE PREDECESSOR AND THE REGISTERING ENTERPRISE FOR A TRANSFER TO THE REGISTERING ENTERPRISE OF THE PENNSYLVANIA UNEMPLOYMENT COMPENSATION EXPERIENCE RECORD AND RESERVE ACCOUNT BALANCE OF THE PREDECESSOR WITH RESPECT TO THE TRANSFER.

WE HEREBY CERTIFY THAT THE TRANSFER REFERENCED IN SECTION 14 HAS OCCURRED AS DESCRIBED THEREIN AND THAT THE REGISTERING ENTERPRISE IS CONTINUING ESSENTIALLY THE SAME BUSINESS ACTIVITY AS THE PREDECESSOR.

COMPLETE THIS SECTION ONLY IF YOU WANT TO APPLY FOR THE PREDECESSOR'S EXPERIENCE RECORD AND RESERVE ACCOUNTBALANCE.

| 1. PREDECESSOR NAME | | DATE |
|---|---|---|
| AUTHORIZED SIGNATURE | TYPE OR PRINT NAME | TITLE |
| 2. REGISTERING ENTERPRISE NAME | | DATE |
| AUTHORIZED SIGNATURE | TYPE OR PRINT NAME | TITLE |

## SECTION 16 - UNEMPLOYMENT COMPENSATION PARTIAL TRANSFER INFORMATION

COMPLETE THIS SECTION IF THE REGISTERING ENTERPRISE ACQUIRED ONLY PART OF THE PREDECESSOR'S PENNSYLVANIA (PA) BUSINESS OPERATION AND IS MAKING APPLICATION FOR THE TRANSFER OF A PORTION OF THE PREDECESSOR'S EXPERIENCE RECORD AND RESERVE ACCOUNTBALANCE.

COMPLETE REPLACEMENT UC-2A FOR PARTIAL TRANSFER (FORM UC-252). THE PREDECESSOR'S PAPAYROLL RECORDS FOR THE TWO YEARS PRIOR TO THE QUARTER OF THE TRANSFER AND/OR ACQUISITION MUST REMAIN AVAILABLE TO THE REGISTERING ENTERPRISE TO ENABLE THE REGISTERING ENTERPRISE TO PROVIDE REQUIRED INFORMATION REGARDING SEPARATED AND/OR TRANSFERRED EMPLOYEES.

UNEMPLOYMENT COMPENSATION (UC) TAXABLE WAGES ARE THOSE WAGES THAT DO NOT EXCEED THE UC TAXABLE WAGE BASE APPLICABLE TO A GIVEN CALENDAR YEAR.

1. NUMBER OF EMPLOYEES WHO WORKED IN THE PART OF THE PREDECESSOR'S PABUSINESS OPERATION THAT WAS TRANSFERRED TO OR ACQUIRED BY THE REGISTERING ENTERPRISE:

2. DATE WAGES FIRST PAID BY PREDECESSOR OR PRE-PREDECESSOR(S) IN THE PART OF THE PABUSINESS OPERATION TRANSFERRED (ACQUIRED) FOR WHICH CONTRIBUTIONS WERE PAID UNDER THE PROVISIONS OF THE PAUC LAW.

DATE:

3. CHECKMARK THE CALENDAR QUARTERS IN THE YEAR OF TRANSFER AND IN THE PRECEDING FIVE CALENDAR YEARS IN WHICH PAUC CONTRIBUTIONS WERE **PAID IN THE PART OF THE PABUSINESS OPERATION THAT WAS TRANSFERRED.** ENTER A ZERO IN EACH QUARTER WHEN NO CONTRIBUTION WAS DUE AND PAYABLE IN THE PART TRANSFERRED.

| YEAR_____ | YEAR_____ | YEAR_____ | YEAR_____ | YEAR_____ | YEAR_____ OF TRANSFER |
|---|---|---|---|---|---|
| QUARTERS | QUARTERS | QUARTERS | QUARTERS | QUARTERS | QUARTERS |
| 1 2 3 4 | 1 2 3 4 | 1 2 3 4 | 1 2 3 4 | 1 2 3 4 | 1 2 3 4 |
| | | | | | |

4. CHECKMARK THE CALENDAR QUARTERS IN THE YEAR OF TRANSFER AND IN THE PRECEDING FIVE CALENDAR YEARS IN WHICH PAUC CONTRIBUTIONS WERE PAID IN THE **PART OF THE PA BUSINESS OPERATION THAT WAS NOT TRANSFERRED.** ENTER A ZERO IN EACH QUARTER WHEN NO CONTRIBUTION WAS DUE AND PAYABLE IN THE PART RETAINED.

| YEAR_____ | YEAR_____ | YEAR_____ | YEAR_____ | YEAR_____ | YEAR_____ OF TRANSFER |
|---|---|---|---|---|---|
| QUARTERS | QUARTERS | QUARTERS | QUARTERS | QUARTERS | QUARTERS |
| 1 2 3 4 | 1 2 3 4 | 1 2 3 4 | 1 2 3 4 | 1 2 3 4 | 1 2 3 4 |
| | | | | | |

5a. PREDECESSOR'S PAUC **TAXABLE** PAYROLL IN THE **PART OF THE PA BUSINESS OPERATION TRANSFERRED FOR THE PERIOD OF THREE CALENDAR YEARS PRIOR TO THE YEAR OF TRANSFER (ACQUISITION).**

5b. IF THE **PART OF THE PABUSINESS OPERATION TRANSFERRED** WAS NOT IN EXISTENCE FOR THREE CALENDAR YEARS PRIOR TO THE YEAR OF THE TRANSFER, ENTER THE PA **TAXABLE** PAYROLL FOR THE PERIOD OF ITS EXISTENCE TO DATE OF TRANSFER.

OR

$ _____                 $ _____

6. PREDECESSOR'S ENTIRE PAUC **TAXABLE** PAYROLL FOR SAME PERIOD INDICATED IN ITEMS 5a OR 5b.

7. PREDECESSOR'S ENTIRE PAUC **TAXABLE** PAYROLL FOR THE PERIOD FROM THE BEGINNING OF THE QUARTER OF TRANSFER TO THE DATE OF TRANSFER

$ _____                 $ _____

9

| ENTERPRISE NAME | DEPARTMENT USE ONLY |
|---|---|
| | |

## SECTION 17 – MULTIPLE ESTABLISHMENT INFORMATION

### PART 1   ESTABLISHMENT INFORMATION

COMPLETE THIS SECTION FOR EACH ADDITIONAL ESTABLISHMENT CONDUCTING BUSINESS IN PA OR EMPLOYING PA RESIDENTS. PHOTOCOPY THIS SECTION AS NECESSARY.

| 1. ESTABLISHMENT NAME (doing business as) | | | 2. DATE OF FIRST OPERATIONS | 3. TELEPHONE NUMBER ( ) |
|---|---|---|---|---|
| 4. STREET ADDRESS | CITY/TOWN | COUNTY | STATE | ZIP CODE + 4 |
| 5. SCHOOL DISTRICT | | 6. MUNICIPALITY | | |

### PART 2   ESTABLISHMENT BUSINESS ACTIVITY INFORMATION

*REFER TO THE INSTRUCTIONS TO COMPLETE THIS SECTION.*

1. ENTER THE PERCENTAGE THAT EACH PA BUSINESS ACTIVITY REPRESENTS OF THE TOTAL RECEIPTS OR REVENUES AT THIS ESTABLISHMENT. LIST ALL PRODUCTS OR SERVICES ASSOCIATED WITH EACH BUSINESS ACTIVITY. ENTER THE PERCENTAGE THAT THE PRODUCTS OR SERVICES REPRESENT OF THE TOTAL RECEIPTS OR REVENUES AT THIS ESTABLISHMENT.

| PA BUSINESS ACTIVITY | % | PRODUCTS OR SERVICES | % | ADDITIONAL PRODUCTS OR SERVICES | % |
|---|---|---|---|---|---|
| Construction | | | | | |
| Manufacturing | | | | | |
| Retail Trade | | | | | |
| Wholesale Trade | | | | | |
| Finance | | | | | |
| Insurance | | | | | |
| Real Estate | | | | | |
| Transportation | | | | | |
| Warehousing | | | | | |
| Communications | | | | | |
| Agriculture, Forestry, Fishing | | | | | |
| Mining, Quarrying Oil/Gas Extraction | | | | | |
| Utility or Sanitary Service | | | | | |
| Services (Personal or Business) | | | | | |
| Domestic | | | | | |
| TOTAL | 100% | | | | |

2. ENTER THE PERCENTAGE THAT THIS ESTABLISHMENT'S RECEIPTS OR REVENUES REPRESENT OF THE TOTAL PA RECEIPTS OR REVENUES OF THE ENTERPRISE.

_____ %

3. ESTABLISHMENTS ENGAGED IN CONSTRUCTION MUST ENTER THE PERCENTAGE OF CONSTRUCTION ACTIVITY THAT IS NEW AND/OR RENOVATIVE.

_____ % NEW          _____ % RENOVATIVE

4.  ☐ YES          ☐ NO          IS THIS ESTABLISHMENT SOLELY ENGAGED IN THE PERFORMANCE OF SUPPORT ACTIVITIES FOR OTHER ESTABLISHMENTS OF THE SAME ENTERPRISE? IF YES, LIST THE NAME(S) OF THE SUPPORTED ESTABLISHMENT(S) AND CHECK THE APPROPRIATE BOX TO DESCRIBE THE SUPPORT ACTIVITY.

_____

_____

☐ ADMINISTRATION          ☐ RESEARCH/DEVELOPMENT          ☐ STORAGE/WAREHOUSE          ☐ OTHER (SPECIFY) _____

10

| ENTERPRISE NAME | DEPARTMENT USE ONLY |
|---|---|
| | |

## PART 3  ESTABLISHMENT SALES INFORMATION

1. ☐ YES  ☐ NO  IS THIS ESTABLISHMENT SELLING TAXABLE PRODUCTS OR OFFERING TAXABLE SERVICES TO CONSUMERS FROM A LOCATION IN **PENNSYLVANIA**? IF YES, COMPLETE SECTION 18.

2. ☐ YES  ☐ NO  IS THIS ESTABLISHMENT SELLING CIGARETTES **IN PENNSYLVANIA**? IF YES, COMPLETE SECTIONS 18 AND 19.

3. LIST EACH COUNTY **IN PENNSYLVANIA** WHERE THIS ESTABLISHMENT IS CONDUCTING TAXABLE SALES ACTIVITY(IES).

COUNTY _____  COUNTY _____  COUNTY _____

COUNTY _____  COUNTY _____  COUNTY _____

**ATTACH ADDITIONAL 8 1/2" x 11" SHEETS IF NECESSARY.**

## PART 4a  ESTABLISHMENT EMPLOYMENT INFORMATION

1. ☐ YES  ☐ NO  DOES THIS ESTABLISHMENT EMPLOY INDIVIDUALS WHO WORK IN **PENNSYLVANIA**? IF YES, INDICATE:
   - a. DATE WAGES FIRST **PAID** ............ _____
   - b. DATE WAGES RESUMED WHEN FOLLOWING A BREAK IN EMPLOYMENT ............. _____
   - c. TOTAL NUMBER OF EMPLOYEES ............. _____
   - d. NUMBER OF EMPLOYEES PRIMARILY WORKING IN NEW CONSTRUCTION ............ _____
   - e. NUMBER OF EMPLOYEES PRIMARILY WORKING IN RENOVATIVE CONSTRUCTION ..... _____
   - f. ESTIMATED GROSS WAGES PER QUARTER ................ $ _____ .00

2. ☐ YES  ☐ NO  DOES THIS ESTABLISHMENT EMPLOY PA RESIDENTS WHO WORK **OUTSIDE OF PENNSYLVANIA**? IF YES, INDICATE:
   - a. DATE WAGES FIRST **PAID** ............ _____
   - b. DATE WAGES RESUMED WHEN FOLLOWING A BREAK IN EMPLOYMENT ............. _____
   - c. ESTIMATED GROSS WAGES PER QUARTER ................ $ _____ .00

3. ☐ YES  ☐ NO  DOES THIS ESTABLISHMENT PAY REMUNERATION FOR SERVICES TO PERSONS YOU DO NOT CONSIDER EMPLOYEES?
   IF YES, EXPLAIN THE SERVICES PERFORMED _____

## PART 4b

1. ☐ YES  ☐ NO  IS THIS REGISTRATION A RESULT OF A TAXABLE DISTRIBUTION FROM A BENEFIT TRUST, DEFERRED PAYMENT OR RETIREMENT PLAN FOR PA RESIDENTS? IF YES, INDICATE:
   - a. DATE BENEFITS FIRST **PAID** ............ _____
   - b. ESTIMATED BENEFITS PAID PER QUARTER ................ $ _____ .00

## SECTION 6A - ADDITIONAL OWNERS, PARTNERS, SHAREHOLDERS, OFFICERS, RESPONSIBLE PARTY INFORMATION

PROVIDE THE FOLLOWING FOR **ALL** INDIVIDUAL AND/OR ENTERPRISE OWNERS, PARTNERS, SHAREHOLDERS, OFFICERS AND RESPONSIBLE PARTIES. IF STOCK IS PUBLICLY TRADED, PROVIDE THE FOLLOWING FOR ANY SHAREHOLDER WITH AN EQUITY POSITION OF 5% OR MORE. *PHOTOCOPY IF ADDITIONAL SPACE IS NEEDED.*

| 1. NAME | 2. SOCIAL SECURITY NUMBER | 3. DATE OF BIRTH * | 4. FEDERAL EIN |
|---|---|---|---|
| 5. ☐ OWNER ☐ OFFICER ☐ PARTNER ☐ SHAREHOLDER ☐ RESPONSIBLE PARTY | 6. TITLE | 7. EFFECTIVE DATE OF TITLE | 8. PERCENTAGE OF OWNERSHIP % | 9. EFFECTIVE DATE OF OWNERSHIP |
| 10. HOME ADDRESS (street) | CITY/TOWN | COUNTY | STATE | ZIP CODE + 4 |

11. PERSON RESPONSIBLE TO REMIT:  ☐ SALES TAX  ☐ EMPLOYER WITHHOLDING  ☐ MOTOR FUEL TAXES

SIGNATURE _____

| 1. NAME | 2. SOCIAL SECURITY NUMBER | 3. DATE OF BIRTH * | 4. FEDERAL EIN |
|---|---|---|---|
| 5. ☐ OWNER ☐ OFFICER ☐ PARTNER ☐ SHAREHOLDER ☐ RESPONSIBLE PARTY | 6. TITLE | 7. EFFECTIVE DATE OF TITLE | 8. PERCENTAGE OF OWNERSHIP % | 9. EFFECTIVE DATE OF OWNERSHIP |
| 10. HOME ADDRESS (street) | CITY/TOWN | COUNTY | STATE | ZIP CODE + 4 |

11. PERSON RESPONSIBLE TO REMIT:  ☐ SALES TAX  ☐ EMPLOYER WITHHOLDING  ☐ MOTOR FUEL TAXES

SIGNATURE _____

* DATE OF BIRTH REQUIRED ONLY IF APPLYING FOR A CIGARETTE WHOLESALE DEALER'S LICENSE, A SMALL GAMES OF CHANCE DISTRIBUTOR LICENSE OR A SMALL GAMES OF CHANCE MANUFACTURER CERTIFICATE.

11

| ENTERPRISE NAME | DEPARTMENT USE ONLY |
|---|---|
| | |

## SECTION 18 – SALES USE AND HOTEL OCCUPANCY TAX LICENSE, PUBLIC TRANSPORTATION ASSISTANCE TAX LICENSE, VEHICLE RENTAL TAX, TRANSIENT VENDOR CERIFICATE OR PROMOTER LICENSE

**PART 1**   SALES USE AND HOTEL OCCUPANCY TAX, PUBLIC TRANSPORTATION ASSISTANCE TAX OR VEHICLE RENTAL TAX

ENTERPRISES APPLYING FOR A SALES, USE AND HOTEL OCCUPANCY TAX LICENSE, PUBLIC TRANSPORTATION ASSISTANCE TAX LICENSE AND/OR VEHICLE RENTAL TAX, COMPLETE PART 1.

**IF THE ENTERPRISE IS:**

- SELLING TAXABLE PRODUCTS OR SERVICES TO CONSUMERS **IN PENNSYLVANIA,** ENTER DATE OF FIRST TAXABLE SALE _____

- PURCHASING TAXABLE PRODUCTS OR SERVICES FOR ITS OWN USE **IN PENNSYLVANIA** AND INCURRING NO SALES TAX, ENTER DATE OF FIRST PURCHASE _____

- SELLING NEW TIRES TO CONSUMERS **IN PENNSYLVANIA,** ENTER DATE OF FIRST SALE _____

- LEASING OR RENTING MOTOR VEHICLES, ENTER DATE OF FIRST LEASE OR RENTAL _____

- RENTING FIVE OR MORE MOTOR VEHICLES, ENTER DATE OF FIRST RENTAL _____

- CONDUCTING RETAIL SALES IN PENNSYLVANIA AND NOT MAINTAINING A PERMANENT LOCATION IN PA, ENTER DATE OF FIRST TAXABLE SALE _____ (COMPLETE PART 2)

- ACTIVELY PROMOTING SHOWS IN PENNSYLVANIA WHERE TAXABLE PRODUCTS WILL BE OFFERED FOR RETAIL SALE, ENTER DATE OF FIRST SHOW _____ . (COMPLETE PART 3)

SALES TAX COLLECTED MUST BE SEGREGATED FROM OTHER FUNDS AND MUST REMAIN IN THE COMMONWEALTH OF PENNSYLVANIA UNTIL REMITTED TO THE DEPARTMENT OF REVENUE. (COMPLETE PART 4)

**PART 2**   TRANSIENT VENDOR CERTIFICATE

IF THE ENTERPRISE PARTICIPATES IN ANY SHOWS OTHER THAN THOSE LISTED, PROVIDE THE NAME(S) OF THE SHOW(S) AND INFORMATION ABOUT THE SHOW(S) TO THE DEPARTMENT OF REVENUE AT LEAST 10 DAYS PRIOR TO THE SHOW.

IF THE ENTERPRISE IS NOT ASSOCIATED WITH A PA LICENSED PROMOTER FOR EACH SHOW, A $500 SECURITY DEPOSIT MUST BE SUBMITTED WITH THIS FORM.

PROVIDE THE FOLLOWING INFORMATION FOR **EACH SHOW:**

| 1. PROMOTER NUMBER | 2. SHOW NAME | 3. COUNTY | |
|---|---|---|---|
| 4. SHOW ADDRESS (STREET, CITY, STATE, ZIP) | | 5. START DATE | 6. END DATE |
| 1. PROMOTER NUMBER | 2. SHOW NAME | 3. COUNTY | |
| 4. SHOW ADDRESS (STREET, CITY, STATE, ZIP) | | 5. START DATE | 6. END DATE |

**ATTACH ADDITIONAL 8 1/2 X 11 SHEETS IF NECESSARY.**

**PART 3**   PROMOTER LICENSE

PROVIDE THE FOLLOWING INFORMATION FOR **EACH SHOW:**

| 1. SHOW NAME | 2. TYPE OF SHOW | 3. START DATE | 4. END DATE |
|---|---|---|---|
| 5. SHOW ADDRESS (STREET, CITY, STATE, ZIP) | 6. COUNTY | | 7. NBR OF VENDORS |
| 1. SHOW NAME | 2. TYPE OF SHOW | 3. START DATE | 4. END DATE |
| 5. SHOW ADDRESS (STREET, CITY, STATE, ZIP) | 6. COUNTY | | 7. NBR OF VENDORS |

**ATTACH ADDITIONAL 8 1/2 X 11 SHEETS IF NECESSARY.**

**PART 4**   LOCATION OF SALES TAX COLLECTED

PROVIDE THE FOLLOWING INFORMATION ABOUT THE PENNSYLVANIA FINANCIAL INSTITUTION OR OTHER LOCATION WHERE SALES TAX FUNDS WILL BE PLACED PENDING REMISSION TO THE DEPARTMENT OF REVENUE.

| 1. NAME OF FINANCIAL INSTITUTION | 2. ACCOUNT NAME | 3. ACCOUNT NUMBER | | |
|---|---|---|---|---|
| 4. TYPE OF ACCOUNT: ☐ SAVINGS | ☐ CHECKING | ☐ CD | ☐ ESCROW | |
| 5. FINANCIAL INSTITUTION STREET ADDRESS | CITY/TOWN | COUNTY | STATE | ZIP CODE + 4 |
| 6. OTHER LOCATION | CITY/TOWN | COUNTY | STATE | ZIP CODE + 4 |

12

ENTERPRISE NAME

DEPARTMENT USE ONLY

## SECTION 19 – CIGARETTE DEALER'S LICENSE

### PART 1    LICENSE TYPE

CHECK THE APPROPRIATE BOX(ES) TO INDICATE LICENSE TYPE REQUESTED. A SEPARATE LICENSE MUST BE OBTAINED FOR EACH ESTABLISHMENT THAT SELLS RETAIL, OVER-THE-COUNTER CIGARETTES. A SEPARATE DECAL MUST BE PURCHASED FOR EACH VENDING MACHINE LOCATION. A CHECK OR MONEY ORDER MUST BE SUBMITTED WITH THIS APPLICATION.

| LICENSE TYPE | NUMBER | FEE | AMOUNT REMITTED |
|---|---|---|---|
| ☐ RETAIL OVER-THE-COUNTER | _____ | @ $    25   EACH LOCATION | $_____ |
| ☐ VENDING MACHINE (ATTACH A LISTING OF LOCATIONS) | _____ | @ $    25   EACH DECAL | $_____ |
| ☐ WHOLESALER | | @ $    500 | $_____ |
| ☐ CIGARETTE STAMPING AGENT AND WHOLESALER | | @ $   1,500 | $_____ |
| | | TOTAL AMOUNT REMITTED | $_____ |

### MAKE CHECKS PAYABLE TO PA DEPARTMENT OF REVENUE

### PART 2    CIGARETTE WHOLESALER

LIST CIGARETTE STORAGE LOCATION(S) (P.O. BOXES ARE NOT ACCEPTABLE).

1. STREET ADDRESS

| CITY/TOWN | COUNTY | STATE | ZIP CODE + 4 |
|---|---|---|---|
| | | | |

2. ☐ YES        ☐ NO        HAS ANY OWNER, PARTNER, OFFICER, DIRECTOR OR MAJOR STOCKHOLDER BEEN CONVICTED OF ANY VIOLATION OF THE PENNSYLVANIA CIGARETTE TAX ACT OR ANY MISDEMEANOR OR FELONY?

IF YES, LIST ALL CONVICTIONS WITHIN THE PREVIOUS 10 YEAR PERIOD. ATTACH ADDITIONAL 8 1/2 X 11 SHEETS IF NECESSARY

3. THE APPLICANT HAS COMPLIED WITH ARTICLE II-A OF THE CIGARETTE SALES AND LICENSING ACT. UNDER PENALTY OF PERJURY, OF ADHERENCE TO STATE PRESUMPTIVE MINIMUM PRICES OR APPROVAL TO SELL AT A DIFFERENT PRICE, IN ACCORDANCE WITH THE ACT:

☐ CIGARETTES WILL BE SOLD AT OR ABOVE THE PRESUMPTIVE MINIMUM PRICE.

☐ CIGARETTES WILL BE SOLD AT AN APPROVED MINIMUM PRICE.

### PART 3    CIGARETTE STAMPING AGENT

1. ☐ YES        ☐ NO        DOES THE ENTERPRISE PURCHASE OR SELL ANY CIGARETTES WHICH ARE NOT PA STAMPED?

IF YES, LIST STATES: _____    _____    _____    _____    _____

13

ENTERPRISE NAME

## SECTION 20 – SMALL GAMES OF CHANCE LICENSE/CERTIFICATE

### PART 1    DISTRIBUTOR AND/OR MANUFACTURER

TO BE COMPLETED BY ALL APPLICANTS (DISTRIBUTOR AND/OR MANUFACTURER)

APPLICANTS MUST SUBMIT A COPY OF THE CERTIFICATE OF INCORPORATION, ARTICLES OF INCORPORATION, CERTIFICATE OF AUTHORITY(NON-PA CORPORATIONS), BY-LAWS, CONSTITUTION OR FICTITIOUS NAME REGISTRATION.

APPLICANTS FOR A MANUFACTURER CERTIFICATE MUST SUBMIT A COPY OF THE COMPANY LOGO(S).

1.    CHECK APPROPRIATE BOX(ES) TO INDICATE TYPE OF LICENSE/CERTIFICATE REQUESTED

| LICENSE/CERTIFICATE TYPE | FEE | AMOUNT REMITTED |
|---|---|---|
| ☐ DISTRIBUTOR LICENSE | $ 1,000 | $_____ |
| ☐ MANUFACTURER REGISTRATION CERTIFICATE | $ 2,000 | $_____ |
| ☐ REPLACEMENT LICENSE | $ 100 | $_____ |
| ☐ REPLACEMENT CERTIFICATE | $ 100 | $_____ |
| NUMBER OF BACKGROUND INVESTIGATIONS FOR OWNERS/OFFICERS, ETC. _____ @ | $ 10 | $_____ |
| | TOTAL AMOUNT REMITTED | $_____ |

### MAKE CHECKS PAYABLE TO PA DEPARTMENT OF REVENUE

IF THE DEPARTMENT DENIES AN APPLICATION, A $100 APPLICATION PROCESSING FEE SHALL BE RETAINED BY THE DEPARTMENT. NO PART OF THE REGISTRATION OR LICENSE FEE SHALL BE SUBJECT TO PRORATION. NO INVESTIGATION FEE SHALL BE REFUNDED.

2.    MANUFACTURERS AND DISTRIBUTORS LIST ALL INDIVIDUALS RESPONSIBLE FOR TAKING ORDERS AND MAKING SALES OF SMALL GAMES OF CHANCE MERCHANDISE. IF AN INDIVIDUAL RESIDES IN PENNSYLVANIA, INDICATE IF COMMISSION OR NONCOMMISSION.

| NAME | TITLE | ☐ SELLS FOR DISTRIBUTOR ☐ SELLS FOR MANUFACTURER | ☐ COMMISSION ☐ NONCOMMISSION |
|---|---|---|---|
| HOME ADDRESS (STREET) | CITY/TOWN | STATE | ZIP CODE + 4 | TELEPHONE NBR. ( ) |
| NAME | TITLE | ☐ SELLS FOR DISTRIBUTOR ☐ SELLS FOR MANUFACTURER | ☐ COMMISSION ☐ NONCOMMISSION |
| HOME ADDRESS (STREET) | CITY/TOWN | STATE | ZIP CODE + 4 | TELEPHONE NBR. ( ) |

### ATTACH ADDITIONAL 8 1/2 X 11 SHEETS IF NECESSARY

MANUFACTURERS ONLY MUST SUBMIT A CATALOG OF THE SMALL GAMES CHECKED BELOW. IF CATALOG IS UNAVAILABLE, PROVIDE NAME OF GAME(S) AND FORM NUMBER(S), NUMBER OF TICKETS PER DEAL, HIGHEST INDIVIDUAL PRIZE VALUE AND PERCENTAGE OF PAYOUT.

3.    CHECK THE APPROPRIATE BOX(ES) TO INDICATE THE TYPES OF SMALL GAMES DISTRIBUTED OR MANUFACTURED.

☐ DAILY DRAWINGS    ☐ PULL-TABS    ☐ PUNCHBOARDS    ☐ RAFFLES    ☐ DISPENSING MACHINES

### PART 2    DISTRIBUTOR

LIST ALL SMALL GAMES OF CHANCE MANUFACTURERS WITH WHOM THE DISTRIBUTOR DOES BUSINESS

| MANUFACTURER'S LEGAL NAME | MANUFACTURER'S CERTIFICATE NBR. M- | TELEPHONE NBR. ( ) |
|---|---|---|
| STREET ADDRESS | CITY/TOWN | STATE | ZIP CODE +4 |
| MANUFACTURER'S LEGAL NAME | MANUFACTURER'S CERTIFICATE NBR. M- | TELEPHONE NBR. ( ) |
| STREET ADDRESS | CITY/TOWN | STATE | ZIP CODE +4 |

### ATTACH ADDITIONAL 8 1/2 X 11 SHEETS IF NECESSARY

14

## PART 3 SMALL GAMES OF CHANCE CERTIFICATION

**MUST BE COMPLETED BY ALL SMALL GAMES OF CHANCE APPLICANTS.**

I CERTIFY THAT THE FOLLOWING TAX STATEMENTS ARE TRUE AND CORRECT

- ALL PA STATE TAX REPORTS AND RETURNS HAVE BEEN FILED, AND
- ALL PA STATE TAXES HAVE BEEN PAID, OR
- ANY PA STATE TAXES OWNED ARE SUBJECT TO TIMELY ADMINISTRATIVE OR JUDICIAL APPEAL; OR ANY DELINQUENT PA TAXES ARE SUBJECT TO DULY APPROVED DEFERRED PAYMENT PLAN (COPY ENCLOSED).

I CERTIFY THAT NO OWNER, PARTNER, OFFICER, DIRECTOR, OR OTHER PERSON IN A SUPERVISORY OR MANAGEMENT POSITION OR EMPLOYEE ELIGIBLE TO MAKE SALES ON BEHALF OF THIS BUSINESS:

- HAS BEEN CONVICTED OF A FELONY IN A STATE OR FEDERAL COURT WITHIN THE PAST FIVE YEARS; OR
- HAS BEEN CONVICTED WITHIN TEN YEARS OF THE DATE OF APPLICATION IN A STATE OR FEDERAL COURT OF A VIOLATION OF THE BINGO LAW OR OF THE LOCAL OPTION SMALL GAMES OF CHANCE ACT OR A GAMBLING-RELATED OFFENSE UNDER TITLE 18 OF THE PENNSYLVANIA CONSOLIDATED STATUTES OR OTHER COMPARABLE STATE OR FEDERAL LAW; OR
- HAS NOT BEEN REJECTED IN ANY STATE FOR A DISTRIBUTOR LICENSE OR MANUFACTURER REGISTRATION CERTIFICATE, OR EQUIVALENT THERETO.

I DECLARE THAT I HAVE EXAMINED THIS APPLICATION, INCLUDING ALL ACCOMPANYING STATEMENTS, AND TO THE BEST OF MY KNOWLEDGE AND BELIEF IT IS TRUE, CORRECT AND COMPLETE.

| NOTARY | AUTHORIZATION |
|---|---|
| SWORN AND SUBSCRIBED TO BEFORE ME THIS<br><br>DAY OF _____ , 19 ___ | |
| | _____  _____<br>SIGNATURE OF AN OWNER, PARTNER, OFFICER   SOCIAL SECURITY NUMBER<br>OR DIRECTOR |
| _____<br>NOTARY PUBLIC | _____  _____<br>PRINT NAME                              DATE |
| MY COMMISSION EXPIRES _____ | _____<br>TITLE |
| | ( )_____<br>TELEPHONE NUMBER |
| NOTARY SEAL | CORPORATE SEAL |

15

| ENTERPRISE NAME | DEPARTMENT USE ONLY |
|---|---|

## SECTION 21 – MOTOR CARRIER REGISTRATION & DECAL/MOTOR FUELS LICENSE & PERMIT

### PART 1  VEHICLE OPERATIONS

A DECAL IS REQUIRED IF AN ENTERPRISE IS OPERATING A QUALIFIED MOTOR VEHICLE, SEE PAGE 25, PART 1 - VEHICLE OPERATIONS.

CHECK THE APPROPRIATE BOX(ES) TO DESCRIBE THE ENTERPRISE OPERATIONS:

☐ COMMON CARRIER  ☐ CONTRACT CARRIER  ☐ FOR HIRE CARRIER  ☐ PRIVATE CARRIER

INDICATE THE FUEL TYPES FOR PENNSYLVANIA BASED QUALIFIED MOTOR VEHICLES:

☐ DIESEL  ☐ GASOLINE  ☐ ETHANOL/GASOHOL  ☐ LPGAS  ☐ CNG/LNG

### MOTOR CARRIER ROAD TAX/IFTA VEHICLE DECAL REQUESTS

COMPLETE THE FOLLOWING FOR EACH QUALIFIED MOTOR VEHICLE YOU INTEND TO OPERATE IN PENNSYLVANIA DURING THE ENSUING CALENDAR YEAR.
**NOTE: DECALS ARE $5.00 PER SET OF TWO.**

1. **IFTA** DECALS (NUMBER OF VEHICLES THAT TRAVEL IN PA AND OUT OF STATE) _____

2. **NON IFTA** DECALS (NUMBER OF VEHICLES THAT TRAVEL IN PA EXCLUSIVELY) _____

3. TOTAL DECALS REQUESTED (ADD LINES 1 AND 2) _____

4. TOTAL AMOUNT DUE (MULTIPLY LINE 3 BY $5) $_____

**REMITTANCE SUBMITTED:**

5. AUTHORIZED ADJUSTMENT (ATTACH ORIGINAL CREDIT NOTICE) $_____

6. CHECK OR MONEY ORDER AMOUNT $_____

### MAKE CHECKS PAYABLE TO PA DEPARTMENT OF REVENUE

CHECK THE APPROPRIATE BOX(ES) TO INDICATE THE JURISDICTION(S) WHERE:

**COLUMN A** – QUALIFIED MOTOR VEHICLES ARE OPERATED
**COLUMN B** – BULK STORAGE OF DIESEL FUEL IS MAINTAINED
**COLUMN C** – BULK STORAGE FOR GASOLINE IS MAINTAINED
**COLUMN D** – BULK STORAGE OF ANY OTHER MOTOR FUEL IS MAINTAINED

| A B C D | | A B C D | | A B C D | | A B C D | |
|---|---|---|---|---|---|---|---|
| ☐ ☐ ☐ ☐ | AK – ALASKA | ☐ ☐ ☐ ☐ ☐ | ID – IDAHO | ☐ ☐ ☐ ☐ | MT – MONTANA | ☐ ☐ ☐ ☐ | RI – RHODE ISLAND |
| ☐ ☐ ☐ ☐ | AL – ALABAMA | ☐ ☐ ☐ ☐ ☐ | IL – ILLINOIS | ☐ ☐ ☐ ☐ | NC – NORTH CAROLINA | ☐ ☐ ☐ ☐ | SC – SOUTH CAROLINA |
| ☐ ☐ ☐ ☐ | AR – ARKANSAS | ☐ ☐ ☐ ☐ ☐ | IN – INDIANA | ☐ ☐ ☐ ☐ | ND – NORTH DAKOTA | ☐ ☐ ☐ ☐ | SD – SOUTH DAKOTA |
| ☐ ☐ ☐ ☐ | AZ – ARIZONA | ☐ ☐ ☐ ☐ ☐ | KS – KANSAS | ☐ ☐ ☐ ☐ | NE – NEBRASKA | ☐ ☐ ☐ ☐ | TN – TENNESSEE |
| ☐ ☐ ☐ ☐ | CA – CALIFORNIA | ☐ ☐ ☐ ☐ ☐ | KY – KENTUCKY | ☐ ☐ ☐ ☐ | NH – NEW HAMPSHIRE | ☐ ☐ ☐ ☐ | TX – TEXAS |
| ☐ ☐ ☐ ☐ | CO – COLORADO | ☐ ☐ ☐ ☐ ☐ | LA – LOUISIANA | ☐ ☐ ☐ ☐ | NJ – NEW JERSEY | ☐ ☐ ☐ ☐ | UT – UTAH |
| ☐ ☐ ☐ ☐ | CT – CONNECTICUT | ☐ ☐ ☐ ☐ ☐ | MA – MASSACHUSETTS | ☐ ☐ ☐ ☐ | NM – NEW MEXICO | ☐ ☐ ☐ ☐ | VA – VIRGINIA |
| ☐ ☐ ☐ ☐ | DC – DIST. OF COLUMBIA | ☐ ☐ ☐ ☐ ☐ | MD – MARYLAND | ☐ ☐ ☐ ☐ | NV – NEVADA | ☐ ☐ ☐ ☐ | VT – VERMONT |
| ☐ ☐ ☐ ☐ | DE – DELAWARE | ☐ ☐ ☐ ☐ ☐ | ME – MAINE | ☐ ☐ ☐ ☐ | NY – NEW YORK | ☐ ☐ ☐ ☐ | WA – WASHINGTON |
| ☐ ☐ ☐ ☐ | FL – FLORIDA | ☐ ☐ ☐ ☐ ☐ | MI – MICHIGAN | ☐ ☐ ☐ ☐ | OH – OHIO | ☐ ☐ ☐ ☐ | WI – WISCONSIN |
| ☐ ☐ ☐ ☐ | GA – GEORGIA | ☐ ☐ ☐ ☐ ☐ | MN – MINNESOTA | ☐ ☐ ☐ ☐ | OK – OKLAHOMA | ☐ ☐ ☐ ☐ | WV – WEST VIRGINIA |
| ☐ ☐ ☐ ☐ | HI – HAWAII | ☐ ☐ ☐ ☐ ☐ | MO – MISSOURI | ☐ ☐ ☐ ☐ | OR – OREGON | ☐ ☐ ☐ ☐ | WY – WYOMING |
| ☐ ☐ ☐ ☐ | IA – IOWA | ☐ ☐ ☐ ☐ ☐ | MS – MISSISSIPPI | ☐ ☐ ☐ ☐ | PA – PENNSYLVANIA | | |

| A B C D | | A B C D | | A B C D | | A B C D | |
|---|---|---|---|---|---|---|---|
| ☐ ☐ ☐ ☐ | AB – ALBERTA | ☐ ☐ ☐ ☐ | NB – NEW BRUNSWICK | ☐ ☐ ☐ ☐ | NT – N W TERRITORY | ☐ ☐ ☐ ☐ | PQ – QUEBEC |
| ☐ ☐ ☐ ☐ | BC – BRITISH COLUMBIA | ☐ ☐ ☐ ☐ | NF – NEWFOUNDLAND | ☐ ☐ ☐ ☐ | ON – ONTARIO | ☐ ☐ ☐ ☐ | SK – SASKATCHEWAN |
| ☐ ☐ ☐ ☐ | MB – MANITOBA | ☐ ☐ ☐ ☐ | NS – NOVA SCOTIA | ☐ ☐ ☐ ☐ | PE – PRINCE EDWARD IS. | ☐ ☐ ☐ ☐ | YT - YUKON TERRITORY |

### PART 2  FUELS

CHECK THE APPROPRIATE BOX(ES) IF THE ENTERPRISE WILL SELL, USE OR TRANSPORT ANY FUELS IN PENNSYLVANIA.

☐ LIQUID FUELS AND FUELS TAX - YEARLY PERMIT REQUIRED BY WHOLESALE DISTRIBUTORS (i.e. ONE LICENSED TO HANDLE TAX FREE LIQUID FUELS OR FUELS IN PA) OR AN IMPORTER OR EXPORTER OF LIQUID FUELS OR FUELS.
ESTIMATED DATE OF FIRST TAX-FREE LIQUID FUELS PURCHASE OR SALE _____

☐ ALTERNATIVE FUELS TAX - YEARLY PERMIT REQUIRED BY ALTERNATIVE FUEL DEALER-USERS FOR THE REMISSION OF TAX ON ALTERNATIVE FUELS (HIGHWAY FUELS OTHER THAN LIQUID FUELS OR FUELS) PLACED INTO THE SUPPLY TANK OF A MOTOR VEHICLE FOR USE ON PA HIGHWAYS.
ESTIMATED DATE OF FIRST FUELING OF VEHICLES _____

PROVIDE A LIST OF ALL PA LOCATIONS WHERE LIQUID FUELS OR FUELS WILL BE SOLD.

| STREET ADDRESS | CITY/TOWN | COUNTY | STATE | ZIP CODE + 4 |
|---|---|---|---|---|
| STREET ADDRESS | CITY/TOWN | COUNTY | STATE | ZIP CODE + 4 |

ATTACH ADDITIONAL 8 1/2 x 11 SHEETS IF NECESSARY

16

| ENTERPRISE NAME | DEPARTMENT USE ONLY |
|---|---|
| | |

## SECTION 22 – SALES TAX EXEMPT STATUS FOR CHARITABLE AND RELIGIOUS ORGANIZATIONS

### PART 1

ACT55 OF 1997, KNOWN AS THE INSTITUTIONS OF PURELY PUBLIC CHARITY ACT, WAS SIGNED INTO LAW ON NOVEMBER 26, 1997. THIS LAW HAS CODIFIED THE REQUIREMENTS AN INSTITUTION MUST MEET IN ORDER TO QUALIFY FOR EXEMPTION, OUTLINING FIVE CRITERIA THAT MUST BE MET. EACH INSTITUTION MUST: (1) ADVANCE A CHARITABLE PURPOSE; (2) DONATE OR RENDER GRATUITOUSLY A SUBSTANTIAL PORTION OF ITS SERVICES; (3) BENEFIT A SUBSTANTIAL AND INDEFINITE CLASS OF PERSONS WHO ARE LEGITIMATE SUBJECTS OF CHARITY; (4) RELIEVE THE GOVERNMENT OF SOME BURDEN; (5) OPERATE ENTIRELY FREE FROM PRIVATE PROFIT MOTIVE.

**ORGANIZATIONS OF THE FOLLOWING TYPE DO NOT QUALIFY FOR EXEMPTION STATUS:**

- AN ASSOCIATION OF EMPLOYEES, THE MEMBERSHIP OF WHICH IS LIMITED TO THE EMPLOYEES OF A DESIGNATED ENTERPRISE

- A LABOR ORGANIZATION

- AN AGRICULTURAL OR HORTICULTURAL ORGANIZATION

- A BUSINESS LEAGUE, CHAMBER OF COMMERCE, REAL ESTATE BOARD, BOARD OF TRADE OR PROFESSIONAL SPORT LEAGUE

- A CLUB ORGANIZED FOR PLEASURE OR RECREATION

- A FRATERNAL BENEFICIARY SOCIETY, ORDER OR ASSOCIATION.

TO APPLY OR RENEW SALES TAX EXEMPTION STATUS A REV-72 APPLICATION **MUST** BE COMPLETED. THIS APPLICATION MAYBE OBTAINED BY COMPLETING THE BELOW FORM OR CALL (717) 783-5473, TTD# (717) 772-2252 (HEARING IMPAIRED ONLY).

IF THE ORGANIZATION CONDUCTS SALES ACTIVITIES AND IS NOT REGISTERED FOR COLLECTION OF PA SALES TAX, REFER TO SECTION 18 OF THIS BOOKLET.

✂ -------------------------------------------------------------------------------------------------------------------------

### PART 2  REQUEST FOR SALES TAX EXEMPT STATUS APPLICATION

NAME

| MAILING ADDRESS | CITY/TOWN | STATE | ZIP CODE + 4 |
|---|---|---|---|
| | | | |

## RETURN COMPLETED FORM TO:

PA DEPARTMENT OF REVENUE
BUREAU OF BUSINESS TRUST FUND TAXES
DEPT. 280909
HARRISBURG, PA 17128-0909

REV-1220 AS+ (2-93)

# PENNSYLVANIA EXEMPTION CERTIFICATE

## CHECK ONE:

☐ STATE OR LOCAL SALES AND USE TAX
☐ STATE OR LOCAL HOTEL OCCUPANCY TAX
☐ PUBLIC TRANSPORTATION ASSISTANCE TAXES AND FEES (PTA)

(Please Print or Type)

COMMONWEALTH OF PENNSYLVANIA
DEPARTMENT OF REVENUE
BUREAU OF BUSINESS TRUST FUND TAXES
DEPT. 280901
HARRISBURG, PA 17128-0901

**This form cannot be used to obtain a Sales Tax License Number, PTA License Number or Exempt Status.**

**Read Instructions On Reverse Carefully**

## THIS FORM MAY BE PHOTOCOPIED - VOID UNLESS COMPLETE INFORMATION IS SUPPLIED

CHECK ONE:
☐ **PENNSYLVANIA TAX UNIT EXEMPTION CERTIFICATE** (USE FOR ONE TRANSACTION)
☐ **PENNSYLVANIA TAX BLANKET EXEMPTION CERTIFICATE** (USE FOR MULTIPLE TRANSACTIONS)

Name of Seller or Lessor

| Street | City | State | Zip Code |
|---|---|---|---|

Property and services purchased or leased using this certificate **are exempt** from tax because:
(Select the appropriate paragraph from the back of this form, check the corresponding block below and insert information requested.)

☐ 1. Property or services will be used directly by purchaser in performing purchaser's operation of:

_____ .

☐ 2. Purchaser is a/an:_____ .

☐ 3. Property will be resold under License Number _____ . (If purchaser does not have a PA Sales

Tax License Number, include a statement under Number 7 explaining why a number is not required.)

☐ 4. Purchaser is a/an: _____ holding Exemption Number _____

☐ 5. Property or services will be used directly by purchaser performing a public utility service. (Complete Part 5 on Reverse.)

☐ 6. Exempt wrapping supplies, License Number _____ . (If purchaser does not have a PA Sales Tax License
Number, include a statement under Number 7 explaining why a number is not required.)

☐ 7. Other _____
(Explain in detail. Additional space on reverse side.)

I am authorized to execute this Certificate and claim this exemption. Misuse of this Certificate by seller, lessor, buyer, lessee, or their representative is punishable by fine and imprisonment.

| Name of Purchaser or Lessee | Signature | Date |
|---|---|---|

| Street Address | City | State | Zip Code |
|---|---|---|---|

## 1. ACCEPTANCE AND VALIDITY:

For this certificate to be valid, the seller/lessor shall exercise good faith in accepting this certificate, which includes: (1) the certificate shall be completed properly; (2) the certificate shall be in the seller/lessor's possession within sixty days from the date of sale/lease; (3) the certificate does not contain information which is knowingly false; and (4) the property or service is consistent with the exemption to which the customer is entitled. For more information, refer to Regulation 200, Exemption Certificates (Title 61 PA Code §32.2). An invalid certificate may subject the seller/lessor to the tax.

## 2. REPRODUCTION OF FORM:

This form may be reproduced but shall contain the same information as appears on this form.

## 3. RETENTION

The seller or lessor must retain this certificate for at least four years from the date of the exempt sale to which the certificate applies. **DO NOT RETURN THIS FORM TO THE PA DEPARTMENT OF REVENUE.**

## 4. EXEMPT ORGANIZATIONS:

This form may be used in conjunction with form REV-1715, Exempt Organization Declaration of Sales Tax Exemption, when a purchase of $200 or more is made by an organization which is registered with the PA Department of Revenue as an exempt organization. These organizations are assigned an exemption number, beginning with the two digits 75 (example 75-00000-0).

# GENERAL INSTRUCTIONS

Those purchasers set forth below may use this form in connection with the claim for exemption for the following taxes:

   a. State and Local Sales and Use Tax;
   b. PTA rental fee or tax on leases of motor vehicles;
   c. Hotel Occupancy Tax if referenced with the symbol (●);
   d. PTA fee on the purchase of tires if referenced with the symbol (+)

## EXEMPTION REASONS

1.) Property and/or services will be used directly by purchaser in performing purchaser's operation of:

   A. Manufacturing      B. Mining      C. Dairying      D. Processing      E. Farming      F. Shipbuilding

This exemption is not valid for property or services which are used in: (a) constructing, repairing, or remodeling of real property, other than real property which is used directly in exempt operations; or (b) maintenance, managerial, administrative, supervisory, sales, delivery, warehousing or other nonoperational activities. Effective October 1, 1991, this exemption does not apply to certain services and PTA tire fee.

   2.) Purchaser is a/an:

   + A. Instrumentality of the Commonwealth.
   + B. Political subdivision of the Commonwealth.
   + C. Municipal Authority created under the "Municipal Authority Acts of 1935 or 1945."
   + ● D. Electric Co-operative Corporation created under the "Electric Co-operative Law of 1990."
   + ● E. Co-operative Agricultural Association required to pay Corporate Net Income Tax under the Act of May 23, 1945, P.L. 893, as amended (exemption not valid for registered vehicles).
   + ● F. Credit Unions organized under "Federal Credit Union Act" or State "Credit Union Act".
   + ● G. Federal Instrumentality
   ● H. Federal employe on official business (Exemption limited to Hotel Occupancy Tax only. A copy of orders or statement from supervisor must be attached to this certificate.)
   I. School Bus Operator (This Exemption Certificate is limited to the purchase of parts, repairs or maintenance services upon vehicles licensed as school buses by the PA Department of Transportation. For purchase of school buses, see NOTE below.)

3.) Property and/or services will be resold or rented in the ordinary course of purchaser's business. If purchaser does not have a PA Sales Tax License Number, complete Number 7 explaining why such number is not required. This Exemption is valid for property or services to be resold: (1) in original form; or (2) as an ingredient or component of other property.

4.) Special exemptions

   A. Religious Organization
   B. Volunteer Fireman's Organization
   C. Nonprofit Educational Institution
   D. Charitable Organization

   E.    Direct Pay Permit Holder
   + ● F.    Individual Holding Diplomatic ID
   + G.    School District
   H.    Tourist Promotion Agency
   (Exemption limited to the purchase of promotional materials for distribution to the public.)

Exemption limited to purchase of tangible personal property or services for use and not for sale. The exemption shall not be used by a contractor performing services to real property. An exempt organization or institution shall have an exemption number assigned by the PA Department of Revenue and diplomats shall have an identification card assigned by the Federal Government. The exemption for categories "A, B, C and D" are not valid for property used for the following: (1) construction, improvement, repair or maintenance or any real property, except supplies and materials used for routine repair or maintenance of the real property; (2) any unrelated activities or operation of a public trade or business; or (3) equipment used to maintain real property.

5.) Property or services will be used directly by purchaser in the production, delivery, or rendition of public utility services as defined by the PA Utility Code.

   ☐ PA Public Utility Commission and/or   ☐ Interstate Commerce Commission

A contract carrier is not entitled to this Exemption and a "Schedule of Charges" filed by such carrier does not satisfy this requirement. This Exemption is not valid for property or services used for the following: (1) construction, improvement, repair or maintenance of real property, other than real property which is used directly in rendering the public utility services; or (2) managerial, administrative, supervisor, sales or other nonoperational activities; or (3) tools and equipment used but not installed in maintenance of facilities or direct use equipment. Tools and equipment used to repair "direct use" property are exempt from tax.

6.) Vendor/Seller purchasing wrapping supplies and nonreturnable containers used to wrap property which is sold to others.

7.) Other (Attach a separate sheet of paper if more space is required.) _____

_____

_____

_____

NOTE: Do not use this form for claiming an exemption on the registration of a vehicle. To claim an exemption from tax for a motor vehicle, trailer, semi-trailer or tractor with the PA Department of Transportation, Bureau of Motor Vehicles and Licensing, use **FORM MV-1**, "Application for Certificate of Title", for "first time" registrations and **FORM MV-4ST**, "Vehicle Sales and Use Tax Return/Application for Registration", for all other registrations.

# INDEX

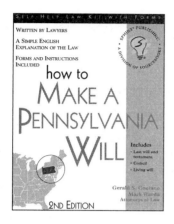

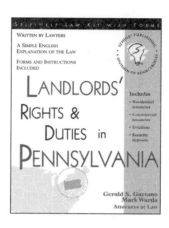

# Sphinx® Publishing's National Titles
*Valid in All 50 States*

## Legal Survival in Business

| | |
|---|---|
| How to Form a Delaware Corporation from Any State | $24.95 |
| How to Form a Limited Liability Company | $22.95 |
| How to Form a Nevada Corporation from Any State | $24.95 |
| How to Form a Nonprofit Corporation | $24.95 |
| How to Form Your Own Corporation (3E) | $24.95 |
| How to Form Your Own Partnership | $22.95 |
| How to Register Your Own Copyright (3E) | $21.95 |
| How to Register Your Own Trademark (3E) | $21.95 |
| Most Valuable Business Legal Forms You'll Ever Need (2E) | $19.95 |
| Most Valuable Corporate Forms You'll Ever Need (2E) | $24.95 |

## Legal Survival in Court

| | |
|---|---|
| Debtors' Rights (3E) | $14.95 |
| Grandparents' Rights (3E) | $24.95 |
| Help Your Lawyer Win Your Case (2E) | $14.95 |
| Jurors' Rights (2E) | $12.95 |
| Legal Research Made Easy (2E) | $14.95 |
| Winning Your Personal Injury Claim (2E) | $24.95 |

## Legal Survival in Real Estate

| | |
|---|---|
| How to Buy a Condominium or Townhome | $19.95 |
| How to Negotiate Real Estate Contracts (3E) | $18.95 |
| How to Negotiate Real Estate Leases (3E) | $18.95 |

## Legal Survival in Personal Affairs

| | |
|---|---|
| Como Hacer su Propio Testamento | $16.95 |
| Guia de Inmigracion a Estados Unidos (2E) | $24.95 |
| Como Solicitar su Propio Divorcio | $24.95 |
| How to File Your Own Bankruptcy (4E) | $19.95 |
| How to File Your Own Divorce (4E) | $24.95 |
| How to Make Your Own Will (2E) | $16.95 |
| How to Write Your Own Living Will (2E) | $16.95 |
| How to Write Your Own Premarital Agreement (2E) | $21.95 |
| How to Win Your Unemployment Compensation Claim | $19.95 |
| Living Trusts and Simple Ways to Avoid Probate (2E) | $22.95 |
| Most Valuable Personal Legal Forms You'll Ever Need | $19.95 |
| Neighbor v. Neighbor (2E) | $16.95 |
| The Nanny and Domestic Help Legal Kit | $22.95 |
| The Power of Attorney Handbook (3E) | $19.95 |
| Social Security Benefits Handbook (2E) | $16.95 |
| Unmarried Parents' Rights | $19.95 |
| U.S.A. Immigration Guide (3E) | $19.95 |
| Your Right to Child Custody, Visitation and Support | $22.95 |

*Legal Survival Guides are directly available from Sourcebooks, Inc., or from your local bookstores.*
*Prices are subject to change without notice.*

*For credit card orders call 1–800–432–7444, write P.O. Box 4410, Naperville, IL 60567-4410*
*or fax 630-961-2168*

# SPHINX® PUBLISHING ORDER FORM

| BILL TO: | | SHIP TO: | |
|---|---|---|---|
| | | | |
| | | | |
| Phone # | Terms | F.O.B. Chicago, IL | Ship Date |

**Charge my:** ☐ VISA  ☐ MasterCard  ☐ American Express

☐ **Money Order or Personal Check**

| | | | | | | | | | | | | | | | | | | | |
|---|---|---|---|---|---|---|---|---|---|---|---|---|---|---|---|---|---|---|---|

Credit Card Number                    Expiration Date

| Qty | ISBN | Title | Retail | Ext. |
|---|---|---|---|---|
| | | **SPHINX PUBLISHING NATIONAL TITLES** | | |
| ___ | 1-57248-148-X | Como Hacer su Propio Testamento | $16.95 | ___ |
| ___ | 1-57248-147-1 | Como Solicitar su Propio Divorcio | $24.95 | ___ |
| ___ | 1-57071-342-1 | Debtors' Rights (3E) | $14.95 | ___ |
| ___ | 1-57248-139-0 | Grandparents' Rights (3E) | $24.95 | ___ |
| ___ | 1-57248-087-4 | Guia de Inmigracion a Estados Unidos (2E) | $24.95 | ___ |
| ___ | 1-57248-103-X | Help Your Lawyer Win Your Case (2E) | $14.95 | ___ |
| ___ | 1-57071-164-X | How to Buy a Condominium or Townhome | $19.95 | ___ |
| ___ | 1-57071-223-9 | How to File Your Own Bankruptcy (4E) | $19.95 | ___ |
| ___ | 1-57248-132-3 | How to File Your Own Divorce (4E) | $24.95 | ___ |
| ___ | 1-57248-100-5 | How to Form a DE Corporation from Any State | $24.95 | ___ |
| ___ | 1-57248-083-1 | How to Form a Limited Liability Company | $22.95 | ___ |
| ___ | 1-57248-101-3 | How to Form a NV Corporation from Any State | $24.95 | ___ |
| ___ | 1-57248-099-8 | How to Form a Nonprofit Corporation | $24.95 | ___ |
| ___ | 1-57248-133-1 | How to Form Your Own Corporation (3E) | $24.95 | ___ |
| ___ | 1-57071-343-X | How to Form Your Own Partnership | $22.95 | ___ |
| ___ | 1-57248-119-6 | How to Make Your Own Will (2E) | $16.95 | ___ |
| ___ | 1-57071-331-6 | How to Negotiate Real Estate Contracts (3E) | $18.95 | ___ |
| ___ | 1-57071-332-4 | How to Negotiate Real Estate Leases (3E) | $18.95 | ___ |
| ___ | 1-57248-124-2 | How to Register Your Own Copyright (3E) | $21.95 | ___ |
| ___ | 1-57248-104-8 | How to Register Your Own Trademark (3E) | $21.95 | ___ |
| ___ | 1-57071-349-9 | How to Win Your Unemployment Compensation Claim | $19.95 | ___ |
| ___ | 1-57248-118-8 | How to Write Your Own Living Will (2E) | $16.95 | ___ |
| ___ | 1-57071-344-8 | How to Write Your Own Premarital Agreement (2E) | $21.95 | ___ |
| ___ | 1-57071-333-2 | Jurors' Rights (2E) | $12.95 | ___ |
| ___ | 1-57071-400-2 | Legal Research Made Easy (2E) | $14.95 | ___ |
| ___ | 1-57071-336-7 | Living Trusts and Simple Ways to Avoid Probate (2E) | $22.95 | ___ |

| Qty | ISBN | Title | Retail | Ext. |
|---|---|---|---|---|
| ___ | 1-57071-345-6 | Most Valuable Bus. Legal Forms You'll Ever Need (2E) | $19.95 | ___ |
| ___ | 1-57071-346-4 | Most Valuable Corporate Forms You'll Ever Need (2E) | $24.95 | ___ |
| ___ | 1-57248-130-7 | Most Valuable Personal Legal Forms You'll Ever Need | $19.95 | ___ |
| ___ | 1-57248-098-X | The Nanny and Domestic Help Legal Kit | $22.95 | ___ |
| ___ | 1-57248-089-0 | Neighbor v. Neighbor (2E) | $16.95 | ___ |
| ___ | 1-57071-348-0 | The Power of Attorney Handbook (3E) | $19.95 | ___ |
| ___ | 1-57071-337-5 | Social Security Benefits Handbook (2E) | $16.95 | ___ |
| ___ | 1-57071-399-5 | Unmarried Parents' Rights | $19.95 | ___ |
| ___ | 1-57071-354-5 | U.S.A. Immigration Guide (3E) | $19.95 | ___ |
| ___ | 1-57248-138-2 | Winning Your Personal Injury Claim (2E) | $24.95 | ___ |
| ___ | 1-57248-097-1 | Your Right to Child Custody, Visitation and Support | $22.95 | ___ |
| | | **CALIFORNIA TITLES** | | |
| ___ | 1-57248-150-1 | CA Power of Attorney Handbook (2E) | $18.95 | ___ |
| ___ | 1-57248-151-X | How to File for Divorce in CA (3E) | $26.95 | ___ |
| ___ | 1-57071-356-1 | How to Make a CA Will | $16.95 | ___ |
| ___ | 1-57248-145-5 | How to Probate and Settle an Estate in California | $26.95 | ___ |
| ___ | 1-57248-146-3 | How to Start a Business in CA | $18.95 | ___ |
| ___ | 1-57071-358-8 | How to Win in Small Claims Court in CA | $16.95 | ___ |
| ___ | 1-57071-359-6 | Landlords' Rights and Duties in CA | $21.95 | ___ |
| | | **FLORIDA TITLES** | | |
| ___ | 1-57071-363-4 | Florida Power of Attorney Handbook (2E) | $16.95 | ___ |
| ___ | 1-57248-093-9 | How to File for Divorce in FL (6E) | $24.95 | ___ |
| ___ | 1-57071-380-4 | How to Form a Corporation in FL (4E) | $24.95 | ___ |
| ___ | 1-57248-086-6 | How to Form a Limited Liability Co. in FL | $22.95 | ___ |
| ___ | 1-57071-401-0 | How to Form a Partnership in FL | $22.95 | ___ |
| ___ | 1-57248-113-7 | How to Make a FL Will (6E) | $16.95 | ___ |
| ___ | 1-57248-088-2 | How to Modify Your FL Divorce Judgment (4E) | $24.95 | ___ |

*Form Continued on Following Page*     **SUBTOTAL**

To order, call Sourcebooks at 1-800-432-7444 or FAX (630) 961-2168 (Bookstores, libraries, wholesalers—please call for discount)

*Prices are subject to change without notice.*

# SPHINX® PUBLISHING ORDER FORM

| Qty | ISBN | Title | Retail | Ext. |
|-----|------|-------|--------|------|
| ____ | 1-57248-081-5 | How to Start a Business in FL (5E) | $16.95 | ____ |
| ____ | 1-57071-362-6 | How to Win in Small Claims Court in FL (6E) | $16.95 | ____ |
| ____ | 1-57248-123-4 | Landlords' Rights and Duties in FL (8E) | $21.95 | ____ |
| | | **GEORGIA TITLES** | | |
| ____ | 1-57248-137-4 | How to File for Divorce in GA (4E) | $21.95 | ____ |
| ____ | 1-57248-075-0 | How to Make a GA Will (3E) | $16.95 | ____ |
| ____ | 1-57248-140-4 | How to Start a Business in Georgia (2E) | $16.95 | ____ |
| | | **ILLINOIS TITLES** | | |
| ____ | 1-57071-405-3 | How to File for Divorce in IL (2E) | $21.95 | ____ |
| ____ | 1-57071-415-0 | How to Make an IL Will (2E) | $16.95 | ____ |
| ____ | 1-57071-416-9 | How to Start a Business in IL (2E) | $16.95 | ____ |
| ____ | 1-57248-078-5 | Landlords' Rights & Duties in IL | $21.95 | ____ |
| | | **MASSACHUSETTS TITLES** | | |
| ____ | 1-57248-128-5 | How to File for Divorce in MA (3E) | $24.95 | ____ |
| ____ | 1-57248-115-3 | How to Form a Corporation in MA | $24.95 | ____ |
| ____ | 1-57248-108-0 | How to Make a MA Will (2E) | $16.95 | ____ |
| ____ | 1-57248-106-4 | How to Start a Business in MA (2E) | $16.95 | ____ |
| ____ | 1-57248-107-2 | Landlords' Rights and Duties in MA (2E) | $21.95 | ____ |
| | | **MICHIGAN TITLES** | | |
| ____ | 1-57071-409-6 | How to File for Divorce in MI (2E) | $21.95 | ____ |
| ____ | 1-57248-077-7 | How to Make a MI Will (2E) | $16.95 | ____ |
| ____ | 1-57071-407-X | How to Start a Business in MI (2E) | $16.95 | ____ |
| | | **NEW YORK TITLES** | | |
| ____ | 1-57248-141-2 | How to File for Divorce in NY (2E) | $26.95 | ____ |
| ____ | 1-57248-105-6 | How to Form a Corporation in NY | $24.95 | ____ |
| ____ | 1-57248-095-5 | How to Make a NY Will (2E) | $16.95 | ____ |
| ____ | 1-57071-185-2 | How to Start a Business in NY | $16.95 | ____ |
| ____ | 1-57071-187-9 | How to Win in Small Claims Court in NY | $16.95 | ____ |
| ____ | 1-57071-186-0 | Landlords' Rights and Duties in NY | $21.95 | ____ |
| ____ | 1-57071-188-7 | New York Power of Attorney Handbook | $19.95 | ____ |
| ____ | 1-57248-122-6 | Tenants' Rights in NY | $21..95 | ____ |

| Qty | ISBN | Title | Retail | Ext. |
|-----|------|-------|--------|------|
| | | **NORTH CAROLINA TITLES** | | |
| ____ | 1-57071-326-X | How to File for Divorce in NC (2E) | $22.95 | ____ |
| ____ | 1-57248-129-3 | How to Make a NC Will (3E) | $16.95 | ____ |
| ____ | 1-57248-096-3 | How to Start a Business in NC (2E) | $16.95 | ____ |
| ____ | 1-57248-091-2 | Landlords' Rights & Duties in NC | $21.95 | ____ |
| | | **OHIO TITLES** | | |
| ____ | 1-57248-102-1 | How to File for Divorce in OH | $24.95 | ____ |
| | | **PENNSYLVANIA TITLES** | | |
| ____ | 1-57248-127-7 | How to File for Divorce in PA (2E) | $24.95 | ____ |
| ____ | 1-57248-094-7 | How to Make a PA Will (2E) | $16.95 | ____ |
| ____ | 1-57248-112-9 | How to Start a Business in PA (2E) | $18.95 | ____ |
| ____ | 1-57071-179-8 | Landlords' Rights and Duties in PA | $19.95 | ____ |
| | | **TEXAS TITLES** | | |
| ____ | 1-57071-330-8 | How to File for Divorce in TX (2E) | $21.95 | ____ |
| ____ | 1-57248-114-5 | How to Form a Corporation in TX (2E) | $24.95 | ____ |
| ____ | 1-57071-417-7 | How to Make a TX Will (2E) | $16.95 | ____ |
| ____ | 1-57071-418-5 | How to Probate an Estate in TX (2E) | $22.95 | ____ |
| ____ | 1-57071-365-0 | How to Start a Business in TX (2E) | $16.95 | ____ |
| ____ | 1-57248-111-0 | How to Win in Small Claims Court in TX (2E) | $16.95 | ____ |
| ____ | 1-57248-110-2 | Landlords' Rights and Duties in TX (2E) | $21.95 | ____ |

**SUBTOTAL THIS PAGE** _____

**SUBTOTAL PREVIOUS PAGE** _____

Shipping — $5.00 for 1st book, $1.00 each additional _____

Illinois residents add 6.75% sales tax _____

Connecticut residents add 6.00% sales tax _____

**TOTAL** _____

To order, call Sourcebooks at 1-800-432-7444 or FAX (630) 961-2168 (Bookstores, libraries, wholesalers—please call for discount)

*Prices are subject to change without notice.*